CHILD GROWTH
AND DEVELOPMENT
IN THE ELEMENTARY SCHOOL YEARS

CHILD GROWTH
AND DEVELOPMENT

IN THE ELEMENTARY
SCHOOL YEARS *Revised Edition*

CECIL V. MILLARD

*Head of Department of Education and Director of
Division of Education, Michigan State College*

D. C. HEATH AND COMPANY·BOSTON

For permission to reprint copyright material, grateful acknowledgment is made to the following publishers and authors:

UNIVERSITY OF MINNESOTA PRESS, Minneapolis, for Figure 14, from *The Measurement of Man* by J. H. Harris and others, 1930.

COURTIS, S. A., for Figures 15, 16, 17, 18, 24, and 28, "Growth and Development in Children," *Report of the Seventh Annual Health Education Conference,* Ann Arbor, American Child Health Association, 1933.

CHILDREN'S BUREAU, for Figure 25, United States Government Printing Office, from *Posture Exercises* by A. Klein and L. C. Thomas, 1926.

APPLETON-CENTURY-CROFTS, INC., New York, for Figure 27, from *Life and Growth* by Alice Keliher, 1941.

COURTIS, S. A., for Figure 29, Unpublished Material.

CHILD BEHAVIOR AND DEVELOPMENT, for Figures 35, 38, 48, and 49, edited by Barker, Kounin, and Wright, 1943.

JOHN WILEY & SONS, INC., for Figure 36, from *Manual of Child Psychology* by L. Carmichael.

UNIVERSITY OF IOWA PRESS, Iowa City, for Figure 37, from data in *An Investigation of the Sentence and the Extent of Vocabulary in Young Children,* University of Iowa Studies in Child Welfare, Vol. III, No. 5, by M. E. Smith, 1926.

A. T. JERSILD AND S. F. BIENSTOCK, for Figure 40, from "A Study of the Development of Children's Ability to Sing," *Journal of Educational Psychology,* Vol. 25: 481–503, 1934.

MERLE H. ELLIOTT, for Figure 41, from "Patterns of Friendship in the Classroom," *Progressive Education,* Vol. 18: 383–390, 1941.

JOSEPHINE R. HILGARD, for Figure 42, from "Learning and Maturation in Pre-School Children," *Journal of Genetic Psychology,* Vol. 41: 36–56, 1932.

COURTIS, S. A., for Figure 43, from "The Goals of Health Education," a paper read before the Physical Education Section of the Schoolmasters Club, Ann Arbor, 1930.

K. M. B. BRIDGES, for Figure 50, from "Emotional Development in Early Infancy," *Child Development,* Vol. 3: 340, 1937.

MACMILLAN CO., New York, for Figure 51, from *Studies in the Organization of Character* by H. Hartshorne, M. A. May, and F. K. Shuttleworth, 1930.

PREFACE

THE general concept of child development has had a dynamic impact on elementary school organization and instruction in recent years. It is a concept which enters into almost all educational discussions, and it is imperative for all who are concerned with the instruction and guidance of elementary school children to know more about it — its principles, its generalizations, and its implications for instruction.

The specialist consequently is under constant pressure to satisfy this need. Information is now available which, when understood and applied, can revolutionize current teaching methods and the handling of children in school. Fortunately child development, as a science, is something more than a philosophy or a point of view about instruction. It thereby sidesteps the traditional progressive controversy and gives signs of becoming basic knowledge in pre-service and in-service training of teachers. In this sense the science of child development offers teacher training the opportunity it has long sought to become a true profession. For a time it seemed that the methodology of the 1920's had given professional stature to education. The ensuing years of disagreement and argument between the progressives and the traditionalists regarding proper methods of teaching and the selection of subject matter seemed to indicate that methodology and curriculum selection were entirely contingent upon the purposes of education and consequently were but the fringes of basic professional knowledge.

It appears that the science of child development, in the application of its findings, may direct the development of methods which will be universally accepted and thereby provide a common understanding of the prerequisites of good teaching. This is necessary if teaching is going to raise its professional level.

This book attempts to bring to pre-service and in-service teachers an over-all concept of the findings of child development that concern the elementary school child. It begins with an exploration of its principles, follows with discussions of its better known phases, and concludes with several chapters on those aspects of child development which are accompaniments or concomitants of growth rather than measurable and direct phases of it — emotion, moral and ethical behavior, personality, discipline, and mental hygiene from the standpoint of growth.

Throughout the entire volume emphasis has been placed on change in the child and on the relationship between the school environment and such change. An effort has been made to present an accurate picture of the processes governing child development which have meaning and implication for the elementary school teacher.

The selection of materials and their organization in this presentation are the result of twenty years of clinical experience and research in child development. As a prelude to the author's current responsibility for direction of a child development observation center, ten years were given to study and research with four hundred children during which time some 200,000 observations were made and recorded. Utilization of this material in undergraduate and graduate courses in child development has had a direct influence on the selection of materials for this volume. It is believed that such a volume will prove helpful to teachers, administrators, and others interested in child development. In addition to its use as a textbook this volume should stimulate the direct observation and study of children. The volume itself represents only an introduction to the subject. Real knowledge will result when the teacher is sufficiently skilled to base his knowledge of child development on his own observation of the children he teaches. It is to be hoped that this book will contribute in some measure to the teacher's achievement of that goal.

Cecil V. Millard

CONTENTS

vii

6

7

8

9

10

PART III: *Concomitants of Growth and Learning*

11

LIST OF FIGURES

LIST OF TABLES

PART I:

BASIC GROWTH CONCEPTS

ORIGIN OF THE ORGANISMIC VIEWPOINT

INTRODUCTION

The current concept of child development, frequently referred to as the organismic, has a long and interesting history (12). Many of the early beliefs have been discarded, and as experimentally sound concepts have evolved, they have been accepted and made the basis for further experimentation. Armchair and authoritarian methods of child study are beginning to give way to studies made under controlled laboratory conditions. The empirical is yielding to the scientific (6, 8, 13).

LIMITATIONS IN EARLY STUDIES

Emphasis on Statistical Interpretations. The study of child development has rapidly accumulated background. As in other scientific fields, its students have sought guidance and direction from related sciences which already had prestige. This manner of progress serves to give a new field a start, but at the same time it limits it in various ways as, for example, the tendency of the 1920's to study childhood from the standpoint of specific traits and capacities. Data reported from these studies bristled with correlations and other current statistical procedures. Laboratory investigation of the human being was confined to studies which lent themselves primarily to statistical treatment. Although great care was used in selecting large group samples, investigations were limited to one or two aspects which were often inconsequential and frequently in disagreement with previous studies. As stated by Frank (6):

. . . . the data thus obtained were often extensive and
yielded results that were statistically significant but also gave
rise to perplexities and anomalies which could rarely, if ever,
be resolved because so little was known about the child subjects beyond sex and chronological age and the one or two
measurements that had been obtained.[1]

Another limitation was that children were selected for study, not
because there was any hope of doing anything directly for them
but with the idea that they would provide data on a specific problem — learning, for example. Sometimes two or more investigators were using the same children as subjects for studies entirely
unrelated to each other (6):

. . . . these produced findings on discrete aspects of child behavior that are difficult to add up to or integrate into any
comprehensive picture of children's activity or the ongoing
process of growth and development in which many events occur simultaneously but at different rates.[1]

This practice is a far cry from current studies, wherein emphasis
is on understanding growth processes by using data compiled by
investigators from various professions (5).

THE CONTRIBUTION OF ANATOMISTS AND PEDIATRICIANS

Direct Contact with Children. The main contributions of anatomists and pediatricians were two in number. First was the fact
that they were working in direct contact with children. This
would seem to be obvious and routine practice, but it is not. The
earlier studies of children carried on by psychometrists were based
entirely on children's records. Frequently investigators had no
contact with the children themselves, and consequently the records
were never compared with the subjects under observation. On the
other hand, pediatricians had the opportunity to compare their
statistical interpretations with the child.

Questionable Validity of Norms. A second contribution of the
anatomists and pediatricians resulted from the attempt to estab-

[1] From *Child Behavior and Development,* edited by Barker, Kounin, and Wright,
1943. Courtesy of McGraw-Hill Book Company.

lish norms. The frequency with which they found variation in their results led them to admit the difficulty of setting clearly defined norms, and as a result, they were among the first to question the validity of norms. It became apparent that it would be more profitable to shift attention to studies of change in developmental status, of the type of growth pattern evolving, and of certain other aspects of the *growing* child. The idea was slowly but gradually accepted. Eventually this procedure gave direction to all types of child study and probably was the beginning of the trend toward continued study of the same children year after year.

THE CONTRIBUTION OF GUIDANCE CLINICS

Beginnings of Personality Studies. At about the same time that physicians, anatomists, and others interested in child growth were beginning to take continued measurements, another group, the workers in various child study centers throughout the country, began to contribute greatly to our growing knowledge of the child. Most of the subjects under their observation were "behavior" children of one kind or another. Children who were extremely poor in school and children thought of as delinquents or court cases were finding their way to children's clinics. In most instances a psychiatrist was in charge, and his problem was the solving of emotional and personality difficulties.

This group made four chief contributions to our knowledge of child development. 1. Norm comparison was of little value in the diagnosis of the child's difficulty. 2. The clinician withheld interpretation until he had all the data available. 3. He diagnosed and predicted future behavior in terms of the operative factors and the treatment prescribed. 4. He handled the case entirely on the basis of the individual's total life pattern. The last is probably the most important contribution of all, and it established a precedent for child study. Using all possible techniques for quantitative analysis of various aspects of the individual's personality, the clinician made the complete diagnosis and prognosis with reference to the individual's personality within its own particular environment (10).

THE ORGANISMIC VIEW

The current view, which interprets all aspects of development in respect to a life pattern, is frequently called the *organismic* concept. Teachers with this viewpoint recognize the child as a dynamic organism that furnishes as much data as the observer is ingenious enough to measure and record. They realize that such data are related, if different, aspects of the total organismic pattern. From the standpoint of research, the emphasis has shifted from studies which seek to ascertain the relation between two variables measured in a large group of children at a given time to studies of growth processes made by many cumulative observations of the same child or children (8). The part that time plays in the development of a child is recognized, and the sequence of developmental aspects of his growth is recorded.

Emphasis on Study of Change. The recent organization of many studies bears testimony to the interest of observers in the changing structure, behavior, and development of the individual child. This viewpoint is far removed from the earlier one, which assumed that growth could be studied by making generalizations based on the average measurements of large groups of children at different age levels.

The Challenge of Studying the Total Child. This point of view is not the result of chance popularity. Basically, it presents its challenge in the fact that comprehensive individual study permits solution of individual problems, unanimity in generalization, and insight into the laws of growth and learning (14).

Growth of Child Study Centers. During the past twenty years both public and private funds have been committed to some kind of study of children. In many instances outstanding leaders in all professions concerned with the welfare of human beings have cooperated in these studies. Child study centers are maintained cooperatively by public and private support. In schools of education and medicine and in other institutions throughout the country, appraisals of continuous measurement data have been undertaken. Now in progress for some time, these studies have been pursued with skill, intelligence, and insight. A well-defined program of data collection on children during critical phases of their development promises results that have far greater implications for teaching than the earlier studies. Although the questions and their answers are not all on the table, enough is now known to revolutionize education.

A New Viewpoint in Teaching. Our present knowledge is a far cry from the idea that the child was born "that way." We have learned much concerning the child's potentiality, his assets and liabilities, and his tendencies toward certain behavior patterns in a given environment. Teaching is looked upon as a reordering of the environment rather than a series of tasks quite unrelated to the child's life outside the school.

Many of the implications of child study, however, are quite unexplored. How the school can best assist in releasing the full potentialities of the growing individual is the main point of child study for the classroom teacher. This is the problem educators now face.

Implications for Schools. Child study has implications for school administration and organization, but these implications have until recently had but little impact. Many schools are still organized on an "ability" system, and evaluation is made exclusively in terms of achievement.

Effect on Health Programs. In health work much progress can be noted. Medical supervision of the school child exists in a constantly increasing number of communities. In many schools nurses work with teachers in supervising the general health of school children. Mental hygiene, the psychology of the child, the relation of the child in his play to other children are aspects of child study which have caught the public fancy. The reader may feel that these developments do not necessarily prove the acceptance of the organismic concept of child growth, but stress on nutrition, the study of physiological defects, and recommendations for their correction are all practical applications of this theory. All these testify to the realization that a child's capacity to learn is frequently affected by his physical health.

Depression and war have delayed other applications which will undoubtedly win easy public recognition. Nevertheless where funds were available, schoolroom lighting has been greatly improved. Sanitary drinking fountains are the rule rather than the exception. Ventilation is improved, and in a few instances, sound-proofing allows a given group to live and work without the noise of the former classroom, where it seemed that only a quiet child is a good child. It is now possible, too, to discover occasionally a classroom painted some other color than tan or brown.

Implications for Curriculum Making. Child growth and development will also make a great impact on curriculum selection. It must be admitted that the traditions of curriculum selection are old and well established, whereas child development is one of the most recent of the sciences. Earliest knowledge was in the physical sciences, hence our emphasis on the study of scientific subjects. If tradition were not enough to account for the academic character-istics of curricula, certainly the psychology of an earlier day, its attitude toward children, and discipline make the present situa-tion understandable. There is a significant and heartening trend away from this background. Attention is being directed more and more toward research findings from sociology, anthropology, and psychology as a guide for curriculum reorganization. The present generation, probably as a result of experience in the war, realizes the inaccuracy and the incompleteness of much of what was learned about mankind and civilization. Cause and effect are be-ing studied in the social sciences with far greater insight than ever before. And as information is collected and organized concerning human nature — its capacities and limitations — it will begin to be reflected in school curricula. The social studies are assuming greater and greater importance in the educational diet of the child with the purpose of giving him a better understanding of himself and his relations with his fellow man.

Effect on Methods. It may be anticipated that the findings of child growth and development will bring about more rapid change in methodology than in the other fields mentioned. Educational psy-chology has always been considered the field of study for the im-provement of instruction, but adaptations in method have fre-quently gone further than the findings justified. Intelligence testing, a real tool for needed research, brought about a recogni-tion of individual differences. Educators, however, often went be-yond sensible limits in applying the idea. The adaptation of nar-row subject matter assignments to the child's ability to learn, rather than adaptation of experience to his stage of development, is an illustration of the point. Today, further insight into individuality has caused informed educators to withdraw the emphasis placed on the idea of fixed performance levels. Through our knowledge of maturing patterns of growth, of the sequence of phases of growth, and of the general relatedness of all aspects of growth, teachers find a new concept of individual instruction, remedial work, and the like. Today teachers speak of "learning activities" rather than "teaching activities." Exploration and study of problems within the classroom and within the greater, more complex, out-of-classroom environment are challenging the emphasis formerly placed on rote learning. Educators are realizing more and more the effectiveness of instruction related to the child's natural interests, the importance of committee work and group planning in enhancing the social climate most conducive to personality development. This kind of change in instructional procedure can be attributed in part to the findings on growth and development.

IMPORTANCE TO TEACHER TRAINING

Child Study Necessary. The tremendous educational significance of the findings convinces one that no teacher is adequately trained without an understanding of this knowledge. As professional material in teacher training, the literature of the child development movement is prerequisite to teaching. To be effective, an understanding of children must be derived from direct study and observation of them rather than from a study of the literature. In this way alone, child study will become a part of the everyday responsibility of the classroom teacher. Educational psychology has proved inefficient to the extent that, as a professional study, it often dissociates itself from direct observation of children. Thus its point becomes vague, its implications misunderstood, and its content academic.

Child development gives promise of not going the same way. This is not entirely the result of more efficient organization; its promise to remain practical is inherent. Child study is characterized by continuous observation of few children, whereas the findings of educational psychology are based mainly on cross-sectional conclusions from large groups. A small group of children is almost always available, and the opportunity to study is always at hand.

SELECTED REFERENCES

1. ANDERSON, J. E., "Child Development: an Historical Perspective," *Child Development,* 27:181–196, 1956.
2. FREEMAN, F. S., "The Study of Individual Differences in the Education of Teachers," *Journal of Educational Psychology,* 41:366–372, 1950.
3. BRADBURY, D. E., "The Contribution of Child Study Movement in Child Psychology," *Psychological Bulletin,* 34:21–38, 1937.
4. COURTIS, S. A., *Toward a Science of Education,* Detroit: Courtis Ratio Tests, 1950.
5. DEARBORN, W. F., AND ROTHNEY, J. W. M., *Predicting the Child's Development.* Cambridge: Sci-Art, 1941.
6. FRANK, L. K., "Research in Child Psychology: History and Prospects," *Child Behavior and Development,* edited by R. G. Barker, J. S. Kounin, H. F. Wright. New York: McGraw-Hill, 1943.
7. JONES, H. E., "The Replacement Problem in Child Development," *Child Development,* 27:237–240, 1956.
8. KERLINGER, F. H., "The Statistics of the Individual Child: The Use of Analysis of Variance With Child Development Data," *Child Development,* 25:265–275, 1954.
9. KROGMAN, W. M., *The Physical Growth of Children,* Monographs of the Society for Research in Child Development, Inc., Vol. XX, Serial No. 60, No. 1, 1955. Lafayette, Indiana: Child Development Publications, 1956.
10. McLEAN, DOROTHY, "Child Development: A Generation of Research," *Child Development,* 25:3–9, 1954.
11. MARTIN, W. E., and STENDLER, CELIA B. *Child Development.* New York: Harcourt, Brace, pp. 5–30, 1953.
12. MURPHY, GARDNER, *An Historical Introduction to Modern Psychology.* New York: Harcourt, Brace, 1929.
13. NATIONAL SOCIETY FOR THE STUDY OF EDUCATION, *The Scientific Movement in Education,* Thirty-seventh Yearbook, Part II, 1938.
14. TANNER, J. M., "The Assessment of Growth and Development in Children," *Archives of Diseases of Childhood,* 27:10–33, 1952.

2

PRINCIPLES OF GROWTH
AND DEVELOPMENT

DEFINITION AND TERMINOLOGY

To many teachers growth means change which takes place without direction and control. To others it designates a process that best occurs only under careful guidance and supervision. In between these two extremes are many gradations of meaning. The parent generally regards growth as a physiological process which has but little relationship to learning, to personality, to social adaptability, or to emotional stability.

From the scientific viewpoint growth is somewhat narrower and, paradoxically, more comprehensive. In the technical sense it may be defined as (6):

> . . . progress toward a definite maturity brought about in an immature organism by the action of appropriate environmental forces . . .

According to this viewpoint *growth* may refer either to increase in reading test scores or to biological change such as growth in height.

The word *development* has often been used synonymously with the word *growth*. In all of the research dealing with physical change, of which there is a tremendous output, no clear-cut differentiation has been proposed (12). The suggestion has been made, however, that *growth* may be described as cellular multiplication, whereas development may be defined as an organization of all the parts which growth and differentiation have produced (8).

Such a distinction is acceptable but somewhat difficult to interpret. With only slight changes in meaning these concepts may be stated more clearly as follows: *Development* may be implied when its usage refers to an over-all process of change, whereas the word *growth* may be used when only one component is under consideration. The child may *grow* in height, for example, but only the whole child *develops*. Such a distinction will be found practical in the longitudinal approach to child study.

Maturity is another word which will be given a special meaning throughout this text. In common usage the word refers to growth or development which has reached its ceiling, or to growth or development which is greater than that expected for a child at a given age. If a five-year-old child resembles a seven-year-old in his behavior, he is said to be "mature for his age." In this text the word *maturity* has a more flexible meaning. It may be used to describe either growth or development at any stage between the zero and the one hundred per cent mark. Thus it will be deemed appropriate to depict a child as having attained ten per cent maturity, or eighty per cent maturity, etc. The word *maturity,* then, may be used to express a definite point of arrival in a stated time sequence.

BASIC PRINCIPLES OF GROWTH

A. GROWTH IS QUALITATIVE AS WELL AS QUANTITATIVE

One of the simplest and most common ways to describe growth is to use the word *change* (16). *Change,* generally, merely implies a quantitative meaning. For example, we may say that "Bruce has grown." What we mean to connote is that he is taller or heavier than he was at some previous time. Such a description is entirely quantitative in its meaning.

An illustration of the *qualitative* aspect of growth may be found in the weight curve of an early-elementary school boy, Figure 1. From February in the kindergarten year to October in the first grade no *quantitative* evidence of gain in weight can be detected. In the instance of this particular child, as also reflected in his height curve (not shown here), a cycle of growth is being completed. Other data testify that there were no illnesses, no family disturbances, no emotional involvements, nor any other influences which might artificially have produced the plateau phenomenon. Obviously the child must be passing through a natural period of development which may suitably be designated as "qualitative" change.

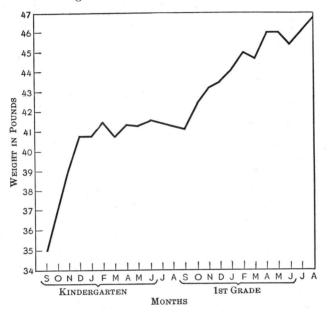

OBSERVED MEASUREMENTS

	Kindergarten				First Grade		
Mo.	*Wt.*	*Mo.*	*Wt.*	*Mo.*	*Wt.*	*Mo.*	*Wt.*
Sept.	35.0	Feb.	41.5	Sept.	41.2	Feb.	45.0
Oct.	——	Mar.	40.7	Oct.	42.5	Mar.	44.7
Nov.	39.2	Apr.	41.2	Nov.	43.2	Apr.	46.0
Dec.	40.7	May	41.2	Dec.	43.5	May	46.0
Jan.	40.7	June	41.5	Jan.	44.2	June	45.5

FIGURE 1. Weight Curve of Early-Elementary School Boy: Case B.F.[1]

The idea, however, is not limited to physiological growth. Figure 2 contains two similar demonstrations of this phenomenon in two entirely different growth processes. In the one instance reading scores present a leveling-off period, and in the other demonstration a similar picture evolves by plotting mental-growth

[1] Dearborn Data, Child Development Laboratory, Michigan State College.

measurements. What happens during the leveling-off, or what we have called the *qualitative,* period, is not too clear. Added maturity is gained, to be sure. This is not to say that quality in growth

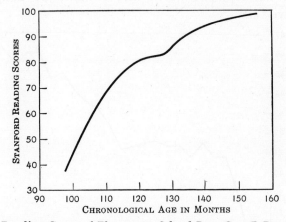

A. Reading Curve of Elementary School Boy: Case R.B.—40M

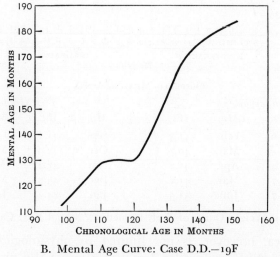

B. Mental Age Curve: Case D.D.—19F

FIGURE 2. Growth Curves Showing Leveling-off Periods

is limited to the natural slowing down, or plateau, period. It is in effect at all times. However, the word "qualitative" seems appropriately chosen to indicate that even during the slowed approach to its maximum, growth is still dynamic and beneficial.

B. GROWTH IS CONTINUOUS

One of the most encouraging concepts for teachers is the idea that growth naturally follows a cyclic pattern as long as environmental and organismic factors remain relatively constant. This means that when there are no abrupt changes in conditions, growth proceeds rather smoothly and evenly toward definable maxima: Adequate evidence is available to suggest that the principle is universal. The principle appears to be valid even though each individual has his own unique growth curves in reference to beginning and end points of cycles, maxima toward which they are progressing, and rates of growth. *Continuity*, in this sense, refers to adherence of the growth impetus to an unfolding design which early in the cycle begins to manifest its over-all characteristics. Much evidence is available to suggest the appropriateness of the use of the word as found in the nature of the individual to revert to an original pattern following removal of an environmental or organismic frustration (17). A child who shows deviation due to illness or emotional upset will tend to return to his original pathway of progress following recovery. Children given special attention in spelling can be boosted above the pattern suggested by previous growth data but more often than not will return to the appropriate place on an extrapolation of their earlier curve after being relieved of the extra motivation or after a vacation coming at the end of a remedial period.

Another way of expressing the idea of continuity is to say that the growth impulse constantly functions during the life of the individual. This concept should tend to clarify the thought and prevent debate on the idea that belief in *continuity* is inimical to the cycle concept. There is no dichotomy when growth is seen as both a quantitative and qualitative process acting under a continuous self-impelled organismic drive.

C. GROWTH VARIES AMONG INDIVIDUALS

Great differences are to be found among children. No two grow quite alike. Children differ in their readiness for learning a particular skill, in their rate of growth, or in the maximum toward which they are progressing. Some children are taller at one time than others and on a later date may be shorter.

Norms have been used to characterize individuality; consequently there has arisen the tendency to describe as individual, or individualistic, those children who deviate considerably from the average. To think that only that individual is unique who is "different" or extreme in his behavior is to admit ignorance of the full meaning of individuality. The most "normal" child of all children in a group is unique in many ways. Among a group of children in a given grade who have approximately equal "intelligence quotients," many differences may be found. Equivalent I.Q.'s or mental ages bespeak very little as to rates of growth, maxima toward which each individual is progressing, and ages at which maxima may be achieved.

Timing, rate of growth, and maximum have previously been mentioned as aspects of individual difference. These make up what might be called in a somewhat casual parlance the "three-dimensional" concept of growth, in which each dimension must be given consideration in appraising learning, growth, or development. This is a much more complex procedure than the utilization alone of the concept of status in explaining or accounting for individual difference. Status is the common and oversimplified idea of individual difference on which most experimentation has built its very unstable foundations. A child is short or a child is retarded in reading as compared with other children in his grade. Such an interpretation describes individuality in only a limited sense and tends to imply a constancy which does not exist. The short child *may* be tall tomorrow. In a year's time the "retarded" reader *may* be "average" or "superior."

Timing: Some children may be described as "dull" in reading at one time but at a later period be found to be excellent readers. To the fully informed student such categorization as "dull" or "excellent" represents oversimplification. Assuming no untoward factors in operation, many children characterized as "dull" while in the early grades may more adequately be described as following a naturally evolving pattern and thereby demonstrating an inevitably late starting point. Other children, following different patterns, demonstrate earlier starting points. In reference to reading, a range of approximately four years (50 months) is found between the time of the earliest and the latest starter (13).[2]

Rate: Differences among children may be found in rates of all kinds of growth and learning. A child may require a long or a short time to achieve optimum maturity. Two children with quite divergent intelligence quotients may be growing at approximately equal rates toward different maxima — cases 5M and 8M in the data listed below (13). Two children with equal I.Q.'s may be growing at the same rate toward different maxima — cases 13M and 14M. Other likenesses and differences may also be discovered.

Case	I. Q.	Maximum (score)	Rate (isochrones)	Starting Age	Finishing Age	Time Required (months)
1M	111	67.6	1.064	64.5	136.0	71.5
2M	111	79.4	1.207	69.4	63.0	132.4
3M	111	95.5	.745	63.6	165.5	101.9
4M	107	85.1	.868	69.7	136.5	87.4
5M	86	51.3	1.371	90.7	146.1	55.4
7M	90	57.5	.981	70.7	148.0	77.3
8M	106	69.2	1.382	81.2	136.1	54.9
9M	115	72.4	1.254	66.4	127.0	60.6
10M	115	95.5	.844	56.0	146.0	90.0
11M	105	74.1	1.198	74.0	137.5	63.5
12M	122	75.9	1.391	64.3	145.2	80.9
13M	111	63.1	1.485	74.1	125.2	51.2
14M	111	72.4	1.413	81.8	135.6	53.8
15M	106	60.3	1.170	68.2	133.2	65.0

Some of the facts about rate may be summarized as follows:

a. Rate is governed by starting point and the maximum toward which growth is progressing.

b. A child with a lesser annual incremental increase may be growing at a greater rate, in reference to his starting point and maximum, than another child with a greater annual incremental increase.

c. Gross annual increments alone are valueless in scientifically determining benefits of remedial procedures or in evaluating instruction.

[2] Age of beginning reading was defined as the age at the one per cent point in the Courtis equation (6).

    d. Rate of growth changes from cycle to cycle even when environmental conditions are constant.

    e. Adolescent rates are usually greater in reference to maxima and starting points although gross increments may be lesser.

Maximum: Each child in a given cycle progresses toward a specific maximum as long as the conditions under which he is growing or learning are maintained. This means in reference to a given environment for learning and the child's potentiality to be affected by it that he is traveling toward individualized limits. Under standardized conditions just so much proficiency, optimally, may be attained in reading, spelling, height, etc. This fact is generally rejected by teachers, counselors, and measurement personnel. It is entirely unknown to parents except in a vague way in respect to physical growth. Most teachers and parents believe that a child's achievement is entirely governed by the amount of energy and effort expended, limited somewhat by intellectual ability.

Children may naturally grow toward the same maximum but with quite different rates. Cases 9M and 14M in the preceding group are progressing toward exactly the same maximum of 72.4. They have approximately equal I.Q.'s but differ in both rate and timing aspects. The most striking difference between them is in the matter of starting points. 9M begins to read at 66.4 months, 14M at 81.8. This is a difference of 15.4 months, and yet they are both progressing toward the same maximum.

Some of the facts about maximum may be stated as follows:

    a. Each cycle of growth has its own maximum.

    b. Some children who are early starters may grow with lesser rates toward higher maxima.

    c. A high maximum does not necessarily imply a rapid rate of growth.

    d. Intelligence as it is conventionally conceived is more closely related to maximum than to rate or to starting or finishing point.

    e. Adolescence adds an increment to the preadolescent maximum.

D. GROWTH IS MODIFIABLE

The impulse to grow is innate and is a powerful force in the growth pattern. Nevertheless, under specific conditions, growth may be modified in terms of rate, timing, or maximum. Timing, probably, is the one dimension of growth which is least susceptible to environmental change.

The idea of modification has common acceptance. What is often misunderstood is the manner in which it may be brought about most effectively. Attempts at modification, usually considered as change in status of the child in a particular skill, through pressure, excessive drill, and extensive practice periods, are usually ineffectual or downright harmful when measured in terms of permanent learning. Pressure tactics have varying effects. If applied during a pre-readiness period, frustration or serious psychological damage may result. When applied during the growth upswing, specious gain may take place which will tend to recede to the original rate of growth when pressure is released.

In the ideal situation, modification results with the greatest permanent benefits by continuous work on improvement of the total culture surrounding the child.

SCIENTIFIC ASPECTS OF GROWTH

A. THE GROWTH DESIGN

Growth follows a describable design. When the conditions under which growth takes place are constant, it progresses in a regular sequence marked by a slow beginning followed by a rapid rise which gradually levels off into what is conventionally called a *plateau*. Measurement, frequently, does not accompany the entire growing period and, consequently, the *design* is not clear. For example, reading tests are usually not administered to children until skill in reading is sufficiently advanced to respond to the test stimulus. As a result reading is, more often than not, seen by the observer as without its slow, halting beginning.

The regularity of progress in the curve depends upon the consistency of the individual and the environment throughout the growth period. Changed conditions in testing, physical or mental well-being, and possibly temperament, produce variation. The curve instead of progressing smoothly goes up by spurts and losses. Nevertheless the trend is upward for an overwhelming per cent of school children. Height growth and mental and other growths are generally curvilinear, under the conditions stated above.

B. THE CYCLIC NATURE OF GROWTH

Some growths begin at birth and end early in the child's life. Others begin at birth and continue to six, seven, or eight years of age. Some begin at two and continue until twelve, thirteen, or fourteen. Many of the learning skills begin in childhood and continue through adolescence. Any learning or growth curve that continues through periods of internal organismic change not only shows design as described but also shows a new pattern (cycle), determined by inner organismic change, which endures until a later organismic change takes place. One or more designs, then, following in a sequence, result in what has been designated as *cycles* (6).[3]

This fact was apprehended for some time before it had much scientific verification. Psychologists and biologists wrote and spoke of early childhood, preadolescent, and adolescent cycles at about the time that learning and mental growths were pictured as curvilinear from their beginning to maturity without any noticeable break in the pattern. Baldwin apparently saw the multicyclic pattern of the curve by admitting a difference in preadolescent and adolescent growth rates (1). In their study of mental development Flory and Freeman found numerous cases in which rate positively accelerated from about ten or eleven years of age to about fifteen (9).

Currently there is much more recognition of the "paralleling" of all kinds of growth curves in children. Thorpe goes so far as to say that every major study in which data were collected regularly on the same children reported that growth is cyclic, proceeding by a series of accelerations and decelerations (19). The most con-

---

[3] Cycles are something more than deviations in the data. Deviations of data in the way of curves may be considered only as cycles when the deviations and shifts parallel natural organismic changes.

vincing statement of all is one made by Shuttleworth (18). In studying twenty-two kinds of growth he concluded:

> . . . . First, all twenty-two dimensions exhibit two major growth cycles consisting of accelerating and decelerating phases. Second, the growth phases of the first cycle are initiated at different ages and are of different durations such that the growth trends of the twenty-two dimensions are not synchronized. Third, the growth phases of the second cycle, in respect to a given menarcheal or M. G. — age group, are initiated at approximately the same ages and are of similar durations such that the growth trends of the twenty-two dimensions are synchronized.

The question can legitimately be raised as to the total number of cycles in the life of the individual. Courtis, earlier, charted four distinct cycles — the prenatal, infancy or early childhood, childhood or preadolescence, and adolescence (6). Although determination of the exact number is an important problem, of more significance to our discussion is the acceptance of the idea of cyclic growth.

C. CONSTANTS IN THE GROWTH CYCLE

The names used to describe the characteristics of the growth cycle have already been partially discussed. They are *starting point* (incipiency), *rate,* and *maximum.* Measurement persons have long talked of *rate* of growth, but *starting point* and *maximum* are relatively new concepts. Unfamiliarity with these two terms is the result of failure to think of growth as a cyclic affair, particularly in the realm of school achievement.

The term *starting point* is becoming better known through research on reading readiness and on individual and sex differences in the ages at which children arrive at pubescence (21). An interesting and significant needed study is one which will compare the effects of organismic change on both the academic and the physiological curve. In a pilot study based on observations of reading growth, it was found that changes in reading performance presaged the beginning of adolescence just as conclusively as physiological changes, both in respect to time of its advent and with similar sex differences (14).

Rate: Rate is the one aspect in the growth or learning curve of an individual which is not entirely unfamiliar to teachers. Teachers often use the word *rate* to compare one child with another. When such comparisons are made in school achievement, the implication is made that the fast learner is the superior performer. This may or may not be true, depending on the child. Quite often a fast learner is growing toward a low maximum, and a slow learner is growing toward a high one. Or, for another example, two children may be growing at different rates toward approximately equal maxima. Three cases present interesting comparisons. Doris and Dorothy are children with equivalent I.Q.'s (100, 102), whereas Betty's average I.Q. is 81. All three showed approximately equal biannual gains on the Stanford Reading Test ranging from 24 to 27.

Case	I.Q. (*Ave.*)	Scores			Biannual Gains		
		2A	4A	6A	2A to 4A	4A to 6A	Average
Doris (1F)	100	31	61	84	30	23	26.5
Betty (11F)	81	19	47	67	28	20	24.0
Dorothy (43F)	102	23	59	77	36	18	27.0

There are other ways, however, of demonstrating rate of growth than by computing increase in score from year to year. It is the latter method which is best known and which leads to oversimplification. The other, less-known method, demands consideration of length of time of the growth period in reference to the peak toward which the child is growing. When these are taken into consideration we find quite different rate computations on these children (13):

	PREADOLESCENT DATA			ADOLESCENT DATA [4]		
Case	Max.	Rate	Starting Pt.	Max.	Rate	Starting Pt.
Doris	63.1	.895	72.6	50.4	.543	125.9
Betty	50.1	.951	77.6	52.8	.495	123.8
Dorothy	67.6	1.735	95.0	38.3	.650	143.5

Dorothy, equivalent in I.Q. to Doris and showing equivalent biannual increments, now achieves almost a doubling of Doris' rate in the preadolescent cycle — 1.735 units to .895 units. How

[4] Adolescent data did not appear in the original study.

can this happen? In these particular cases it was mainly a matter of starting points. Doris began to read at 72.6 months, whereas Dorothy did not begin until she was 95.0 months of age. To arrive at about the same maximum, which was the case, Dorothy necessarily progressed at a much higher rate.

Maximum: The maximum in a cycle of growth is the term used to describe the point toward which a growth curve is progressing. In a sense it corresponds to what was formerly referred to as *physiological limit,* although it has a much broader connotation. Defined specifically it may be termed the point a growth curve is approaching as it levels off and decreases in score-unit increments. It is the one aspect in the growth design least affected by teaching and, apparently, most affected by heredity.

RELATION OF GROWTH TO LEARNING

A. GROWTH AND LEARNING ARE COMPLEMENTARY

Growth in height of an individual is not an isolated effect, nor is the growth in reading an isolated effect. The lay person and many teachers often consider growth and learning as separate entities of individuality. Organismic drive produces change in the height of an individual. The same drive likewise produces an achievement increase over and beyond learning or teaching efforts. Growth and learning therefore are inseparable, representing a unity which is present throughout the entire period of development. Case after case could be marshaled to point out that it is impossible to distinguish one growth pattern from another when several are reduced to growth ages and graphed in comparable age units. A reading curve and a weight curve, for example, when placed together, are strikingly similar (Figure 3).

In the illustration given, Jack made remarkable gains after being given considerable teacher attention in the last half of the third grade (3A). The teacher was given much credit for the reading gain. It is clearly obvious that there was much improvement. But in looking at the weight curve one may make some interesting observations. Weight resulted in vastly greater increments after a previous year of very little gain. The total picture suggests that this child was a late grower. The assumption can be reasonably made that improvement in reading would have resulted without the extra effort.

The illustration is offered to demonstrate that the *interrelations* of growth and learning are ignored most of the time in evaluating instruction. The illustration also suggests that when the child reaches a satisfactory maturity status, learning takes place rather easily.

B. LEARNING BEST AT CERTAIN PERIODS OF MATURITY

There are definite degrees of maturity necessary for various kinds of learning. The teacher who tries to force learning in

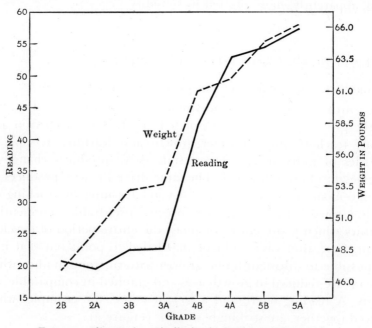

FIGURE 3. Illustrating Similarity in Design of Curves in Reading and Weight: Jack (144M)

Data

Grade:	2B	2A	3B	3A	4B	4A	5B	5A
Reading:	21	19	22	22.5	42	53	54	58
Weight:	47	48.2	53.2	54.2	61.2	61.5	65.5	66

advance of essential general maturity is not only inefficient but is setting up an inhibitory situation which may immediately affect the child's personality in such a way as to cause him to rebel against learning when the time for its natural beginning arrives (17).

A new word coined to show the relationship is *pacing*. It refers to the presentation of learning experiences in terms of difficulty, scope, and sequence according to the child's maturity. The teacher who uses *pacing* effectively is careful to see that the job to be done is interesting enough to challenge the child, simple enough to be performed with reasonable effort, and meaningful enough to provide functional application.

C. LEARNING BEST AS PART OF A TOTAL PATTERN

Learning is always most effective, other factors properly considered, when it takes place in a total environment rather than in just a part of one. This is another way of saying that personal needs can be best met only when the individual identifies himself as part of that total. A good illustration may be found in the way in which a young boy learns the motor skills necessary in playing baseball. He learns these skills best by first playing the game. It is only after playing that he wants to practice batting, throwing, sliding, or pitching. When he needs practice in some of these elements, he will practice the skills he needs most, but it is always the game that is the motivating factor. In other words, the total environment provides him with the most effective learning opportunity. Teachers will readily see the application of this point to motor learning. They will also appreciate the ease with which the environment can be provided to bring out the necessary motivation for motor-skill improvement. To see the point in relation to reading, arithmetic, etc., and to provide the identifying and motivating environment is more difficult.

D. UNRELATED AREAS OF LEARNING INEFFICIENT

Schools traditionally have emphasized the acquisition of specific, discrete skills. Skill learning is not necessarily harmful. The wrong done is in the method used and in the assumption that unrelated learnings automatically become a part of a whole. If children are failing to learn — as is said in every generation, but more vociferously in some generations than in others — the fault proba-

bly lies in the deficiencies of traditional teaching rather than in
the idea that all schools have gone "progressive."

Discrete skills, after all, are worthwhile only as they contribute
to total performance. They are tools to be used in the achievement of physical, mental, vocational, and emotional well-being.

IMPLICATIONS OF GROWTH FOR INSTRUCTION

A. THE CHILD MUST BE TREATED AS AN INDIVIDUAL

Respect for Individuality Essential: The most important implication for instruction from our knowledge of child growth and development comes from the fact of individuality. Each child is
unique. Each child is himself and quite unlike any other.

Measurement of instruction, if not handled with caution, tends
to obliterate this concept. It urges the interpreter to think of an
individual in categories and as a deviant, above or below, from a
concept of normalcy. If the efforts of all those working in counseling, testing, and remedial work, and if all those teachers who are attempting to make the child into something that he isn't, or are
attempting to produce conformity of behavior or performance,
were successful all at once, we would certainly have a strange
world. Conformity within reason must be achieved, but not at the
expense of reasonable individual expression.

Faulty Use of Averages: Measurement people, among others, have
not yet come to grips with the total problem of diagnosis as seen
from the longitudinal point of view. A recent bulletin, for example, appropriately enough suggests three areas of investigation
for diagnosing sources of learning difficulty — (1) extent of mastery of the tools of learning, (2) personality or mental health,
and (3) appraisal of ability (20). On the basis of this hypothesis
it then suggests that a minimum program of educational diagnosis
demand three tests. One should deal with basic skills, one with
personality appraisal, and one with intelligence.

The application of such a program to Jack, shown in Figure 3,
would have been of but little help had it been applied while
Jack was in the second grade or in the first half of the third grade.
Jack would have produced low scores in basic skills, but no relation between these would have been found with his mental health,

which was good, or with his ability (I.Q. measurement), which was high. Jack's case is merely typical of the many children who mature slowly and therefore must be handled in a more comprehensive manner than by evaluation of status deficiency.

During recent years longitudinal studies have done much to weaken faith in the practice of normative comparison. The graph of the averages of hundreds of six-, seven-, eight-, or nine-year-old children is quite different from that of an individual child (7). Individual curves tend to be more curvilinear. The deviations from norms of large numbers of individual children show the obvious unfairness of carrying such a comparison too far.[5] Some children approach the norm at one point and pull away at a later period, and they do so when developing under relatively constant environmental conditions (2).

B. COMPLEXITY OF GROWTH INDICATES THE UNFAIRNESS OF CONVENTIONAL INTERPRETATION

Inadequacy of Single Measures: When only one measurement or even a battery of single measurements is used, accurate and valid interpretation of individual children is almost impossible. This is true for two reasons. First, because at least one of every four measurements taken in the public schools is faulty, and second and more important, status interpretation gives but a slight clue as to progress or design of the growth aspect under scrutiny.

Two girls with different reading scores may be used to illustrate the point that growth is a very complex process and does not lend itself to simple interpretations. Case histories reveal that Girl B received "F's" in reading in both the first and second grades. In grade three she was given "C's," in grades four and five her marks were "B's," and finally, in grade six, "A's." Girl A's marks followed a reverse pattern. In terms of growth, each girl was found to be following a rather precise sequence. This would indicate consistent growth throughout all grades. There were no deviations from the curves that would justify special explanations. Thus, the marks given had no reliable interpretative values regarding the growth of either child.

[5] See Figure 17, p. 65.

In analyzing the curves, it was discovered that Girl A started reading sufficiently early to seem superior, whereas Girl B started so late as to be considered dull. In regard to maxima, Girl B was definitely "superior," but for three years this potentiality was unrecognized. Adequate measurement and an ensuing study of the pattern would have singled out this child as having high reading potentiality.

Injustice of Status Analysis: Both girls achieved adequately at all points. There was a slight difference in the two rates of growth, a considerable difference between maxima, and a difference in starting points. Such an analysis shows the inherent error in comparisons of status only, and, incidentally, illustrates the complete inadequacy of marks for appraising and evaluating achievement in relation to potentiality. The analysis also points out that the concepts of the meanings of "superior," "inferior," etc., need an overhauling.

C. STUDY OF CYCLES IMPORTANT

Obviously, the curvilinear nature of growth and its manifestation in cycles have important implications for those who would undertake interpretation of measures of elementary school children.

In the first place the cycle design practically relegates all single measurements on a given child or group of children to the most elementary of interpretations. Single measures may be used in the aggregate to obtain grade or school norms but are almost useless for individual interpretation regardless of the claims made for them. It is now known that mere immaturity can easily become confused with deficiencies or weaknesses. And even "real" deficiencies are often products of anomalies of behavior. Consequently, and second in our list of implications, is the idea that identification of cyclic growth requires a series of measures — annual, semiannual, or monthly. Identification of *design,* as described above, prescribes a measurement series which has as its goals (1) determination of the nature of the curve — past and present, and (2) determination of the child's current status in reference to that design.

Third, knowledge of the precise nature of a given growth curve for one child is important, but in addition it is necessary to determine other growth designs for that child in order to further evaluate the particular design under study. The child who demonstrates a slow-moving curve in reading through the first and second grades, for example, may be undergoing normal growth or be demonstrating growth far below his optimum. A study of various other growths may demonstrate a similar phenomenon or the curves, contrarily, may depict a swift upsurge at this time quite different from that of the curve under scrutiny.

Fourth, for the technician in instructional evaluation, the principles of child development as portrayed in this text offer suggestions for highly important research in determining basic growth interrelations. By a combination of the Olson and Courtis techniques, it is possible to determine specific mathematical relationships between various aspects of growth, with the possibility of arriving at verifiable findings concerning them which are almost entirely unapproachable by conventional usage. Ability to predict from one growth phase to another for *an individual child* is the reward promised for success in this venture.

Fifth, complete instructional measurement should contribute not only to accurate estimates of the child's growth and development but likewise should provide a means for explaining variation from the pattern. In this thought there can emerge a goal in diagnostic procedure which is a far cry from current attempts to explain by reference to norms.

D. IMPORTANCE OF PRINCIPLES

A knowledge of the principles of child growth is of great importance to the person interpreting child development data (10). The observer who has had the opportunity to study the normal course of maturation and who understands the data so collected has a much better basis for dealing justly and intelligently with the child (3).

Teachers readily accept the facts regarding the physical development of children. They are aware of varying growth rates and varying maxima which children attain. No teacher would risk appearing so ridiculous as to attempt to force all children to approximate a given height norm. All teachers know that physiological development is determined by factors over which they have little control.

In regard to measures of achievement in school subjects, their attitudes are quite different. The idea persists that children below the norm represent teaching failures, and children above the norm represent teaching successes. Longitudinal testing of children and the findings of child development are beginning to make an impact (11). Continuous testing of individual children produces results which indicate that scores on tests have little meaning unless appraised in terms of each child's developmental pattern.

There is some danger that the principles of child growth and development will be given too little or too much attention. The facts as presented may give the impression that such growth as takes place is inevitable and that there is little to do about it one way or another. Because of strong individuality in the growth sequences, teachers may come to believe that forces beyond their control are too potent and that if a child is ready to learn he will learn.

The only answer to the dilemma is further understanding and continued efforts to apply findings to classroom procedure. Measurement has a great responsibility in improving the situation. The wise teacher knows that she can expect no more growth or learning than that which represents a reasonable advance on the child's own growth pattern. She need not use pressure and disciplinary methods on the slow learner, nor does she overpraise the child whose status is high but who achieves easily because he is an early-maturing child. As Courtis has said (5):

> . . . Wisdom, plus records, and faith, spell inspiration and power; ignorance and inadequate equipment generate conflict, disaster, tragedy. . . .

SELECTED REFERENCES

1. BALDWIN, B. T., *The Physical Growth of Children from Birth to Maturity.* Iowa City: University of Iowa, Studies in Child Welfare, I, 1:92, 1921.
2. BAYLEY, NANCY, "Individual Patterns of Development," *Child Development,* 27, 1:45–74, March, 1956.
3. BRANDT, R. M., AND PERKINS, H. V., *Research Evaluating a Child Study Program.* Monographs of the Society for Research in Child Development, Inc., Vol. XXI, Serial No. 62, No. 1, 1956. Lafayette, Indiana: Child Development Publications.

4. BRECKENRIDGE, M. E., AND VINCENT, E. L., *Child Development*. Philadelphia: Saunders, 1949.

5. COURTIS, S. A., "Discipline under the Growth Concept," *Child Growth in an Era of Conflict,* edited by C. V. Millard, Fifteenth Yearbook, Department of Elementary School Principals. Lansing: Michigan Education Association, 1944, p. 6.

6. ——, "What Is a Growth Cycle?", *Growth*, I, 13:160, May, 1937.

7. ——, "Major Growth Concepts," *Pupil Development and the Curriculum*. Ann Arbor: Bureau of Educational Reference and Research, University of Michigan, 1937-38.

8. FRANK, L. K., "What is Growth?", Radio Forum on Growth and Development of the Child, 1936-37.

9. FREEMAN, F. N., AND FLORY, C. D., Growth in Intellectual Ability as Measured by Repeated Tests, Monographs of the Society for Research in Child Development, Vol. II, Serial 9, No. 2. Lafayette, Indiana: Child Development Publications.

10. GARRISON, K. C., *Growth and Development*. New York: Longmans, Green, 1952, pp. 61-79.

11. HENDERSON, R. L., "Do Teachers Profit from Self-directed Child Study?", *Elementary School Journal*, 56:152-157, 1955.

12. MEREDITH, H. V., "An Empirical Concept of Physical Growth," *Child Development*, 9, 2:166-167, June, 1938.

13. MILLARD, C. V., "The Nature and Character of Preadolescent Growth in Reading Achievement," *Child Development*, 11, 2:71-114, 1940.

14. ——, "A Comparison of Organismic Concordance-Discordance Ratings with Projective Appraisals of Personal Adjustment," *Merrill-Palmer Quarterly*, 3, 3:198-210, February, 1957.

15. NALLY, THOMAS P. F., *The Relationship between Achieved Growth in Height and the Beginning of Growth in Reading*. East Lansing, Michigan: College of Education (doctoral dissertation), 1953.

16. OLSON, W. C., "Meaning of Growth," *Child Growth in an Era of Conflict,* edited by C. V. Millard. Fifteenth Yearbook, Department of Elementary School Principals. Lansing: Michigan Education Association, 1944, p. 1.

17. ——, *Child Development*. Boston: D. C. Heath and Company, 1949.

18. SHUTTLEWORTH, F. K., *The Physical and Mental Growth of Girls and Boys Age Six to Nineteen in Relation to Age at Maximum Growth,* Monographs of the Society for Research in Child Development, Vol. IV, Serial 22, No. 3. Lafayette, Indiana: Child Development Publications, 1939.

19. THORPE, L. P., *Child Psychology and Development*. New York: McGraw-Hill, 1946, pp. 262-272.

20. TIEGS, E. W., "Educational Diagnosis," California Test Bureau, 1948.

21. UDOH, E. A., *Relationship of Menarche to Achieved Growth in Height*. East Lansing, Michigan: College of Education, Michigan State University (doctoral dissertation), 1955.

3

INTERRELATIONS OF GROWTH—
AN APPROACH TO A STUDY OF
THE CHILD AS A WHOLE

THE NEED FOR STUDY

Most of the approaches to our knowledge of the child have been made from detailed and systematic study of some one phase of the child's total development. At best not more than two or three aspects of the child as a whole have been investigated over any considerable period of time. It is true that the same children have been studied in respect to many types of growth. In reference to the total child these have been additive rather than integrative. Studies of physical growth, mental growth, and educational achievement have been made and published, and the results are now well known, but since generalizations about the whole child tend to go beyond complete verification, there is great need for a new type of study in which the interrelationships of many phases of development are investigated. In such studies the child's total growth will be observed rather than many discrete growths. It should be obvious to anybody that the child as a whole is affected by school. We know enough about the various influences affecting growth to know that physical growth, or the lack of it, has some relationship to other kinds of growth. There is no question among investigators as to the intimate interrelations of many aspects of the organism's activity in the child's total environment. Disease, malnutrition, emotional disturbances, injury, and shock are not limited in their effects to a single kind of growth but influence total development. It is therefore true that observations, measures, and performance scores represent something more than the specific growth being evaluated.

The purpose of this chapter is to point out and describe evolving techniques for studying growth interrelations, to discuss briefly the generalizations that apply to instruction, and to suggest further work to be done in this field.

STUDY TECHNIQUES

Techniques for child study can be classified in many ways. The simplest is to classify method of study under two headings. The one may be called *status study,* in which single testings on a large number of cases are used, and the second, *longitudinal study,* in which fewer cases are studied over a long period of time. The length of time for longitudinal study varies. It may be assumed that cases are followed as long as they are available and most satisfactorily when the period of study covers complete cycles of development.

A. STATUS STUDIES

Ever since psychologists became familiar with statistical techniques, the problem of determining growth relationships has been a popular one. Using cross-sectional data such as averages, the procedure for computing correlations among different types of measurements for the same children became standardized.

Early Correlation Studies of Physical and Mental Growth. Probably the most investigated problem is the relationship between physical and mental growth. In general, this type of study produced positive, but low, statistical correlations. The majority of these were below .30 and in the main are to be found between .10 and .20.

In some instances height was compared with mental growth. In other instances, the physical variable was weight, or dentition, or sitting height, etc. The resulting correlations, from .10 to .30, are positive, of course, but too low to indicate much relationship. The degree of physical growth (as measured) seemed to have no value in predicting or determining mental status. Nor does mental status data have any value in determining or predicting physical status when studied from this approach. Boynton and Parsons, for example, studied data on intelligence, height, weight, lung capacity, and head circumference. Some forty correlations were computed (3). All of these were positive but low, with an approximate range of .10 to .30.

University of Chicago Studies. Other studies of this type yielded similar results. At the University of Chicago, Abernethy arrayed physical and mental measurements of 340 girls and boys about equally divided (1). Measurements were collected each year and correlations were reported for each age level from eight to seventeen years of age. Again these ranged from .15 to .30. Intelligence was studied in connection with height, weight, ossification ratio, lung capacity, and chest girth. The highest correlation was found between intelligence and standing height. Considering all the data, the correlations for girls were lower than those for boys. Another interesting finding was the fact that the correlations were lower as the children approached college age.

University of California Studies. Similar results were reported from the University of California (11). Scores were obtained from 250 boys and girls on the California Pre-School Mental Scale with the young children and on the Stanford-Binet Test with the older children. These data were correlated with measurements of height and weight. Correlations ranged between .15 and .20, with no sex differences noted.

The problem has also been approached through a study of physical defects in connection with mental status. These investigations were based on the idea that malnutrition or disease might be direct causes of mental deficiency. The general procedure followed was to administer preliminary tests, correct the defect, and remeasure. Reports of almost all the experiments showed that there was no increase in mental ability after correction. It was concluded that the physical defect *per se* had little connection with the mental status of the children concerned.

On the other hand, there is much evidence to indicate that mentally retarded children have more than the normal number of physical defects of various kinds.

Conclusions regarding Physical Defects. It is no exaggeration to say that in reference to mental defectives investigators are generally agreed on the following (10) :

 1. Growth proceeds more slowly.
 2. Dental development is retarded.
 3. There are more and graver physical defects.

The statistical correlations, however, do not strongly underwrite these assumptions. What conclusion can be made? Can one infer that physical defects cause mental deficiency or that low intelligence leads to a greater incidence of physical deficiency? The only inference rightfully drawn is that on our present evidence neither can be proved to be the cause or the effect of the other. Both may be accompaniments or results of some general environmental conditioning. On the other hand, it may be that, since it is impossible to control all the factors in such research, the results cannot be considered definitive.

B. LONGITUDINAL STUDIES

The low correlations among various phases of mental and physical growth and other data dealing with the problem have not discouraged further research among students of child development. They feel that these low correlations with cross-sectional data are inevitable, since individual differences in the sequences of growth are obscured by the technique of "averaging" used in status studies.

Cyclic development in all growth suggests definite interrelations and thereby encourages wider and more intensive experimentation (9, 12).

Courtis argues that individual mental growth parallels physiological growth, showing the same cycles and certain common points of acceleration, timing, and deceleration (8). This seems to imply that a general factor is operative throughout all maturational periods.

Findings that would completely validate these statements are not yet available. Considerable progress has been made, however, and much more is known than is generally applied in classroom instruction. A major difficulty lies in the problem of deciding whether efforts should be pointed toward the discovery of principle or toward interpretations on individual children. At present, although it is little realized, research has made greater progress in discovery of principle than in explaining differences in behavior among individual children.

A number of techniques have been employed in interpreting longitudinal data. Some of these involve a very simple handling of growth measurements; others necessitate more complex procedures. Both kinds require continuous, cumulative study and, in the main, represent an effort to arrive at principles as well as an attempt to interpret the growth and development of individual children (4, 23).

It is not the purpose of this chapter to give a detailed analysis of each technique, but to point out that there are more complex and scientific methods for studying the child than one would infer from much of the current educational literature. We shall discuss techniques for analyzing growth patterns rather than those aimed at interpreting status.

1. Minot's Arithmetic Method

Percentage of Advance during Given Intervals. Minot's method has been used considerably in clinical study and in a general way by interpreters who describe growth in terms of the percentage of advance during a given interval of time. A description of its usage points out its simplicity (19):

> Take the weight at a given age, and the weight at the next older age for which there are observations . . . then express the daily (quarterly or annual) increase as a percentage of weight at the beginning of the period.

The argument advanced for this technique is based on its simplicity and rapidity and on the fact that it precludes smoothing or interpolation of data.[1] This technique provides data on individual growth but does not provide leads for analysis in the exact way possible in certain other techniques.

[1] See Figure 7, p. 42, for explanation of "smoothing."

2. Graph-Tangentmeter-Ratio Method

The graphical method offers possibilities for reasonably accurate interpretations of growth. The *tangentmeter* is a specially constructed graph to which the measured data can be applied. The Wetzel Grid is an illustration of this approach to analysis of performance (25). Wetzel has provided a means for plotting weight in relation to height and provides seven channels on a grid graph to record this relationship. Normal progress is the diagnosis when the measures so plotted ascend within any one of several channels. The seven channels provided represent a range from obesity to undernourishment. Deviation within a channel is not judged abnormal, but crossing from one channel to another is regarded as an indication of a problem deserving attention.

3. The Olson Technique

Organismic Age. One of the most popular methods for studying various interrelations was originated by Olson. Careful longitudinal studies of achievement in relation to other aspects of growth have been carried on for a number of years at the University of Michigan (20). Dr. Olson has directed attention toward the interrelations of such phases of growth as achievement in school subjects, height, weight, dental and carpal growth, growth in grip, and mental age. In order to make comparison easier, he translates all measures into an "age" category. Thereby, all ages can be averaged and an over-all, or *organismic,* age computed.

This method is simple, readily understood, and quickly applicable to individual cases. There is considerable logic in his idea that the expression of measurements in terms of age gives a maturity meaning and time significance to various measures and permits comparison of various kinds of growth for a given child.

His technique involves plotting growth ages in each area of growth above the point on the chronological ages at which they were taken and then connecting the points. A straight-line diagonal is drawn through the chart at the intersection of the scales for the same chronological and growth ages. A mental age of ten years, when the child is ten years old chronologically, would fall on the line. The diagonal assumes a year of growth for each year of life and provides a point of reference but is not necessarily considered a norm.[2]

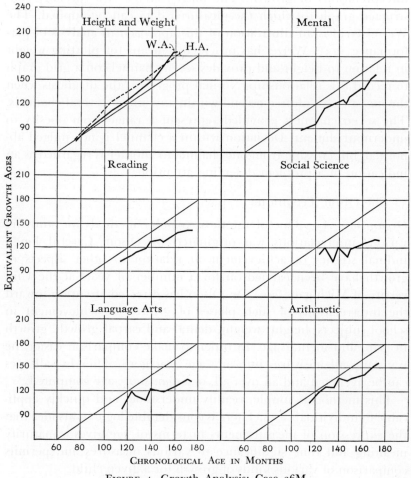

FIGURE 4. Growth Analysis: Case 36M

4. Growth Analysis (Olson Variation)

It is possible to utilize the Olson technique with variation as to the kind of data to be graphed. This can be done satisfactorily, however, only when there is no attempt to determine organismic

2 See Figures 4, 5, and 6.

age and the data is graphed for certain other purposes. Recommended scores for plotting are those obtained from cumulative achievement tests and from measures of height, weight, and mental age.

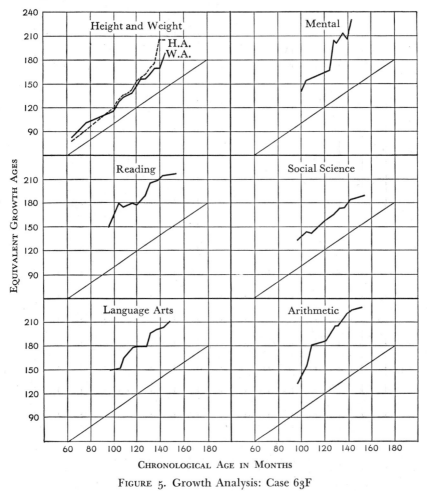

FIGURE 5. Growth Analysis: Case 63F

Advantage of Growth Analysis. This technique has the advantage of utilizing data available to the classroom teacher. Few schools at present are equipped to collect grip measures, carpal measures, dental measures, etc. It is possible that this concession to the practical leads the investigator even further from the discovery of the true curve of organismic or general development. Figures 4, 5, and 6 represent several illustrations of the use of the technique.

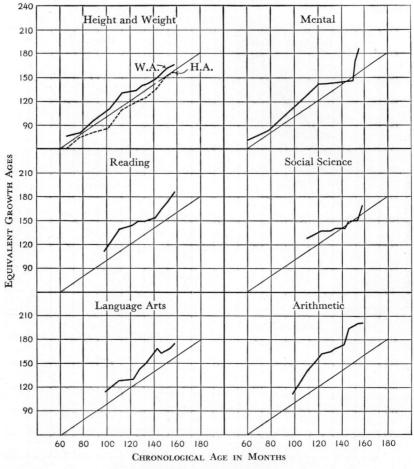

FIGURE 6. Growth Analysis: Case 70F

These three cases are respectively two girls and a boy. The boy represents a low level of school achievement and the two girls are representative of high normal and very high achievement. Data shown in the three figures illustrate the following general conclusions:

1. A gradual spread of growth as the child grows older.
2. A period of leveling or rounding off of all curves of an individual child, at an age segment approximating the child's pubescent period, followed by a second rise.
3. A marked period of fluctuation occurring at the beginning of the pubescent stage of development.

Practical Uses. The practicality of this technique is obvious. It is a simple device by which all growth measures can be translated into common denominators and thus made comparable. In any one of the figures, height age can be compared with mental age, reading age, or any of the other ages included. Since the data are reduced to a common denominator, it is possible to determine the spread of the child's growing abilities and to evaluate his general developmental pattern.[3]

5. Curve Fitting and Algebraic Differentiation

Although a number of techniques have been used in the biological sciences for evaluating growth, educators and those whose research involves the study of human beings have made little use of them. Courtis is outstanding as an educator who has studied the possibilities of using these techniques. Since he has undoubtedly been influenced by the work of biologists, we shall give a brief description of one of the better known systems that they employ and a somewhat more elaborate description of the Courtis method.

a. The Brody Method

Uses of the Exponential Formula. Brody's method enables the investigator to determine percentage values of growth based on rate (5). By the use of a formula, amounts of percentage increment or decrement are computed over given units of time. Brody makes no claims for the use of his formula on human data, but since it has been so used by some investigators, the following comment from Meredith is pertinent (15) :

---

[3] A study of many of such figures has been made. It has not been agreed upon yet whether a good educational program results in widespread performance or tends to keep individual performances within a limited distance of each other. In some cases a difference of 120 months exists between high and low growths.

> The procedure is economical and reliable. However, the formula is derived from the general equation for a simple exponential curve. Examination of the integral curves presented . . . will show that only two of these curves — those for maximum head length and maximum head breadth — approximate the exponential form. Consequently, this method is rejected as not being valid for use in this study.

In other words Meredith dismisses this method because the equations used do not seem to fit the data with which it has been tried. Since this technique has been used in very few studies, the reader must be content with Meredith's criticisms.

b. The Courtis Method

Isochrons. Courtis, using the Gompertz curve, has coined the word *isochron* to describe growth patterns. An isochron represents one per cent of the total time required to reach maturity in a given cycle of growth (6). Since the equation which he has developed reduces the picture of growth from a curve to a straight-line basis, it is assumed that equal growths are made for each unit of equal time. He has used his equation extensively with a multiplicity of types of growth data in predicting maxima, in pointing out and defining cyclic changes, and in studying the effect of factors influencing growth (7).

ILLUSTRATION OF THE COURTIS METHOD

Possibilities in the Courtis Method. The Courtis technique appears to offer the most complete method for studying growth interrelations. It is superior to the inspectional method and to the technique of norm comparison because it can be applied to any series of growth data and because it is mathematically exact. Possibilities which may be explored with this method are:

1. Possibility of refining the Olson age-curve by providing smoothed curves which rule out chance deviations.
2. Possibility of refining interpretations by comparing all available growth sequences in terms of percentages of development rather than status scores or derived ages.
3. Possibility of discovering the actual mathematical relation

ships between growth sequences which exist at given periods of development of the organism.

4. Possibility of predicting performance from the mathematical relationships so discovered.

To illustrate some of the possibilities just mentioned, the three
cases previously shown in Figures 4, 5, and 6 are used. The three
children selected represent one boy, apparently slow in growing
and with low normal mentality (36M) and two girls. One of the
girls is unusually bright, with a fine personality, quite mature at
an early age, and seemingly superior in all aspects of her development (63F). The other is a rather small girl, somewhat shy, and
with a high-normal intelligence (70F). Utilizing the actual data,
two-cycle equations were computed for each of the growth sequences for the three cases.

Advantage of Smoothed Curves. In Figures 4, 5, and 6 the actual
scores without any smoothing or interpolation were transmuted
into age equivalents and graphed. The advantage of such a graphical representation without smoothing is that it provides a clue to
individual consistency of performance. In comparing one individual with another it may be assumed that the reliability and validity of the test is constant and that the individual, rather than the
test, reflects deviations in performance.

The purpose of smoothing is to get down to the true pattern of
growth. For example, if a child has five mental scores, as follows:

Age at Testing *in Months*	*Mental Age* *in Months*
60	55
70	78
80	72
90	90
100	93

it may be safely assumed that the testing at 80 months of age does
not represent a real measure of the child at this time. Smoothing
would obscure this score, and a graph of this child's mental development would result in the second curve shown in Figure 7.

Utilizing the equations for smoothing, the original growth sequences appear as shown in Figures 8, 9, and 10. The advantage

of the smoothed curve is obvious. It portrays what the investigator believes is the true pattern of growth, and therefore gives more accurate data for studying the relation of one curve to another. On the other hand, the advantage of the picture of individual variability is eliminated.

The Courtis equation also provides an opportunity to study growth relations in an entirely new way, namely, in terms of the percentages of the maximum toward which the child is growing.

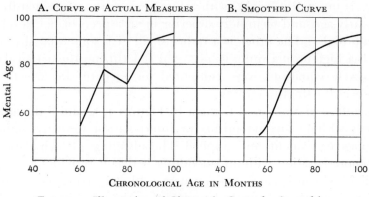

FIGURE 7. Illustration of Change in Curve by Smoothing
Technique

These are shown graphically for the three cases (Figures 11, 12, and 13).

Smoothing Brings Out Cycle Effect. The most interesting conclusion shown by the figures is the definite two-cycle picture especially indicated by the two girls (63F and 70F). This is not so obvious in regard to the boy (36M). Other phenomena are also brought out. For example, in the three cases, each child acquires a height maturity of 65 to 72 per cent before reading begins.

This kind of picture tends to give a clearer concept of the relations of achievement to mental maturity, to physiological development, etc. than the techniques previously described.

This type of portrayal also reverses the most obvious generalization drawn from the growth-age graph. In the typical growth-age portrayed, the curves for the individual begin within a narrow range of each other and tend to spread farther and farther apart as the child becomes older. In the percentage of development

graph, they begin with wide ranges, and as they approach maturity
the curves come closer together.

The possibility of discovering exact mathematical interrelations

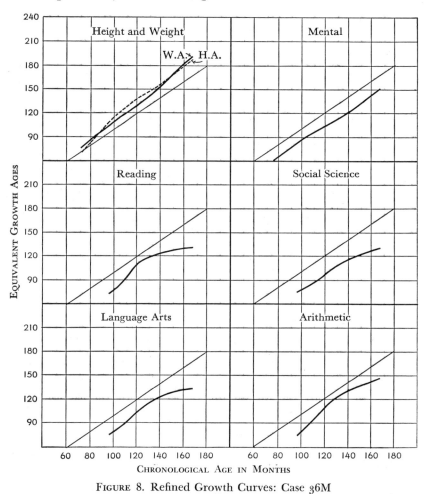

FIGURE 8. Refined Growth Curves: Case 36M

has never been fully explored. In the three cases used for illustrative purposes, as has just been noted, a height maturation of
between 65 and 75 per cent occurs before a child begins to read.
Is there, then, a definite mathematical relationship between physical growth and reading growth which might serve as a basis for
predicting when reading should begin? The discovery and utiliza-

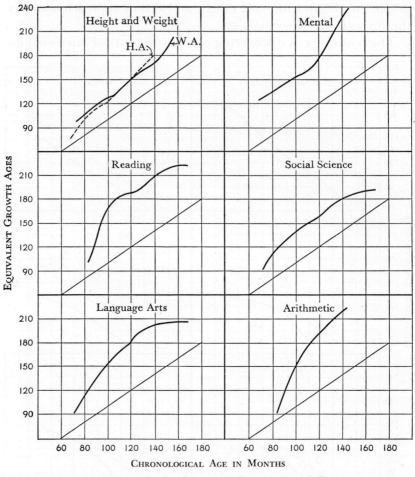

FIGURE 9. Refined Growth Curves: Case 63F

tion of such a ratio, if there is one, would do much to alleviate pressure in teaching and to reduce to a minimum the number of reading failures. This idea is not new. Teachers today talk about relating instruction to the maturity of the child, but they do not really know the maturity of the child. The current practice is a guess technique. The possibility suggested here would be in the realm of exact science. Let us illustrate further by posing certain problems and attempting their solution.

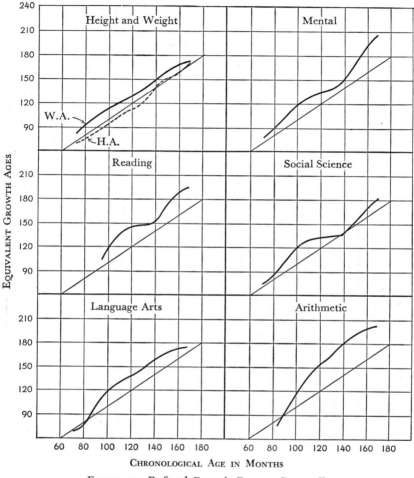

FIGURE 10. Refined Growth Curves: Case 70F

a. To What Extent Is There a Definiteness to Individuality of Growth?

Individuality in Cycle Patterns. Individuality may be reflected in several ways. One of the most striking aspects is the age at which the various cycles begin. For example, a child who enters puberty late should show a late adolescent spurt in all kinds of growth. A child who is precocious physically should show early starting points in all of his learning curves. In the three cases already mentioned, the beginning points in the achievement curves (reading,

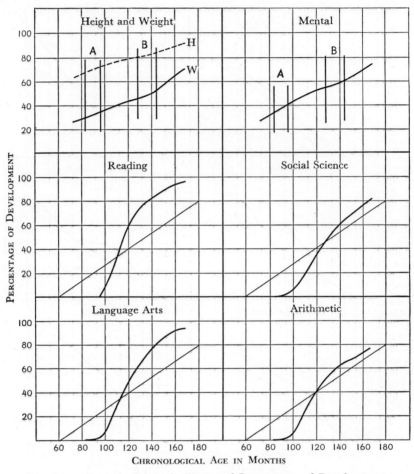

FIGURE 11. Growth Curves in Terms of Percentages of Development: Case 36M

A. Area of Physical and Mental Development for the Beginning of Pre-adolescent Learning

B. Area of Physical and Mental Development for Beginning of Adolescent Learning

language arts, social science, and arithmetic) were computed (7) as well as the beginning ages for the adolescent spurt for all the data (achievement, mental growth, height, and weight). Considerable individuality was found in the three cases. The boy (36M) with an I.Q. of 86 started all learning curves within two months

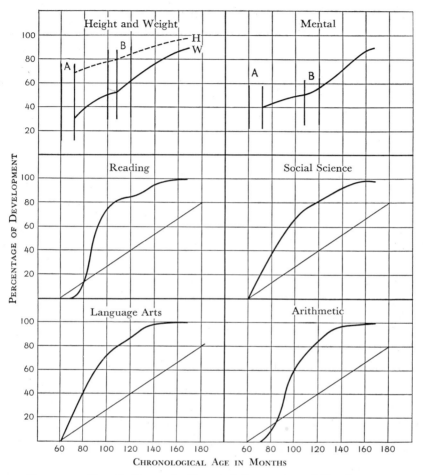

FIGURE 12. Growth Curves in Terms of Percentages of Development: Case 63F

A. Area of Physical and Mental Development for the Beginning of Pre-adolescent Learning

B. Area of Physical and Mental Development for Beginning of Adolescent Learning

of 92.4 months of age (7 years, 8.4 months). One of the girls (70F) started all curves within 5.6 months of a 76.8 average; whereas the other girl, the brightest child of all (63F), began all learning curves within 10.1 months of an average age of 64.9 months (Table I).

Individuality was also reflected in the ages at which the adolescent cycle began (Table I). The greatest variability from any child's average was found for Case 36M. All of this boy's adolescent cycles started within 12.9 months of his average of 131.3 months (10 years, 11.3 months).

TABLE I

AGES AT WHICH CYCLES STARTED

Trait Studied	Case 36M I.Q. 86	Case 70F I.Q. 114	Case 63F I.Q. 173
AVERAGE STARTING POINT OF PREADOLESCENT LEARNINGS	92.4	76.8	64.9
AVERAGE DEVIATION OF STARTING POINTS	2.0	5.6	10.1
AVERAGE STARTING POINT OF ALL ADOLESCENT GROWTH	131.3	123.7	110.7
AVERAGE DEVIATION OF STARTING POINTS	12.9	8.4	9.4

It is interesting to note that among these cases the starting point is earlier if the child is brighter. This holds for both the preadolescent and adolescent cycles.

b. To What Extent Can Generalizations Be Made concerning All Children?

It is unreasonable to assume that generalizations concerning growth interrelationships can be made on the basis of only three cases. Nevertheless, some similarities in growth relations of the three children indicate the possibility of determining exact ratios. Utilizing the equations again, percentages of maturity were computed for height, weight, and mental development for the ages at which the average learning curves (reading, language arts, social science, and arithmetic) began.[4] The results show quite striking uniformity for three children with such widely varying intelligence quotients (Table II). The average height maturity at the time when reading began was 66.8 per cent.

Uniformity of Results. Not one of the children showed more than a 3.1 per cent deviation from the average of the three cases in any

[4] Averaged for each child from the preadolescent equations of these curves.

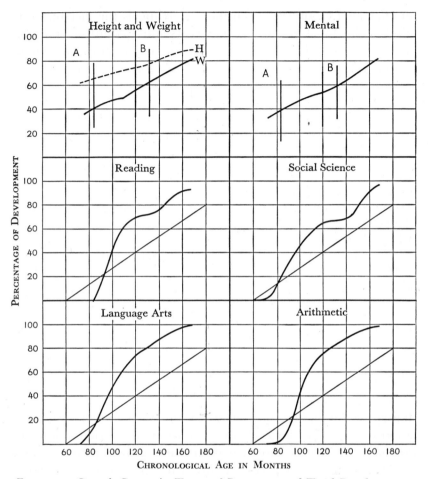

FIGURE 13. Growth Curves in Terms of Percentages of Total Development: Case 70F

A. Area of Physical and Mental Development for the Beginning of Pre-adolescent Learning

B. Area of Physical and Mental Development for Beginning of Adolescent Learning

one of the three interrelations. The similarities shown seem the more remarkable in view of the striking individual differences among the three children. In the first place, one child is a boy and the other two are girls, and there is a wide range of difference in the ability of the three children. One child has an I.Q. of 86 and another an I.Q. of 173. Even more startling is the fact that one child begins his skill learning at 5 years and 5 months (64.9 mo.) and the slowest child begins at 8 years and 9 months (92.4 mo.) (Table I).

TABLE II

UNIFORMITY OF VARIOUS GROWTH RELATIONS
AMONG THREE CHILDREN

Trait Studied	Case 36M I.Q. 86	70F 114	63F 173	*Average*
PER CENT OF HEIGHT GROWTH AT BEGINNING OF AVERAGE PRE-ADOLESCENT LEARNING CURVE	70.8	63.7	66.0	66.8 A.D.* ± 2.7
PER CENT OF WEIGHT GROWTH AT BEGINNING OF AVERAGE PRE-ADOLESCENT LEARNING CURVE	33.4	38.0	34.6	35.3 A.D. ± 1.9
PER CENT OF MENTAL GROWTH AT BEGINNING OF AVERAGE PRE-ADOLESCENT LEARNING CURVE	38.9	35.3	36.6	36.9 A.D. ± 1.3

* Average deviation.

PROGRESS OF RESEARCH IN GROWTH RELATIONSHIPS

In recent years considerable experimental progress with longitudinal techniques has been made in discovering exact growth relationships. These range all the way from correlation studies to prediction of mental status based on height-growth patterns (16). Experimentation has dealt mainly with physiological, mental, and school achievement studies. In contrast, little has been accomplished in relating emotional and social growth to other aspects of development. Experimentation in this field has failed to produce conclusive results, more because of the lack of techniques for longitudinal measurement than because of failure to recognize their importance. Through the methods available, progress has been made in the direction of discovering the extent of individual differences among children. So far, no scales have been constructed that would enable investigators to plot changes against age and experience. In spite of this gap in experimental procedure we now have enough knowledge to question many of the practices conventionally used in the elementary school. One of the outstanding conclusions obtained with these newer techniques, regarded as having considerable validity, is that a growth curve based on one set of data, such as height, for example, tends to express an underlying individuality also reflected in other growth measures, such as reading or mental growth. This point has been made by Courtis (8) for a number of years and by Olson (21). Millard, by calculating "height quotients" for forty boys, was able to predict intelligence quotients about as accurately as they were measured by intelligence tests (16). Much more work needs to be done in this area. Enough is known, however, to question seriously remedial work, drill, and other teaching devices. The idea that a child's learning curve is the product merely of perseverance, plus teacher effort or special method, can be seriously challenged (21).

Achievement as a Part of Total Growth. A second conclusion about the newer methods, sufficiently validated to provide many implications for instruction, concerns the nature of school achievement. The experiments of Bergman, Olson (20), and Courtis (8) all indicate that any phase of school achievement is a function of the total growth of the child. Under specific conditions that are relatively constant, such as a uniform curriculum, individual differences, according to individual design, maintain their unique characteristics. Height, weight, or carpal patterns, studied longitudinally (in contrast to status studies) are more predictive of a child's school achievement than the kind of teaching he receives, the course of study he takes, or the kind of drill or remedial work he does (24).

In a previous section, it was pointed out that growth is modifiable. This is true under certain conditions, but improved achievement is most difficult to bring about through teacher effort alone. Tilton's study shows the futility of diagnostic and remedial activities in producing permanently improved achievement (24).

Experiments on the relationship of affective or emotional states to various growth patterns seriously suggest that improvement can best be brought about by releasing stress and strain instead of adding it to the motivating factors. Studies to date indicate that there is more than a chance relationship between growth anomalies and disturbing behavior.

CONCLUSION

Purpose to Motivate Study. This chapter has been written to serve two purposes: (1) to present to students and to teachers in the field some of the little-known possibilities of understanding the growth and development of children; (2) to point out that what is needed now is not more detailed information but recommendations and procedures for using the data now available.

For Classroom Teachers. Students in training to become teachers and teachers in the field have been kept in mind in presenting the material of this chapter. It is recognized that in many teaching situations all the teacher need do is to keep fairly good control of children, to follow the text, and to pass or fail children who do or do not come up to the standards of a given school or community. In this kind of situation no time is provided for anything more than superficial child study and nothing is done with data obtained. In such a school a knowledge of child development produces minimum results.

Opportunity in Child Development Studies. Because of the findings becoming available and because of their scientific implications for teaching, child development now offers a broad field for technical study. If all teachers were trained in it, there would be much greater progress in applying the findings of child study to instructional reorganization. With such knowledge, parents would easily recognize teachers as a professional group rather than as "keepers" of children. The technical knowledge of child development is so vast that acquisition of it would require a type of professional training comparable to the study of law and medicine in its comprehensiveness.

Need for Expanded Teacher Training Program. It must also be clear that if teachers are to acquire this knowledge and training they must go beyond the present limits of teacher training programs. The only alternative is to have in the schools experts who study children, arrive at conclusions, and make decisions regarding implications for instruction for the larger group who are without these skills.

Need for Research. For the research worker or the expert in child development, this chapter indicates the need for research which will lead to broad generalizations concerning growth. The most recent findings on growth interrelations tend to challenge much of the work now classified as studies of readiness. Too much attention is given to a vague concept of maturity and too little toward determining "how much."

Moreover, some of the equations and techniques for precise analysis of individual growth need much further study and investigation. Incredibly few educators have experimented even slightly with them. Investigators studying child development from an educational viewpoint have tended to emphasize the social forces influencing growth, development, and learning at the expense of the biological. Both need to be given equal emphasis.

It is not possible to give a thumbnail sketch of growth and development, nor is there a mass approach to child study. The attempts of teachers and educators to devise simple forms for recording growth data are either pitiable, or more optimistically, a step in the right direction.

SELECTED REFERENCES

1. ABERNETHY, M. E., *Relationships between Mental and Physical Growth*, Monographs of the Society for Research in Child Development, Vol. I, No. 7. Washington: National Research Council, 1936.
2. ASMUSSEN, ERLING, AND HEEBOL-NIELSEN, K. R., "A Dimensional Analysis of Physical Performances and Growth in Boys," *Journal of Applied Psychology*, 7:593–603, 1955.
3. BOYNTON, P. L., AND PARSONS, R. F., "Pupil Analysis in the Peabody Demonstration School," *George Peabody College Bulletin*, 1935.
4. BAYLEY, NANCY, "Individual Patterns of Development," *Child Development*, 27:45–74, 1956.
5. BRODY, SAMUEL, *Growth and Development with Special Reference to Domestic Animals, III. Growth Rates, Their Evaluation and Significance*. Columbia: University of Missouri, Agricultural Experiment Station, Research Bulletin 97, 1927.
6. COURTIS, S. A., "Maturation Units for the Measurement of Growth," *School and Society*, 30:683–690, 1929.
7. ——, *The Measurement of Growth*. Ann Arbor: Brumfield, 1932.
8. ——, "Maturation as a Factor in Diagnosis," *Educational Diagnosis*, Thirty-fourth Yearbook, National Society for the Study of Education, 169–187, 1935.
9. FALKNER, F., "Measurement of Somatic Growth and Development in Children," *Courrier*, 4:169–181, 1954.

10. Flory, C. D., *The Physical Growth of Mentally Deficient Boys,* Monographs of the Society for Research in Child Development, Vol. I, No. 6. Washington: National Research Council, 1936.
11. Honzik, M. P., and Jones, H. E., "Mental-Physical Relationships during the Pre-School Period," *Journal of Experimental Education,* 4:139–146, 1937.
12. Jennings, C. G., and Pyle, S. I., "The Merrill-Palmer Logarithmic Developmental Graph," *Merrill-Palmer Quarterly,* 1:99–110, 1955.
13. Jones, Mary C., and Bayley, Nancy, "Physical Maturing Among Boys as Related to Behavior," *Journal of Educational Psychology,* 41:129–148, 1950.
14. Krogman, W. M., "Biological Growth as it May Affect Pupils' Success," *Merrill-Palmer Quarterly,* 1:90–98, 1955.
15. Meredith, H. V., *The Rhythm of Physical Growth,* Iowa City: University of Iowa, Studies in Child Welfare, VI, No. 3. 1935.
16. Millard, C. V., "Further Comments on the November Issue" (I.Q.'s), *Educational Method,* XIX, No. 8:445–447, May, 1940.
17. Krogman, W. M., "The Growth of the 'Whole Child' in Relation to Dental Problems," *Journal of Oral Surgery, Oral Medicine, and Oral Pathology,* 3:427–445, 1950.
18. ——, Gruelich, W. W., Wechsler, D., and Wishik, S. M., "The Concept of Maturity from the Anatomical, Physiological and Psychological Points of View," *Child Development,* 21:25–60, 1950.
19. Minot, C. S., *The Problem of Age, Growth, and Death: A Study of Cytomorphosis, Based on Lectures at Lowell Institute.* New York: Putnam, 1908.
20. Olson, W. C., and Hughes, B. O., "The Concept of Organismic Age," *Journal of Educational Research,* 36:525–527, 1942.
21. ——, *Child Development.* Boston: Heath, 1949.
22. Smith, Gudmond, "Development as a Psychological Reference System," *Psychological Review,* 59:363–369, 1952.
23. Tyler, F. T., "Organismic Growth: P-technique in the Analysis of Longitudinal Growth Data," *Child Development,* 25:83–90, 1954.
24. Tilton, J. W., "An Experimental Effort to Change the Achievement Test Profile," *Journal of Experimental Education,* 15:318–323, 1947.
25. Wetzel, N. C., "Physical Fitness in Terms of Physique, Development, and Basal Metabolism," *Journal of the American Medical Association,* 116:1187–1195, 1941.

PART II:
ASPECTS OF DEVELOPMENT

4

THE PHYSICAL GROWTH
OF THE CHILD

THE SCOPE OF THE RESEARCH

1. Many Studies in This Field

Studies of physical growth are more numerous than those on any other aspect of development. Every category of physical change subject to measurement is under investigation. Such studies serve a variety of purposes. Pediatricians and others are seeking the rate and rhythm of growth, hygienists are interested in the relation of exercise and diet to organismic well-being, and educators are looking through this mass of data to ascertain the implications for mental progress and general learning (25).

Study Categories. The classification of studies reported in the Child Development Abstracts (7) will serve to illustrate the comprehensiveness of the research.

a. Morphology: Anatomy; Embryology; Anthropometry; Somatic Constitution
b. Physiology and Biochemistry: Growth; Endocrines; Hormones; Nutrition; Vitamins
c. Clinical Medicine and Pathology: Dentistry; Immunology; Diagnostic Tests
d. Psychology: Behavior; Intelligence; Learning; Personality
e. Psychiatry and Mental Hygiene: Crime; Delinquency
f. Public Health and Hygiene: Epidemiology; Morbidity; Mortality
g. Human Biology and Demography: Genetics; Natality and Fertility; Population; Race and Sex Differences

h. Education: Class Curriculum; Vocational Guidance
i. Sociology and Economics: Laws; Family; Marriage and Divorce

Of these nine areas, five touch directly upon some category of physical growth and well-being. It is from this broad classification of experimental data that educators are seeking the classroom implications of physical growth.

Many outstanding child-study centers have been active for years in collecting data on children. Working in several of the study categories mentioned above are the clinical centers at Yale, Harvard, the State University of Iowa, and the Universities of Michigan, Chicago, California, and Minnesota.

Research Center at Harvard. One of the most outstanding centers is that at Harvard University, which originated as the Center for Research in Child Health and Development sponsored by the Department of Child Hygiene of the Harvard School of Public Health. To give the reader a concept of its breadth of interest in child development and particularly in physical growth, the following is quoted from its statement of purpose :

Purpose of the Harvard Center.

The scope of the research activities at the center is very broad and deals with problems within, or impinging upon, many different disciplines. *The project has become a coordinated research in the borderland fields of human biology and has as its central theme the more precise understanding of the phenomena of human development and their relations to problems of child health.* Although there has been emphasis on problems of health and fitness, an attempt has been made to explore, in so far as possible, all major aspects of development in the same children and all forces which may have bearing upon the developmental progress of these children. With this evidence in hand, important relationships between the various aspects of development, or between any one of them and physical well-being, should be brought to light. Although the center is interested in investigating problems of significance to but a single field, in appropriating time and facilities preference has been given to those projects which give promise of procuring information having a significant relation to studies in other fields.

Emphasis has been placed primarily *upon progress* — that is, upon growth and developmental changes. The project is concerned both with the pattern of human growth as revealed by the analysis of group material at succeeding age periods and with the differences which are encountered in the nature and extent of these changes in different children as revealed by the study of individual records. All investigations, therefore, have been planned as longitudinal studies of the same children.

Harvard University and others have for some time now been collecting data periodically and issuing reports and conclusions (7).

2. Most Studies of a Longitudinal Nature

Effect of the Harvard Approach. Until the last decade or so, interpretations of physical development were limited by the fact that children were not generally available for follow-up study. Thus, practically all research was based upon averages of children's measurements — average height, average weight, or averages of other physical measurements. With the impetus given to longitudinal study at Harvard and other centers, it soon became evident that growth curves based on averages were inadequate as criteria for interpreting individual growth. It is now rather generally accepted that cross-sectional data have resulted in misinterpretations in the prediction and analysis of individual growth rhythms.

Value of Norms. On the other hand, conventional norms do have certain values and there is no reason why the use of one type precludes use of the other when both fit into a program for really understanding the child. As Thorpe says (32) ". . . . measurement procedures serve different yet complementary purposes. One (cross-sectional) provides a background for discerning growth tendencies within groups, races, populations, and either of the sexes. The other (longitudinal) makes it possible to compare an individual with himself at different stages of growth and with groups of which he may be a member."

Advantages of Longitudinal Data. Thorpe's recommendation, concurred in by the writer, seems to be the result of expediency and the desire to do the best possible job of analysis with the tools available. In time, however, it is likely that the longitudinal approach will displace many of the older methods of comparing an individual with a norm.[1] As stated by Courtis, there are a great many advantages in the use of longitudinal data. Some of them are given in the list which follows below (9).

1. They reveal the natural patterns of growth which average out in mass data.
2. They make possible the interpretation of a child's growth curve in terms of his own natural standards.
3. They increase the reliability of interpretations of test scores.
4. Fewer cases are needed for a given reliability.
5. They are powerful diagnostic instruments.
6. They eliminate the effect of selective factors.
7. They permit comparisons and correlations between different types of measurement.

3. Aspects of Physical Development

A glance at the broad general headings under which research is being continuously pursued should make it obvious that the following discussion is highly selective, including only such material as will be immediately useful to the classroom teacher and will motivate child study without requiring too much equipment and expenditure of time. Hence the material concerns chiefly the exterior aspects of physiological growth. It can therefore be quite accurately classified as quantitative rather than qualitative in its nature.

Attention will be given to utilization of height and weight data. Treated more generally and with less statistical support will be the topics of posture and cranial and skeletal growth, as well as the more refined and less obvious growth of the sensory organs. Certain generalizations on physical growth will serve as an introduction to the more detailed discussions and the topics to be treated in the following pages.

[1] Courtis has advocated a "Curve of Constants" (*see p. 65*), which may be called a norm but retains the curvilinear nature of individual growth. Such a curve as he proposes, however, is constructed from cumulative data taken from records on the same children.

THE GENERAL NATURE OF PHYSICAL GROWTH

1. General Development

Shifts in Growth Patterns. Young children grow very rapidly. Increase in height is accompanied by increase in weight. As children increase in stature their legs become longer in relation to trunk length and hands and feet show rapid growth. This means change

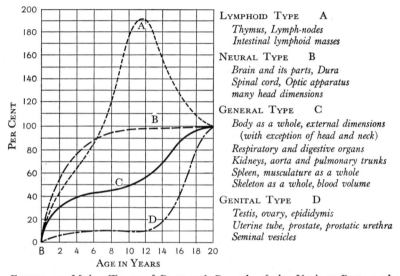

FIGURE 14. Major Types of Postnatal Growth of the Various Parts and Organs of the Body

in rates and a shift in the rhythm of development during certain periods of maturation. From five to seven, for example, growth of all parts of the body progresses at given ratios. From twelve to fifteen, a new growth pattern seems to replace the earlier rhythm or paralleling of growth sequences. New rhythms appear in each cycle of growth, but remain at constant ratios during any one cycle. Certain types of growth are dormant during some periods of maturity and active at others. Throughout all periods, however, normal development is harmonious and characteristically individualistic.

Normal Growth Is Always Rhythmic. It is quite probable that a basic potential functions in the development of each individual's total organismic pattern. Normalcy might be thought of as the presence of such an integrative relationship. This does not mean that normalcy disappears at adolescence, when certain types of growth, dormant during preadolescence, proceed at advanced rates. Normalcy exists unless disintegrative factors prevent growth according to the pattern. Certain shifts in the pattern, occurring at certain periods of maturity, are normal and represent an integrative action at newer and more complex levels (28).

Although organs, tissues, and skeleton all mature according to a particular rhythm, each has a certain specificity. Specificity may refer to rate, age at time of starting and end points, or the maximum toward which each is growing. The central nervous system and the sex organs grow at different rates with different timing or rhythm. The nervous system develops rapidly from birth to adolescence and then progresses less rapidly. Growth of the genital system also begins early but proceeds slowly from birth to adolescence and then increases in rate. In contrast to these the sensory and neural growths both mature rapidly during the prenatal period. Further specificity is illustrated in Figure 14 (16).

2. Growth in Size

Conventional Generalizations on Increase in Size. In general, children grow rapidly during the early and middle elementary school years. A marked decline in the rate of growth in height, weight, and certain other types of body growth begins at about ten or eleven years of age. This is conventionally explained as ". . . a period of consolidation of earlier gains and a breathing spell before the changes incident to pubescence begin . . ." (13). Undoubtedly it is a period of "consolidation," but in terms of growth concepts it is a period in which all types of growth are reaching preadolescent maturity.

3. Increases at Adolescence

Increased Rates during Pubescence. All investigations show that pubescence results in increased rates of growth at a time in which new rhythms or new relationships are established. It is pertinent then to discuss the age at which children arrive at this stage.

For some children pubescence begins at eight years of age and for others it does not begin until the child is sixteen years old. In general the range for girls is from eight to fourteen and from eleven to sixteen for boys. Courtis (9), however, shows considerable extension on the upper limits of both groups (Figure 15). Presenting in another light approximately the same data, Courtis shows occurrence identical with growth patterns (Figure 16).

Effect of Sexual Maturity on Size. The first overt signs of sexual maturity are the menarche in girls and the appearance of pubic

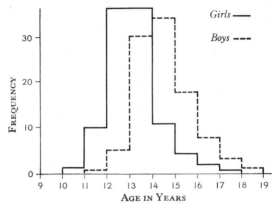

FIGURE 15. Distribution of Ages at Which Pubescence Occurs

and axillary hair in boys. Studies indicate that the rate of growth in both height and weight correlates with the degree of sexual maturity. It is generally concluded that the children who are the most advanced for a given chronological age are taller and heavier than those who have not progressed so far. Dimock reports that among boys of fourteen years of age the postpubescent were 4.6 inches taller and 22.6 pounds heavier than the prepubescent (10). Studies reported for girls show that the average girl of twelve years who menstruates before her thirteenth birthday is almost 4.5 inches taller and over 24 pounds heavier than the average girl menstruating at fourteen or older (6).

Shuttleworth also presents some interesting findings in this connection (26). According to his data the beginning of the period of rapid growth in height is usually found between two and one half and three and one half years before the first menstruation. He also reports that the year of most rapid growth is within the two-year period preceding the menarche. To illustrate this point, he states that of the girls studied those who had menstruated for the first time at eleven years of age had had their most rapid growth in the preceding year, that is, between the tenth and eleventh birthdays. On the other hand, the later the age for first menstruation, the greater the interval between the year of most rapid growth and the menarche. The girls who had menstruated

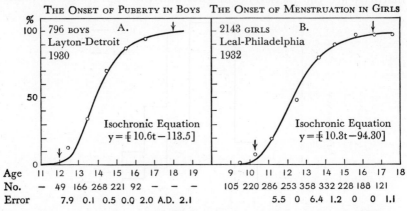

FIGURE 16. The Onset of Puberty in Boys and Menstruation in Girls

for the first time at fifteen had had their record growth between 12.5 and 13.5 years. This would indicate that such a distinctive sign of sexual maturity is somewhat late in the adolescent growth cycle. It also obviously indicates that pubescence begins before menstruation.

PROGRESS IN HEIGHT AND WEIGHT

1. General Pattern of Growth

The practice of cumulative or longitudinal study of the child has necessitated considerable revision of concepts as to how a given child grows and develops, since the earlier curves based on averages obscure considerably the individual character of growth (9). This is clearly illustrated by a comparison of the curve of constants taken from longitudinal data with the typical curve of averages (Fig. 17).

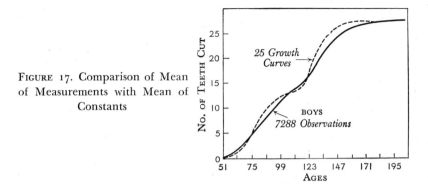

FIGURE 17. Comparison of Mean of Measurements with Mean of Constants

Variation from Cycle to Cycle. For an individual child, growth proceeds at different rates in different cycles. Stated conventionally, there are two periods of rapid growth, with one period in between of slower growth. The periods of rapid growth are early infancy and adolescence. The period of less rapid growth is late childhood or, as it is sometimes called, the preadolescent cycle (Fig. 18) (9).

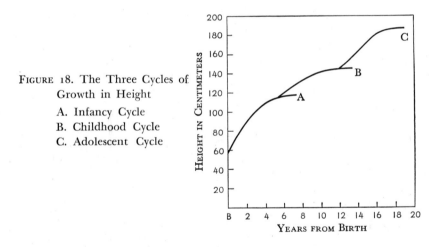

FIGURE 18. The Three Cycles of Growth in Height

A. Infancy Cycle
B. Childhood Cycle
C. Adolescent Cycle

2. The Typical Child

It is difficult to describe the average child. The average is really a mythical concept, for there are few average children. In order, however, to evaluate gains made by the individual child, it seems desirable to describe his progress in terms of the "average" child, although the measured characteristics of the "average" child do

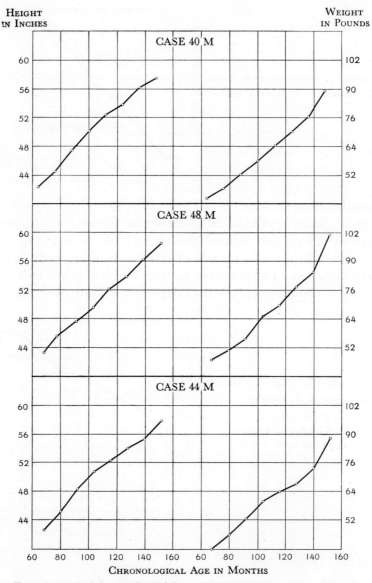

FIGURE 19. Heights and Weights of Typical Elementary School
Boys from Kindergarten through Grade Six

not necessarily represent criteria by which the normalcy of all other children should be judged (24).

Typical Height. In general the average child is about 21 inches long at birth. At five years of age he is approximately 42.5 inches tall and at twelve to twelve and a half years, when he enters the junior high school, he is about 58 inches in height. The typical child roughly doubles his height between birth and the time of entering the elementary school. By the time he enters junior high school he has just about tripled his birth length. The three boys shown in Figure 19 all approximate this height upon completion of the sixth grade and show but little variation from the standard 42.5 inches on entering the kindergarten.

The typical child gains about 10 inches in height during his first year. The following year his gain is approximately 5 inches. In the elementary school years, he gains from 2 to 2.5 inches before he reaches the fifth and sixth grades (Table III). During these years his gains are slightly less, but they increase during the junior high school period.

Typical Weight. The child at birth weighs around 7 pounds. By the time he is one year of age his weight has tripled. Weight at entrance to the kindergarten ranges for most children between 38 and 43 pounds. Between twelve or twelve and a half, when he enters the junior high school, his weight ranges between 80 and 95 pounds. Among the typical boys (Figure 19) Case 48M is somewhat larger both in the kindergarten and at the end of his year in the sixth grade. The other two are quite typical.

Gains made by the typical child amount to approximately 12 to 15 pounds during the first year of life. In the elementary school years, he gains between 4.5 and 6.5 pounds per year. At the sixth grade level he gains from 12 to 18 pounds (Table III).

Children show much steadier rate of gain in height than they do in weight. This difference is not indicated by yearly measurements but is most marked when measurements are taken monthly.

Normal Ranges. The point has been made that there is no single criterion for normalcy in height and weight, and the above description of a typical child should be used with proper caution. Faber has provided a satisfactory solution by constructing a table of weight ranges for specified heights and ages (11). He recommends that no child be considered abnormal in height or weight unless his measurements fall outside a range which includes the middle 80 per cent of weights for his particular age.

TABLE III

GAINS IN HEIGHT AND WEIGHT OF SELECTED ELEMENTARY SCHOOL BOYS

	GRADES												
	K		1		2		3		4		5		6
CASE	Ht.	Wt.	Ht.	Wt.	Ht.	Wt.	Ht.	Wt.	Ht.	Wt.	Ht.	Wt.	Ht.	Wt
40M	2.1	4.4	2.6	4.8	2.9	6.1	2.2	7.0	1.7	6.0	2.1	5.9	1.4	12.9
44M	2.6	5.9	3.0	7.0	2.8	7.8	1.7	4.2	1.6	4.1	1.0	6.0	2.7	12.8
48M	2.3	3.9	1.9	5.0	2.1	8.8	2.6	5.2	1.7	7.8	2.2	6.0	2.3	17.2

Height in Inches; Weight in Pounds

3. Monthly Gains in Weight [2]

How to Evaluate Gains. The amount a child should gain can be determined only after consideration of a great many factors. Generally speaking, a weight gain needs to be evaluated in terms of the initial weight at the beginning of the period of gain. For example, a big, heavy child is likely to gain more per unit of time than a smaller child. The amount of gain must be interpreted in terms of the child's period of development or cycle. Children in the sixth grade, girls in particular, show greater monthly increases than they do in any of the first three grades (Tables IV, V, VI, and VII). [3]

A study of monthly gains is very interesting. Among the cases shown, selected at random as typical cases, it is obvious that it is not unusual for children to show occasional losses in weight, sometimes slight losses for two or three months in succession. This is particularly true after an excessive monthly gain.

Children in the early elementary grades gain about one half a pound each month. During the year this amount of gain is spread from zero to approximately a pound gain in one month (Table VIII). In the upper elementary grades the average gain per month

[2] This topic has not been treated for height data because growth from month to month is too slight to be measured accurately by schoolroom techniques.
[3] Data taken from the Child Development Laboratory at Michigan State College.

is approximately seven tenths of a pound with ranges from zero to one and one half pounds.

TABLE IV

GAINS IN WEIGHT OF TEN GIRLS OF GRADES I TO III

MIDMONTH MEASUREMENTS

LONGITUDINAL DATA

| GRADE | MONTH | CASES | | | | | | | | | | AVERAGE |
		102F	120F	154F	198F	399F	110F	130F	148F	90F	127F	
	SEPT.-OCT.	1.2	1.5	0.0	0.2	0.7	1.9	1.1	1.3	1.0	3.7	1.3
	OCT.-NOV.	0.5	—0.5	0.2	1.5	0.3	0.2	1.2	—0.1	1.7	1.2	0.6
	NOV.-DEC.	—0.2	1.0	—0.2	—1.0	0.4	0.4	—0.3	0.0	1.2	0.5	0.2
	DEC.-JAN.	1.5	0.5	2.7	1.7	1.5	—1.0	—0.5	0.0	0.5	—0.2	0.7
I	JAN.-FEB.	1.2	—0.7	1.5	—0.2	0.5	0.2	2.2	1.0	—0.7	1.2	0.6
	FEB.-MAR.	—3.0	1.5	0.0	1.2	0.2	1.0	0.2	0.7	1.7	—0.2	0.4
	MAR.-APR.	0.7	0.5	1.2	—0.5	—1.0	—0.2	—1.0	0.5	0.0	0.5	0.1
	APR.-MAY	1.2	0.5	—0.2	0.5	1.0	0.2	0.5	0.2	0.2	0.7	0.5
	MAY-JUNE	2.5	—0.5	—0.5	—0.5	0.5	—0.2	0.0	—0.2	—1.2	0.0	0.0
	JUNE-SEPT.	—0.2	—0.1	0.3	1.5	—0.2	2.7	1.2	—0.5	1.0	1.7	0.7
	SEPT.-OCT.	0.7	2.2	0.0	1.2	0.5	0.7	2.2	1.0	0.5	1.5	1.1
	OCT.-NOV.	1.2	0.8	0.8	1.0	1.0	0.0	1.5	1.0	0.5	0.2	0.8
	NOV.-DEC.	—0.2	0.9	1.6	0.5	1.5	0.7	1.0	1.0	—0.5	1.0	0.8
	DEC.-JAN.	—2.5	0.5	0.7	1.0	0.2	—0.2	0.7	—0.5	0.7	1.7	0.2
II	JAN.-FEB.	3.7	0.7	0.7	0.0	0.7	1.0	—0.2	0.5	—0.5	—0.7	0.6
	FEB.-MAR.	—1.5	0.5	0.7	1.2	0.7	0.0	1.0	0.2	2.2	1.5	0.7
	MAR.-APR.	1.2	0.7	0.2	—0.2	1.2	0.7	0.7	0.7	0.5	0.2	0.6
	APR.-MAY	1.0	—0.2	1.0	1.5	—1.0	0.0	0.2	1.0	0.2	—0.7	0.3
	MAY-JUNE	0.5	—1.0	0.0	—0.2	0.2	—0.2	1.0	—0.2	—0.7	0.5	0.0
	JUNE-SEPT.	1.7	0.2	2.5	2.0	1.0	1.7	0.2	1.7	1.7	0.2	1.3
	SEPT.-OCT.	1.0	1.0	1.7	1.7	0.0	1.5	0.7	0.5	0.0	1.3	0.9
	OCT.-NOV.	1.2	1.2	0.7	1.5	0.2	1.2	0.7	0.0	2.2	1.8	1.1
	NOV.-DEC.	0.7	0.2	—2.2	—1.0	1.7	—0.2	—0.2	0.5	—0.3	0.1	0.0
	DEC.-JAN.	0.0	0.0	0.0	0.7	1.5	—0.2	2.5	0.0	1.0	0.5	0.6
III	JAN.-FEB.	1.0	1.2	2.5	0.7	1.0	0.5	—0.2	0.2	1.2	0.7	0.9
	FEB.-MAR.	0.0	0.2	2.2	1.7	0.5	0.7	0.5	—0.7	0.5	0.7	0.6
	MAR.-APR.	1.2	1.2	0.7	2.5	0.5	—0.5	0.0	0.2	—0.2	0.5	0.6
	APR.-MAY	1.0	—0.7	0.5	0.0	—1.2	0.0	1.2	1.7	1.2	—0.2	0.4
	MAY-JUNE	—0.7	0.7	—0.7	—1.0	1.2	—2.0	0.0	—0.5	0.0	0.0	—0.3

4. Seasonal Effects

Weight. Most interesting is the relation of weight gain to the seasons (Figure 20). This, of course, has implications for those who plan and are responsible for the physical well-being of chil-

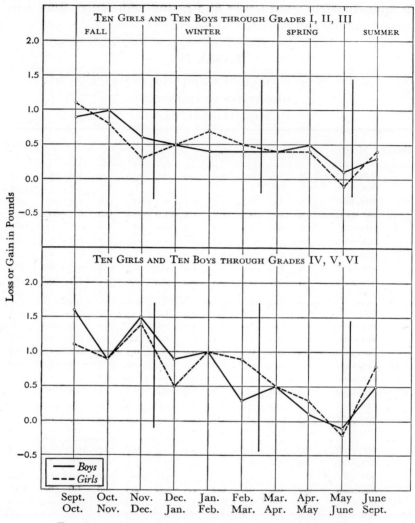

FIGURE 20. Seasonal Gains in Weight for Girls and Boys

dren in school. A regional survey made by the author shows that
children in the elementary grades make the greatest gains of the
year during the fall.[4] Whereas the spring season shows the lowest

[4] Olson, on the basis of a national survey, reports a similar conclusion, noting that
the average gain per month gradually decreases during the school months from September to May. From February to May, the last part of the period of less gain per
month, the rate of illness inexplicably declines.

TABLE V

GAINS IN WEIGHT OF TEN GIRLS OF GRADES IV TO VI
MIDMONTH MEASUREMENTS
LONGITUDINAL DATA

GRADE	MONTH	103F	19F	22F	24F	25F	31F	32F	38F	42F	43F	AVERAGE
	SEPT.-OCT.	1.8	0.9	1.1	1.0	2.3	2.0	1.9	—0.8	1.4	2.0	1.4
	OCT.-NOV.	0.0	0.2	0.9	—0.1	1.7	0.8	1.0	0.1	0.6	—1.3	0.4
	NOV.-DEC.	1.1	0.9	1.0	1.9	0.1	1.2	2.0	3.8	1.0	2.1	1.5
	DEC.-JAN.	0.2	0.0	1.2	—1.0	—0.1	—1.2	0.1	2.0	0.1	1.9	0.3
IV	JAN.-FEB.	0.0	—0.1	1.1	0.0	0.5	0.2	1.0	0.1	0.0	1.3	0.4
	FEB.-MAR.	0.7	0.2	0.9	1.1	1.7	0.7	0.8	—1.9	1.2	1.8	0.7
	MAR.-APR.	1.0	1.1	0.0	—1.8	0.2	0.0	—0.7	—0.2	—0.3	2.1	0.1
	APR.-MAY	1.2	0.7	1.0	1.8	2.1	—0.7	0.9	—0.1	—1.0	—1.9	0.4
	MAY-JUNE	0.9	0.3	0.9	0.0	—1.1	0.9	1.1	2.0	—0.7	2.0	0.6
	JUNE-SEPT.	1.0	0.9	—0.8	1.0	2.1	2.1	5.0	1.1	2.1	2.7	1.7
	SEPT.-OCT.	0.1	0.9	1.0	0.1	1.7	—0.3	0.9	0.9	1.7	2.3	0.9
	OCT.-NOV.	1.0	0.9	1.8	—0.2	1.3	1.3	1.9	1.3	0.0	1.8	1.1
	NOV.-DEC.	1.3	1.2	2.9	1.0	1.2	0.4	—0.3	0.9	1.2	2.9	1.3
	DEC.-JAN.	—0.7	—1.7	—1.7	3.0	2.7	—0.2	2.7	0.1	0.0	2.2	0.6
V	JAN.-FEB.	2.0	1.0	3.2	—1.0	2.2	1.5	0.5	—0.9	—0.3	0.8	0.9
	FEB.-MAR.	2.7	0.2	0.5	0.7	—0.2	1.2	0.7	—0.1	—0.7	1.1	0.6
	MAR.-APR.	—0.2	—0.5	1.0	1.0	1.5	0.7	0.5	—0.1	1.7	2.1	0.8
	APR.-MAY	0.5	0.5	—1.0	0.5	0.0	—0.5	1.0	—0.8	0.0	—0.1	0.0
	MAY-JUNE	0.5	0.5	—0.2	—0.2	—1.5	—0.5	1.0	—0.2	—0.8	—2.0	—0.3
	JUNE-SEPT.	—0.7	1.2	4.9	2.0	4.0	3.5	5.0	4.9	0.8	7.1	3.3
	SEPT.-OCT.	2.5	1.5	1.0	0.0	0.2	0.2	2.2	1.3	0.2	0.0	0.9
	OCT.-NOV.	1.7	—0.5	3.2	1.2	1.5	0.7	0.5	1.8	2.0	—1.0	1.1
	NOV.-DEC.	1.7	1.2	0.2	1.5	1.5	—3.2	0.7	1.6	1.3	6.3	1.3
	DEC.-JAN.	1.2	—0.7	—1.5	—0.5	1.5	4.7	0.7	1.5	—1.0	0.7	0.7
VI	JAN.-FEB.	1.0	1.5	0.5	1.7	3.2	2.0	1.7	1.5	0.7	2.5	1.6
	FEB.-MAR.	—0.7	0.7	2.5	0.2	4.0	1.7	3.2	—0.5	1.6	2.2	1.5
	MAR.-APR.	2.5	—0.2	0.5	0.7	—1.5	—0.2	2.0	1.0	0.0	0.2	0.5
	APR.-MAY	0.2	1.0	0.7	—1.2	—1.0	1.2	1.0	0.5	2.5	0.5	0.5
	MAY-JUNE	1.7	—1.0	0.5	0.2	—1.2	0.7	—0.5	—0.5	—2.0	—6.5	—0.9

gains per month, the summer vacation months show a pickup, culminating in maximum gains not later than December. The fact that school activities increase in tempo during the spring months, finally culminating in promotion, is rather incongruous in view of these facts. It would seem, rather, that the spring program should be the time when motivation toward children's activities, both play and study, should be minimized. On the other

TABLE VI

GAINS IN WEIGHT OF TEN BOYS OF GRADES I TO III
MIDMONTH MEASUREMENTS
LONGITUDINAL DATA

Grade	Month	Cases										Average
		101M	102M	82M	88M	93M	220M	96M	97M	114M	116M	
	SEPT.-OCT.	0.2	0.7	0.0	0.3	0.2	2.0	1.2	2.0	2.0	3.0	1.2
	OCT.-NOV.	0.2	—0.2	0.3	1.8	0.9	2.1	0.8	1.0	1.3	1.9	1.0
	NOV.-DEC.	0.7	1.0	0.2	0.1	—0.1	—0.6	0.0	0.5	0.7	0.3	0.3
	DEC.-JAN.	—0.2	1.2	1.7	0.5	0.0	—0.2	0.7	—1.0	0.2	0.0	0.2
I	JAN.-FEB.	0.0	0.2	1.5	0.5	1.7	1.5	0.5	1.7	0.5	0.5	0.9
	FEB.-MAR.	—0.2	0.5	0.0	—0.5	2.5	1.7	—0.2	0.5	0.0	1.5	0.6
	MAR.-APR.	1.7	—0.5	—2.5	1.2	0.2	1.5	1.0	—0.5	—0.7	—0.2	0.0
	APR.-MAY	0.0	0.7	1.7	0.5	—0.2	0.5	0.7	0.0	1.7	—0.2	0.5
	MAY-JUNE	0.5	3.5	0.0	—0.7	0.2	—0.2	1.5	—0.5	—0.5	0.5	0.4
	JUNE-SEPT.	0.0	—3.5	0.5	1.0	3.5	3.7	—0.5	1.7	0.2	0.7	0.7
	SEPT.-OCT.	1.7	1.0	2.5	1.2	1.0	—1.0	0.2	0.5	1.0	0.5	0.9
	OCT.-NOV.	1.0	2.1	—0.7	—0.7	1.2	2.0	0.0	1.0	—0.5	0.5	0.6
	NOV.-DEC.	0.5	—0.5	1.0	2.5	1.5	2.2	0.8	0.2	2.2	1.5	1.2
	DEC.-JAN.	0.0	0.2	—0.2	0.2	0.2	—1.2	1.2	2.0	0.7	0.2	0.3
II	JAN.-FEB.	0.5	1.2	0.0	1.2	—1.5	0.2	1.2	—0.5	0.2	—0.2	0.2
	FEB.-MAR.	1.0	0.2	1.0	0.2	1.2	1.5	0.0	0.5	0.0	0.0	0.6
	MAR.-APR.	—3.0	0.7	—0.5	0.7	0.5	—1.5	0.7	0.2	1.2	0.7	0.0
	APR.-MAY	4.2	—0.2	0.5	0.0	—0.7	—0.2	—0.5	2.2	—1.0	1.5	0.6
	MAY-JUNE	0.2	—0.2	1.7	0.0	—0.7	1.2	0.5	—1.5	0.0	—1.2	0.0
	JUNE-SEPT.	—0.2	0.0	0.7	1.7	0.7	2.7	1.7	4.2	2.5	0.0	1.4
	SEPT.-OCT.	1.5	1.5	0.5	0.0	1.0	1.5	—0.2	—1.0	0.2	1.0	0.6
	OCT.-NOV.	0.0	1.0	1.2	1.2	4.2	0.7	0.2	1.2	1.5	1.5	1.3
	NOV.-DEC.	1.7	0.7	—0.5	0.5	0.5	—0.7	0.7	0.7	0.5	0.2	0.4
	DEC.-JAN.	—0.2	1.2	1.7	1.0	2.0	—0.5	1.5	1.5	0.7	0.7	1.0
III	JAN.-FEB.	1.7	—2.5	1.0	—0.2	—1.2	3.0	—1.5	—0.5	—0.7	1.2	0.1
	FEB.-MAR.	—0.7	3.0	—0.7	0.0	—1.2	0.5	1.0	—1.0	0.0	—1.2	0.0
	MAR.-APR.	1.7	0.7	0.7	1.0	2.5	2.0	—0.2	1.2	2.0	0.5	1.2
	APR.-MAY	—0.7	0.7	—0.7	0.0	0.2	2.5	1.5	—1.5	2.7	—0.2	0.5
	MAY-JUNE	—0.2	1.5	1.2	—0.7	—0.5	1.7	—0.7	1.0	—2.0	0.0	0.0

hand, this may be nothing more than a demonstration of a natural phenomenon. The human system may need to be at low ebb during some part of the year, and perhaps the spring is the best time. Schools that conduct summer programs have the opportunity to study this problem and to determine whether less gain during the spring is natural or whether it represents a period of comparative exhaustion, perhaps affected or encouraged by highly motivating

TABLE VII

GAINS IN WEIGHT OF TEN BOYS OF GRADES IV TO VI
MIDMONTH MEASUREMENTS
LONGITUDINAL DATA

GRADE	MONTH	CASES										AVERAGE
		18M	19M	93M	21M	23M	94M	24M	25M	26M	18M	
IV	SEPT.-OCT.	0.1	2.0	2.2	2.0	1.0	3.0	2.0	—0.2	2.8	0.1	1.5
	OCT.-NOV.	0.2	0.9	3.9	1.2	1.0	1.2	—0.8	—1.1	1.3	0.2	0.8
	NOV.-DEC.	0.8	0.9	1.0	0.8	1.7	0.5	1.1	1.3	0.8	0.8	1.0
	DEC.-JAN.	0.2	0.1	1.8	1.8	1.3	2.5	—0.3	0.7	0.9	0.2	0.9
	JAN.-FEB.	1.0	—0.2	2.0	1.1	1.7	0.5	0.2	1.0	0.0	1.0	0.8
	FEB.-MAR.	0.7	0.3	2.0	0.7	1.0	—0.2	1.0	2.0	1.1	0.7	0.9
	MAR.-APR.	—0.7	2.7	—2.7	—1.7	—0.9	—0.5	—1.9	—1.7	—0.1	—0.7	—0.8
	APR.-MAY	1.0	—0.7	—0.1	—0.2	1.1	0.7	—0.1	1.8	0.0	1.0	0.3
	MAY-JUNE	—0.1	—0.2	—2.0	—0.9	—0.1	—0.2	—2.0	—2.0	0.2	—0.1	—0.7
	JUNE-SEPT.	0.0	1.2	4.1	1.0	1.9	—0.8	—1.8	0.0	1.8	0.0	0.6
V	SEPT.-OCT.	2.0	1.9	0.8	1.1	2.2	2.8	.7	3.1	1.0	2.0	1.9
	OCT.-NOV.	0.0	0.8	3.2	0.9	0.8	0.1	1.0	0.0	1.0	0.0	0.8
	NOV.-DEC.	1.8	0.7	3.7	3.2	1.5	2.2	2.2	1.3	0.2	1.8	1.8
	DEC.-JAN.	—1.2	1.2	1.7	—1.0	2.0	1.5	0.7	1.0	0.9	—1.2	0.6
	JAN.-FEB.	2.2	1.0	—0.2	3.5	0.0	0.5	—0.7	1.2	0.2	2.2	1.0
	FEB.-MAR.	—1.0	—1.5	—2.2	—0.2	0.5	1.2	—0.5	—1.0	0.0	—1.0	—0.6
	MAR.-APR.	1.0	1.5	0.7	1.0	—0.2	—0.5	2.2	2.5	—0.3	1.0	0.9
	APR.-MAY	0.0	—1.2	1.7	1.5	—0.5	0.5	—1.2	0.5	0.3	0.0	0.2
	MAY-JUNE	0.7	0.0	1.5	—1.7	0.7	—1.0	—1.0	—0.5	—1.0	0.7	—0.2
	JUNE-SEPT.	1.0	2.2	8.0	1.7	0.0	0.2	5.5	1.5	2.0	1.0	2.4
VI	SEPT.-OCT.	1.0	2.0	0.7	—0.5	2.0	2.7	2.5	0.0	1.7	1.0	1.3
	OCT.-NOV.	1.0	0.2	2.5	0.2	2.0	—0.2	3.2	0.0	1.3	1.0	1.1
	NOV.-DEC.	1.0	0.7	3.0	1.2	1.2	2.0	2.2	2.5	1.7	1.0	1.6
	DEC.-JAN.	0.5	1.7	2.7	0.0	3.7	1.0	2.0	1.2	—1.0	0.5	1.2
	JAN.-FEB.	—0.7	0.2	4.5	3.2	1.7	—0.5	2.0	—0.5	1.5	—0.7	1.1
	FEB.-MAR.	1.0	0.2	—2.0	—1.7	2.0	2.0	3.5	1.2	—0.2	1.0	0.7
	MAR.-APR.	0.7	1.7	0.5	3.5	—1.0	—1.7	2.0	8.0	—0.2	0.7	1.4
	APR.-MAY	0.2	—2.2	—0.2	—1.7	0.5	0.7	2.0	—2.0	0.0	0.2	—0.3
	MAY-JUNE	0.7	—0.7	1.7	—0.5	1.5	—0.7	1.5	—0.2	1.0	0.7	0.5

spring activities. It is certainly desirable that vacation periods come when they do, and it will be interesting to see whether schools maintaining summer programs promote or impede the rehabilitation which seems to occur during the summer, when school is not in session. The value of summer camps can also be studied in relation to the rhythm of gain and loss of weight. It is highly questionable whether the great expenditure of energy in

TABLE VIII

AVERAGE WEIGHT GAINS PER MONTH OF TEN BOYS AND TEN GIRLS
OF GRADES 1, 2, AND 3, AND AVERAGE GAINS OF TEN OTHER
BOYS AND TEN OTHER GIRLS OF GRADES 4, 5, AND 6

		Months									
Sex	Grades	*Sept. to Oct.*	*Oct. to Nov.*	*Nov. to Dec.*	*Dec. to Jan.*	*Jan. to Feb.*	*Feb. to Mar.*	*Mar. to Apr.*	*Apr. to May*	*May to June*	*Summer per mo.*
BOYS	1, 2, 3	0.9	1.0	0.6	0.5	0.4	0.4	0.4	0.5	0.1	0.3
BOYS	4, 5, 6	1.6	0.9	1.5	0.9	1.0	0.3	0.5	0.1	—0.1	0.5
GIRLS	1, 2, 3	1.1	0.8	0.3	0.5	0.7	0.5	0.4	0.4	—0.1	0.3
GIRLS	4, 5, 6	1.1	0.9	1.4	0.5	1.0	0.9	0.5	0.3	—0.2	0.8

highly competitive camps contributes to the physical well-being of the child. There is no doubt that summer camp activities for some children should include a great deal of time for rest periods and for more quiet work in such activities as arts and crafts. The same is true of physical education programs in the schools. Spring activities could well move toward more socialization and fewer competitive sports. There is no doubt that some space in the school should be set aside for cots, and supervised rest periods should be as much a part of the program as big-muscle activity is now.

5. Individual Differences

Sex. Even the most naive student of child development knows that all children do not grow in the same way. There are differences between the sexes as well as differences among children of the same sex. Investigators are inclined to think that boys are taller and heavier than girls, except for a period of time during the late elementary and junior high school grades. This observation is substantiated by measurements of a small group of children going through school together (Figure 21). Of the children selected (at random), the averages for the boys are greater than those for the girls throughout the kindergarten and the first six grades. In weight, however, the girls exceed the boys from the beginning of the sixth grade to the end of the seventh grade. In the cases selected, the differences are also affected by age, since the boys average five months older than the girls. An age matching of groups would show a difference other than that noted. Boys and girls would be nearly equal in size during the early grades, and the superiority of girls in weight during the later elementary grades would be much more marked.

Pubescent Differences. In the junior high school there are further differences in the growth curves of the two sexes. Most outstanding is the earlier maturing of the girls, a concomitant of which is the

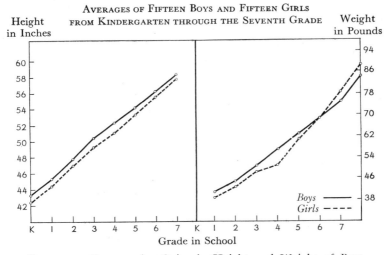

AVERAGES OF FIFTEEN BOYS AND FIFTEEN GIRLS
FROM KINDERGARTEN THROUGH THE SEVENTH GRADE

Height in Inches · Weight in Pounds · Grade in School

FIGURE 21. Comparative Gains in Height and Weight of Boys and Girls

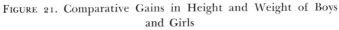

Beginning Ages at Kindergarten
Boys 66.8   Girls 61.8

fact that girls on the average achieve their year of most rapid growth a little more than two years sooner than boys.

Differences in Size between Bright and Dull Children. An interesting subject of study has been the relationship between "brightness" and size. The popular idea has been that bright children are small and that the big children are somewhat stupid. The exact opposite of this viewpoint is nearer the truth. Thorndike was about the first to argue that the brighter children were physically superior. Terman, well known for his studies of bright children, gives considerable factual documentation to the idea (30). In his study of children with minimum I.Q.'s of 140, he reports that as a group the brighter children are physically superior to other

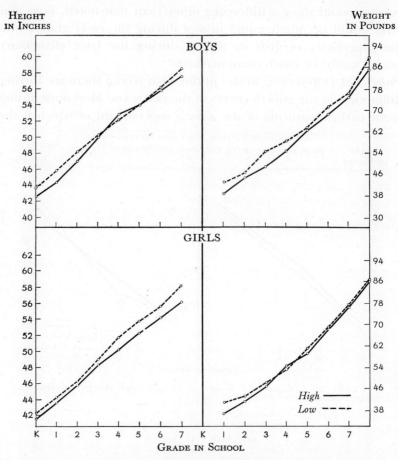

FIGURE 22. Comparison of Heights and Weights of Groups of Children with Differing Intelligence Quotients (Graphed according to Grade Placement)

Beginning Ages at Kindergarten

Boys: High — 60.8;   Low — 74.4
Girls: High — 59.0;   Low — 66.2

children. Jones, on the basis of his University of California research, reports that in general desirable physical development correlates positively with desirable mental development. He adds, however, that the statistical correlations obtained are too low for prediction values (18).

But this does not present quite the picture that the teacher faces in school. Among children progressing from grades one through six, twenty boys and twenty girls were selected and placed in contrasting groups. One group for each sex was called the high intelligence group and the other the low intelligence group. Since these children progressed together, it was possible to compare the averages of the groups according to their September measurements in each of the elementary grades (Figure 22). Results seemed at first to disprove the theory that bright children are larger, since the lower intelligence group were taller and heavier. But when the investigators studied the individual data on these children, they discovered that the brighter children in the various grades were much younger in both instances. Among the selected cases, during September of the kindergarten year, the groups differed as noted below:

	AGE AT BEGINNING OF KINDERGARTEN	
	Boys	*Girls*
HIGHER INTELLIGENCE	60.8	59
LOWER INTELLIGENCE	74.4	66.2

When the average curves were plotted with age held constant, the brighter children were the larger in each curve except one (Figure 23).

Increase in Differences as Children Progress in School. Differences between children of the same sex and age is a commonly recognized fact. Differences may be found at any age level but are most marked during the period of early adolescence. As children become older the differences between the extreme cases become greater. As they become older and larger they tend to maintain, however, approximately the same relative position in regard to the total group. Some small children may approach the average of the group, but short children are very unlikely to become tall or tall children to become short (23).

Effect of Maturation Differences. Early and late maturing children show considerable differences in their height and weight growth patterns. Shuttleworth claims that children who mature early begin their "pubescent spurt" earlier, grow faster, and complete their growth a few months earlier, but do not necessarily grow to greater maxima (31). The converse, obviously, is that

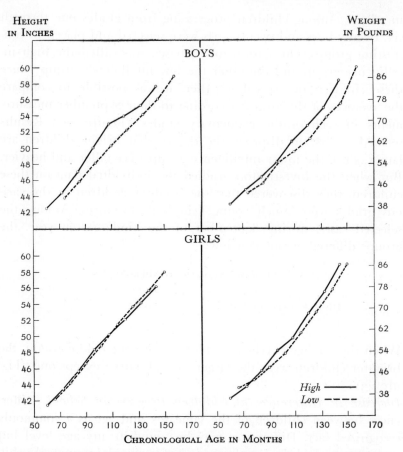

HEIGHT
IN INCHES

WEIGHT
IN POUNDS

FIGURE 23. Comparison of Heights and Weights of Groups of Children
with Differing Intelligence Quotients (Graphed according to Age)

Beginning Ages at Kindergarten		*Average Intelligence Quotients*	
Boys: High — 60.8;	Low — 74.4	Boys: High — 114;	Low — 88
Girls: High — 59.0;	Low — 66.2	Girls: High — 120;	Low — 101

children who mature later in their preadolescent development
grow more slowly, but not necessarily to lesser maxima. Further,
there are exceptions to the rule. Some children who grow slowly
and mature later in preadolescence also become bigger than those
whose early childhood growth was more rapid. This fact, long re-
marked by lay observers, has been substantiated by scientific studies.

BODY DEVELOPMENT

1. The Developing Framework

Bones Are Protective. The body framework is mainly a skeletal arrangement of bones bound together by strong connective tissues called ligaments. Attached to this framework are the muscles. The bones and muscles hold the body together and form a protective agency for the organs of the body. It is needless to do more than point out how the bones of the head serve to protect such a delicate structure as the brain so that nothing except a severe blow causes it any particular damage. Likewise, the chest is so built structurally as to afford fine protection for the heart and lungs, and the unique pelvic skeletal structure provides the essential support for the abdominal organs. Aside from providing protection and the necessary framework, the various bones also aid in the production of essential blood cells and provide a source of calcium when other parts of the body require this constituent for their proper functioning.

Characteristics of Children's Bones. In comparison with the bones of the adult, the bones of a child contain a proportionately greater part of water and soft proteinlike materials and a considerably lesser portion of mineral substances. Likewise the skeletal constituents contain much more cartilage and fibrous tissue during the early years. Because of this fact the bones of the child are more pliable and elastic than the adult's. While this characteristic is desirable, in that fracture is less likely, it does provide more opportunity for deformity and imperfection since the bones resist less successfully the many stresses and strains of muscles and tissues. Consequently the child needs to be observed and guided to prevent unnecessary tensions and pulls tending to create deformities which would weaken his total structural strength.

How Bones Develop. It is interesting to study a series of X-ray pictures of a child's skeletal structure as he matures. They illustrate very clearly that in the young child the bones are not firmly grown together. Between the ends of bones there is much space.

The amount of space is in practically an inverse ratio to age and his ligaments are longer and less firmly attached.

Children's bone structures are affected by the amount of blood which flows through them and to their covering. Because of the creative needs of growth, a greater amount of blood is found in children's bones than in the adult. And also, children's bones have a much thicker covering. These characteristics, of course, are designed by nature for the good of the child. The thicker covering, elastic connections, and soft structure prevent him from the consequences of much of his irrational, exploratory, and random muscular activity. The greater blood flow provides the chemical constituents for necessary materials for growth. Nature sometimes penalizes, however. Bone disease due to infection is more prevalent among children because their bones are more vascular than those of adults.

Methods of Study. Considerable research has been done on skeletal maturation. Age-development norms have been constructed, and it is now possible to compare an X-ray with a standard, thereby arriving at a definite skeletal age similar to mental age, reading age, height age, etc.

X-ray Studies. The most popular technique of clinicians is to compare with a norm a standard X-ray picture of the contour of the ends of the bones and the epiphyses [5] and the growth toward union of the epiphyses with the bone shaft. There are two methods of utilizing the data obtained from these comparisons. The first attempts to determine progress in terms of the child's chronological age. The other is that used by Olson, in which carpal growth is resolved to an age base as one aspect of total organismic development. In this connection some of the pertinent facts on skeletal growth will be of interest to the teacher.

Skeletal Development. The child at birth has a bony structure which lacks epiphyses. There are large spaces between the long bones of the wrist. From birth to the time when the child begins school, the epiphyses begin and wrist bones are adjacent but not in contact with each other. During the elementary school grades

[5] The bony masses adjacent to the ends of the long bones and separated from them by cartilage.

all bones grow toward each other and the adjacent epiphyses grow larger and assume definite shapes.

Not until a girl is nine and a boy approximately eleven does the last wrist bone appear. There is, however, a bone called the sesamoid which indicates growth at the pubescent level. For girls this bone appears in the hand between eleven and twelve years and for boys between thirteen and fourteen years of age.

Characteristics of Maturity. Complete maturation occurs when all the bones unite. This final stage begins when the epiphyses and the bone shaft come together at approximately thirteen to fourteen for girls, and between fifteen and sixteen for boys. Maturity or near-joining is completed in girls at about sixteen and in boys at nineteen (1).

Qualitative Aspects of Skeletal Growth. Skeletal development is qualitative as well as quantitative. It has been found, for example, by many observers that there appears to be a change in the density of bone structure at certain stages of maturity. The periods of decreasing density are particularly marked at adolescence. This phenomenon is thought to result from an increased need of minerals brought on during new cycles of growth by increased growth rates. As a result the supply, unless maintained in the diet, is depleted. According to this viewpoint, diets rich in calcium are necessary at these ages.[6]

Differences in Skeletal Maturation. Although it is generally believed that skeletal growth is quite regular as compared with other phases of growth, it is nevertheless true that individual differences are reflected here as elsewhere. In agreement with the general conclusion that individual differences are greatest during the periods of greatest growth, skeletal differences are most marked at adolescence in the early teens.

Differences between the sexes are about the same as for other types of growth. The slight differences noted at birth increase during the school years until at the ninth-grade level, girls are approximately two years accelerated over boys.

Differences among a given sex are also to be found. According to Flory, large, well-developed children are more likely to reach

[6] This view concurs with the general theory of instability at the beginning of new cycles of growth.

skeletal maturity before other children (12). Flory also notes that these children finish high school ahead of those less mature in this aspect of growth.

2. Cranial Development

Growth of the Head. The growth rate of the head is only of passing interest to teachers, since this phase of the child's development is relatively complete before he begins school. As everyone knows, the newborn child has a larger head for his size than the adult. In proportion to the total, the greatest prenatal growth occurs in that part of the head which holds his brain. His face is smaller by comparison. During early infancy the face grows rapidly, the cranium slowly. As the face develops, the child takes on his own individual facial characteristics, which become more and more marked as he progresses toward maturity.

3. Teeth and Jaw

Growth of Teeth. At birth the child has no teeth. However, both his "baby" and his permanent teeth are in the process of growth. This is true in reference to both the outer (enamel) and the inner (dentine) portion. Before the tooth erupts, the enamel is fully formed. This is not true of the dentine, which continues to form until the root is completed. All of the baby, or deciduous, teeth appear normally by the age of three or four.

The growth of the permanent teeth requires a much longer period of time. Calcification begins at birth and continues through infancy, the preschool and school years. The last teeth to mature are the so-called wisdom teeth, which make their appearance between seventeen and twenty-five years of age.

Growth Pattern in Tooth Eruption. Of considerable interest to clinicians is the type of growth curve representative of the number of teeth at given stages of development. In Figure 24, tooth eruption follows the familiar pattern already illustrated by height and weight data. The curve has a slow beginning, rapid acceleration, with a slowing down between nine and ten years, followed by a second rapid growth between eleven and thirteen (9).

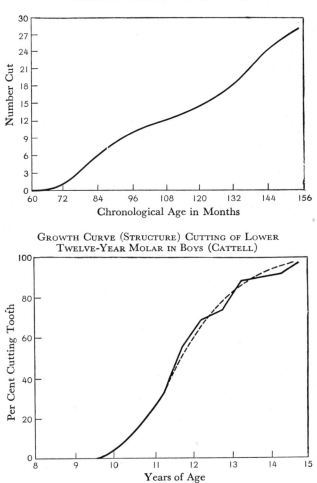

DEVELOPMENT CURVE FOR THE CUTTING OF
PERMANENT TEETH IN BOYS (CATTELL)

GROWTH CURVE (STRUCTURE) CUTTING OF LOWER
TWELVE-YEAR MOLAR IN BOYS (CATTELL)

FIGURE 24. The Eruption of Teeth as a Form of Growth

Meaning of Integration. Data on the time of tooth eruption may
be used to compare stages of maturity with a child's chronological age and his grade placement and are important in evaluating the uniformity of the total developmental pattern in regard to timing. No one has investigated the point fully, but it is
likely that good integration for a given child would present a

series of growth curves with considerable uniformity in starting points, periods of acceleration, plateaus, and times of reaching the various maxima.

Eruption of Teeth. The first tooth generally appears at about six months of age. Other deciduous teeth appear during the following two or three years. There is no obvious further development from this time to around the age of six. Since this tooth usually erupts behind the second molar and without the advance notice of a vacancy, it is frequently not recognized as a permanent tooth and consequently is neglected.

The sequence of growth is not too generally known and should be of interest to teachers who today are becoming more and more sensitive to the need for a program of dental care.

Sequence of Eruption. Even before the appearance of the first molar, all of the permanent teeth are growing and maturing. This happens at the same time that the roots of the deciduous teeth are disappearing. This process is called resorption. Under normal circumstances, when a permanent tooth is about ready to erupt, the only part of the deciduous tooth which remains is the crown.

A child entering school at six has usually lost some of his early teeth. Examination of the spaces usually shows the beginning eruption of permanent incisors. Some children already have their six-year molars. During the school years, until the age of twelve or thirteen, most children have spaces here and there as early teeth are lost and replaced by permanent ones.

Effect on Personality. From the standpoint of good oral hygiene, proper sequence is more important than the child's age at the time of eruptions. Missing teeth, of course, cause some embarrassment at later than normal ages, but as far as oral hygiene is concerned, this is not deleterious.[7] Irregular growth and poor synchronization may result in poor alignment. Good alignment depends upon retaining the deciduous teeth until the permanent teeth begin to erupt. Consequently, good dental care with the first teeth is important for immediate good nutrition and health as well as for good occlusion and jaw development later.

[7] Late development is usually a sign of immaturity and may be anticipated if immaturity is reflected in other growth patterns.

Individual Differences. There are individual differences in the time required for growth and in the ages at which teeth appear. Girls are more precocious, cutting their teeth a little earlier than boys. Normally, as teeth appear, the jaw also grows so as to properly adjust to the number of teeth that it must accommodate. Sometimes, however, tooth eruption and jaw growth are not synchronized. In some instances, jaw growth is inadequate and consequently some teeth do not erupt, or they may erupt and be forced out of proper alignment. In other instances, the jaw may grow more than is necessary and teeth become badly spaced. Another irregularity is the lack of synchronization of the two jaws in their growth. One may grow more than the other so that the teeth of the upper and lower jaws do not come together properly. This condition is referred to as *malocclusion.*

Effect of Growth Differences between Teeth and Jaw. Malocclusion may be the result of differences in the width or the length of the jaws. If there are width differences the grinding surfaces do not function properly. In length differences the grinders are badly fitted and the bite of the front incisors is bad.

Good occlusion is of great importance to children. It is necessary for the establishment of good eating habits as well as for the best possible personality development. Whether occlusion is good or bad depends upon the growth pattern of the jaw and influencing factors. The jaw, for example, may be growing normally, but because of dietary deficiencies the teeth may not grow as expected. This throws jaw development out of its natural rhythm, and the problem becomes complex. Another cause of difficulty may be premature loss of deciduous teeth. In many instances premature loss may result in an irregular eruption of the permanent teeth depending upon the growth of the jaw at that time. Other factors contributing to malocclusion are lip- and thumb-sucking. It is quite generally agreed, however, that for most children if the habit is broken before the age of five, previous bad effects are likely to disappear.

Necessity for Record of Growth of Teeth and Jaw. In some instances oral irregularities may be self-corrective. On the other hand, minor deficiencies may become increasingly worse. As in other phases of growth there are wide individual differences.

Because of such differences it is advisable that teachers become aware of the indications of good and bad growth. It is important, therefore, that the growth of the jaws and teeth be carefully watched. Since most children have a different teacher each year it is essential that some notation or record of development be available among the child's health records.

4. Establishing and Maintaining Good Body Posture

Good posture may be defined simply as good body balance. Good body balance and good body mechanics are the result of

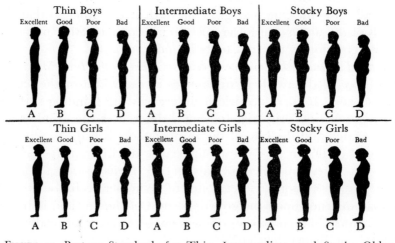

FIGURE 25. Posture Standards for Thin, Intermediate, and Stocky Older Boys and Girls

proper integration of muscular and skeletal growth. Good balance is indicated by easy and graceful body movement.

Importance of Observation. Since posture can be easily observed by teachers and since so much of the child's time is spent in school, it seems advisable to emphasize this aspect of physical growth and to point out some of the posture problems of which teachers should be cognizant (Figure 25) (20).

Effect of Poor Posture. Poor posture may affect not only the normal outward evidences of growth — tallness, straightness, rhythm of movement, etc. — but also the condition of internal organs. Round shoulders, a slumped standing or sitting position resulting in a deflated chest, may reduce the potential maximum chest space in which the lungs expand. The beneficial result of maximum lung space is obvious. It gives the child sufficient storage capacity for oxygen. Cramped physical conditions of any part of the young growing body are harmful. They, according to their location, may affect circulation or digestion, or produce disturbances associated with the nervous system.

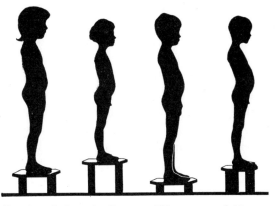

FIGURE 26. Sample Posture Silhouettes of Young Children Four and One-half Years Old

Relation of Posture to Personality. Posture is not only a cause of poor body functioning but frequently an effect as well. Poor internal conditioning or malfunctioning of the organs may produce poor posture. Frequently, feelings of inferiority or inadequacy reflect themselves in the outward carriage of the body. The child may assume a slinking inconspicuous rhythm of movement, or he may key his body movements toward what he considers a brave, cocky, or bullying type of physical personality. On the other hand, a healthy, energetic child usually has a well-poised, natural rhythm of movement.

Constituents of Good Posture. Good rhythm in physical movement is contingent upon body alignment, muscles, and nerves. Since the body is subject to gravity, the individual who moves freely must be well balanced. He must be developed symmetrically about a vertical line passing through his center of gravity. Nature tends to provide a balance around this center. If a part of the body projects too far beyond this line in one direction, it must be balanced by a projection in the opposite direction (Figure 26) (13). In the picture of four-year-old children, the protuberance of the abdomen is balanced by the projection of the buttocks. The line of balance normally passes through the ear, the tip of the shoulder, the hip joint, and a point slightly in front of the ankle.

Pairing of Muscles. Muscular placement and function augment natural structural uprightness. Nature has arranged all muscles in pairs so that they work opposite each other. If one of a pair becomes stronger than the other the unequal pull tends to draw the affected part of the body away from a natural symmetrical position. In a program of physical development or in corrective work on posture, it is essential to consider the relative strength of different muscles as well as muscle strength in general.

Necessity of Proper Interpretations. Probably of greatest importance to teachers is a complete understanding of what is normal and what is a bad deviation from normalcy. As in many other fields a little knowledge is a dangerous thing. Teachers might better ignore posture than attempt to fit all children into what they consider a normal pattern. Our earlier warning about the use of norms can be repeated here. There is no single standard by which all children can be appraised. Body development that is good for one child is not necessarily good in another child. Good balance and rhythm of movement can result from a number of types of body developments. A heavy, stocky child has a body balance and bodily alignment quite different from that of a slender, wiry individual (Figure 25).

Of equal importance to teachers is the shift in body balance and alignment as the child matures. Teachers unacquainted with the posture profile of the maturing child may attempt to encourage a body carriage that is quite unnatural for him at a particular age.

A. PHASES OF POSTURE CONTROL

Preschool Child. The time from about fourteen months until the child is approximately six is an age of increasing stability in movement. Babies' legs are bowed to a considerable degree, but they should straighten out rapidly when walking begins. The young walker usually has a knock-kneed, toed-out support, which gradually decreases and disappears at about the beginning of the preadolescent cycle of growth — near six years of age for most children. The young child, however, presents a straight upper back, a protruded abdomen. This is natural because of the weakness of the abdominal muscles and the type of diet to which he is accustomed (Fig. 26).

Early Childhood. Upon entrance to school the child still has a prominent abdomen with its accompanying lordosis. His knee support is good, his feet and arches normal. Head, neck, and shoulders show good symmetry. Most children present such a posture picture during this period of development. Since the child at this age is generally active, his physical training motivations should be diversified and informal.

Adolescence. During the adolescent period the child begins to show his adult posture characteristics. Normally, the abdomen has been drawn in and the accompanying back line has straightened (Figure 25). Marked individual differences at this stage of development begin to appear, accentuated by individual interests in physical activity. During adolescence, instability in coordination and rhythm may be expected again, because this is a period of new growth.

Adolescents are naturally very much interested in their physical growth patterns. Satisfaction, dissatisfaction, or even surprise at their individual development has various effects. Girls, for example, may become self-conscious in regard to breast development and try to conceal this growth by hunching or holding their shoulders forward. Others may go to the opposite extreme. A tall boy or girl may slouch to appear more nearly like his peers. Such behavior may be only temporary, but if it seems to continue it should be discouraged. On the other hand, many of the developmental changes at these ages provide motivations which automatically lead to good posture and body balance. The desire on the part of most boys to excel athletically and the desire of girls to be attractive and socially adequate motivates activities conducive to good posture.

Corrective Work Incidental. This period is important, since it is the proper time, from the standpoint of growth, to bring about corrections that will become permanent. Teachers should realize, however, that they will obtain better results by directing posture development through interesting physical and social activities rather than through formal posture exercises.

5. Growth of Organs

The organs most directly affected by educational activities are the heart, the eyes, and the ears. Because of the social implications of sexual maturation, it is desirable that this topic also be given some attention. Growing up includes the following phenomena. The heart beat is stronger but slower. The assimilation of food takes longer, and digestive conditions become more stable and less susceptible to upset. Respiration, like the pulse, becomes slower, deeper, and more regular as the child gets older. The bladder holds urine for a longer period of time, and the content of the blood is less subject to variation in composition. Body temperature stabilizes. The picture in general is one of greater stability and efficiency. To teachers this implies that young adults and older children are less affected by environmental change than young children and consequently have a greater power to adjust to new circumstances. It is essential, however, that teachers understand certain exceptions in physical abilities to adjust, so that the planned demands of instruction can be made compatible with the physiological limitations of the children concerned (22).

Heart. Since there is considerable functional heart disturbance among adolescents, it may be well to point out the nature of the heart pattern of growth. There is considerable difference in the rate of growth of the heart and the body as a whole. Between the approximate ages of four to ten the heart grows more slowly. In comparison to over-all body size, the heart is smaller in proportion at these times than at any other period. The greatest difference exists at approximately seven years of age. From this point the two tend to parallel in growth rate, but at adolescence the heart is still unready to support all the activities that the body in this developmental stage is prepared for. Children can easily be overstimulated at these ages in such a way as to cause difficulties that may have permanent ill effects.

6. Ears and Eyes

The ears and eyes are organs with which teachers may well be concerned. Both of these are primary assets in the child's learning program and are constantly in use. Their protection is important and therefore pertinent for discussion.

Ear. At birth the ear is quite fully developed, and both the inner and the middle ear have reached nearly adult proportions. The main difference in ear structure between the infant and the grown adult is in the Eustachian tube. In children this tube connecting the ear with the throat is a short, wide, straight passage. As a result, the young child is continuously threatened with ear infections which develop in the throat.

The importance of guarding against all kinds of throat infections cannot be overstressed. Teachers should also be sensitive to deficiencies in hearing and should become sufficiently well acquainted with available health data to make the necessary seating arrangements for children with the slightest difficulties.

Early Growth of the Eye. Of still greater importance in the learning situation is the eye. At birth the newborn child is farsighted. During early childhood this condition is gradually modified. Normal, or *binocular,* vision is characterized by the cooperation of both eyes, resulting in single vision with a proper perception of depth. Although normal for them, many children are slow in arriving at this stage of maturation, some as late as eight years of age — an age beyond the normal introduction to reading. Under these circumstances, when maturation is late, the child is certain to have reading difficulty. Incidentally, there are some individuals who never attain this degree of maturation.

Vision Difficulties. The child who does not achieve binocular vision is commonly known as "cross-eyed." The child then has double vision, or *strabismus.* At an early age the condition is not unusual, most often appearing around two years of age, and is frequently periodic. If it persists, the child either develops the habit of using one eye or using both alternately. Such usage exerts undue strain, and the child is handicapped in not having the full advantage of depth perception. His judgment of distances and of moving objects is bad. He is greatly handicapped in play and from the safety point of view is endangered. Parents who are aware of the condition should have it treated and corrected before the child begins school. Teachers should be alert to the symptoms and should be able to detect those who get into school without the proper correction and treatment. And further, in a good child-study program, the child will be tested as to the extent of binocular vision and tested as to his dominant eye. This information is important in interpreting the readiness of the child for reading, writing, and other school activities.

7. Reproductive System

Knowledge of the development of the child's reproductive system is important to teachers because of its personal and social implications. Since the child's prestige in the upper elementary grades and in the junior high school is always partially contingent upon his physical development, this problem needs discussion.

Immaturity of Reproductive System during Childhood. The reproductive organs remain immature during early childhood. This growth begins at around ten years of age and proceeds rapidly when the girl begins to ovulate and the boy is capable of producing spermatozoa. As in other phases of development, growth here shows marked sex differences (Figure 27) (19).

The implications for personal and social behavior as a result of the changing sexual development of the members of a group are of great importance to teachers. A well-ordered, well-adjusted sociometric group may become entirely disarranged in the upper elementary grades. A few girls whose development is precocious are likely to become bored and uninterested in the activities of the group. Boys who previously held status because of certain physical or social qualifications may find their leadership challenged if they develop slowly.

Effect on Personality. Other problems may arise to threaten the social solidarity of the group and can easily cause difficulties of adjustment to the usual instructional order. Boys, for example, may produce some quite harmless obscenity by writing on lavatory walls, and girls may become more interested in older boys, much to the distress of the teacher who fails to understand their natural, unfolding, sexual curiosity.

Irregularity Should Be Explained. The menarche and menstruation have already been discussed in relation to physical growth. Because of the uncertainty and fear of many young girls when this condition first appears, one further point should be made concern-

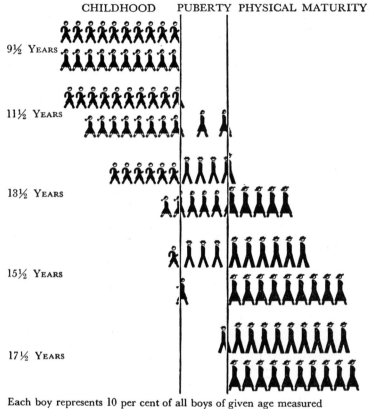

CHILDHOOD   PUBERTY PHYSICAL MATURITY

9½ Years

11½ Years

13½ Years

15½ Years

17½ Years

Each boy represents 10 per cent of all boys of given age measured
Each girl represents 10 per cent of all girls of given age measured

FIGURE 27. Differences in Timing of Maturity for Boys and Girls

ing the natural irregularity of the menstrual flow during adolescence. Knowledge of this point is important to teachers. Because of either the ignorance or taboo-attitude of parents who fail to inform their children properly, they must act as parent substitutes and provide necessary guidance.

Menstruation is a phase of maturation produced by the activity of certain endocrine glands. In spite of some information to the contrary, the length of the menstrual cycle varies between girls and at different periods with the same girl. Irregularity is to be expected in the first years after its initial appearance. According to Arey the usual cycle is twenty-eight days (2). For young girls the average length of the cycle amounts to approximately thirty-four days — an average based on the great variation among some of the girls in the study. Some girls were found to vary no more than six days from their average, whereas a few varied as much as 211 days. In the latter instances there was an interval of approximately eight months between menstruations. Between the first years of menstruation and nineteen years of age, it was found that deviations from the mean among two-thirds of the girls were reduced from twenty to four days.

Causes of Irregularity. The cause of individual variation is of interest. In general, menstruation fits into the general developmental pattern of girls. Familial differences, nutritional, climatic, and general health conditions affect this pattern as well as the beginning time of menstruation. There is some evidence that girls whose mothers menstruated early also tend to menstruate early. Daughters of mothers whose first menstruation occurred between twelve and thirteen also menstruated at this age. Daughters of women who menstruated somewhat later than normal tended to resemble their mothers in this respect (14).

CONCLUDING IMPLICATIONS

A. GENERAL PURPOSE

It seems desirable to draw certain implications of a general nature dealing with physical growth and well-being of the child as well as to consider certain matters related to his emotional and social well-being.

1. Teachers need to understand physical growth in terms of the child's outlook on life. One of the greatest influences in the development of social attitudes is his own size, conformation, and physical status. Teachers, of course, may attempt to gain such information through interviewing children, or through observing them, and draw certain conclusions of their own. The teacher may conclude, for example, that John has become unsocial, introspective,

or insecure. The root of the problem, however, lies in the reason for such behavior. The answer, or clue to the answer, if it is to be found among physiological factors, cannot be obtained without some sort of study of the child's developing physiological pattern. Perhaps a tendency toward nearsightedness has rendered him inefficient in playing baseball. Perhaps he is beginning to lose status through an increasing incompetency in general physical skills because he is growing slowly at a time when other children are growing at increased rates. The more the teacher knows about physical growth, the better her position in dealing with him. Knowledge of this kind makes it possible to determine whether a child needs to be shifted to a more immature group, aided in adjusting to his deficiency, or encouraged to establish status through other means.

2. Teachers need to *aid* children in understanding physiological growth and the problems it creates. If one were to record the various behavior problems of normal children traceable to physical or physiological phenomena occurring during the elementary and early adolescent school years, the number and significance would be amazing. Teachers can aid children and give necessary security only by thoroughly understanding the nature and character of physical growth (15).

B. USE OF HEIGHT AND WEIGHT MEASURES

Height and weight measures, as conventionally used, have very little value for child study. Teachers frequently watch weight gains and losses and make value judgments accordingly. It was pointed out previously that weight gains must be judged according to the season and that from month to month no child seems to show a constant pattern. Consequently, the practice of comparing gains between any two consecutive months is not in accord with any known meaningful facts on growth. A teacher who inherits height and weight data which have been kept up to date by previous teachers and continues such a collection has a somewhat better opportunity to evaluate a child's physical progress. If the total pattern shows progress, monthly deviations may be ignored.

This kind of record, when available, lends itself to further significant usage. The total pattern can be studied in terms of growing periods, leveling-off periods, and new cycles of growth. It can also be compared with other kinds of recorded measures of the same child. Curves of one phase of growth may be studied for similarities with other phases of growth, or all may be drawn to a single scale by use of various age-growth tables, and interpretations made accordingly.

C. GENERALIZATIONS FROM PHYSICAL GROWTH DATA

A study of height and weight data brings to light certain general truths which are helpful and necessary in understanding total development. 1. These data illustrate the fact that growth is a continuous process. 2. Such growth as one observes in this phase of development leads one to conclude that about all that is necessary for growth is immaturity and a normal environment in which to grow. In this connection, then, it would seem that the nearest approach to a curriculum that has any meaning lies in determining the relation between opportunity and stage of maturity. 3. Studies of physical growth indicate considerable stability in the achievement of a child's projected or "predicted" pattern. Growth curves studied by the author during the depression, when many new factors emerged, seemed only slightly affected over the entire period of school attendance by these changes. Olson has frequently spoken of the lack of a continuing effect on the growth pattern of illness, emotional shock, and similar factors. This should not encourage carelessness in dealing with the child's health and physiological problems. It does challenge the wisdom of certain health practices aimed at producing immediate change in the growth pattern. Among the procedures which may well be questioned are short-time health plans, intense remedial instruction, and other temporary teacher activities instituted to bring about permanent, marked change.

The child's natural growth pattern seems to resist change and maintain itself despite both harmful and advantageous forces. After experiencing unusual environmental or organismic factors of either positive or negative character, the organism tends to resume its original pattern. The only motivating factors the organism can endure are those of a natural kind which permeate a child's environment throughout his period of growth. Added assignments, special attention, and other remedial procedures, frequently prescribed, may temporarily change the growth pattern but when terminated have little continuing effect. These are valuable mainly when they contribute to the child's psychological well-being. Special attention which develops a success attitude or rescues the child from a temporary slump in either mental or physical health is, of course, desirable.

Finally, in the face of the available evidence, one must conclude that growth and development are strongly influenced by a general emerging pattern. Individuality, which cannot be entirely accounted for by environmental factors, as shown by close adherence to definite and individual cycles, provides striking validity for such a generalization. This would indicate that physical and instructional benefits should not be presented too early or too late to produce maximum general benefits. One may then infer that the child is limited in the amount of environmental influence that he can effectively utilize.

SELECTED REFERENCES

1. BAYLEY, NANCY, AND PINNEAU, S. R., "Tables for Predicting Adult Height from Skeletal Age: Revised for Use with the Gruelich-Pyle Hand Standards," *Journal of Pediatrics*, 40:423–441, 1952.

2. AREY, L. B., "The Degree of Normal Menstrual Irregularity," *American Journal of Obstetrics and Gynecology*, 37:13–29, 1939.

3. BLISS, C. I., AND YOUNG, M. S., "An Analysis of Heart Measurements of Growing Boys," *Human Biology*, 22:271–280, 1950.

4. BLUM, L. H., AND FIELDSTEEL, N. D., "Method for Objective Measure of Developmental Progress," *American Journal of Diseases of Children*, 83:306–308, March, 1952.

5. BOOKWALTER, K. M., AND OTHERS, "Grip Strength Norms for Males," *Research Quarterly*, 21:249–273, 1950.

6. BRYAN, A. H., AND GREENBERG, B. G., "Methodology in the Study of Physical Measurements of School Children, Part II, Sexual Maturation, Determination of Immaturity Points," *Human Biology*, 24:117–144, 1952.

7. *Child Development Abstracts and Monographs.* Society for Research in Child Development, Inc., Lafayette, Indiana: Child Development Publications.

8. CLEMENTS, E. M. B., "The Age of Children When Growth in Stature Ceases," *Archives of the Diseases of Childhood*, 29:147–151, 1954.

9. COURTIS, S. A., "Growth and Development in Children," *Report of the Seventh Annual Health Education Conference.* Ann Arbor: American Child Health Association, 1933.

10. DIMOCK, H. S., "A Research in Adolescence, I. Pubescence and Physical Growth," *Child Development*, 6:176–195, 1935.

11. FABER, H. K., "A Weight Range Table for Children from 5 to 15 Years of Age," *American Journal of Diseases of Children*, 38:758–761, 1929.

12. FLORY, C. D., *Osseous Development in the Hand as an Index of Skeletal Development,* Monographs of the Society for Research in Child Development, Vol. I, No. 3. Washington: National Research Council, 1938.

13. FRANK, ALMA, "A Study in Infant Development," *Child Development*, 9:8–16, 1938.

14. GOULD, H. N. AND M. R., "Age of First Menstruation in Mothers and Daughters," *Journal of American Medical Association*, 98:1349–1352, 1932.

15. FRANK, L. K., KROGMAN, W. M., GRUELICH, W. W., WECHSLER, DAVID, AND WISKEK, S. M., "The Concept of Maturity from the Anatomical, Physiological and Psychological Points of View" *Child Development*, 21:19–60, 1950.

16. HARRIS, J. A., AND OTHERS, *The Measurement of Man*. Minneapolis: University of Minnesota Press, 1930.

17. GRUELICH, W. W., AND PYLE, S. I., *Radiographic Atlas of Skeletal Development of the Hand and Wrist*. Palo Alto: Stanford University Press, 1950.

18. JONES, H. E., "Relationships in Physical and Mental Development," *Review of Educational Research*, III:150–162, 177–181, 1933.

19. KELIHER, ALICE, *Life and Growth*. New York: Appleton-Century, 1938.

20. KLEIN, A., AND THOMAS, L. C., *Posture Exercises,* Children's Bureau, Publication No. 165. Washington: U. S. Government Printing Office, 1926.

21. Harding, V. V., "A Method of Evaluating Osseous Development from Birth to Fourteen Years," *Child Development*, 23:247–271, 1952.

22. ILIFF, A., AND LEE, V. A., "Pulse Rate, Respiratory Rate, and Body Temperature of Children Between Two Months and Eighteen Years of Age," *Child Development*, 23:237–245, 1952.

23. KOCH, W., AND KAPLAN, D., "Testing of Trend in Bodily Development of School Children," *American Journal of Diseases of Childhood*, 80:541–544, 1950.

24. KROGMAN, W. M., *A Handbook of the Measurement and Interpretation of Height and Weight in the Growing Child,* Monographs of the Society for Research in Child Development, Vol. XIII, Serial No. 48, No. 3, 1950. Lafayette, Indiana: Child Development Publications.

25. ——, *The Physical Growth of Children: An Appraisal of Studies 1950–1955*. Monographs of the Society for Research in Child Development, Inc., Vol. XX, Serial No. 60, No. 1, 1956.

26. SHUTTLEWORTH, F. K., *Sexual Maturation and the Physical Growth of Girls Aged Six to Nineteen,* Monographs of the Society for Research in Child Development, Vol. II, No. 5. Washington: National Research Council, 1937.

27. MASSLER, M., AND SUHER, T., "Calculation of 'Normal' Weight in Children by Means of Nomograms Based on Selected Anthropometric Records," *Child Development*, 22:75–94, 1951.

28. MEREDITH, H. V. AND E. M., "Annual Increment Norms for Ten Measures of Physical Growth on Children Four to Eight Years of Age," *Child Development*, 21:141–147, 1950.

29. NICOLSON, A., AND HANLEY, C., "Indices of Physiological Maturity: Deviation and Interrelationships," *Child Development*, 24:3–38, 1953.

30. TERMAN, L. M., *Genetic Studies of Genius, Vol. I, Mental and Physical Traits of a Thousand Gifted Children.* Palo Alto: Stanford University Press, 1925.

31. SHUTTLEWORTH, F. K., *The Adolescent Period: I. A Graphic Atlas. II. A Pictorial Atlas.* Monographs of the Society for Research in Child Development, Serial Nos. 49 and 50, Nos. 1 and 2, 1951. Lafayette, Indiana: Child Development Publications.

32. THORPE, L. P., *Child Psychology and Development.* New York: Ronald Press, 1946.

33. WATSON, E. H., AND LOWRY, G. H., *Growth and Development of Children.* (2nd edition) Chicago: Yearbook Publishers, 1954.

5

ASPECTS OF MOTOR GROWTH

INTRODUCTION

Separate discussion of general physical growth and motor growth by no means implies that the two are independent of one another. Motor growth is one of the elements of general physical growth and development and is contingent upon the child's utilization of his physical apparatus. Teachers are often more aware of general physical growth than of motor growth, and in the elementary school consideration of motor development is likely to be quite incidental and is quite frequently ignored in instructional planning.

Learning, Controlling, and Integrating Motor Response. Motor development, both simple and complex, may be defined as the process of learning, controlling, and integrating maturing motor responses. Fine responses, such as those of the fingers, hand, or forearm, or those involved in hand-eye coordination depend on small muscles. On the other hand, the gross responses, especially those of the trunk, the legs, and the shoulders, are dependent on large-muscle activity.

Physiological, Physical, and Psychological Factors. Where motor performance is mainly a physical or physiological phenomenon, its quantitative and qualitative aspects are affected by another factor — the psychological condition of the organism (22). Physical size and proportion are essential in the framework through which motor ability is to function. Organic capacities limit the potentiality of performance, and psychological factors provide motivation and direction. The individual is capable of a large number of motor performances, all dependent upon the relationship of these basic factors to one another.

PATTERN OF MOTOR GROWTH

Cycle Pattern. Motor growth follows the same pattern of maturation as all other growth sequences. Certain skills are learned early and at an early age show complete maturation; other skills begin and mature later. Still others start early and do not mature until late adolescence, thereby continuing through two cycles of growth.

FIGURE 28. Single-Cycle Motor Skill

Example of a Simple Skill. An example of a fairly simple skill is that of turning a somersault. This skill begins at approximately five, and it reaches its peak of efficiency at between ten or twelve years of age (Figure 28) (9). The curve covers a single-cycle growth period but indicates deterioration because of lack of practice. Consequently it never quite reaches complete maturity. This is probably due to the fact that turning somersaults is no longer a natural activity for twelve-, thirteen-, and fourteen-year-old children.

Example of a Complex Skill. An example of a skill requiring a longer period of time for maturation is handwriting (Figure 29) (8). This skill clearly shows the two-cycle period and requires approximately twelve years for full maturation.

Other skills follow a similar pattern, beginning slowly, rising rapidly to a leveling-off period, and, if complex, demonstrating these same characteristics during adolescence.

One of the problems which have proved interesting to investigators is whether motor ability is general or specific in nature. This question has been approached through correlation studies involving many kinds of performance.

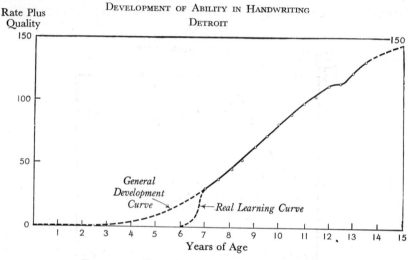

FIGURE 29. Growth of Ability in Handwriting

Range of Correlations. Carpenter, testing children in grades one to three, utilized a number of measures, including right and left grip, broad jump, dash, hop, and baseball throw. Correlations were then calculated which ranged from a —.10 to .77. In the main, these correlations were between .20 and .50 (6,7).

Using some seventeen different tests with college students, Perrin collected data including such simple measures as reaction time, tapping, and a number of others much more complex (27). In order to check the validity of general versus special ability, correlations were computed between the simple and the complex tasks. Results, although positive, were low. Consequently Perrin concluded that motor ability is a specialized, rather than a general, skill. In a like experiment Barton obtained similar results but found correlations as high as .55 between skills which seemed analogous (1). In general, correlations were positive but low. Other experimenters who concluded from their results that there is no such entity as a general motor ability were Ragsdale and Breckenfield, who said, "it is probably incorrect to speak of general motor ability in the same sense that we speak of general intelligence" (28).

Evidence of a General Ability. Evidence to the contrary has been presented by a number of investigators. Farmer gave tests to over 1300 adults. Consistently high correlations were found between certain tests. A sufficient total of these induced him to state that there must be some common element in motor abilities (13). Lerquin in working with boys aged nine to eleven concluded that there is no common motor factor among all reactions but possibly a basic factor of speed and accuracy (23). McFarlane, obtaining correlations between .40 and .45, concluded that in the more complex motor performances there is a general skill (26). McCloy and others obtained results which seem to justify general factors of strength and velocity (25), whereas Wendler identifies factors of motor educability and sensorimotor coordination (31).

Why Correlations Vary. Inconsistencies are to be expected, since there are variables in the scores which have not been given consideration. Performance is a product of rate and time in relation to a definite starting point and a definite maximum. Up to this point these concepts have not been taken into consideration in the studies. It is likely that greater consistency, as well as higher correlations, would have resulted had the various experimenters determined correlations between such aspects of motor growth as per cents of development, ages of maturation, and maxima toward which the skills were maturing. The evidence of interrelationships between such unrelated aspects of development as reading, physical development, and mental development would indicate that the field of motor growth, in which types of growth are more comparable, would have rendered positive evidence had data been collected longitudinally and studied by either the Olson or Courtis techniques. Such approaches to the data would enable investigators to reach more consistent conclusions regarding the question of general, versus specific, skill. Perhaps this question is less important than the question of individual uniqueness in motor growth. Without the evidence one can only speculate as to the answer.

MOTOR GROWTH DURING THE ELEMENTARY SCHOOL YEARS

Many Skills Learned before Entering School. In most instances motor growth occurs in an orderly developmental pattern (2). It follows a definite plan of integration from control first in head movements, then to the arms, hands, upper trunk, and finally to the lower trunk, legs, and feet.

Before the child comes to school, simple motor skills have matured and many others of a more complex nature are well on their way to maturity (24). These include feeding, walking, running, and other skills. During the school years he learns other skills of coordination such as writing, riding a bicycle, dancing, playing the piano (3).

Basic Skills Should Be Learned Early. It is advantageous to the child to learn the basic skills as early as possible. After one skill is learned another can be attempted, each one building upon the other. Motor learning, fortunately, is very easy for most children. About all they need is opportunity (16). Where this is delayed, perhaps because of illness, learning becomes difficult. In the early years nature provides a random muscular explorature which gives the proper motivation at a time when growth needs are most demanding. Long delay in the opportunity finds the child at a stage of development where self-consciousness restricts the earlier, natural, explorational, and often unrealized motivations.

COMMON MOTOR SKILLS

With the possible exception of girls in the upper grades, all elementary school children take great pride and joy in physical performance. Nearly every child finds pleasure in running and jumping, bicycle riding, roller skating, hiking, camping, and swimming.

Actually the elementary school child learns very few new motor skills. His time is given over to practicing skills already learned and extending and combining them. Children progress very rapidly in coordinating simple motor skills into the more complex patterns. Of great interest in this connection is the tendency to stunt and to show off when a skill has been reasonably well learned. After several experiences in which they have gained courage and some control, two- and three-year-old children will go down a slide backwards, on their stomach, and in any other way that is different. The baby who walks fairly well will try to run, and if his venture leads to an abrupt sit-down, he laughs and has a great time, especially if he is being watched by others. Young children will whirl until they fall down, run on tiptoe, and experiment with all kinds of variations of the normal performance of the skill. This is a common accompaniment to skill learning.

Role of Maturation in Development of Speed and Strength. Most observers agree that maturation involves increases in speed and strength, and this becomes obvious as children progress from the preschool years into the elementary school group. During this period they also begin to learn more complicated patterns.

The elementary school age is the time when motor skills are put to more practical use. Children in the early stages of learning such a skill as riding a bicycle, at first start, stop, get off, race, and ride without touching the handlebars. After the skill is mastered, they are more content to use the bicycle to travel from place to place (11).

Relation of Games to Interests. One of the most common skills of all children is that of playing ball. According to Breckenridge and Vincent, ". . . skill in handling balls of all kinds is almost a *sine qua non* for good gang contacts in the elementary school years. . . ." The children of the early elementary years generally show a preference for games involving chasing and running, but they are also intrigued with games in which a large ball is used. For the older children more complex games are appealing. The team game with group competition assumes importance for boys. At the upper elementary level they become very skillful in the various phases of baseball. The older girls like soccer and field hockey; many of them are interested in softball and some, even, in touch football. Other games which appeal are ping-pong, volley ball, and tennis, all requiring a high degree of coordination, rhythm, and timing.

Early elementary and kindergarten children are most interested in running, climbing, and dancing. Jumping rope, a seasonal activity, very popular with girls, makes its appearance as a skill with the five- and six-year-olds and remains popular for several years. Children at the early elementary school age begin to roller-skate but ice skating invites tumbles, falls, and consequently, considerable difficulty in mastering necessary skills. Six and seven years is the proper time for this. If there has been some preliminary experience, the five- and six-year-olds are ready for the two-wheel bike. The seven- and eight-year-old children become very competent both on the bicycle and on ice skates.

COMPLEX MOTOR LEARNING

The two types of fine motor learning of greatest significance to teachers are the coordination and control of eye movements and the control of hands and fingers. In the discussion to follow the development of proper eye movements will include consideration of (a) the early development of the eye, (b) visual acuity and discrimination, (c) eye-mind organization, and (d) eye-hand preference. The discussion of manipulative skills will emphasize the desired relationship between the manipulative maturity of the child and instructional activity, a relationship, unfortunately, which is often ignored (14).

A. DEVELOPMENT OF EYE MOVEMENTS

Essential Muscular Skills. Children are born with the mechanical equipment for vision, but it is some time before they master two very fine, essential muscular abilities. The one skill is involved in the process by which light is focused on the proper spot of the retina, and the other is the skill of coordinating the movements of the two eyeballs. The first skill is usually demonstrated by the time the baby is five or six months of age. This skill results in control of the very small muscles which govern the adjustment of the lens in the focusing of light. The child is several months old before he masters the second skill of turning both eyes together toward an object. Some children do not acquire this skill until they are three or four years of age. Obviously, if a child seems unusually retarded in developing either one of these skills, parents should consult an oculist.

B. VISUAL ACUITY

Development of Visual Acuity. Evidence from child study centers indicates that most children can distinguish a small cube at four months of age and an object as small as a hair on a rug at about six months. When the child is a year old he will show an interest in picture books which have one large picture per page. At two and a half to three, he will be interested in stories associated with pictures. When the child reaches school age there is still a great diversity of visual ability. Some children will be interested in books and have the ability to direct the eye horizontally across the page while concentrating on one line of print. Other children will have difficulty doing this without using a finger to guide them or an aid such as a small strip of cardboard placed immediately below the line to be followed.

Beginning Reading Requires Maturation of Primary Skills. It is essential that such primary skills be well developed before a child starts reading in order that the habits of regular and rhythmic horizontal eye movements can be established. The child who is pushed into reading before he has these controls will develop tensions and faulty eye habits which tend to become permanent. Moreover a story has meaning and interest only to the child whose eyes move smoothly and freely across the page. Research shows that the child whose eye movements are halting and confused, although he may be unaware of his lack of freedom in eye movement, gains only piecemeal, rough, and uneven ideas and impressions.

C. EYE-MIND COORDINATION

Skills Required for Reading. Eye-mind coordination, required for a successful beginning in reading, includes the ability to see likenesses and differences in word forms and the ability to remember word forms. These two are actually part of the same general skill. No child can remember word forms who cannot distinguish likenesses and differences. It is by growth in ability to differentiate that words are finally recognized and retained in the memory.

Most Eye Testings Inadequate. It is obvious that eye development must be adequate before the child is ready to read. And unfortunately, too few school authorities are sufficiently trained in determining visual readiness for reading. It is customary for school health authorities to examine acuity at the standard twenty-foot distance, but unless some obvious weakness is discovered no other check on acuity of visual sensation and perception is made. Any further routine calls for a separate check on each eye, to determine the efficiency of binocular vision and balance, but usually none is made. The Betts visual sensation and perception tests are beginning to be known and increasingly used for this purpose. Incidentally, this is the best known test used in schools to determine the efficiency of each eye when both are being used.

Method of Checking for Defects. Defects in vision greatly hinder the child in beginning to read. If the defect is of such a nature as to result in a blurred retinal image, the child cannot distinguish the letter pattern presented. Consequently he confuses similar words, such as *cat, mat, pat.* In addition to his discomfiture in discovering that he is making mistakes, he feels insecure, loses confidence, and becomes nervous and fatigued. The confusion also frustrates the development of the rhythmic and regular eye movements essential for later comprehensive reading. Preliminary tests of visual acuity and perception should enable the observer to distinguish children who are simply immature from those who have serious defects which should be called to the attention of a specialist.

The following special defects may be detected with the telebinocular, and they need attention before desirable reading habits can be developed:

Binocular vision: two-eyed vision

Visual acuity: keenness of vision

Fusion abilities: mental blending of right and left eye images into one composite image

Lateral imbalance: tendency for one or both eyes to deviate inward or outward from their normal position

Vertical imbalance: tendency of one eye to deviate upward or downward

Stereopsis level: depth perception or three-dimension vision

Amatropia: an error of refraction, such as farsightedness, nearsightedness, or astigmatism

D. EYE-HAND PREFERENCE

Teachers are interested in the problem of whether or not to compel the use of the right hand in school activities. Undoubtedly there is considerable pressure toward training children to become right-handed. The argument has gone first one way, then another. At present the general attitude is that there is no particular harm in encouraging left-handed children to become right-handed, but rather that harm may result through the method used. Encouragement, approval, acceptance of lower standards of performance at the beginning may be cited as proper methods in contrast to scolding, constant criticism of results, and undue drill.

Other research indicates that in the natural order of events in the child's experiences, there is a gradual increase of dominance of the right hand over the left hand (19).

How Preferences Develop. It seems desirable to point out how hand-eye preferences arise. Children in the first year of life indicate no hand preference. Between one and a half years and two years of age the child begins to use one hand more than another, although at times he appears to be ambidextrous. Preference in the use of one hand actually begins when he has developed some skill in the use of each hand. From the time preference is first indicated, the child shows a rapidly developing superiority in the use of the preferred hand (19).

How does preference come about? Is the tendency one way or the other inherent, or is it an acquired characteristic? Early behavioristic psychologists claimed that handedness was the result of training and experience. Somewhat later, neurologists announced that handedness had a structural motivation which was influenced only by practice and experience. This idea was based upon experimentation which related handedness to cerebral dominance inherent in the individual. From this point of view it was regarded as proper to change a child's handedness if his preference was slight and not too firmly fixed (5). It was also believed that if left hand dominance was outstanding, change would produce emotional tension, stuttering and other speech defects, or would even result in nail biting, facial tics, and other nervous symptoms.

Research today has brought about some change in this theory. Cerebral dominance is still recognized as important. Whereas formerly it was regarded as inherent, it is now looked upon as the result of training and practice in the use of the left and the right hand. Consequently, retraining is thought to have no bad effects as long as proper methods are used. However, retraining is not regarded as too important and probably should not be attempted unless the child wishes to make the change or, for some special reason, a change is desirable.

Most Children Right-Handed. Casual as well as expert study indicates that most children seem to prefer the right hand. In a survey reported by Thorpe, it was discovered that only six to eight per cent of the children were left-handed (30). According to some authorities about one-fifth of children can be trained to use either hand. Nevertheless, some can only be changed with great effort and unjustified nervous strain.

Many teachers believe that handedness can be determined by ascertaining the "eyedness" of the individual. Undoubtedly it is wise to know which eye is dominant in dealing with cases of handedness which prove troublesome, but there is no evidence that eye dominance gives a reliable determination.

DEVELOPMENT OF MANIPULATIVE SKILLS

The activity of children with paints and crayons before three years of age is mainly of a scribbling, exploratory nature. At three or four years of age children are usually delighted when given the opportunity to create a riot of color on a large sheet of paper. At this time they are also ready to express some initiative in design and pattern. Such concepts usually take shape in the making, and it is not until the child is four or five years of age that he can project a design and then carry it out.

Early Experiences Desirable. Because of the popularity of nursery schools and child study groups, many children learn the preliminary skills of hand and finger manipulation before they enter elementary school. If children do not have these earlier experiences, they go through the various stages a little more slowly when they enter kindergarten.

Late Childhood and Adolescent Development. Control in manipulation approximating that of an adult is reached between the ages of six and twelve. Shoulder, arm, and wrist controls develop rapidly during this period, while the finer manipulatory and delicate finger controls are achieved around twelve years of age. From twelve onward development continues toward general coordination and rhythm of movement.

Principles Common to All Development. The principles of growth previously outlined apply to motor learning as they do to any kind of growth and learning. Certain of these will be elaborated upon here, with certain subsidiary principles that need attention and analysis. The reason for stressing the point is that teachers generally give little attention to motor learning, except incidentally in helping a child meet extracurricular needs. That motor learning has some broader implications is a new thought for most teachers.

A. LEARNING AND GROWTH COMPLEMENTARY

In motor skills, as in no other kind, the relationship between growth and learning is most clearly brought out. Constant improvement in learning a motor skill cannot take place without continued growth and maturation, nor can maturation and growth result without experience, practice, and learning. Through growth influences, the child is placed in a position to learn, and through his motor learning experiences the best possible maturation is facilitated (10).

B. MOTOR LEARNING AFFECTED BY PERIOD OF
   PHYSICAL DEVELOPMENT

There is undoubtedly a definite relationship between motor and physiological growth. It is therefore possible to generalize that motor learning is most efficient when the activity involved is appropriate to the individual's stage of general maturity (Figure 30).

Specific Relationships as Yet Undiscovered. Although they are not yet determined, there are definite degrees of physical and physiological maturity essential for efficient and satisfying motor learning. The teacher who tries to force learning in advance of these is not only inefficient, but is setting up an inhibitory situation which will immediately react unfavorably on the child's personality and inhibit learning when the time arrives for it.

The proper procedure should utilize what is called *pacing*. In teaching motor skills, the parent or teacher has the problem of re-

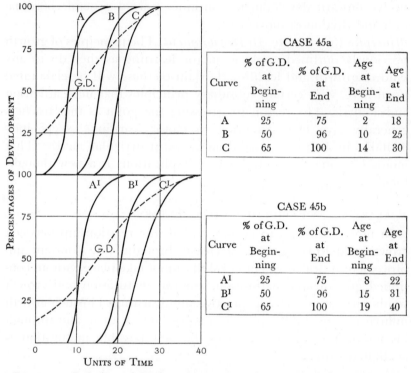

CASE 45a

Curve	% of G.D. at Beginning	% of G.D. at End	Age at Beginning	Age at End
A	25	75	2	18
B	50	96	10	25
C	65	100	14	30

CASE 45b

Curve	% of G.D. at Beginning	% of G.D. at End	Age at Beginning	Age at End
A^I	25	75	8	22
B^I	50	96	15	31
C^I	65	100	19	40

FIGURE 30. Relation of Various Motor Learnings to Periods of General Development

(Illustrating differences in timing of three curves involving two boys. In each case the same relationships between general development and specific growths are maintained.)

quiring practice and drill, but also of being certain that the skill practiced is compatible with the child's stage of maturity. As the child becomes more mature he is ready for more complex and difficult motor learnings. Pacing promotes efficient learning and has favorable psychological effects on the child. The child who learns adequately by proceeding from simple to complex skills develops a feeling of adequacy and confidence that contributes to his learning efficiency and to his personal-social development.

C. MOTOR LEARNING PROVIDES A MEANS FOR SOCIAL ADJUSTMENT

The boy or girl who is skillful in games, who has developed manipulative skill in art, music, and playground activities makes desirable social contacts (20). He is sought out by other children and seldom has to face the inhibiting effect of poor performance, so detrimental to the development of social adequacy. The acquisition and development of skills based on motor learnings contribute to the child's security and social poise. For this reason games and recreational skills are stressed in programs which seek to combat delinquency among older boys and girls (15).

D. MOTOR LEARNING FACILITATES CREATIVE LEARNING AND
    EXPLORATION AS WELL AS INTEGRATION

Most of the psychologists who accept the organismic point of view of growth and learning insist that the "whole" child reacts to any given environmental stimulus. Learning is always an over-all rather than a discrete process; it affects the entire organism and contributes to the complete reorganization of the individual's pattern of behavior. Stated educationally, learning is most effective and satisfying when the child's interests, attitudes, and needs are given consideration.

Need for Motor Activity in Academic Learning. Many teachers realize this but fail to see the contribution of motor activity to the child's total education. Some teachers are unaware that certain kinds of motor activity, properly applied, can entirely revitalize an academic learning situation. The emphasis given to this point is not primarily to demonstrate to health and physical education teachers how best to develop motor skills in games. Nor is its purpose that of pointing out that making boys skillful in games helps to prevent delinquency, although these are important. The main point of the emphasis is to show that more motor activity is needed in the total school learning situation.

Restriction Reduces Effectiveness. In the elementary school any program of instruction which restricts motor activity without purpose runs counter to what is known about the developmental needs of children.

Creative impulses are almost entirely associated with motor activity. As the child becomes adult, he may do creative work without any accompanying motor activity. The young child, however, thinks and creates with movements. He does not write a play abstractly or reflectively by sitting down and thinking things through. By acting it out he makes discoveries which cannot be made in any other manner. Children demonstrate, imitate, and create to the accompaniment of motor activity. Even in academic learning, it is virtually impossible for a child to eliminate motor accompaniments. If a child is having difficulty with number combinations and is not allowed to count, he will develop a tapping with his foot of which he may become quite unconscious. Learning to read or spell is frequently accompanied by lip movements or by an inaudible tongue movement. Such motor activity should be eliminated, but not by mandate or through punishment. Where such "crutches" are used, it is frustrating to attempt to force abandonment of them. Special aids such as combination charts in arithmetic or the use of a dictionary in spelling may be profitably used. In broader curriculum activity, however, motor expression should be encouraged rather than repressed, since it is such a natural response of children. In situations where it is not desired it should be discouraged.

Creative Activities Require Motor Accompaniments. It is reasonable to assume that most children, varying individually, of course, are motivated to create in some form or another. Creation may take place in painting a mural, originating a dance, or drawing a picture of the trip "we took last Thursday." The most worthwhile educational experiences emerge in abundance when motor expression is adequately joined with intellectual opportunity. Without adequate room space, materials, and the opportunity for elasticity in organization, the teacher is greatly handicapped in building the proper instructional program.

Motor Accompaniments Necessary in Core Program. The motor activities involved in dramatization, the dance, the manipulatory skills involved in the arts and in manuscript writing have another value. This value results in program and curriculum enrichment in the broad social sciences and language arts fields. Unless materials are available and motor activity is encouraged, these areas are likely to break down into nothing more than one large consolidated course in the social sciences, for example, with specific time given to geography, history, and current events, and no general coordinating activity. This does not imply that there should be a special activity period during which children merely let off excess energy in random spontaneous motor expression. The argument is for more motor expression in the entire elementary program. In most kindergartens this point is applied in actual practice. In the first grade and from there on the child is abruptly and meaninglessly introduced to the sit-down-now-be-quiet procedure of most conventional teachers with curriculum activity specifically scheduled to various subject matter areas.

SIGNIFICANCE TO TEACHERS

Teachers may question the importance of a knowledge of motor development. Height and weight measurement and interpretation is fairly acceptable as one of the responsibilities of the classroom teacher in child study. But what more does the teacher need to know about the child's physical-motor development? What is the significance of the fact that Johnny is well coordinated and Hazel is not?

Aids in Determining Maturity. Paralleling the child's physical development as indicated by height and weight is the extent of his rhythm and motor coordination. A tall and heavier than normal child might by a casual inspection appear to be more mature than he really is. Further observation might point out a lack of coordination and rhythm which would lead one to question the first conclusion and decide that the child is, instead, both young and immature. In other words, a large child is more likely to be generally mature and advanced if he also manifests maturity in coordination. The extent of a child's motor development, then, provides an additional index of his maturity.

Aids in Determining Security. It is common knowledge among the investigators of child behavior that physical growth — oversize, undersize, immaturity, or precocity — may be the source of peculiar behavior. The child whose physical development is decelerated or accelerated, or who lacks muscular control and rhythm of movement, may show social deviations. Nothing gives a child more security within his social grouping than physical and motor adequacy. Unsatisfactory behavior in many instances, at first thought traceable to a disturbed or abnormal personality, mishandling in school or at home, or poor environment, may result from a feeling of physical or motor inferiority. Other records, such as personality inventories, interview data, and anecdotal or behavior journals are helpful in making such determinations. Nevertheless, the most accurate diagnoses require information and observation of the child's evolving motor pattern.

Aids in Interpreting Diagnostic Problems. Students interested in the clinical phases of reading have concerned themselves frequently with the question of hand-eye dominance as a factor in reading, spelling, or writing ability or disability. Teachers who have followed these studies become alert to the child's hand and eye preference and also note reading or spelling difficulties in relation to these.

Aids in General Instructional Improvement. Because of the great urge to physical activity most children have considerable difficulty in adjusting to the conventional school's practice of sitting down, being quiet, and walking quietly. If it is true, as most psychologists state, that this developmental period is a time when children are most interested in the use of their bodies, then the school is particularly negligent if it provides too little time for meeting this need.

Knowledge of these facts has significance for instructional planners. In the area of motor growth, the classroom must be regarded as a proper environment for developing manipulative skill, particularly for the six- to twelve-year-old child. Secondly, as clearly stated, the encouragement of motor development must be regarded as an aid to social growth and the development of creativity. Certainly these facts represent a substantial validation of the usage of a great many types of supplementary instructional activity of a nonacademic nature.

This information is greatly needed by the kindergarten teacher who must provide the setting suitable for the development of rhythm and coordination. This information is necessary in interpreting a good performance, or a poor one, in arts and crafts activities. And it is most essential for health and physical education teachers who have available a repertoire of games, exercises, and activities aimed at the development of rhythm and coordination. And lastly, it is important for all who are helping the child achieve adequate personal and social adjustment.

SELECTED REFERENCES

1. BARTON, E., *Correlation among Motor Abilities* (unpublished thesis) Madison: University of Wisconsin, 1926.
2. BAYLEY, NANCY, *The Development of Motor Abilities during the First Three Years,* Monographs of the Society for Research in Child Development, No. 1. Lafayette, Ind.: Child Development Publications, 1935.
3. BLUM, LUCILLE H., AND FIELDSTEEL, NINA D., *Blum-Fieldsteel Developmental Charts,* Based on the Norms and Observational Methods of the Gesell Development Schedules. Yonkers on the Hudson: World, 1952.
4. BUELL, CHARLES, "Motor Performances of Visually Handicapped Children," *Journal of Exceptional Children,* 17:69–72, 1950.
5. BURGE, IVAR, "Some Aspects of Handedness in Primary School Children," *British Journal of Educational Psychology,* 22:45–51, 1952.
6. CARPENTER, AILEEN, "Tests of Motor Educability for the First Three Grades," *Child Development,* 11, No. 4:293–299, 1940.
7. ——, "The Differential Measurement of Speed in Primary School Children," *Child Development,* 12, No. 1:3–12, 1941.
8. COURTIS, S. A. (unpublished material)
9. ——, "Growth and Development in Children," *Report of the Seventh Annual Health Education Conference.* Ann Arbor: American Child Health Association, 1933.
10. DUSENBERRY, LOIS, "A Study of the Effects of Training on Ball Throwing by Children Ages Three to Seven," *Research Quarterly,* Vol. 23, No. 1:9, 1952.
11. LATCHAW, MARJORIE, "Measuring Selected Motor Skills in Fourth, Fifth, and Sixth Grades," *Research Quarterly of the American Association of Health and Physical Education,* 25:439–449, 1954.
12. McCRAW, L. W., "A Factor Analysis of Motor Learning," *Research Quarterly of the American Association of Health and Physical Education,* 20:316, 1949.
13. FARMER, J., "A Group Factor in Sensory Motor Tests," *British Journal of Psychology,* 17:327–334, 1927.
14. SEILS, L. G., "The Relationships between Measures of Physical Growth and Gross Motor Performance of Primary-Grade School Children," *Research Quarterly of the American Association of Health and Physical Education,* 22:244–260, 1951.
15. HARRIS, D. B., "A Play Activities Blank as a Measure of Delinquency in Boys," *Journal of Abnormal and Social Psychology,* 37:546–559, 1942.

16. SMITH, S. L., AND GOSS, A. E., "The Role of the Acquired Distinctiveness of Cues in the Acquisition of a Motor Skill in Children," *Journal of Genetic Psychology*, 87:11–24, 1955.

17. TAYLOR, C. M., BAL, M. E. P., LAMB, M. W., AND MACLEOD, GRACE, "Mechanical Efficiency in Cycling of Boys 7 to 15 Years of Age," *Journal of Applied Psychology*, 2:563–570, 1950.

18. WALTERS, C. ETTA, *Scientific Foundation of Motor Learning*, Workshop Report. Washington: National Association for Physical Education for College Women, 1956.

19. JONES, H. E., "Dextrality as a Function of Age," *Journal of Experimental Psychology*, 14:125–143, 1931.

20. ——, "Physical Ability as a Factor in Social Adjustment in Adolescence," *Journal of Educational Research*, 40:287–301, 1946.

21. ——, *Motor Performance and Growth*. Palo Alto: Stanford University Press, 1948.

22. WENAR, CHARLES, "The Effects of a Motor Handicap on Personality: I. The Effects of Level of Aspiration," *Child Development*, 24:123–130, 1953.

23. LERQUIN, R., "Étude Expérimentale sur L'Habileté Motrice," *L'Année Psychologique*, 30:106–143, 1929.

24. MCCASKILL, CLARA L., AND WELLMAN, BETH, "A Study of Common Motor Achievements at the Pre-School Ages," *Child Development*, 9:141–150, 1938.

25. MCCLOY, C. H., "The Measurement of General Motor Capacity and General Motor Ability," *Research Quarterly of the American Physical Education Association*, Supplement 1, V:46–61, March, 1934.

26. MCFARLANE, MARGARET, "A Study of Practical Ability," *British Journal of Psychology*, Monograph No. 8, 1925.

27. PERRIN, F. A. C., "An Experimental Study of Motor Ability," *Journal of Experimental Psychology*, 4:24–57, 1921.

28. RAGSDALE, C. E., AND BRECKENFIELD, I. J., "The Organization of Physical and Motor Traits in Junior High School Boys," *Research Quarterly of the American Physical Education Association*, V:47–55, October, 1934.

29. ZUBECK, J. P., AND SELBERG, PATRICIA A., *Human Development*. New York: McGraw-Hill, 1954.

30. THORPE, L. P., *Child Psychology and Development*. New York: Ronald Press, 1946.

31. WENDLER, A. J., "A Critical Analysis of Test Elements Used in Physical Education," *Research Quarterly of the American Physical Education Association*, IX:64–76, March, 1938.

6

THE GROWTH OF INTELLIGENCE

INTRODUCTION

The purpose of this chapter is (1) to present a picture of the maturing mental pattern, and (2) to point out ways and means by which such knowledge leads to a better understanding of the total child. Such information and understanding should improve a child guidance program and provide cues for better teaching. Since the material presented is for classroom teachers, the discussion will be directed primarily toward their interests.

Intelligence is a subject which has challenged a long line of investigators. Certain problems, hypotheses, and conclusions have provoked lively controversy (16). It is not our purpose to analyze in detail issues of interest chiefly to research workers. Consequently the material offered will be determined (1) by the level of teacher opportunity for studying intelligence and (2) by its possible implications for instruction.

THE NATURE OF INTELLIGENCE

A. THEORIES OF INTELLIGENCE

What is intelligence? Investigators have been interested in this question for decades without being able to agree upon a single definition. One of the earliest, by Binet, described intelligence as directness of thought, capacity for making adaptations, and the power of self-criticism (33). Stern, in a like vein, described intelligence as a general mental adaptability to new problems and adjustments (9). Both of these definitions stressed the generality of intelligence, but numerous later research studies tended to challenge this viewpoint.

The early idea noted above became known as the *unit-factor* theory, which generally considered intelligence as mainly dependent upon hereditary factors.

G *and* S *Theory*. Spearman has been the chief advocate of a second theory (31). His view accepts two factors as involved in an intellectual performance or task, which he calls respectively *g* and *s*, referring to general and specific powers. The general factor *g* is regarded as underlying all mental functioning and is thereby considered the common denominator in all sorts of mental performance. This factor may vary from individual to individual but is consistent in all types of mental functioning of a given individual.

Since mental functioning in unrelated types of situations calls for different kinds of mental accompaniments, there must be a specific factor which is also operative in each type of situation. This factor or power is specific to a given type of functioning and may be entirely different from those used in other types of situations. This factor *s* not only varies from individual to individual but within the individual according to the ability called for by the task at hand.

The *g* and *s* theory has one point in common with the unit-factor theory. Similarity is found in the idea that a general ability is operative in any kind of intellectual performance. It does differ, however, in that it recognizes the possible existence of special abilities. The two viewpoints are acceptable to child study observers to the extent that performance is recognized as an over-all activity rather than a functioning of a special ability or aptitude.

Thorndike Theory. The third point of view is a variation of the general ability theory. Instead of regarding performance as contingent upon an over-all power functioning in all types of specific situations, this viewpoint holds that intelligence is comprised of distinct abilities, all operating in a definite interrelation brought about by the quantity of neural connections involved (36). Thorndike has since modified this view by pointing out that the quality of the neural connections is a factor as well as the quantity. He calls this an *integrative* relationship.

Gestalt Theory. Thorndike's theory is not entirely in opposition to Spearman's. A fourth, however, suggested by the Gestalt phychologists, is considerably different. According to this group, intelligence functions to the extent that the elements of a given situation are seen in relation to a meaningful whole. Thus this school of psychology has placed much emphasis upon integration. This seems quite reasonable and not too out of harmony with the others. In its attempt to explain the functioning of intelligence in reference to special abilities such as perception it departs from the other theories and loses its point in a maze of terminology. Instead of using accepted terms to explain behavior, it coins new terms which evade analysis and interpretation.

What does all this imply for the teacher-observer of child behavior? In the main it points out that in spite of fervent and extensive study and research, investigators have not yet reached a common understanding and agreement on the exact nature of what we measure and call intelligence. Observers should be cautioned to study the relationships of intelligence to other aspects of behavior which are observable and measurable (24). In the light of the disagreement among experts as to the meaning of intelligence, it is certainly obvious that the importance given I.Q.'s should be lessened.

B. CHARACTERISTICS OF INTELLIGENCE

Intelligence, insofar as it has been investigated and studied, is said to have four characteristic functions (36). Thus it is defined not by what it is, but by what it can do.

Difficulty. The first is thought of as that characteristic which is defined by the intellectual *difficulty* or level at which intelligence performs. From this point of view the more difficult the task a person can achieve, the greater his intelligence.

Range. The second characteristic, proposed by Thorndike, is what he calls *range*. Range is determined by the number of types of tasks which can be performed at a given level of difficulty. This point of view is logical enough, but since difficulty is defined for so few tasks, it resists scientific analysis and experimentation.

Area. Area is the third characteristic. It may be described as the summation of tasks achieved as defined by their difficulty and range. A person with a wide area of intellectual ability would be one who could solve tasks at a high level of difficulty and on a broad range. This again is a theoretical concept as far as our skill in accurate measurement is concerned. It does serve, nevertheless, to give ideas about the meaning of intelligence.

Speed. Speed is the fourth characteristic. Most investigators agree that that intellect is superior which performs a given task with ease and dispatch as compared with another which functions less easily and with less directness. Speed is commonly evaluated by the number of situations correctly solved in a given unit of time. On the other hand, some intellects are efficient in terms of range and difficulty but approach a problem cautiously and carefully. In the main, speed is an attribute of intelligence, but in most groups there will be a few who are overly cautious and careful. It is obvious that in such situations other factors are operative which cannot be entirely separated in evaluating intelligence (22).

C. KINDS OF INTELLIGENCE

Are there "kinds" or "types" of intelligence? From the lay point of view, and quite possibly from the point of view of the practical teacher, the answer is definitely affirmative. Every teacher knows of children who, though "academically" bright, have trouble in getting along with other children or are inadequate in certain social situations. Also, every teacher knows of children who have special skills but are inept in academic matters. According to Broom, a classification of types of intelligence consists of (5):

1. Abstract or academic intelligence
2. Social intelligence
3. Concrete (including mechanical) intelligence
4. Esthetic intelligence

It is likely that most teachers can readily accept such a classification, since it seems to parallel their experiences with children. The studies of Thurstone seem to validate the idea that intelligence is complex and consists of a variety of abilities (37). Utilizing the technique of factor analysis, he has identified several aspects of intelligence through intercorrelations. The question can justifiably be raised, however, whether intelligence can be isolated sufficiently to be broken down into categories. It would seem to many that experience, training, and conditioning are influential and frequently are not given adequate attention in arriving at conclusions.

SOME FACTORS AFFECTING INTELLIGENCE

A. INHERITANCE

Kinds of Studies. Many techniques have been used to study the effect of inheritance upon intelligence (7). These include correlation techniques, historical analyses of families through many generations, and co-twin study. Included among these are correlations between intelligence measures of members of families in various relationships, for example, correlations between scores for twins, for brothers and sisters, and for parents and their children. Such correlations range from .40 for parents and children to .90 for identical twins (4).

High Correlations in Same Families. These data indicate that the closer the family relationship, the higher the correlation (2). Some investigators assume that with the effect of heredity so significant other factors are rather unimportant. These people fail to see that the high correlations do not necessarily indicate the superiority of heredity as a factor but may also reflect identity of environment.

Historical Studies. The historical investigation of families has been a very interesting approach to the problem. Among the best known are the Kallikak-Jukes-Edwards family studies. Data on these people have been used to point out that mental superiority, or deficiency, persists in related stocks. In one family line, for example, it was discovered that, of 480 descendants of a feeble-minded woman, only 46 were of normal intelligence.

Using a similar technique, Galton in 1892 reported his famous analysis of 977 men of genius (11). Of this group, over 500 had distinguished relatives while a similar number of so-called normal men had but four eminent relatives. Again, the reader must be warned that such data do not rule out the effect of environment.

Family Likenesses in Growth Patterns. One of the most recent approaches is the comparison of growth curves of parents and children. Olson and Hughes have studied data on parents, collected when the parents were children, with similar data on offspring. These results are interesting and do much to point out the powerful influence of heredity, not only on status but also on the over-all pattern of growth (19).

B. ENVIRONMENT

Co-Twin Studies. Co-twin study has also provided a technique for getting at the effect of environment on intelligence. Gesell probably did the most to popularize this type of investigation, which uses groups with similar inherited traits so that differences in environment, changed at will, can be studied. According to Gesell, who observed a small number of cases given special training during relatively short periods, original similarities are but little changed by special training (12). Other investigators have studied the question of differences in intelligence between identical twins raised in considerably different environments. Schweisinger reported in 1933 on ten pairs of identical twins who met these conditions (28). Briefly, he found that among six pairs there were no significant differences. Four pairs varied as follows: in two pairs twelve-point differences in I.Q. were found, whereas in the other two pairs there was a difference of approximately fifteen points.

C. ENVIRONMENT VERSUS HEREDITY

Teachers for a long time have wondered about the relative effect of heredity and environment. The emphasis swings first one way then the other (13).

Conflict in Reported Results. In a number of instances, as pointed out previously, scientific studies have demonstrated the importance of inherited potentialities. On the other hand, many more studies than those reported here demonstrate the importance of environment in conditioning human growth (30). The impartial observer now calls the battle a draw. The two are actually complementary in the total growth process. Heredity can function only in a given environment, and environmental factors are contributory only to an organism which is dynamic, that is, has genic potentialities and is able to grow.

To overemphasize one point of view is to ignore the facts supporting the other. Regardless of the bias with which the problem is approached, the findings always illustrate the great variability to be found among people. Although it is true that the average children of privileged groups excel underprivileged children, it is also true that a large percentage of children of the lower social group excel the average of more privileged children.

D. RACE

The literature dealing with the relation between race and intelligence is interesting, although as yet without many implications for teachers in the classroom.[1] The typical procedure of most investigators is to test a number of individuals in each racial group, compute average scores and range, and then compare with available age or grade norms.

Conventional Approach Used. Such studies were begun, in the main, during World War I. From the data it was concluded that the intelligence of such people as the Poles, Italians, Greeks, and Russians was somewhat lower than those of the English, Americans, Scotch, and Germans. Although much has been said to point out that under test conditions which utilized the English vocabulary nothing else could be expected, nevertheless the studies are quoted as authoritative.

Weaknesses in Data. A further weakness of the data is that in most instances the environmental influences have been ignored. To be thoroughly reliable, test results may be used to study racial differences only when the groups tested have had common motivations, experiences, and backgrounds.

Generalizations Need Further Study. Great caution should be exercised in accepting generalizations from inadequate data regarding the superiority of any race. The later investigations which tend to point out individual differences among a racial group. rather than the study of relative brightness of several races, are making much greater contributions to instruction. Of this type is the study made by Witty and Jenkins who report that among 8000 Negro children, twenty-six had I.Q.'s beyond 140 (39). Such studies, which indicate abilities and spread of intelligence among given racial groups, do more to define educational problems than do the earlier studies which present a questionable comparative picture of racial groupings.

Need for New Approach. Further research involving the collection of longitudinal data may throw new light on the problem. Few

---

[1] This problem is a social problem rather than a growth problem.

of these, however, have been undertaken to date. Such studies should look into the total developmental picture of, for example, the Negro child in school. In terms of mental growth, the major problems which investigators need to solve are these:

a. How do the developmental intelligence curves of Negro children differ from others?

c. Do they differ to such an extent that growth ranges in the various grades need to be widened?

b. What do the developmental curves show in relation to periods of readiness for learning, periods of rapid growth, etc.?

If it is discovered that the developmental patterns of any special racial group fall within the normal range, there is no special instructional or administrative problem, aside from the social problem involved. Teachers, then, need to consider any child from a minority group only as an individual who should be treated according to his special growth needs.

THE DISTRIBUTION OF INTELLIGENCE

A Classroom Distribution. Distribution of intelligence is the spread of its quantitative measurement in reference to the general population. For example, if an intelligence test is properly administered to one hundred typical, and otherwise unrelated, school children of the same age, very high and very low scores will be obtained, with the majority found between these extremes (11). The discrepancy between the highest and the lowest in mental age units will range over several years. In a rather typical city school situation the following distribution of twenty-six children was found in October in a certain third grade. The distribution of intelligence is shown with the distribution of the same children by chronological age (Figure 31). The figure is interesting because of the two types of distributions. Among the twenty-six children reported, the chronological age distribution represents a range of from seven to ten and a half years — an approximation of a normal curve. Three children are definitely overage and one underage. The mental age distribution is skewed, including children from six and a half to nine and a half years approximately. The sharp drop in distribution indicates that the school promotion policy is to accelerate children who are more than one and a half years advanced, and not to demote or fail, unless absolutely necessary, children who are slow.

Reason for Skewed Distributions. In actual school situations there is usually, then, a somewhat skewed distribution (Table IX, p. 128).

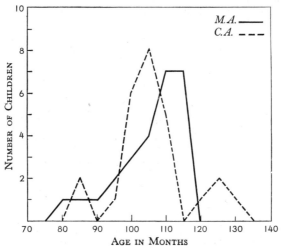

FIGURE 31. Comparison of Mental and Chronological Age Ranges in a Typical Third Grade

Since children who are below normal drop out of school, either because the typical school program is geared to a higher level, or because certain children are so far below normal as to need to be institutionalized, there are more superior children in school than dull. This is indicated in each column in Table IX (p. 128), except for Sandiford's hypothetical distribution.

THE NATURE AND CHARACTER OF THE MENTAL GROWTH CURVE

A. THE DATA AVAILABLE

Classification of Individual Differences. Other factors being equal individual differences express themselves in three ways: (1) differences in ages at the beginning and ending of a growth cycle,

TABLE IX

PERCENTAGE DISTRIBUTION OF INTELLIGENCE QUOTIENTS OF
UNSELECTED CHILDREN [2]

Classification	I.Q. Range	Witty[a]	Millard[b]	Madsen[c]	Terman-Merrill[d]	Sandiford[e]
NEAR GENIUS OR GENIUS	Above 140	0.03	0.77	0.2	1.33	0.25
VERY SUPERIOR	120–140	8.5	8.33	9.8	11.30	6.75
SUPERIOR	110–120	14.3	24.07	17.4	18.10	13.00
NORMAL, OR AVERAGE	90–110	56.9	54.01	51.6	46.50	60.00
DULL, RARELY FEEBLEMINDED	80–90	10.8	9.72	12.4	14.50	13.00
BORDERLINE, SOMETIMES FEEBLEMINDED	70–80	7.2	2.16	6.4	5.60	6.00
FEEBLEMINDED	Below 70	2.2	0.92	2.3	2.63	1.00
Total	—	99.93	99.98	100.1	99.96	100.00

[a] Witty: 1000 Unselected Children, Grades 1–8
[b] Millard: 648 Unselected Children, Grades 3, 5, 7
[c] Madsen: 880 Elementary School Children, Grades 1–8
[d] Terman-Merrill: 1937 Revision Unselected Population
[e] Sandiford: Hypothetical Normal Population

(2) differences in the maxima attained at maturity in a given
cycle, and (3) differences in rates of growth. To point out these
differences in detail and also to determine the pattern of mental
growth, the data on sixty girls and fifty-four boys were studied.
The girls had received a total of 566 tests covering an average age
span of 97.6 to 164.8 months, and the boys had been given a total
of 466 tests from an average age of 102.2 months to 171.3 months.
The average number of tests per child was 9.4 for the girls and 8.7
for the boys. The tests given were the Kuhlman-Anderson group
tests of intelligence. The following general procedure was carried
out with the data for each child (6):

Step 1. An equation for the mental growth of each individual
was derived from the actual measurements.

Step 2. These equations were then solved for values for each
individual at the ages at which the tests were given.

Step 3. Comparisons were then made between the equation
values and the actual scores and the differences noted.

[2] Revised from Witty, P. A., and Others, Elementary Educational Psychology, New
York, Prentice-Hall, Inc., 1945, p. 106.

Step 4. The average I.Q. for each child was computed from available data and predictions from this average were made at ages when the tests were given.

Step 5. Comparisons were then made between mental ages predicted from average I.Q.'s and the actual mental ages measured by the tests.

Step 6. Comparison of the deviations computed as described under Step 3 were made with the deviations computed as described under Step 5.

Step 7. Consolidated equations were made for each sex by averaging the constants in the equations.

The cases selected for study were somewhat above average intelligence. The mean for the girls' group was represented by an I.Q. of 109.4, standard deviation of 14.0, and for the boys by 104.4, standard deviation of 13.9.

B. ADEQUACY OF EQUATIONS IN DESCRIBING MENTAL GROWTH

Mental Growth Follows Definite Patterns. Many teachers will find it difficult to believe that it is possible to describe a child's growing

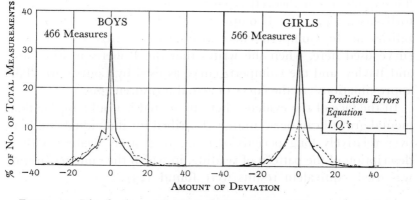

FIGURE 32. Distribution of Boys' and Girls' Mental Measurements from Equation (and I.Q.) Predictions

mental pattern in exact mathematical terms (10). The equations derived picture the two-cycle growth over an age span of nearly six years with a mean deviation of less than one month. Approximately two-thirds of all the actual measurements fell within 7.5

months of a zero error from the equation prediction (Table X).
Equations for Mental Growth. In comparison with the predictions
from the average I.Q.'s of each child, the equation predictions
presented considerably less error (Figure 32).

Average I.Q. Ineffective in Describing Growth. A study of Table
X gives further evidence that the two-cycle equation describes the
pattern of growth better than the conventional I.Q.

TABLE X

COMPARISON OF ERRORS OF PREDICTED SCORES FROM EQUATIONS
WITH PREDICTED SCORES FROM MEAN I.Q.'S

| | BOYS | | GIRLS | |
	Equation Error	I.Q. Error	Equation Error	I.Q. Error
MEAN ERROR	—0.86	—0.20	.73	—.88
STANDARD DEVIATION	7.5	10.7	7.2	11.00
MEAN ERROR WITHOUT SIGN	5.1	8.5	4.7	8.0

The data presented here tend to refute the statement of Helen
Thompson that a theoretical curve of growth cannot be satisfactorily used (35). Dr. Thompson does admit, however, the possibilities in the Gompertz curve as used by Courtis, which is the
curve used here, when she writes that the Robertson, the Jenss
and Bayley, and the Gompertz curve as used by Courtis are "fair
approximations" to the curve of actual measurements.

In the face of the evidence here presented it would appear that
mental growth can be accurately described for individual children
over relatively long periods of time. In a study dealing with a
description of the pattern of reading, in which the same technique
was used, equivalent results were found (23).

C. THE COMPOSITE PICTURE OF MENTAL GROWTH

Curve of Constants Used. As described under Step 7, a composite
equation for each sex was obtained. Working through each composite equation so derived, at various age levels, a curve of growth
for boys and girls was constructed (Figure 33).

Curve Shows Two Cycles. The pattern of growth shows the two-cycle characteristic with the break, seemingly, between 120 and 140 months of age. It is interesting to note the shifting around the straight line representative of a constant I.Q. The greatest shift occurred during adolescence at approximately fifteen years of age.

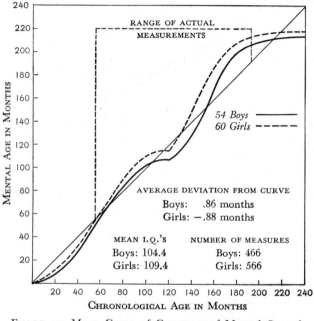

FIGURE 33. Mean Curve of Constants of Mental Growth for Selected Boys and Girls

Equations

Boys: $Y = 150.5 [.258t + 14.69] + 65.0 [.786t − 92.10]$

Girls: $Y = 153.0 [.270t + 14.61] + 66.3 [.797t − 88.47]$

D. COMPOSITE SEX DIFFERENCES

1. Differences in Maxima

Each Cycle Has a Maximum. Since the composite equations for these boys and girls result in two-cycle curves, it is obvious that there is a maximum toward which each group is growing before reaching adolescence and a second maximum toward which each is growing during adolescence. Since the second maximum is expressed by values in the equation over and beyond the first maximum, the sum of the two would represent the absolute maximum as determined by the Kuhlman-Anderson tests. Comparison of these by each sex group is shown (Table XI).

TABLE XI

MEAN PREADOLESCENT, ADOLESCENT, AND TOTAL MENTAL
MAXIMA OF BOYS AND GIRLS (IN MONTHS)

| | PREADOLESCENT | | ADOLESCENT | | TOTAL MAXIMUM | |
	Mean	S.D.*	Mean	S.D.	Mean	S.D.
BOYS	149.4	8.0	64.0	22.2	216.6	30.6
GIRLS	153.0	7.7	66.5	19.6	218.6	28.8

* Standard Deviation.

Girls Maximum Greater. In each instance the mean maximum of the girls was slightly greater than that of the boys. Of more interest, perhaps, is the fact that the mean total maximum of each group is close to a mental age of eighteen (216 months) years.

2. Differences in Rates of Growth

The two-cycle concept of mental growth is considerably different from the idea that mental growth proceeds most rapidly during infancy and early childhood. The two-cycle curve also sharply differentiates from the logarithmic form proposed by Gesell and the parabolic curve suggested by Thorndike, in which mental growth is described as progressing from zero at birth to a midvalue at approximately three years of age and attaining its final maximum at about twenty-one years of age.

Negative Acceleration in Both Cycles. The mean rates of the boys and girls in this study show the characteristic of negative acceleration, but in both cycles of growth. In more direct opposition to the parabolic or single-cycle concept with its consequent continuous negative acceleration is the picture of growth of these children in which rate is two or three times greater during adolescence than in the preceding cycle. Growth in this instance is described in value terms of the maximum toward which each cycle is progressing, rather than in terms of increment from one age to another.

Girls Rate Greater. It is interesting to note that the rates of growth in both cycles were slightly greater for girls than for boys. It is also significant that the range of rates during adolescence was much greater for both boys and girls than during the preadolescent cycle. This gives further evidence of a fundamental characteristic of individual differences, namely, that they increase with age.

E. OTHER FACTS CONCERNING MENTAL GROWTH [3]

In utilizing the equation technique in the study of growth, it is possible to consider data from many approaches. It seemed advisable in this instance to seek solutions to three problems:

1. The distribution of ages at which the adolescent cycle begins
2. The distribution of per cents of development within the preadolescent cycle when adolescence begins
3. The distribution of ages at which adolescent mental maturity is reached

Beginning of Adolescence Earlier than Expected. According to the data the mean age of beginning the adolescent cycle was 106.1 for girls and 108.8 for boys (Table XII). For both groups these ages correspond roughly to nine years of age, which is much younger than is generally considered the age for the beginning of adolescence.[4]

Girls More Mature on Beginning Adolescence. The girls, although they began at a younger age, were slightly more mature in their preadolescent development when it started, 74.8 to 72.6, and in their adolescent cycles reached maturity (99.0 per cent) almost two years before the boys (Table XII). This seems to be the outstanding sex difference found in these data and can be accounted for mainly by the difference in rates of growth. The fact that the girls had slightly higher I.Q.'s should not be entirely dismissed in accounting for this difference.

[3] To be elaborated upon in a forthcoming study.
[4] Obvious breaks, however, do not begin to appear until between ten and twelve years of age (Fig. 33).

TABLE XII

SEX COMPARISONS IN TIMING OF MENTAL GROWTH
(AGE IN MONTHS)

	Age at Beginning of Adolescence		Preadolescent Development at Beginning of Adolescence		Age at Adolescence Mental Maturity	
	Mean	*S.D.*	*Mean*	*S.D.*	*Mean*	*S.D.*
BOYS	108.8	21.9	72.6 pct.	15.1	226.0	39.4
GIRLS	106.1	20.1	74.8 pct.	7.9	203.0	35.4

THE QUESTION OF CONSTANCY OF THE INTELLIGENCE QUOTIENT

High Correlations in Early Data. In the early days of the great popularity of mental testing, there rapidly accumulated much literature testifying to the constancy of the intelligence quotient. The concept was formulated after it was found that children re-tested at intervals of one to three years obtained about the same intelligence quotients as before. Such variation as was discovered was attributed to unreliable testings rather than to changes in intelligence. The correlations were high, often ranging between .80 and .90 for the two testings. These data were accepted as valid and the general belief developed that the I.Q. was fixed. Naturally such a concept gave impetus to organization of levels of instruction based on the child's ability to learn, and set up a pattern of intelligence testing such that two or three tests evenly spaced throughout the entire elementary and secondary school years were regarded as sufficient. The more recent correlation studies between intelligence test results point out weaknesses both in the earlier concepts and in the practices which they motivated. Bradway, testing with an interval of ten years, reports correlations in the sixties. As interpreted by Olson, this means (26).

> . . . the chances are about one in four that when a child is four or five years old, and one in three that when the child is two or three years old, the intelligence quotient will have changed 15 points or more in the following ten years. About one fourth of the two- and three-year-old group and one third

of the four- and five-year-old group changes less than 5 points. About one half of the two- and three-year-old group and about three-fifths of the four- and five-year-old group change less than 10 points.

Low Correlations in Recent Studies. Goodenough and Mauer point out even greater variation (15). Utilizing several tests over a period of twelve years the correlations obtained were less as the time interval became greater. Coefficients between .40 and .50 were computed between the Minnesota tests, given before three years of age, and the Stanford-Binet, given five years later. A correlation of only .12 was found between preschool tests and American Council tests given twelve to fourteen years apart.

Such evidence, joined with the type of mental curve earlier portrayed (Fig. 33), indicates that there can be but little remaining foundation for the theory that the I.Q. is fixed. Unfortunately there is no great trend toward accepting the conclusion that such changes are a natural unfolding of the particular child's pattern of growth. Olson is among the few who believe that "the individual growth curves indicate systematic changes as if the expression of intelligence were under the influence of an unfolding design." However, he holds no brief for prediction possibilities. Nor does he state that such changes as occur might be due to the curvilinear and cyclic nature of that pattern (26).

Faulty Concept of Mental Growth. Others, while recognizing possibilities for change, ignore the fact that the normal mental growth curve constantly varies in its I.Q. ratio. Differences found are attributed to differences in the reliability of the two testings, particularly when one of them is given at the preschool level. Another explanation given is that the difference on a later testing is to be expected when the child is sufficiently mature to understand what is wanted of him in terms of test performance. Differences in health, attitude, rapport, and emotional status are also quoted as reasons for later change. And then, there is the general belief that children who test low at first will later show gains, whereas children who test high at first will later show losses. The point of view of this writer is that one or more of these factors may be operative at some time or another. Nevertheless, these are factors that cause variation from the true curve rather than change in the direction of the curve. Temporary effects may accentuate or modify the real picture of change, but they do not necessarily affect or influence the true emerging pattern. From this viewpoint it may be concluded that an intelligence test not only measures what we call intelligence but when utilized longitudinally provides some insight into the effect of such factors as emotion, temperament, and other similar aspects of personality. These are shown by the amount of variation from the over-all curvilinear pattern. When the point of view of natural shift is accepted, variation from the emerging pattern becomes as important in interpretation as the shift in status from one testing to the next (29).

THE MEANING OF MENTAL AGE

Error in Homogeneous Grouping. The question of the constancy of the I.Q. naturally challenges certain conventional practices which are quite universally employed (14, 42).

A challenge may be directed toward the view held by most teachers regarding the meaning and significance of mental age. Mental age has always been looked upon as a criterion of performance. If a child has a mental age of six, he is labeled as ready to begin reading. If he has a mental age of ten, he is expected to do the school work normally expected of a child of ten. In making such judgments, it is immaterial whether the first child mentioned is five, six, or seven years old chronologically. And in the latter case, chronological age likewise is given little consideration. Grouping children on a mental age basis results in considerable chronological differentiation and differentiation also in reference to I.Q.'s. Acknowledging that this practice may be justified under certain instances, the error results in assuming that the grouping, once made, continues homogeneously in this respect (Figure 34). Although both children shown have a mental age of six when they are six years old chronologically, Child A with a greater maturity at that time is obviously progressing toward a lower preadolescent maximum. The question as to which child is potentially better prepared for reading at the time of the intersection of the two curves is completely unanswered. Such differences in children serve to challenge the validity of the mental age readiness concept and suggest the possibility of maturity as a more effective criterion. Unfortunately, this sort of information is generally unavailable and teachers at present are without the necessary skills to properly interpret it. Under existing circumstances mental age may be employed for grouping purposes if tempered by judgments about the

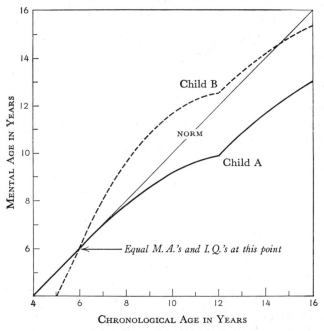

FIGURE 34. Shifts in Homogeneity of Mental Age of Two Children with Equal Chronological Ages

child's maturity and if the teacher keeps in mind the fact that status at a given time frequently shifts to a new relative position. A second step which can be recommended is to start collecting data much more frequently. Only when a pattern begins to be established through the use of cumulative data can a valid judgment be made as to readiness and potentiality.

Homogeneity a Coincidence. A supplementary point which has a bearing on the problem is the danger of using grouping procedures. The picture of mental development shown by the consolidated growth curves (Figure 33), and specifically illustrated in Figure 34, shows that there can be but little validity in any kind of permanent grouping. Homogeneity in mental age between two children is almost invariably a coincidence and cannot be used effectively for a considerable length of time in an instructional program. Consequently, then, potentiality is much more characteristic of an emerging pattern of growth than performance. A child with superior potentiality may often read normally, or achieve in any other manner, somewhat below other children whose potentiality is less (Figure 34). It is almost always incorrect to say that a child is not performing up to his potentiality. Child B has the greater potentiality, even before six years of age, regardless of his relative immaturity and performance status at this time.

Errors in Interpreting I.Q. Teachers are frequently confused by children who score high on intelligence tests but perform rather inadequately as well as by those who test low but perform in better than normal fashion.

In comparing mental age with reading age, it is generally conceded that one is quite predictable of the other. The high correlations between reading scores and intelligence scores represent the findings upon which the practice can be fairly well justified. An error too frequently made is that of interpreting the data for an individual child. Many children have intelligence and reading scores which do not correspond to the general expected relationship. In such cases children who measure at a reading age below their mental age are immediately stigmatized as reading below their potentiality, and children who measure in reading age beyond their mental age are considered either as benefiting from special training, superior background, or from a special aptitude. Frequently in such cases the intelligence test scores may be considered erroneous.

Test Weaknesses. It may well be that the differences result from limitations in the tests used or in our inability to interpret scores or status in terms of comparative maturities. The tests have certain limitations which are not generally understood. The most significant is that mental age cannot be tested longitudinally from birth to maturity by any single test now available. To be entirely valid over this period of time, a test should be so constructed as to show gain in mental age in terms of units which, when the results are graphed, would correspond to, or parallel, periods of over-all development. A test should respond to the phenomena of maturation and should reflect the kind of growth which the organism can demonstrate. No test is so constructed. As a matter of fact, the normal picture of growth which test constructors attempt to achieve through the selection of their test items is a single-cycle curve. Consequently the results often give a faulty picture of an individual child.

Achievement tests, too, provide sources of error for three similar reasons. (1) As in intelligence tests, items are selected which fail to provide a picture of progress corresponding with the pattern of organismic growth. (2) They provide forced ceilings for the brighter children. Many children in the upper fifth, sixth, and seventh grades achieve so closely to the upper limits of such a test that the investigator is unable to discover the true picture of achievement. There is no doubt that in the most widely used achievement tests, the brighter children who attain a high pre-adolescent maximum do not later show nearly the same relative adolescent achievement as do the less able children.

(3) Another source of error in comparing intelligence and achievement may be found in our practice of evaluating a score in terms of a norm rather than in terms of the maximum toward which the child is growing. Even with the limitations in tests already mentioned, comparative maturities are found to agree much more closely than do our current common denominators of age- or grade-level (6,24).

Until the limitations noted are corrected it will be necessary to expect among a great many children considerable difference between mental age and achievement age. With the kind of data now provided a great advance would be made if mental age is given a lessened emphasis in evaluating achievement. If the child gains from grade to grade, his progress should be considered satisfactory unless he is among those who are affected by poor health, emotional maladjustment, or other handicaps. Where cumulative testing is possible and efforts are made to graph results, further conclusions and deductions can be made. No single aspect of growth, not even intelligence, should be considered dominant in a criterion for achievement.

IMPLICATIONS FOR TEACHERS

A. REVISED ATTITUDE TOWARD INTELLIGENCE NECESSARY

Investigations of the meaning of intelligence and the results of investigations dealing with its pattern of growth indicate that teachers who work with intelligence tests must revise their concepts. It seems reasonable to expect that the research available should shake the belief of those who think that a single intelligence testing can predict a mental growth pattern. To speak of the constancy of the I.Q. without giving attention to many conditioning factors certainly cannot be justified in the face of these investigations. In the past this attention was missing in studies of homogeneous grouping, studies of racial differences, and the like. The constancy of the I.Q. was generally accepted, and teachers and clinicians treated children accordingly.

Present Practices Unjustified. The implications of variability in the I.Q. and the suggestions that somewhat large mental changes may occur is certainly startling and will require care, if not great modification, in interpreting intelligence testings. Many school practices, such as the X, Y, Z grouping idea, are based on the earlier extreme concept of fixed intelligence. Consequently, far-reaching and significant changes in instructional organization should result with further substantiation of the newer findings.

B. CONTINUED EXPERIMENTATION WILL CLARIFY
RESEARCH RESULTS

Weakness in Iowa Studies. Such research obviously indicates a possible closer relationship between environment and intelligence than has previously been thought to exist. What this amounts to in a definite quantitative relationship is, of course, unknown. Further clarification of the problem is needed, as is further experimentation which takes into consideration the general curvilinear nature of the growth curve and the concept of cyclic growth of the individual. It may be that some of the changed I.Q.'s reported by the "Iowa Studies" may be nothing more than the change produced by the natural curvilinear character of the curve (Fig. 33).

It is unlikely that any mathematical index of the environmental effect on intelligence will be determined shortly. The difficulty lies in our inability to provide sufficient controls which take into consideration every factor that might be effective. Moreover, it is essential to know the normal growth patterns of the children under consideration before attempting to produce changes in that pattern. Only then is it possible to determine the effect of a planned change in the environment.

C. RECENT EXPERIMENTATION GIVES BROADER MEANING
   TO EFFECT OF INSTRUCTION

Heredity and Environment Supplement Each Other. A sensible viewpoint credits both heredity and environmental stimuli for human behavior. Heredity fixes broad limits through which the environment can be effective and the kind of environment or general cultural surroundings provide the cue to the extent to which the individual is approaching his growth potentials.

Weakness in I.Q. Usage. For the teacher really interested in the improvement of children there is hope in this idea. The I.Q. ceases to be an infallible measure of potentiality and takes its place as only one of a series of indices. Other data such as ratings of socioeconomic background must also be included. If we desired to be truly accurate in respect to this relationship it would be necessary to classify children into socioeconomic categories before judging brightness. This would give an entirely different picture of intelligence.

The longitudinal picture of mental growth and its relation to other aspects of development indicate that an entirely new emphasis needs to be placed on the relationship of intelligence to learning. Formerly children were grouped in various levels according to I.Q. and given assignments according to their level. On this assumption many programs developed which attempted to relate instruction to the child's ability. The pattern of mental growth underscores the futility of this kind of practice, not to mention the undemocratic intellectual smugness which this procedure tends to foster (21).

Pacing Rather than Grouping. A contrary, but infrequently employed, procedure is suggested. This is what has been called a *pacing* of the instructional program and involves emphasis and de-emphasis according to whether mental growth is proceeding rapidly or slowing down.

Problem of Individual Differences. Obviously, all children do not show the same timing in respect to various developmental periods. The problem of individual differences becomes greater rather than less when timing as well as status must be taken into consideration in planning an effective instructional program. Nevertheless this does not necessarily imply that all children need to be working at different tasks, nor does it imply that different children need to be working at various levels of difficulty on the same task.

The major step to be taken in reference to these facts is a shift in objective. Maturation, rather than mastery, then becomes the goal in the instructional program. Children grow toward diversified maxima according to their potentialities and the motivations provided in their environment. This is true even where children undergo the same curriculum requirements. The conventional school has portrayed nothing more clearly than the idea that in spite of rigid requirements all children permanently achieve according to their own specific and peculiar individualities. Recognizing and accepting progress rather than mastery in accordance with the developmental pattern of a given child indicates, strangely enough, that much less "teaching" need be done individually than one would think. Group teaching under good conditions, whenever possible, not only insures necessary motivation for achievement in the specific task at hand, but also provides the motivation in such related learnings as the social or the emotional. This does not necessarily imply that no individual attention should be given the child at any time. It only means that formal arrangements for such instruction should not permeate the whole curriculum offering, and are best provided informally and in relation to specific growth needs.

SELECTED REFERENCES

1. ALTUS, GRACE THOMPSON, "A Note on the Validity of the Wechsler Intelligence Scale for Children," *Journal of Consulting Psychology,* 16:231, 1952.

2. ANASTASI, ANNE, "Tested Intelligence and Family Size; Methodological and Interpretive Problems," *Eugenics Quarterly*, 1:155–160, 1954.

3. ANSBACHER, H. L., "The Goodenough Draw-a-Man Test and Primary Mental Abilities," *Journal of Consulting Psychology*, 16:176–180, 1952.

4. BAYLEY, NANCY, "Some Increasing Parent-Child Similarities during the Growth of Children," *Journal of Educational Psychology*, 45:1–21, 1954.

5. BROOM, M. E., *Educational Measurements in the Elementary School*. New York: McGraw-Hill, 1939.

6. COURTIS, S. A., *The Measurement of Growth*. Ann Arbor: Brumfield and Brumfield, 1932.

7. BLEWETT, D. B., "An Experimental Study of the Inheritance of Intelligence," *Journal of Mental Science*, 100:922–933, 1954.

8. CATALONA, FRANK L., AND MCCARTHY, DOROTHEA, "Infant Speech as a Possible Predictor of Later Intelligence," *Journal of Psychology*, 38:203–209, 1954.

9. CORNELL, ETHEL L., AND GILLETTE, ANNETTE, "Construction and Educational Significance of Intelligence Tests," *Review of Educational Research*, Vol. 20, pp. 17–26, 1950.

10. ——, AND ARMSTRONG, CHAS. M., "Forms of Mental Growth Patterns Revealed by Reanalysis of the Harvard Growth Data," *Child Development*, Vol. 26, No. 3, 169–204, Sept., 1955.

11. GALTON, F., *Hereditary Genius: An Inquiry into Its Laws and Consequences*. New York: Macmillan, 1892.

12. GESELL, ARNOLD, AND OTHERS, "Maturation and the Patterning of Behavior," *Handbook of Child Psychology*, edited by Carl Murchison. Worcester: Clark University Press, 1933.

13. EELS, K., DAVIS, A., HAVIGHURST, R. J., HERRICK, V. E., AND TYLER, R., *Intelligence and Cultural Differences*. Chicago: University of Chicago Press, 1951.

14. ELWOOD, MARY ISABEL, "Changes in Stanford-Binet I. Q. of Retarded Six-Year Olds," *Journal of Consulting Psychology*, 16:217–219, 1952.

15. GOODENOUGH, FLORENCE L., AND MAUER, KATHERINE M., *The Mental Growth of Children from Two to Fourteen Years*. Minneapolis: University of Minnesota Press, 1942.

16. FROMM, ERIKA, HARTMAN, LENORE D., AND MARSCHAK, MARIAN, "A Contribution to a Dynamic Theory of Intelligence Testing of Children," *Journal of Clinical and Experimental Psychopathology*, 15:73–95, 1954.

17. GRIFFITHS, RUTH, *The Abilities of Babies. A Study in Mental Measurement*. New York: McGraw-Hill, 1954.

18. HAGGARD, ERNEST A., "Social-Status and Intelligence: An Experimental Study of Certain Cultural Determinants of Measured Intelligence," *Genetic Psychology Monographs*, 19:141–186, 1954.

19. HUGHES, B. O., "Implications of Heredity for Education," *University of Michigan School of Education Bulletin*, Dec., 1946.

20. HEIM, A. W., AND WALLACE, J. G., "The Effects of Repeatedly Retesting

the Same Group on the Same Intelligence Test: II. High Grade Mental Defectives," *Quarterly Journal of Experimental Psychology*, 2:19–32, 1950.

21. HENDRICKSON, GORDON, "Mental Development During the Preadolescent and Adolescent Periods," *Review of Educational Research*, 20:351–360, 1950.

22. HONZIK, M. P., AND OTHERS, "The Stability of Mental Test Performance Between Two and Eighteen Years," *Journal of Experimental Education*, 17:309–324, 1948.

23. MILLARD, C. V., "The Nature and Character of Pre-Adolescent Growth in Reading Achievement," *Child Development*, 11, No. 2:79, 1940.

24. ——, "Further Comments on the November Issue" (I.Q.'s), *Educational Method*, XIX, 8:445–447, 1940.

25. KENT, GRACE H., *Mental Tests in Clinics for Children*. New York: Van Nostrand, 1950.

26. OLSON, W. C., *Child Development*. Boston: Heath, 1949.

27. KOLSTOE, O. P., "A Comparison of Mental Abilities of Bright and Dull Children of Comparable Ages," *Journal of Educational Psychology*, 45:161–168, 1954.

28. SCHWEISINGER, G. C., *Heredity and Environment*. New York: Macmillan, 1933.

29. LINCOLN, E. A., "Stanford-Binet I. Q. Changes in the Harvard Growth Study," *Journal of Applied Psychology*, 20:236–242, 1936.

30. NISBET, JOHN, "Family Environment and Intelligence," *Eugenics Review*, 45:31–40, 1953.

31. SPEARMAN, C. T., *The Abilities of Man*. New York: Macmillan, 1947.

32. PATTERSON, C. H., *The Wechsler-Bellevue Scales*. Springfield, Illinois: Thomas, 1953.

33. TERMAN, L. M., *The Measurement of Intelligence*. Boston: Houghton Mifflin, 1916.

34. ——, AND ODEN, MELITA H., *The Gifted Child Grows Up*. Palo Alto: Stanford University Press, 1947.

35. THOMPSON, HELEN, "Physical Growth," *Manual of Child Psychology*, edited by Leonard Carmichael, New York: Wiley, 1946.

36. THORNDIKE, E. L., *The Measurement of Intelligence*. New York: Teachers College, Columbia University, Bureau of Publications, 1927.

37. THURSTONE, L. L., *Primary Mental Abilities*. Chicago: University of Chicago Press, 1938.

38. SHERMAN, MANDEL, *Intelligence and Its Deviations*. New York: Ronald Press, 1945.

39. WITTY, P. A., AND JENKINS, M. D., "Intra-Race Testing and Negro Intelligence," *Journal of Psychology*, 1:179–192, 1936.

40. SLOAN, WILLIAM, "Motor Proficiency and Intelligence," *American Journal of Mental Deficiency*, 55:394–416, 1951.

41. SKODAK, MARIE, "Mental Growth of Adopted Children in the Same Family," *Journal of Genetic Psychology*, 77:3–9, 1950.
42. THURSTONE, L. L., AND ACKERSON, L., "The Mental Growth Curve for the Binet Tests," *Journal of Educational Psychology*, 20:567–583, 1929.
43. TYLER, F., "Comments on the Correlational Analysis Reported in 'Intelligence and Cultural Differences'," *Journal of Educational Psychology*, 44:288–295, 1953.
44. WORCESTER, DEAN A., "Mental Development From Birth to Pre-Adolescence," *Review of Educational Research*, 20:345–350, 1950.

7

LANGUAGE DEVELOPMENT

NEED FOR STUDY

Language ability, more than any other skill, enables man to rise above his environment. It empowers him to project his knowledge into the future, and it is his basic tool for cooperation. Animals have methods of communicating with each other, but verbal expression enables man to transmit fine shades of meaning — an expression far beyond the ability of other animals.

Use of Language. The use of language permits man to transmit easily to the new generation his accumulated learnings and thoughts. It makes it possible for him to extend his experiences and generalize from them, to share experiences, seek assistance in discriminating between meanings, control behavior, and conserve, accumulate, and transmit all these to a new generation. Through the use of language man can theorize, experiment, and thereby save time in his own development and improvement. The child whose language development is seriously retarded suffers almost insurmountable barriers to his necessary development. No one will deny that the earlier the child achieves communicative facility, the sooner he is ready to benefit from the use of this instrument in all his personal-social developmental needs.

Importance in Instructional Relationships. Language, certainly, is a most important tool in learning. It is basic to the instructional relationship between pupil and teacher, and between pupil and pupil. Therefore, providing the environment for maximum language development is a fundamental responsibility of elementary education. Reading rapidly and with comprehension, speaking effectively and with desired shades of meaning, and writing intelligently are universal educational objectives.

Basis for Discovering Defects. Another reason for studying the child's language development is to obtain the necessary background for distinguishing between real and borderline speech defectives. Every teacher should be sufficiently trained to determine whether or not a child is a speech defective and whether the assistance of a speech therapist is necessary. Most children progress in their language development through a period of baby talk. The great majority proceed rapidly through this period. Articulatory imperfections may be overlooked in these children. For certain others the problem is more serious. These latter show marked defects which persist well up into the early elementary grades. Teachers should be able to distinguish those who are likely to shed their infantile speech habits in a short time from those whose habits may persist and demand special clinical attention. Teachers who are unable to do this may further solidify the pattern or even help create a problem more difficult to cure. Hasty introduction of formal speech correction with young children whose imperfections are only temporary or merely an indication of emotional immaturity may produce self-consciousness and speech withdrawal.

Parallels General Development. A third reason for studying language development is to learn more about the child's total organismic pattern. The growth of communication skills parallels other phases of development. Some skills begin early and rapidly become effectively used. Others begin late in the child's developmental pattern and continue in their growth into late maturity.

HOW LANGUAGE IS LEARNED

A. EARLY THEORIES

Psychologists and others have speculated considerably concerning the beginnings of language. Some of them have concluded that language came about through evolutionary processes in which it emerged as a step somewhat above earlier forms of nonverbal communication. This, they explain, resulted from the evolution of an increasingly complex nervous system. A considerable number have suggested that language grew out of earlier speech sounds connected with pleasurable or painful experiences. Some evidence of this may be found in the fact that the pleasure sounds of gurgling and cries of pain in the infant appear before speech is possible.

The speech response is entirely learned and entirely possible because the newly born child is an organism potentially capable of modification through reaction with his environment. Specifically, the normal child is born with the equipment for integrating the activity of such mechanisms as the vocal cords, the tongue, teeth, lips, and the nasal and oral cavities. He also inherits the secondary mechanisms for speech which include the lungs and the diaphragm. The integrating activity is itself a maturational process which makes possible the expansion of the earlier gurglings to later comprehensible speech (9).

B. THE ROLE OF IMITATION

Imitation plays a very important role in the child's linguistic development. There is agreement as to the general effect of imitation, but there is some controversy as to whether it is voluntary or not, whether it is accompanied by comprehension, is immediate or deferred, and whether it is exact (18).

Imitation and Repetition. Evidence of learning by imitation is shown by the fact that the child learns the language of his environment and by the fact that the congenitally deaf child cannot learn normal speech because he is unable to hear and therefore cannot imitate others.

Of equal importance to the imitation of others is the imitation by the child of those sounds which he himself has made (18). Nearly everyone is familiar with the continued babblings of the infant. It is believed that a desire to hear himself talk is what contributes to this activity. When the child is in the presence of adults and accidentally or purposely makes sounds, parents are likely to pronounce a word which approximates the sound made. This is a good training procedure, since it provides an auditory strengthening and stimulates the child to remake the sound he has produced. Consequently, he is aided toward more precise perception and rendition of approved pronunciation (19).

C. MATURATION

Effect of Maturation. Maturation, of course, is an important factor in language development. In a training program with twins, Strayer found significant differences in results when one of the twins was delayed for five weeks in beginning his training period (29). The child so delayed not only displayed more effective learning but showed a more mature speech response. From this experiment it was concluded that training cannot overcome differences in maturational levels.

D. UNDERSTANDING

Understanding Aids Learning. Understanding the language of others is of great assistance to the child in learning to use language himself. In a natural environment it is quite clearly established that the child has considerable understanding of what others are saying before he uses words. Such understanding occurs at about the end of his first year. Frequently, however, the child is very attentive to the speech of others at approximately nine months of age.

The infant's use of gestures before he can speak is evidence that he understands adults. Gestures and general body movements, frequently used by infants as a means of expressing themselves, are often accompanied by vocalization. As a matter of fact, such duality of expression is so common that certain psychologists explain speech as a mature means of expression substituted for the earlier gross motor activity.

DEVELOPMENTAL SEQUENCE

A. SIMILARITY OF LANGUAGE GROWTH TO OTHER
   GROWTH SEQUENCES

Curvilinear Pattern. Growth in language, like other growth, follows a curvilinear sequence. Comprehensible speech, a simple language growth, begins early and reaches maturity early (Figure 35). The curve, though lacking in data to show its beginning, rises rapidly but rounds off toward maturity at three years of age. This point is better demonstrated in the curve for increase in the number of words per sentence used by a child as he gets older (Fig. 36). Data for increase in vocabulary follow a curvilinear pattern but, since the data are not shown for children beyond six years of age, the abrupt rounding off toward maturity cannot be demonstrated (Fig. 37).

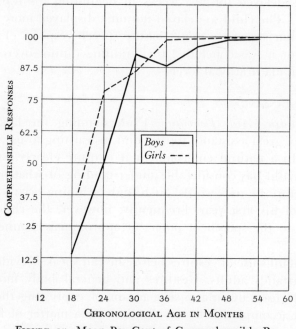

FIGURE 35. Mean Per Cent of Comprehensible Responses by Chronological Age and Sex

Cycles in Complex Curves. The more complicated kinds of growth involved in language development show the cycle pattern, with the second cycle appearing at adolescence. This point is brought out clearly in the curve representing the mean number of words per sentence in the written compositions of the individual from eight years of age to fourteen (Fig. 36). The curve is characterized by a preadolescent cycle clearly leveling off at approximately eleven years of age and rising to a greatly increased maximum by age fourteen. It is obvious from these charts that the effect of adolescence is most marked (13).

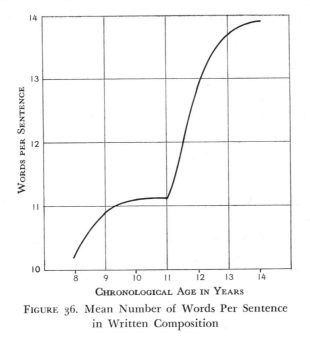

FIGURE 36. Mean Number of Words Per Sentence
in Written Composition

B. PRESPEECH SOUNDS

The beginnings of language have been studied by investigators since the latter part of the seventeenth century. In most instances, investigators have been parents who compiled notes on their child's language expression as it developed. Hence the studies have been individual in nature, and since they varied greatly, generalization has been difficult. Nevertheless, they provided a beginning for the more recent, more scientific observational techniques (18).

Prespeech Responses. It has already been pointed out that non-verbal signs and gestures represent the beginning of formal communication. In the early informal communication pattern, children learn to express themselves, obtain wants, and in a limited sense exercise some sort of control over their environment. It is in these early adaptive responses that investigators find the beginnings of comprehensive and mature language behavior (23).

Babblings. The second stage of expression may be found in the incoherent babblings and other sounds made by the infant. The first sounds are mere vocal responses to feelings of personal comfort or discomfort. In general, however, it is claimed that these rudimentary and incoherent vocalizations are the beginnings of vowel and consonant sounds from which the later comprehensible words evolve (21).

Because elementary school teachers are not particularly interested in this stage of the child's development, the discussion will

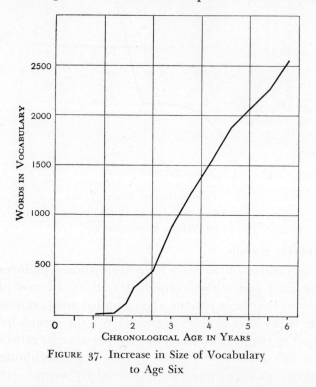

FIGURE 37. Increase in Size of Vocabulary
to Age Six

not go into great detail on the speech habits of the infant preliminary to word usage. But the order in which the infant learns consonants and vowels, and the implication of this order for teaching word usage and phonetics at a later stage of development justify some treatment of the subject. It is believed that the order of difficulty of learning speech responses at this early stage of development persists in the elementary school period, where consonants and vowels are involved in spelling, speech, reading, and in other subject-matter learnings related to communication of all kinds.

First Speech Sounds. There is not entire agreement as to the order in which the child's speech sounds develop, but there is considerable authority for the belief that the vowels, particularly *a* and *u*, are used first. Consonants are first used in the labials *b, p, m, w* and the tip dentals, *t* and *d*. The sounds involving *k* and *g* appear somewhat early and are later followed by the *s* and *z* sounds. There is some evidence that *f, e, r,* and *v* are among the last sounds to be used. It must be realized that these do not appear in actual words but may be identified among the child's sound responses to various stimuli.

C. THE FIRST WORD

By repeating the sounds he hears about him, and particularly those he hears in his own incoherent babblings, the child learns to use words (18).

Many children arrive at the one-word stage by ten months and nearly all between fifteen and eighteen months of age (16). A child reaches this stage earlier if his parents take time to give him names of objects that he can pronounce, as indicated by his earlier sounds, and that have meaning for him. After some successful experiences in this kind of activity, the child becomes interested in the exercise and soon wants a name for everything he sees. Indulgence on the part of parents to his demands for a "name" gives him considerable satisfaction and pleasure. It also provides him with the background for forming one-word sentences, mainly used in making a demand on his elders. The word "Doggy!" may mean "Look at the doggy."

Difficulty of Distinguishing between Babbling and First Words. It is difficult to determine when babblings cease and actual words are substituted. There is a tendency to interpret first sounds as words. Since it is necessary to depend on parents for records, data are not always reliable. The advent of the first word is so anxiously awaited that clearness of the sound is likely to be more imagined than real. The criterion of meaning is consequently difficult to apply. Other criteria are likewise awkward. One, for example, is understanding and another is ability to repeat a word when it is spoken by others.

Age of Appearance. Despite the difficulty of determining exactly when intelligible words are first spoken, numerous studies have dealt with the problem. Age range for this phase of development has already been noted as occurring between ten and eighteen months. Cattell, utilizing parents' data, accepts eleven months as the standard (5), whereas Shirley, judging on the basis of the word spoken before professional examiners, designates fourteen months as the average age (23). Smith reports that none of the children studied had begun to talk at eight months, whereas at ten months seventeen could speak one word (25).

Type of Word Spoken. There is little question as to the type or word-form first spoken. This may be described as a repetitive monosyllable. Universally familiar examples are *mama, dada,* and, of course, *bye-bye.* As soon as parents note this phenomenon they encourage the child, and he soon begins to use such words in specific situations. The great majority of the earliest words are of a definite phonetic form consisting of single or duplicated syllables in which the consonants are either labials (*p, b, m, w*), labio-dentals (*f, v*), or tip-dentals (*t, d, n*). Usually consonants are found only at the beginning of the word, and the word is either monosyllabic or repeated monosyllables.

Part of Speech. Of course it is impossible to state the exact part of speech of the first words, since they are usually isolated or at best occur in the briefest of sentences. In the main, the first words are used as interjections or nouns. Aided by gestures or some affective bodily or mental state, the child is able to convey a variety of meanings utilizing only one word. The single word "dog" may be interpreted as "See the dog," or, in another situation with some limited inflection, "Where is the dog?"

First words have an emotional quality. They may express a wish or a feeling. Or again they may express a real personal need. Interestingly enough, it is believed by some authorities that speaking the word is secondary to the general emotional status of the child at the time of using the word and that as words are learned, they are used to supplement body movements, emotional expressions, and other devices used to express wants.

D. THE GROWTH OF VOCABULARY

Types of Studies. Many studies have been made on the growth of the child's vocabulary. Earlier studies used the method of listing all new words as they were first heard in the child's speech. In more recent years all kinds of approaches have been made to the problem. According to McCarthy, there are the following eight types of studies (18) : [1]

1. Estimates of total vocabulary at specified ages (usually of single children).
2. Analyses of total vocabularies according to parts of speech.
3. Analyses of total vocabularies for subject-matter content.
4. Analyses of the occurrence of the various parts of speech in samples of conversation.
5. Analyses of the occurrences of the various parts of speech in compositions.
6. Estimates of total vocabularies of groups by the use of the free association technique.
7. Estimates of total vocabularies by the use of vocabulary tests.
8. Word frequency counts.

Much is known about the number of words used by children at various ages, the parts of speech of the words used, and the nature of the *cumulative frequency* curve.

Nature of the Curve. After the child first begins to speak, his vocabulary shows rapid progress. At one year of age he can usually speak one word, at three he may use approximately 1000, and at six as many as 2500 words. All children, of course, do not proceed at this rate, nor do all of them reach the same maximum number. The child's total pattern of development, his home background, educational opportunity and experience, and his intelligence all have a great influence. The average boy or girl at graduation from high school is likely to have a complete vocabulary of approximately 14,000 words. Terman provides a somewhat similar standard in his early mental test norms (30).

8 years	3600	words
10 years	5400	words
12 years	7200	words
14 years	9000	words
16 years	11,700	words
18 years	13,500	words

[1] Reprinted by permission from *Manual of Child Psychology* by L. Carmichael, published by John Wiley & Sons, Inc., 1946.

The data on children from one to six indicate that the curve for vocabulary growth is similar to all other growth curves. It begins slowly, increases rapidly, and appears to reach a cycle-maturity between five and six years of age (Fig. 37).

Ideas Expressed by Young Children. Vocabulary studies have frequently been concerned with the ideas expressed in young chil-

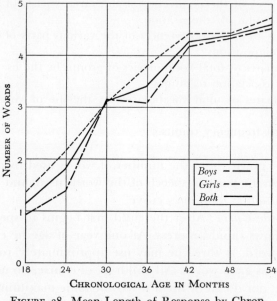

FIGURE 38. Mean Length of Response by Chronological Age and Sex

dren's speech. Typical of this approach is a study made by Shirley in which verbatim records were made for 336 children ranging in age from two to five years (24). The four ideas or concepts most frequently occurring referred to "mother," "father," "home," and "brother" or "sister." Up to eleven, the most common words had an emotional connection, and at least fifty per cent of the total were related to the common needs of children (4).

E. LENGTH OF RESPONSE

There is a very marked difference among children in the number of words used over a given period of time. In general, this number corresponds to the child's age. Correlations between chronological age and the number of remarks per hour range between .50 and .60 (18) .

As has been noted earlier, the child uses increasingly longer sentences as he gets older. The maturity span for spoken words ranges from one-word sentences at eighteen months to sentences of approximately six or seven words in length by the time he is nine to ten years of age. From eighteen months to forty-eight months, the range is from one to about four words per sentence (Fig. 38) .

Standards for Oral Speech. The developmental sequence from the single-word stage to facility with complete sentences is about as follows (20) :

1. The *single-word* stage, which commences at approximately the beginning of the second year and lasts from four to twelve months.
2. The *two-word* stage, which appears by approximately the middle of the second year and which extends to around twenty-seven months. This period is marked by a preponderance of nouns and a concomitant lack of verbs, articles, prepositions, and conjunctions.
3. The *short-sentence* stage (three to four words) , which begins around the twenty-eighth month and lasts until approximately the fourth year. During this period verbs are not inflected and prepositions, conjunctions, auxiliary verbs, articles, and pronouns are often omitted.
4. The *complete-sentence* stage, from around the fourth year on, in which six to eight words, characterized by increased grammatical complexity, and meanings are used. Pronouns, articles, prepositions, and conjunctions come into use.

In the same way, with increased maturity children write longer sentences. The best data now available may be found in two studies undertaken sixteen years apart (11, 28) . The more recent data have been shown previously in graphic form (Fig. 36) . In tabular form, the combined data of the two studies will prove of equal interest to teachers, since the table shows approximate age and grade expectations (Table XIII) .

FACTORS AFFECTING DEVELOPMENT

A. SEX

It will be of interest to teachers to note that girls exceed boys in certain aspects of language growth. This fact holds even during the neonate days. The superiority of girls in speaking plainly between eighteen and fifty-four months of age has also been noted.

TABLE XIII

MEAN NUMBER OF WORDS PER SENTENCE IN WRITTEN COMPOSITIONS

		WORDS PER SENTENCE	
AGE	GRADE	*Heider and Heider*	*Stormzand and O'Shea*
8	3	10.2	
9	4	10.9	11.1
10	5	11.1	
11	6	11.1	12.0
12	7	12.8	13.0
13	8	13.7	15.2
14	9	13.9	17.3
15	10		17.8
16	11		18.0
17	12		19.8
18	College Freshmen		19.9
20	College Upper Classmen		21.5
	Adults		20.9

Girls use longer sentences, and their growth in various other phases of language proceeds more rapidly than that of boys (Fig. 35). The superiority noted is in reference to early beginnings and more rapid progress, but not necessarily toward greater maxima (17).

Superiority of Girls. Among feeble-minded children, girls have been found to talk earlier and have about half the frequency of speech defects. Girls are reported to reach maturity in articulation approximately a year earlier than boys. To teachers this means that the general speech pattern of first-grade girls is about equivalent to that of second-grade boys. Among gifted children, a similar superiority exists, girls using short sentences at a slightly earlier age than boys. According to a study by Davis, covering the period of maturation from five to ten, girls from nine to ten years of age are superior to boys in articulation, word usage, and length, complexity, and grammatical correctness of sentences (7). It was also discovered that girls use more personal pronouns and conjunctions in their speech and less slang.

An interesting summary of many of the differences mentioned has been prepared by Thorpe (32). He reports that girls are considerably superior in articulation at five and again at nine and a half. Whereas a much greater frequency of substitution of *d* for *th, w* for *r* is found among boys, a greater number of girls substitute *t* and *th* for *s*. The two sexes are about equal in number of words per remark, in single-word expressions, and in the use of elaborated sentences. In reference to emotionally toned remarks, in the number of infinitives and auxiliary words, and in the mean number of different words, the frequencies favor girls.

B. INTELLIGENCE

Children of superior intelligence begin to talk at an earlier age than their less gifted contemporaries. On the basis of intelligence test scores, the child judged bright begins to talk during his eleventh month, the average child at fifteen months, and the dull child at thirty-eight months. There are, however, wide individual differences among each group. Among the group of gifted children studied by Terman, some did not talk until two to two-and-a-half, and some did not begin until they were three years of age (31). Therefore it would be inadvisable to attempt to predict mental brightness merely from the fact that the child talks early or late. Speech delay may be caused by many other factors, and it should not be carelessly assumed that it is the result of deficient intelligence.

Relation of Intelligence to Language. This raises a further question regarding the relationship between language and intelligence. The question is whether the greater language maturity among brighter children is the result of greater intellectual potentiality, or whether, as Garrison and Garrison (10) report, the superiority of this group on intelligence tests is due to more advanced language experience. Their argument implies that language is primarily responsible for intellectual development. Through language the individual acquires knowledge from the past which is greatly beneficial to him. With good language and communicative facility he has a superior means of acting and reacting, which thereby influences his intellectual and mental growth.

C. SOCIOECONOMIC FACTORS

It is generally recognized that socioeconomic factors greatly influence language development. Some investigators go so far as to say that while poor socioeconomic background is reflected in all phases of the child's development, the retardation is more marked in reference to language than to any other maturational pattern. Thus it would appear that regardless of intelligence and other factors, maximum language development is contingent upon an adequately stimulating environment.

Need for Enriched Environment. Studies of children from contrasting environments show that children of the upper social classes are decidedly superior in language development to those of lower social strata. Stern goes so far as to say that language differences between children of educated and noneducated parents are equivalent to about eight months in linguistic maturity (27).

Effect of Teachers. Of especial interest to teachers is the study made by Worbois, who compared the language of children in a one-room school with that of children in a consolidated school (37). Cases were selected carefully, and every attempt was made to pair children according to I.Q., age, and home background. The only reported variable in the study was the education of the children's teachers. In the one-room school the teacher had less than one year of training beyond high school, whereas those in the consolidated school had approximately two years or more. Significant differences in vocabulary and in vocabulary effectiveness were found in favor of the children from the consolidated school. These children also were superior in words used in certain picture-analysis tests. Such studies only indicate the interest in the problem and illustrate ways and means of obtaining data. Findings of this kind, in favoring one group over another, are entirely coincidental unless the growth pattern involved in the contrasting groups is determined before, during, and after the study. It is likely that despite efforts to arrive at matched groups, community differences reflect themselves in the data obtained.

Related Environmental Factors. Other environmental factors also influence language growth. Investigators who have studied the problem with a limited number of cases report that travel, explorations, and other experiences are followed by increases in vocabulary. Such data, although limited and concerned with very few cases, indicate the possibility that occupational differences are reflected in the language skills of children, that language deficiency is likely to be due to the restricted environment commonly experienced by children of lower economic backgrounds. Restricted environments also limit the child through the language limitations of parents. Parents in the poorer environments are frequently less gifted and experienced linguistically and consequently afford a more restricted opportunity for the child to profit by imitation. Investigations of the effects of specific environmental experiences are limited in number. There seems to be little question that school activities, like explorations, trips, and new worthwhile experiences, contribute to the opportunity for language learning. Undoubtedly all these have a bearing on growth of vocabulary, sentence structure, and oral and written composition (18).

Age of Associates. The influence on language of the age of the people with whom the child associates seems to have been a controversial subject. There are certain contacts which all agree contribute greatly. One of these is the extent of contact children have with adults. McCarthy, using length of response as a criterion, found that children who associated with adults reached the 70th percentile, whereas those who associated chiefly with either older or younger children ranged between the 42nd and 52nd percentiles (18). The implication that association with adults tends to raise the response level has been substantiated by other investigations. These indicate that children use longer sentences and more complex language patterns in talking to adults and hence are able to practice and accustom themselves to more mature ways of speaking. Outstanding among the findings of this category of investigation are the facts relative to "only" children (7). There seems to be no challenge of the idea that "only" children, especially girls, are the most advanced in all phases of their language development. Although other data indicate that single children are more likely to be found in the higher socioeconomic brackets and have better educated parents, their superiority cannot thereby be entirely explained (14).

Children in Institutions. Further evidence comes from studies of children in institutions who have had a minimum of adult contact (3). Such children are characteristically the most retarded. It is true that most of these children come from the lower socioeconomic levels and seem a little below norms in native ability. Nevertheless, the language retardation shown is as great as the superiority of "only" children, and it is believed that the lack of adult contact has contributed greatly to it.

Effect of Multiple Birth. Certain language problems arise for children of a multiple birth (7). Twins are markedly retarded in all aspects of language. Specifically, the mean length of response of five-year-old twins is approximately equal to that of the average three-year-old child. This would indicate that the rate of growth during the early years is approximately one-half that of the singleton child. Fortunately, this difference begins to decrease after the child enters school. This may indicate that during the years when the children are not in school, twin association is not conducive to normal linguistic growth. One cannot disregard the fact, however, that new cycles of growth begin at about the age of entrance to school. This in itself may be a factor in improved growth rates in language. An interesting sidelight on the discussion is the comparative language development of boy-girl twins. Twin boys who have twin sisters, rather than brothers, are less seriously retarded. It has been explained that the somewhat more rapid development of the twin sister motivates the boy (7). And since they are of different sexes and thereby fraternal twins they tend to depend less upon each other than identical twins and receive less attention from parents toward identity of action. They are therefore more likely to make contacts of greater diversity which motivate individualized speech efforts.

Nursery School. Teachers will be interested in the results of investigations of the effect of nursery school attendance upon language development. One would be justified in concluding that such an experience would be helpful. Nursery school attendance has been cited as tending to improve the I.Q. and has been given credit for other facilitating effects. Most children, however, in the upper socioeconomic levels fail to benefit in the way of improved language patterns. As a matter of fact, it is found that nursery school attendance, especially for only children, may produce a retarding result (18). For twins the situation might produce opposite results. The research is not quite clear on this. Where twins had had considerable isolation from other children and were more retarded than usual as a result, the greater social contact would undoubtedly prove helpful to language improvement (18).

This situation should not be too hastily accepted as an argument against such an experience. The social development which it facilitates may counteract the language retardation resulting from less adult contact.

SPEECH DEFECTS

A. INCIDENCE

Because of differences in the criteria used for determining normal speech habits, it is difficult to estimate accurately the probable number of children needing attention. It is believed that one per cent or more of the school population are persistent stutterers and that as many as fifteen to twenty per cent stutter at some period (32). Unfortunately, the last two decades show no improvement in the general situation. This statement is based on data of studies made in 1927 and in 1936. In the earlier study it was reported from a large city school that 2.8 per cent of the school children had speech defects of one kind or another. Of this group 26.9 per cent stuttered, 57.1 per cent lisped, and the remaining 16 per cent had varied disorders (34). In the latter study, made in Indiana, it was found that the number of school children with speech difficulties represented 3.7 per cent of the total school population (15). More recent studies are available but add nothing to our knowledge of the national situation. Studies of the incidence of speech defects show considerable lack of uniformity in procedure. This is true particularly of the criterion of what constitutes a speech defect. Some of the studies concern speech difficulties exclusive of stuttering; some emphasize stuttering, but exclude other defects. Such lack of uniformity precludes the possibility of getting a clear picture of the national situation.

B. CRITERION FOR THERAPY

Techniques used for determining whether or not a child has a speech defect vary considerably. Success in locating cases depends greatly upon the teacher's sensitiveness to the problem. Many teachers are quite unaware of speech problems; whereas others, particularly those with some training, are able to discriminate between temporary and persisting disorders. Teachers with some training are able to see the difficulty of dividing children into two groups, one containing children with perfect speech and the other children with defective speech. As in other skills, the difference between normal and defective speech is so slight that it is hard to draw an absolute line.

Need for Adequate Tests. Children who need special attention may be located by utilizing a measuring instrument which evaluates and diagnoses the difficulty. Speech specialists are not in agreement regarding a satisfactory test. Probably the best known is the Blanton-Stinchfield Articulation Test. This test includes 100 sounds used in 100 test words accompanied by standardized patterns.

Criterion for Treatment. Springob, in working with preschool children, selected as defectives those over four years of age who made 20 or more errors in the Blanton-Stinchfield Articulation Test. Poole believes that the child who is developing normally is capable of articulating all sounds by the time he is eight years of age and that lack of improvement at the age of six indicates the need for special treatment (21).

Another way of getting at specific difficulties is through an appraisal of the child's general language development. The research shows very little work of this kind. Much of the analysis has been piecemeal and unrelated. Studies have followed the procedure of classifying errors of various kinds, analyzing sentence structure, function, use of language, and analysis of parts of speech. This technique provides such a closed system that relationships can only be inferred from shifts and trends in what is regarded as acceptable in the percentages of occurrence. There is undoubtedly some relationship between disabilities, but no technique has yet been devised for evaluating a given child's general performance (18).

One study may be an exception in this regard (35). This study also gives a cue to teachers who attempt to discover children in need of special attention. The criterion rests in the generalization that various phases of language development parallel each other. According to this study, the child who is progressing poorly in one phase is likely to be progressing poorly in certain others. Such a generalization would indicate that treatment should be broad and directed toward all phases rather than toward specific weaknesses. This suggestion is based on Williams' conclusions that with the exception of vocabulary there is a high positive correlation between measures of various language aspects (35). Particularly high is the correlation between the child's accuracy of speech articulation and such other speech skills as length, complexity, and completeness of the unit of expression. Other investigators are agreed that a child's ability to articulate is closely related to other phases of his language development. Or, stated negatively, prolonged deficiency in articulation is accompanied by other aspects of language deficiency.

C. CUES TO DIFFICULTIES

It is difficult to list all causes for language difficulty in any sort of categorical relationship, since language itself is much broader than mere speech. Language is used in writing and in thinking as well as in speaking. Therefore the classification must be general enough to include the broader aspects of language difficulty. It would seem that the following meet this condition fairly well: (1) deficient environment; (2) sensory or other physical limitations; and (3) emotional maladjustments. Each of these is discussed in the sections following.

1. Deficient Environment

A deficient environmental level is, of course, one of the causes of depressed language development. Such deficiencies may result from the child's lack of opportunity for exploration, travel, and social opportunity, or from lack of opportunity for friendly, loving, adult contact. Institutionalized children, generally, are most representative of such environmental deficiency for achieving maximum growth. Unless he receives full and complete motivation he will not reach his complete potentiality.

2. Sensory or Other Physical Limitations

Unfortunately, many children suffer from sensory or motor deficiencies. In relation to speech or general language development, deafness is one of the most limiting factors. Ten to twenty per cent of the school population are affected to some degree by hearing deficiencies. Children so handicapped certainly cannot be expected to reach maximum potentialities. Of this large number only a small percentage are totally deaf. The remainder suffer only partial loss of hearing, but enough to produce marked language retardation. Hearing defects are difficult to detect at an early age because of the usual babblings of the newborn child. If these children are highly intelligent they are likely to compensate so well for their deficiency that they may be undiscovered well up into the elementary school years (22).

Other defects which cause trouble are those of the speech organs and their supplementary structures. These include defects of the mouth, larynx, or tongue, malformed jaws, irregular or slow appearing teeth, and defective palates. Such deficiencies contribute to poor articulation and will be noticed in connection with this aspect of language performance.

3. Emotional Maladjustments

Emotional maladjustments contribute to stuttering and other speech disorders. In many instances too much encouragement of speech, or too great an emphasis on grammatical correctness may cause the child to strain, to become self-conscious, or to lose confidence in himself. Children who sense the need of success in order to gain favor and status become too tense or too afraid to try. Ridicule, nagging, and unfavorable comparison with other children also have a bad effect. In many instances pressures of this sort lead to stuttering.

Ages When Stuttering Occurs. In the main there are two stages of maturity at which stuttering is most likely to occur — between two-and-a-half to three years of age and again at the age of school entrance. Stuttering is most frequent at the earlier age. Children have achieved sufficient vocabulary — eight hundred to twelve hundred words — and are very eager to use it. It is at this time that they begin the short-sentence stage described earlier. This is also the period of rapid growth in social development, which results in a motivation to communicate and to attract attention. At this age children are unable to select the words they wish to use, and as a result of hesitation in speech and the accompanying conflicting drive for immediate expression, they begin to stutter. This is particularly true for boys and perhaps would explain the drop in "mean length-of-response," which is much greater for boys than for girls (Fig. 38).

Treatment for Stuttering. Among most children stuttering is so slight as to be scarcely noticeable. Other children develop the symptom much more markedly and continue the pattern for several months beyond its normal span. Such children, of course, are the ones whose difficulties are most likely to become serious. For the great majority, stuttering need not be regarded seriously if it is handled in the proper way. It must be considered merely as a stage of language growth which needs positive but casual attention, rather than as a symptom which needs special remedial attention. Above all, the parent must aim to establish the child's confidence and security.

Stuttering upon entering school is quite a different problem. At this stage of maturity it is more serious. The child's vocabulary is sufficient, and his "length-of-response" is adequate for his age. The trouble is likely to occur as a byproduct of nervous strain resulting from unfamiliar environmental impacts. He finds the need to adjust to a new authority, to other children, and to new rules and regulations. Unless this is done successfully — and the school should create an environment that makes the child's adjustment easy — certain immature language responses become fixed and the child exhibits other symptoms of nervous strain.

Relation of Handedness to Stuttering. The relation of handedness to stuttering is not clearly established, and investigators disagree as to the influence of cerebral dominance. It has been established, however, that among stuttering children, many more are ambidextrous as compared to the general school population (twelve to one) and that the ratio of stuttering children to normal children in reference to left-eye dominance is approximately fifty-seven to one (32). It is safe to point out, therefore, that forcing the use of the right hand may lead to trouble.

The main problem of the relationship of speech to emotional development is not generally recognized because it is so simple. One of the first responsibilities of the school is to help the child make normal speech contacts with other children in his group. Although it is a first problem, it is also a continuing problem. It is not one which can be dealt with by the kindergarten and first-grade teacher and then dropped. It is one which must be faced by all teachers in all grades. Every time a child comes into contact with new groups of children he must develop a satisfactory language contact. The assistance of teachers can make a great contribution. That this has not been done to any great extent is illustrated by the lack of poise of a great majority of adults in meeting strangers or talking before an audience. Embarrassment in speech hinders social development.

With a running vocabulary totaling some thirty thousand words, the child beginning elementary school wants and needs to tell about his new experiences and reactions. Rather than give him this opportunity we tend to impose quiet and limit expression to the written word. This procedure undoubtedly hampers full emotional, social, and language development.

INTERRELATIONS WITH OTHER ASPECTS OF THE GROWTH PATTERN

Language research is fragmentary and tends to emphasize status rather than the study of patterns through developmental cycles (18). Conventional research, therefore, has been limited largely to the relationships of aspects of language development to general intelligence and motor learning.

A. LONGITUDINAL VIEWPOINT

It is the thesis of the writer that in every phase of his development each child has his own characteristic paralleling or pacing. All phases of growth have definite interrelations with respect to beginning and end points, periods of rapid rise, and maximum achieved.

Among the language data available, there are numerous incidences that substantiate this outlook. "Mean length-of-response" (Fig. 38) shows a curvilinear pattern reaching a given maximum at approximately six years of age. "Comprehensible speech" presents the same over-all picture, with a maximum again occurring at approximately six years of age. "Mean-number-of-words-per-sentence" in written composition projects a curve which appears to begin after six years of age, approaches an adolescent maximum around twelve, and then continues on a spurt similar in character to previously shown curves of physical, mental, motor, and academic growths.

The only readily available data contrary to such a concept are found in studies comparing learning to talk with learning to walk. McCarthy's mean-length-of-response curve (Fig. 38) shows a depression at three years of age. This age is generally regarded as a time of rapid growth and from the viewpoint previously mentioned should not be the time for such a marked depression. The depression has been previously explained as a possible result of the fact that this is the time of new motor learnings. Or, as stated by Shirley: ". . . . Speech development is held in abeyance at the time when motor progress is most rapid." The literature, however, is not convincing on this point. The seeming need for research workers to isolate various particular aspects of language for study has resulted in a dearth of knowledge of the child's general language development (18). As in other areas of study, it is likely that many interesting relationships are evading discovery. Fortunately there is a general recognition of the deficiencies of research into isolated functions. It is to be hoped that realization of limitations will lead to the development of techniques for discovering relationships between functions.

B. STATUS STUDIES

Correlations between scores on one aspect of motor development (tracing) with ability to pronounce consonants and consonant blends are reported as .67 and .65, respectively (18). Other investigators have reported that speech defective children are

definitely inferior on motor ability performance, and that conversely, children who demonstrate good motor coordination also
exhibit better than average speech development (18).

The relationships between intelligence and language development have earlier been indicated. Other findings not mentioned
are those of Shirley who reports rather high correlations, ranging
from .63 to .76, between Minnesota Preschool Test scores and
various vocabulary and vocalization scores (23).

Undoubtedly the lack of acceptable measuring instruments has
prevented research workers from arriving at conclusions concerning the relation between linguistic and emotional development.
From isolated, clinical studies, however, has come a wealth of
material which indicates that the emotional tone of a child can
greatly influence his emerging language pattern. Many available
studies analyze seemingly unexplainably delayed or interrupted
speech in cases where retardation cannot be attributed to a lack
of mental development, deafness, or various possible pathological
conditions. Among these cases, almost invariably, the only reasonable diagnosis points to severe emotional shock or to some kind of
psychic trauma.

The potential harm in severe adult criticism of the child's early
language behavior has already been mentioned. In many cases
such an attitude has resulted in the child's refusal to talk or at best
has reduced his language response to mere monosyllables. In
many such cases freedom from the contact has resulted in normal
speech.

Other cases which demonstrate a relationship between emotional
status and language proficiency are those involving stuttering.
Certain children stutter only before certain persons and respond
quite normally in the presence of others (18).

Relation to Social Development. Schmidt reports that mental defectives who have received helpful attention with their speech and
language greatly improve in sociability and general gregarious-
ness. A rather significant study conducted by Davis discovered a
positive relationship between maturity of articulation and acceptable social behavior (8). For measuring the latter, the Haggerty-
Wickman-Olson Behavior Rating Schedule was used. The conclusion was that those factors which impair the child's speech

performance are also deleterious to his social development. On the other hand, it may be that the speech difficulty itself is a major factor in reducing the child's ability to make the proper social adjustment.

IMPLICATIONS FOR TEACHERS

Need for Language Data. Language, of course, involves reading, spelling, writing, composition, and certain other aspects of the elementary school curriculum (8). The vocabulary development of a child is of considerable importance in explaining ability to read and spell. The child's mean length of response is certainly of importance in predicting how he will make an oral report, and it will certainly determine how well he may handle a written composition.

Many of the developmental curves portrayed throughout this chapter are from data not ordinarily available on school children. Anyone who has read this chapter will be able to see the many uses that might be made from such data if it were customarily recorded. Intelligence tests concern themselves with vocabulary measures, but the data, although quite frequently on hand, has been but little used in determining or predicting the vocabulary curve of growth. An adequate vocabulary, both written and spoken, is in essence a criterion of readiness for many elementary school learnings.

Responsibility of the School. The second implication relates to the tremendous responsibility of the school for providing the enrichment so essential for maximum language development. From this point of view, the schools that use explorations, broad area projects, new experiences of all kinds, new books, new observations are providing an educational program in harmony with a great majority of the research findings (33).

It can reasonably be concluded that language development is stimulated by broad educational opportunities at any age following the first demonstration of the child's ability to verbalize. Of great importance is the opportunity for creative self-expression if accompanied by suitable experiences. In reference to language, such a program should include the opportunity for frequent conversation, the opportunity to repeat stories, to describe experiences, to listen to others, and to participate in socialized activities. All of these contribute to maximum language usage.

Trend in Research. The final implication of this chapter is reflected in the current trend of education and research, which, probably because of our inability to utilize much of the earlier findings, is shifting away from the idea that language is a form of growth quite apart from other phases of development. The present viewpoint is that language can be characterized as a form of social behavior. In this kind of relationship, research in child development can contribute greatly to an understanding of the child in school. Such an emphasis also will motivate research workers and teachers to seek out the basic relationships of various aspects of language to each other and to the child's general pattern of development. The very important problem of determining such relationships and the problem of discovering ways and means for utilizing such information for better integration of personality is the challenge to all in this field.

SELECTED REFERENCES

1. AMES, LOUISE BATES, "The Sense of Self in Nursery School Children as Manifested by their Verbal Behavior," *Journal of Genetic Psychology,* 81:193–232, 1952.

2. DREGER, RALPH MASON, "Spontaneous Conversation and Story Telling of Children In a Naturalistic Setting." *The Journal of Psychology,* V, 40:163–180, 1955.

3. BRODBECK, A. J., AND IRWIN, O. C., "The Speech Behavior of Infants without Families," *Child Development,* 17:145–156, 1946.

4. GAMMON, AGNES L., "Comprehension of Words with Multiple Meanings," *California Journal of Educational Research,* 3:228–232, 1952.

5. CATTELL, P., *The Measurement of Intelligence of Infants and Young Children.* New York: The Psychological Corporation, 1940.

6. HILDRETH, GERTRUDE, "An Evaluation of Spelling Word Lists and Vocabulary Studies," *Elementary School Journal,* 51:254–265, 1951.

7. DAVIS, E. A., *The Development of Linguistic Skill in Twins, Singletons with Siblings, and Only Children from Age Five to Ten Years,* Monograph Series No. 14. Minneapolis: Institute of Child Welfare, 1937.

8. DAVIS, I. P., "The Speech Aspects of Reading Readiness," *Newer Practices in Reading in the Elementary School,* Seventeenth Yearbook, Department of Elementary School Principals. Washington: National Education Association, 1938.

9. IRWIN, ORVIS C., "Speech Development in the Young Child: 2. Some Factors Related to the Speech Development of the Infant and Young Child," *Journal of Speech and Hearing Disorders,* 17:269–279, 1952.

10. GARRISON, S. C. AND K. C., *The Psychology of Elementary School Subjects.* New York: Johnson, 1929.

11. HEIDER, F. K. AND G. M., "A Comparison of Sentence Structure of Deaf and Hearing Children," *Psychological Monographs,* 52, 1:42–103, 1940.

12. JOHNSON, GRANVILLE B., JR., "Bilingualism as Measured by a Reaction Time Technique and the Relationship Between a Language and Non-Language Intelligence Quotient," *Journal of Genetic Psychology,* 82:3–9, 1953.

13. LODGE, W. J., "Developmental Characteristics of Childhood," *Elementary English,* XXX, No. 2:111–114, 1953.

14. McCARTHY, DOROTHEA, "Factors That Influence Language Growth: Home Influences," *Elementary English,* XXIX, No. 7:421–428, 1952.

15. LOUTTIT, C. M., AND HALLS, E. C., "Survey of Speech Defects among Public School Children of Indiana," *Journal of Speech Disorders,* 1:73–80, 1936.

16. McCARTHY, DOROTHEA, "Organismic Interpretations of Infant Vocalizations," *Child Development,* 23:273–280, 1952.

17. ——, "Some Possible Explanations of Sex Differences in Language Development and Disorders," *Journal of Psychology,* 35:155–160, 1953.

18. ——, "Language Development in Children," *Manual of Child Psychology,* edited by Leonard Carmichael. New York: Wiley, 1946.

19. McCURRY, WILLIAM H., AND IRWIN, ORVIS, "A Study of Word Approximations in Spontaneous Speech of Infants," *Journal of Speech and Hearing Disorders,* 18 (2) :133–139, 1953.

20. NICE, M. M., "Length of Sentences as a Criterion of a Child's Progress in Speech," *Journal of Educational Psychology,* 16:370–379, 1925.

21. POOLE, I., "Genetic Development of Articulation of Consonant Sounds in Speech," *Elementary English Review,* 11:159–161, 1934.

22. REYMERT, M. L., AND ROTMAN, M., "Auditory Changes in Children from Ages Ten to Eighteen," *Journal of Genetic Psychology,* 68:181–187, 1946.

23. SHIRLEY, M. M., *The First Two Years: A Study of Twenty-five Babies; Vol. II, Intellectual Development,* Monograph Series No. 7. Minneapolis: Institute of Child Welfare, 1933.

24. ——, "Common Content in the Speech of Preschool Children," *Child Development,* 9:333–346, 1938.

25. SMITH, M. E., *An Investigation of the Sentence and the Extent of Vocabulary in Young Children.* Iowa City: University of Iowa Studies in Child Welfare, Vol. III, No. 5, 1926.

26. SPRINGOB, J. R., *Factors Influencing the Incidence of Articulatory Speech*

Defects in Preschool Children. Minneapolis: University of Minnesota (unpublished master's thesis), 1930.

27. STERN, W., *Psychology of Early Childhood: Up to the Sixth Year of Age.* New York: Holt, 1930.

28. STORMZAND, M. J., AND O'SHEA, M. I., *How Much English Grammar?* Baltimore: Warwick and York, 1924.

29. STRAYER, L. C., "Language and Growth: The Relative Efficacy of Early and Deferred Vocabulary Training Studied by the Method of Co-Twin Control," *Genetic Psychology Monographs,* 8:209–319, 1930.

30. TERMAN, L. M., AND MERRILL, M. A., *Measuring Intelligence.* Boston: Houghton Mifflin, 1936.

31. ——, AND OTHERS, *Genetic Studies of Genius, Vol. I: Mental and Physical Traits of a Thousand Gifted Children.* Palo Alto: Stanford University Press, 1925.

32. THORPE, L. P., *Child Psychology and Development.* New York: Ronald Press, 1946.

33. STRICKLAND, RUTH G., "Factors That Influence Language Growth: School Influences," *Elementary English,* XXIX, No. 8:474–480, 1952.

34. WALLIN, J. E. W., *Clinical and Abnormal Psychology.* Boston: Houghton Mifflin, 1927.

35. WILLIAMS, H. M., *Development of Language and Vocabulary in Young Children,* Vol. 13, No. 2. Iowa City: University of Iowa Studies in Child Welfare, 1937.

36. TEMPLIN, MILDRED C., "Speech Development in the Young Child: 3. The Development of Certain Language Skills in Children," *Journal of Speech and Hearing Disorders,* 17:280–285, 1952.

37. WORBOIS, G. M., "Language Development in Two Different Rural Environments," *Child Development,* 13:175–180, 1942.

8

THE DEVELOPMENT OF
CREATIVE ABILITY

INTRODUCTION – NEED FOR CREATIVE ACTIVITY

Creative ability is usually regarded as a special talent or aptitude which manifests itself late in adolescence or in adulthood and
somewhat exclusively among young people and adults who are not
quite normal in other respects. This may be true to some degree,
but there is a gradually expanding belief that all children have
creative power (14). Experimental investigation and observation
justify this idea. In the average home or school the development
of creative ability has been greatly ignored. Schools are particularly guilty. The average school, placing its main emphasis on
drilling and learning factual material, has tended to stifle creative
development and has done little or nothing to encourage curriculum activity which would enhance the child's potentialities. In
the main, school procedure has been of a kind that almost inevitably encouraged the unimaginative and stodgy child. Two factors account for this: (1) in our present social order emphasis
has been placed on the acquisition and production of material
goods, rather than upon creative and esthetic expression; (2) experimental psychology so far has progressed but little beyond the
power to analyze, appraise, and evaluate at the mechanical level
of learning. In a way the latter reason resembles the first. Education itself has taken on the earmarks of the culture which it represents. As adults strive for possession of material things and new
scientific means of production, the school has stood for achievement and possession. The mark of the educated man has been too
much that of academic possession. Consequently, the development

of a creative, imaginative individual has been left pretty much to chance.

In most schools variation from this pattern has been well within the borders of "acceptability." Even at the university level, devotion to research and the development of new knowledge is only a little over one hundred years old. Within this span of time, adult originality and creativity have been encouraged and new contributions have been greatly prized. In the lower brackets of the educational scheme, creativity has been a minor objective, and in most instances, conformity rather than originality has won all available honors.

From the standpoint of the development of the individual such neglect at the lower immature stages has been most unfortunate (14). Adults have, in the main, developed fixed patterns of behavior, and consequently, new forms of thought and action have been difficult to formulate. There is no question, however, in the minds of psychologists that creative ability can develop and grow under proper stimulation and guidance, particularly during the child's early years (9). Creative skill, like any other, lends itself to improvement. Assuming that this is true, one cannot help but speculate as to the kind of education or school that might best promote the development of creative skill. There can be but little doubt that had a tradition of inventiveness been in vogue in place of the tradition of mastery, schools today would be far better able to serve the needs of children and adults.

OBJECTIVES IN CREATIVE DEVELOPMENT

Current experimentation with educational programs which give attention to the creative aspects of the child's development are in striking contrast to the efforts of the conventional school. In the typical schoolroom, "creative activities" are frequently planned around the celebration of a national holiday or some other phase of our national life. At best their duration is only a day or two. The only activity involved is likely to be a trite demonstration, reading, or play, usually written by adults. Today, in the better schools, the program for creative development is greatly broadened by being tied in with the entire elementary school activity.

Dramatics, the use of arts and crafts materials, dancing, imaginative and creative writing are used as vehicles for complete development to be utilized throughout the school day, rather than a special or extracurricular opportunity for creative inspiration.

Objectives for promoting creative development are many and varied. Some have been implied in the opening paragraphs of this chapter. Others could be added. Those to be presented in the paragraphs following have been selected in accordance with the point of view that creative development can be realized through the general learning activities of the school, along with special individual attention to the child's particular abilities and experiences. From this viewpoint it appears that creative activity in the school should attempt four developmental goals. Stated briefly, these are (11):

1. To facilitate the learning of basic fundamental skills.
2. To develop maximum manipulative growth.
3. To provide a means for creative expression for all children at all stages of maturity in all cultural areas.
4. To provide the means for integrating activities which broaden the scope and relate the interests of the children involved.

Facilitates Learning. To a considerable degree the activities necessary for creative development can be correlated with regular classroom instruction. Where this has been done, the social science areas, for example, are improved greatly as a result of greater interest and motivation. This happens when regular classroom instruction is made informal, as it is whenever art and other creative media are introduced in the learning scheme. And when diversity of opportunity is provided, the teacher can better relate instruction to the varying maturities of individual children. Creative activity enhances and encourages individual development and expression and provides wide opportunities for children with varying maturities and skills to work cooperatively (21).

The development of manipulative skill is fundamental in certain kinds of creative activity. The manipulative skill of the individual follows three main cycles of growth: the babyhood cycle, the preadolescent, and the adolescent or adult cycle. Manipulative

growth during the first cycle is a matter of large-muscle maturation. At this stage of maturity, art activities, provided for creative
growth, are best when they encourage broad and sweeping, rather
than minute and painstaking, productions. Drawing should be

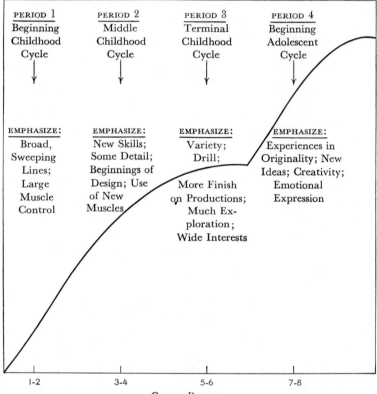

FIGURE 39. Suggested Emphasis and Content for Maximum
Creative Growth

encouraged through broad movements, large and unrestrained, in
order to develop large-muscle control. Children in the early elementary grades, therefore, should not be given assignments which
call for narrow, enforced tracing or coloring, since such activities
are unrelated to the child's maturational stage at that time
(Fig. 39).

There is another purpose in providing opportunity for unrestrained expression than that of exercising the young child's large muscles. This purpose is largely ignored and only by implication appears in the literature of the subject. It may be expressed as that of developing, at an early age, freedom and courage in creative expression (14). Freedom is an essential for the later, more mature aspects of creative activity. As a matter of fact, it is lack of freedom which inhibits those who in adult life are motivated toward creative explorations of one kind or another.

During the preadolescent developmental period the smaller muscles advance from their early formative beginnings, and at about eight to nine years of age begin to show considerable proficiency. This is the proper age for introducing design, more detail, etc. This point holds for work in arts and crafts, in creative writing, in expression involving games, and in motor activity. It is the period when technique may be introduced and much progress expected of the child. Variety should be provided so that all aspects of the child's creative potentiality may be explored. The better conventional schools begin these opportunities in the junior high school. This is too late for maximum creative growth. Such opportunities should be available for most children from eight to eleven years of age, in grades three to six (14). The junior high school period coincides with the beginnings of adolescence. This should be the time for a higher level of expression than mere exploration and orientation to various creative media.

Learning activities at the adolescent cycle (Fig. 39) should place emphasis on originality, creative design, and opportunity for emotional expression. If the child has been given creative opportunities in this sequence, very fine work will be produced in the seventh, eighth, and ninth grades without pressure, and the work of some children will compare favorably with that of more mature individuals.

Encouragement of Creative Expression. Our knowledge of child growth and development leads us to believe that all normal children in varying degrees and with widely divergent interests and abilities possess creative impulses and that significant creative growth is promoted by encouragement as the child progresses through school. It is essential that such opportunity be provided continuously, and it appears that only through broad cultural, artistic, and other creative activity can these results be obtained along with maximum general growth and development.

Research shows that the adult who has missed this opportunity in his early life only rarely achieves adequate expression and is thereby stunted in his development and limited in his capacity for satisfying living. All children have the right to the kind of environment which facilitates the growth and development of their total power for self-expression. Not every child can become an artist, but every normal child inherits the potentialities requisite for creative living in some area (7).

To be more specific, each individual possesses to some degree the ability to fashion from the materials of his environment some form of expression individualized according to his taste and maturity. Many children may realize similar objectives with varying degrees of skill. As potentialities for performance are divergent, so are fields of expression. Children interested in composition may achieve adequate expression through creative writing. Others may find satisfaction in rhythmic media, in utilizing line or color, or in recording ideas on wood, paper, canvas, glass, or fabrics of one kind or another. For other children, expression through manipulation in clay or wood will be most satisfying. Others will develop creative maturity through expression in music. In order to meet the challenge, the school must offer diversified opportunity.

Program Integration. Another value of creative activity is the satisfaction the child experiences when he sees school as an integrated or correlated opportunity, and not as a series of unrelated events, some satisfying and others frustrating in their effect. Where children experience a school day as a totality, the academic and the creative truly complement each other. Nothing does more for an academic program than a well-planned interweaving of all school activities (11).

This viewpoint contrasts sharply with that which sponsors a special creative arts period. Providing the materials and the opportunity for expression at given limited times tends to separate the activity from the total environment so that the activity becomes merely a time for release of pent-up energy.

DEFINITION OF CREATIVE ACTIVITY

A. MISCONCEPTIONS

Before defining what is meant by creative activity, it seems advisable to point out certain misconceptions regarding it. In the first place creative activity does not include every uninhibited word or act. Undoubtedly the idea that it does has gained headway through the efforts of those who wish to discredit any kind of change in school curricula as well as by those who feel that anything different is good. Such acts in and by themselves are not necessarily creative, and teachers should be skeptical of the validity of anecdotal data which so characterize every little personality quirk. Deviations in thought, word, and action provide important insights into personality, and in a sense may be the basis for creativity. Not all such differences in behavior, however, can be called "creative."

Creativity Not Rare. Secondly, there is the existing misconception about the rarity of creativeness. Teachers rather universally feel that any effort to provide the environment for developing creativity is useless, since they consider that relatively few children are creative. These teachers believe that only the genius has creative powers. This idea is entirely faulty. Creative acts are possible to all normal individuals, and it is the responsibility of the school to do everything reasonable to provide the opportunity for creative expression for ordinary children, as well as for the obviously "gifted" person.

B. DEFINITION

Modern psychology leads us to believe that all normal children, in varying degrees and with greatly divergent interests and aptitudes, possess creative impulses. Fundamentally, to create means to endow with meaning a personalized experience (11). Usually such an activity involves the creation of something new to the individual. The writing of a play for a Broadway production is a creative act, as is the writing and planning of a dramatization for a school assembly program. Both of these activities are characterized by a constructive departure from what already exists, motivated by the goal of providing individual or group satisfaction.

C. CHARACTERISTICS

Foundations in Work of Others. 1. Creative acts are not entirely original. Even the more important creations of art, science, and literature are developed from foundations provided by others. The individual contribution rests in rearrangement in some way or another, an "insight projection," new alignment, or "addition-to." In science it frequently means the completion or solving of a problem that has puzzled others.

Social Background. 2. A creative act has a sociocultural background. Creative productions reflect in some way the social backgrounds of which they are a part. One individual may express a criticism of a period. Another may express joyfully a social gain. Artists who live in isolation reflect in some way their environment. They cannot express themselves adequately without referring to the culture which they have abandoned. Society, good or bad as they see it, is their inspiration. Or, more to our point, all creative acts have in common the characteristic that they cannot represent anything more in the way of originality than the reconstruction or new projection of something already existent.

Emotional Coloring. 3. A creative act at its best is accompanied by an affective, emotional state. This, in the main, is what distinguishes creative activity from strictly scientific problem solving or reflective thinking. An emotional accompaniment and expression is perhaps its greatest value to its creator. From the standpoint of evaluation that creative act endures in its influence which arouses similar emotional feelings on the part of those who later share in its appreciation and validation.

Need of Media. 4. Creative expression necessarily involves media. This characteristic is so obvious that it scarcely needs mentioning. The point to be made is that each form of expression needs its own media and raw materials. The inventor, the artist, and the theorist all have special media. This is also true of community planners and all those who work at the highest level of creativity and imagination.

Standards and Form. 5. Creative activity has certain standards and forms. In all creative acts there is considerable uniformity. Likenesses are greater than differences or variations. This fact is important in teaching "appreciations." Real appreciation incidentally is not merely a listening or reading opportunity. At best, appreciation springs from participation and personal experimentation with creative media. This is the explanation for the fact that painters, for example, understand and appreciate music, dancing, dramatics, and other forms of creation than the one in which they work. It is also the explanation of the cold, lifeless, polite, unemotional approval of the arts throughout much of adult society. Appreciation of this kind has been mechanically acquired rather than experienced.

Creative productions of the various arts resemble one another in their emotional affective tone, in the fact that they represent the solution of a problem, and reflect a sociocultural epoch.

Differences consist mainly in the media and skill demanded by a particular field of creative activity.

ANALYSIS OF A CREATIVE ACT

A. STAGES OF ADULT CREATIVITY

In 1926 Graham Wallas, after studying the reported thought processes of distinguished mathematicians, scientists, and artists, concluded that four steps characterize a creative act and that they occur in the following sequence: (1) preparation, (2) incubation, (3) illumination, and (4) verification (22). Actually these categories are little more than a device to organize a discussion of creative activity.

Stage of Preparation. Preparation is the name given to the thought activity which accompanies orientation, exploration, and the assembling of materials for the solution of a problem. The question faced is defined, redefined, related to solutions of similar problems, and the like. Aside from a small group who have achieved successes without preliminary exploration, creative thinkers report the existence of this stage.

The period ends with the discovery of a block to the solution of the problem. This occurs after materials have been assembled, outlines made, and all pertinent matters have been considered. A second characteristic of the period is the fact that the various activities involved may, as far as immediate goal is concerned, be purposeless. At this stage, rambling, diversified, uninhibited activity, such as wide reading or random exploration of ideas, is the rule.

Incubation. Of unusual interest is Wallas' stage of *incubation,* the time during which an idea rests in the mind while one is busy with other activities. During this period relaxation occurs, imperfect possible solutions disappear, and the mind acts apparently without conscious motivation toward one solution. As described, this period provides a means of refreshment and the motivation for a new and vigorous attack on the problem. Those who might attempt to follow this sequence should not assume that the matter is entirely forgotten. In spite of much testimony to the contrary, it is likely that suggestions for the attack are not entirely separated from conscious "mulling" or conscious tentative suggestions for solution.

Illumination. Eventually an idea appears which seems to organize rapidly all the steps necessary for solution. Some of the conditions under which this phase of creative thought takes place are interesting. Insight occurs frequently during dreams, in sickbeds, and other equally unlikely places. This would indicate that all such insight occurs in between periods of intense concentration on a problem.

Verification. Verification is the word given by Wallas to the usual final stage in a complete act of creative thinking. It resembles what might be called a "trial run," or the activity expended in evaluating the "illumination." In the laboratory, illumination is not a final guide until experiments have been made which substantiate its correctness. For the novelist, it requires an expression and evaluation of the idea which "came to him."

This stage, however, does not necessarily result in completion of the creative act. Validation may show that the idea was worthless, the hypothesis without foundation, or the musical score disappointing. In this instance the cycle must be begun again. In other instances, validation on the first trial may produce the desired result.

B. GUIDES FOR MOTIVATING CHILDREN'S CREATIVITY

There is little evidence to substantiate complete application of Wallas' stages to the creative act of a child. It is most encouraging for teachers to realize that mature creators do not seem to create as easily as might be naïvely imagined. In reporting an analysis of the creative work of experts, Patrick points out that in the poet's mind ideas at first are vague, appearing and disappearing over a period of several weeks. Or an idea may come from observing the experience of some other individual. The general idea to be expressed becomes clear, but the details and the proper wording may require months for completion (16).

A musician similarly points out the curious experience of having chords and rhythms unexpectedly become clear in his mind. Melodies and harmonies appeared such as could not be thought through at will. These assumed a superior and exalted quality. First efforts at expressing them in composition were disappointing and quite unlike the first mental concept of them.

Teachers who have read biographies of eminent men and women know that most of them made many attempts before their problems were eventually solved.

From studying the various stages outlined by Wallas and from familiarity with the records of distinguished people who invariably report the elusiveness of the satisfactory production, it is possible to list certain guides for teachers in promoting creativeness in children.

Patience and Time Required. If teachers seriously wish to promote creative development, first of all they must have unlimited patience and be willing always to provide time. In comparison with the labor and time required for adult creative productions, how worthless is the art period which requires a definite time for artistic manifestation, a definite and specific assignment, and a definite adult appraisal of the child's efforts.

Integrated Rather than Special Activity. Because of the time required for an artistic creation, the need for extensive motivation and stimulation, and the necessity of relating creative work to the child's environment, it seems desirable that opportunity for creative activity be more generally available. This implies that special periods at scheduled times during the school day do not entirely meet the need. As far as possible, creative work must be done when the inspiration occurs. Of course a child cannot be allowed to drop everything else and rush to the art room because he feels like painting. It does imply that the reorganization of limited subject-matter areas to broad core programs accomplished in many cities today more nearly satisfies this need (11).

Individual Differences. Individual differences are reflected in children's artistic creations to as great an extent as they are in other aspects of development. Creativeness involves such a combination of potentialities that individual differences are probably greatest in this area of accomplishment. One is quite justified in making this assumption, since the backgrounds for creative expression are so varied. Some children have been encouraged in creative exploration because parents have seen that this phase of development is as beneficial to the child as more traditional phases. When schools provide creative opportunities for all children, it is likely that individual difference spans will cover about the same range as those in the more conventional areas such as reading, physical development, mental development, etc. Until this is done, one may assume an even greater span.

This suggests that areas for expression must be extensive and that media in all areas must be greatly increased. The typical school allots only a small percentage of its complete instructional budget to this area. This amount may with profit be greatly increased.

Program Must Be Elastic. No set program or course of study will provide the proper kind of organization. A fine statement on organization of this sort was made by Rugg in 1933 (17). He emphasized the importance of creative activity, arguing that the creative and appreciative arts should parallel the study of man and that both are most effective when they are closely integrated. Thus creativeness is enhanced and greater opportunity is provided for the child to learn understanding and tolerance of all men. Introduction to literature and the fine arts from their creative aspects should encourage understanding and enjoyment of them in contemporary life and provide emotional and personality expression. In this duality, the use of history is mandatory (17). The impression of the past on the present can thereby be fully understood with emphasis on the creative movements in the modern world and their relation to social life. When developed with understanding of the child, his maturity, interests, and needs, an appreciation of architecture, the theatre, poetry, fiction, racial understanding, etc., can all be approached. So-called areas to be utilized could be the dance, dramatics, painting, sculpture, and the crafts.

Need for Caution in Evaluation. In carrying out an evaluation program on the creative development of the child, great caution must be exercised. The teacher must not lose sight of the fact that the child represents a completeness, or a oneness, in his development. He is not only a unit physiologically, mentally, and creatively, but he functions at all times as a unit. It must be remembered, then, that evaluation of creative development considers only one aspect of this unity. When classifications and divisions of development are provided, they are useful only in limiting and providing direction to discussion.

Evaluation of creative development should also take into consideration the fact that the child grows through various developmental cycles. One cycle of growth ends dramatically when the child is born, and a new one begins. Throughout all cycles many changes are produced which reflect themselves in changed velocities of growth, changing interests, and changing emotional affects.

This idea poses a warning. The child's creative development must be appraised in terms of past growth phases and environmental influences as well as in relation to future potential growth. And further, the teacher must be warned that the creative aspect of development is important not only in itself but in interpreting other phases of development. This means that creative development has meaning for interpreting the child's mental growth, his emotional state, and his personal and social development. To a lesser degree it provides interpretative guides for his social appreciations, understanding of others, breadth of reading and understanding, and his basic environmental and cultural outlook.

CREATIVE POTENTIALITIES OF THE CHILD

Research has not explored the full scope of the child's creative potentiality. Probably because music, art, writing, and the dance are conventionally a part of the school curriculum, the research has concentrated in these areas, and discussion here will be limited to development in music, in the arts, in writing, and in the dance.

A. MUSIC POTENTIALITY

General Findings. Research indicates (1) that creative development in music is closely related to the child's stage of maturity, (2) that individual differences are particularly characteristic, and (3) that maximum development depends greatly on opportunity and participation at home and in school.

Other findings are not quite so unanimous and therefore provide some interesting controversy. One of the issues on which there is considerable disagreement is the question whether musical ability is inborn or acquired. According to Seashore, musical performance is limited by motor capacities of an inherent nature and other skills involving unusually high capacity are also limited by inherent potentialities. No one can disagree with this but many object to his statement that potentialities do not vary with intelligence, age, or training.

Effect of Instruction. Jersild and Bienstock are among the dissenters. In a study of the effect of instruction upon ability to sing tones and intervals, records were kept on children 31 to 48 months of age. Results among the instructed group showed that they were considerably superior to children in the untrained group.

Updegraff and others at the University of Iowa obtained similar results. They found that children from three to five years old made consistent gains under special training. A control group was used to compare results, which favored the group with special training. The control group also showed gain, probably due to increased maturity. Incidental to the experiment, but of great importance to teachers, are certain other findings of the Iowa group. Their study reports that enjoyment, interest, and general satisfaction gave the children self-confidence, a greater motivation for learning, and more enjoyment in musical participation.

Pattern of Growth. In reference to growth of the child's ability to produce tones in the voice range, Jersild and Bienstock report the average increase in relation to age (Table XIV). Unfortunately these investigators could not, in this experiment, provide data from the age of ten years to adulthood. A graph of the data based on a study of 407 children from ages two to ten shows a two-cycle

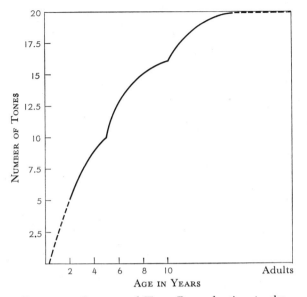

FIGURE 40. Increase of Tone Reproduction in the
Voice Range

TABLE XIV

INCREASE OF TONE REPRODUCTION IN THE VOICE RANGE *

Age in Years	*Number of Tones*	*Age in Years*	*Number of Tones*
2	5	7	14
3	7	8	15
4	9	9	16
5	10	10	16
6	13	Adults	20

* From "A Study of the Development of Children's Ability to Sing," by Jersild and
Bienstock, *Journal of Educational Psychology*, 25:481–503, 1934.

growth curve. Assuming a continuous growth from ten years of
age to adulthood, the total development represents a three-cycle
curve (Fig. 40). Since there were numerous exceptions to them,
the averages portrayed should not be accepted as fixed norms. One
child only four years of age could sing twenty-two tones, a number somewhat equivalent to the adult average. The children in

the study could not necessarily use their complete tonal range in singing. Nevertheless, the study demonstrates that growth of this ability follows the developmental pattern previously indicated and demonstrates a growth effect as well as inherited potentiality.

Heredity Versus Training. In another study, Jersild found that children seem to improve by instruction in relation to initial musical ability (13). The experiment dealt with sight reading and with the playing of musical instruments. Scheinfield, in investigating the inheritance of musical talent, states unequivocally that superior musical achievement is contingent upon unusual hereditary traits (18).

Such conclusions, although they allow for the effect of training, emphasize the importance of heredity and tend to discourage those who feel that creative powers are more common. Enough inconsistency may be found in these conclusions to indicate the failure of these investigators to fully rule out growth potentiality in musical ability. When it is said that improvement may result in proportion to initial ability, the word "proportion" needs definition as does "initial ability." It would be more appropriate to say that improvement proceeds at varying rates, at varying beginning and end points, and toward varying maxima. Such a statement does not rule out heredity as a factor, nor does it minimize or fail to consider its effects. What the child probably inherits is a general potential for growth rather than a special ability. Some children learn to read sooner than others, progress more rapidly, and achieve higher maxima. We do not, however, claim that one child has a greater aptitude for reading than another as we claim aptitude in music, for example.

Providing the Environment. Music can be both creative and appreciative in the elementary school. Sufficient opportunities should be provided to open a vista of wide possibilities for musical expression, and to help children realize the joy and satisfaction of listening, participating, and creating. These three activities provide the motivation for satisfying individual and social goals and teach children that music is part of their cultural inheritance.

Almost all children upon entering school show great enthusiasm for music. They obtain satisfaction and joy from singing repeatedly the songs they have been taught, and they carry into their games and into their lives at home this love of singing. Introduction to instrumental music through simple melodic and percussion instruments is equally thrilling. They learn to perform singly and in groups and consequently they learn to listen seriously and appreciatively. For full developmental opportunity, the dance should be introduced along with music. With this provision children learn to interpret music. All children have a natural love for music in all its forms — dancing, singing, playing, listening, and simple creation. It is the job of the school to orient the child to these various media and to stimulate early his natural appreciation and creative ability.

B. POTENTIALITY IN CREATIVE ART

Children develop some proficiency in producing designs of line and color before they enter school. Children who have the opportunity to experiment with simple art media manifest this ability between three and three and a half years of age (3). Moreover, they show at this age an ability to interpret what they have done. Almost invariably they "name" these early productions. *Developmental Sequences.* At four years of age most children will attempt a production from a preconceived idea. In the face of this evidence, one should not assign the task of drawing, say, a vase or a bunch of flowers. Drawing might much more effectively be introduced by suggesting that the child draw a "picture of the trip taken," or of the "story just read to you." In such an assignment, imagination is given free play and the child is given the opportunity to emphasize what he has seen and heard in relation to his interests, background, and maturity. Other illustrations are provided most adequately in the suggestions of Lowenfeld (14).

With young children simple block building offers opportunity for creative expression. Babies will carry blocks around with them, throw them, and manipulate them in irregular and unplanned masses. At three or four years of age, they will build formal rows or piles and sometimes very simple structures. Very shortly after this period of development, their structures assume more complexity and between four and five years of age, blocks will provide a setting for imaginative, dramatic play. When children reach school age many of them begin to build imitations of structures they see around them (21).

Use of Tools. In the broader fields of crafts a similar developmental pattern occurs. Since more complicated tools than the hands are to be utilized, children need considerable experience in handling them. Even here, time and patience are required of the teacher or parent. A child of two or three years of age will spend considerable time pounding nails in the soft wood block provided. Older children when they first explore more complicated tools will pound nails or saw a board, seemingly to no purpose. They should be given time to explore thoroughly such media of expression before they make a product with design from imagination or from conscious planning. Many children lose their desire for creative work in arts and crafts because they have been "pushed" to make objects or forced to follow a plan before they have become familiar with the tools at their command.

Inhibiting Effects. Nothing inhibits creative development in these fields more surely than overemphasis on tidy, careful work or on perfection of detail. The first objective in the early grades should be joy in manipulation (Fig. 39). From eight to nine years of age, imagination should be allowed full play in planning and design. At this age culmination of a plan will proceed rapidly and efficiently (14).

C. POTENTIALITIES FOR CREATIVE WRITING

Of all the traditional areas for creative expression, creative writing has probably been the most ignored. There are many reasons for this, aside from the fact that the opportunity and environment are so often deficient. Brueckner has clearly pointed out the difficulties involved (4). Before the child can write creatively, he must have at his command both a writing and a speaking vocabulary. When these are inadequate, or when his writing vocabulary is inferior to his speaking vocabulary, he has difficulty in expressing his ideas. Some children are further handicapped by a lack of experience from which ideas may be derived. A further difficulty is the complexity of the handwriting process. Style of writing, English usage, and grammatical correctness are also involved. And to top off a description of what must be faced, the child must master the rules for capitalization and punctuation.

Problem of Skill. Brueckner has stated the problem clearly. The main difficulty in encouraging the development of ability in creative writing is the inhibiting effect of conscious attention to mechanics and the problem of paralleling properly the written and spoken vocabulary of the child. As Breckenridge and Vincent state the problem, it is a matter of pacing instructional opportunities in such a way that the mechanics of writing (penmanship, spelling, handwriting, etc.) drop into the background at the proper time (3). Such pacing makes it possible for writing to become a tool for the expression of ideas. These investigators probably do not imply that the mechanics of writing must be mastered first. If they do, their implication conflicts with the idea that creative writing can begin early in the child's school life. They probably mean that mechanics should be learned in the child's early school years in such a way that creative writing, at any stage of the child's development, should not be inhibited by excessive attention to it (12).

Mechanics and Creative Writing Develop Together. The mechanics of writing and the encouragement of creative writing must be developed together. The conventional schools attempt to teach the mechanics first. This usually results in unsatisfactory growth in mechanical skill, the forgetting of skills learned, and minimized opportunities for utilization. To a considerable degree the process should be reversed. Creative writing should be encouraged at certain stages of the child's development at the expense of mechanics. One experiment, at least, has shown that young children can produce good stories, poems, or other compositions when freed from the fear and inhibition of struggling through mechanics (20).

Creative and Mechanical Relations. In order to demonstrate a possible instructional relationship between some of the mechanical aspects of writing and its creative aspects, the following suggestions are made:

> *Period 1: Beginning Childhood Cycle*
> In this period language and speech activities should receive emphasis. This is a period in which informal conversation should be encouraged without any problem to be solved or

decision to be reached. There should be a beginning in: (a) reporting an experience, personal or otherwise; (b) telling a story previously heard or read; (c) giving directions for going to a specified place or for making something; (d) making an announcement of some school activity or meeting.

In writing, children should be given, first of all, instruction in writing their names. Letter form and movement should be demonstrated in manuscript writing. As children learn letter forms, they may do a little writing in making their scrap books, Christmas cards, and valentines. Labeling can be encouraged. During the latter part of this period, some children may wish to make their own copies of stories dictated to the teacher and written by her. As troublesome letters appear, they should be isolated for some study, but the whole planning should be casual.

The beginning of creative composition at this period should be undertaken through dictation of stories by children to the teacher. This is a period when oral language should be emphasized with the stress on creativeness. The imagination of children should be given free play.

Period 2: Middle Childhood Cycle

This is a period of rapid learning. All language activities not previously introduced should be started. Form, quality, spelling, and writing may be given considerable attention. Skill in discussion of definite topics should be encouraged. The use of the telephone, taking part in formal meetings, a topical report, joke, or ancedote, book reviews, written notices of meetings, the development of description both oral and written, and writing letters are all justifiable activities.

In handwriting, this is a period for increased skill in letter making, phrasing, etc. Individuality will begin to manifest itself in the latter part of the period and should be encouraged.

In reference to creative writing, this period is one in which emphasis may be given to the mechanical without neglecting entirely the creative opportunities. The emphasis on speech gives way to an emphasis on written communication.

Period 3: Terminal Childhood Cycle

In this period there results a leveling off of growth and improvement in mechanical skills. Rather than pressing for new mechanical skills, the teacher should develop activities which polish and perfect at the levels on which the child finds himself.

This period is the "nightmare" period for teachers. Because the idea of a temporary plateau has not been generally recognized they continue to stress mastery and to attempt to push children to reach "grade norms." Thus the opportunity for creative composition is lost.

Period 4: Beginning Adolescence Cycle

In a sense, this period is similar to Period 1. It is a time for new orientation and exploration. Imaginative composition, creative writing, and dramatics should be emphasized. Some attention should be given to skills, since this is the time when previous skills, having gone through a plateau period, will begin to improve.

Quality and taste, rather than form, should be emphasized. In respect to creative writing, differentiation must be made between boys' opportunities and girls'.

Lowenfeld has proposed five stages from the age of two to thirteen (14). Although his classification refers particularly to creative art, it may be applied to other creative developmental stages. He shows some recognition of the cyclic nature of development by his age-level characterization. For the babyhood cycle he names two stages, the "scribbling" and the "preschematic." The period from seven to nine is called the "schematic," and the age level from nine to eleven is called the "gang age" stage. He provides the name "reasoning" for the age level from eleven to thirteen. The main disagreement of this writer would be directed toward his latter two classifications. Nine is somewhat young for the "gang age," and the use of the word "reasoning" at the adolescent age implies that it might be absent in the earlier stages. The important point is that the maturity of the child must be given thorough attention in planning a program for the development of creative expression.

D. POTENTIALITIES IN THE DANCE

The dance, like writing, music, arts and crafts, is a medium for the development of creative ability. Under proper conditions children can express themselves just as intelligibly through dancing as through any other media. It provides an outlet for pent-up physical energy and a means for releasing emotional tension. Rightly used, it becomes a valuable area of experience, which enables children to develop into well-balanced, socially adjusted individuals.

Relation to Music. Fundamentally, the dance is a rhythmic response to music. In this sense it follows the accessory principle for development. Among young children bodily rhythm begins with simple over-all movement. Before a child is a year old, he may move his whole body in response to certain types of music. Though he does not follow the beat of the music, at best he gives a general body response to the stimulation provided.

Nursery School Performance. During the nursery school years only a few children can respond to the rhythmic challenge of music by marching or stamping accurately with the beat. Nearly all children, however, enjoy such exercises and opportunities.

Not all children can develop the muscular and motor coordination necessary for intricate performances. Individual differences are reflected here as elsewhere. Certain children show unusual ability in mastering complicated steps. Others, of course, are not so proficient and should not be discouraged by being forced into routines beyond their maturity and ability levels. Dancing can also aid many children who are somewhat awkward and uncoordinated, and can provide great assistance to the bashful or self-conscious child.

The full creative utilization of dance instruction should not be limited in its scope — it should be cultivated for expression, to provide an emotional outlet, and to offer performance opportunity. Where it remains elastic in its instructional opportunity, it may lead to dramatization, to writing, or to the creation of a play. To limit its boundaries is to limit general enjoyment and development.

As with other forms of expression, the dance should have no set curriculum or fixed sequence of activities. One expresses when he feels, not when commanded. Teachers should have at their disposal a knowledge of the types of dances which children of various ages can enjoy. It is also proper to stimulate children toward activities normal for youngsters of their age. With moods once established and with action started, children may be stimulated to express themselves clearly and forcibly. This form of expression, rightly done, is as understandable and as clear as the canvas, the song, or the printed page.

IMAGINATION IN CREATIVE THOUGHT

A. DEFINITION

Part of a Creative Art. Imagination is part and parcel of creative activity. In whatever area expression is to result, imagination must be employed. Imagination is so closely allied to the whole business of creative activity that definition is difficult. And imagination can be either positive or negative. It can be utilized in the solution of a problem or in a creative production which may be either good or bad for the individual or for society. Consequently differentiation must be made. Constructive imagination seems satisfactorily defined as that phase of thinking which visualizes a tentative solution to a present or future problem.

Imagination probably involves the cerebral process employed in Wallas' period of incubation just before insight is achieved. It is the preliminary to planned action in this respect.

B. DANGERS AND POSSIBILITIES

Danger of Retreat into Fantasy. Imagination has been described as having negative possibilities. It may therefore be utilized in such a way as to be harmful. It is not likely, however, that the young child will so use his power of imagination. The danger to the young child lies in the possibility it offers for retreat into a world of fantasy.

Should Lead to Action. To what extent should the imaginations of elementary school children be employed in their creative development? As long as imagination is profitably utilized in a creative production, it is desirable. When imagination fails to lead to action it is bad for the child. Imagination in a creative act may, in its first stages, lead to pointless, unfounded, and even fantastic stories, plays, or pictures. Eventually it should result in satisfaction and a feeling of achievement.

Much use therefore should be made of the child's imagination through style and variety in storytelling, writing, arts and crafts activities, in the dance, or in improvising new games. A considerable amount of time for combining imagination and creative activity could well replace some of the time devoted to Mother Goose and fairy tales in preschool and early school years.

C. DEVELOPMENTAL PHASES

Increases with Age. Imaginative activities occupy much of the uncontrolled, out-of-school, mental life of most children. During the preschool years imaginative situations increase with advance in age. Markey, in a study in which children were observed for periods of two and one half hours, reports an increase from six and a half imaginative situations for children two and a half years of age, to twenty-six for children three and a half years of age. Other studies and observations report similar increases. Situations in which imaginative powers were used were eating mud pies, pretending that a string of blocks was a train or that dolls were real babies.

Peak Period. Research indicates that the time for entering school represents the period of greatest frequency in imaginative play (3). Up to this point imaginative play has not been utilized, particularly in a creative sense. School entrance demands a beginning of direction to imagination, which previously has been random and exploratory. Imagination may be employed creatively in telling stories, in art work, and in games.

Sympathy Rare among Young Children. Imagination plays other roles in the child's development. It may be employed in a demonstration of sympathy for another child. This demonstration is, however, very rare before four years of age. The power can, and should, be greatly encouraged through the elementary school years. This quality unfortunately demands personal experience in a wide range of situations and is not fully mature before adulthood.

Fantasy Should Be Overcome. Fantasy, belief in magic, and superstition as a phase of imagination should be overcome as the child progresses through the elementary school. Belief in Santa Claus, fairies, and the Easter Bunny should be supplanted by more realistic ideas. This transition should come, however, when the child has sufficient social maturity to substitute personal group satisfactions for the more immature, egotistical daydreams and fantasies.

D. UNCREATIVE IMAGINARY SITUATIONS

Imaginary Companions. An uncreative use of imagination may be found in an undue and prolonged preoccupation with imaginary playmates. Such a creation is usually developed early in the child's life. During nursery school it is not an unusual circumstance to find at least one-fourth of the children so involved. Such a condition results from a lack of satisfying comradeship with other children or poor adjustment with peers. Singletons frequently substitute an imaginary companion for a real one of their own age. Children envious of a companion's baby brother or sister may indulge in this kind of imaginary substitution.

Imaginary companionships that become too real should be discouraged as soon as possible, but not by ridicule or by punishment, since this would only drive the relationship under cover, where the possibility for damage is greatest. An attempt should be made to divert the positive power of imagination into interpretation of drawings, planning of group activities, sharing, and other creative demands and thereby submerge its negative aspects in healthy social relationships.

Daydreaming. Daydreaming, like other phases of imagination, is related to creative development. When teachers show faith in the productive ability of a child they promote his own confidence in his capacity for creative production. For maximum development, this kind of acceptance must be shown toward the individual who wishes to do creative work.

Daydreaming which leads to discontent may cripple creative ability both in respect to the development of goal and in respect to creative production. Love, faith, the establishment of security, and opportunity for self-expression are the requisites for returning such deviates into more normal behavior patterns.

APPRECIATION AS CREATIVE DEVELOPMENT

Participation. Appreciation is in reality nothing more than the understanding resulting from the creative development of the individual. This would imply that the teaching of appreciation requires considerably more activity than occurs in a daily class in music or art. How **any music** teacher would expect to secure much appreciation of music merely by playing records on a phonograph or by having children listen to the radio at specified times is quite beyond understanding. Nor can an appreciation of the creative efforts of others come about through sentimental appeals to children's so-called cultural interests. A child does not learn to appreciate through being told to listen but through actual participation which allows for creative growth and development. Children should have the opportunity to listen but only when listening accomplishes a purpose, and most effectively, when the opportunity for listening provides motivation and understanding of the child's own creative efforts as well as those of others.

Requires Both Emotion and Understanding. Appreciation, when it involves both an emotional and an intellectual response, is indicative of creative motivation. Although emotion is what distinguishes creative work from reflective thinking, creative productions do not result entirely from emotion with little or no intellectual realization or understanding. Appreciation is of the highest order when emotional responses are accompanied by complete intellectual understanding. Maximum appreciation involves a background of experience that enables an individual to distinguish various aspects of excellence. An illustration by Harriman points out how both intellectual understanding and emotional satisfaction may be achieved. An individual who listens to Tschaikovsky identifies the contribution of Beethoven in the various themes and backgrounds. The relationship between the two interests the listener who recognizes it. But real appreciation goes further. Previous experiences with music enable an individual to criticize the quality of a performance. He may also be interested in discussing interesting highlights of the composer's life that may have a bearing on the kind of music produced. And he can describe the personal emotions aroused by the performance.

Environment. In the growth of appreciation as a phase of creative development it must be remembered that school and home are a part of the total community and culture and that the esthetic values they foster are a product of the child's total social situation. Real appreciation conditions the child's total background and changes and influences his environment. Real appreciation therefore brings about change in the environment of which it is a product. No school can develop real appreciation if it presents a fine art room for its "creative" environment and totally ignores corridors, home rooms, and other instructional areas. Real appreciation should result in a group attack on improving the total esthetic surroundings of the school. In one school in which the development of appreciation had such an objective, far-reaching esthetic changes were produced. Home rooms were made restful and attractive. Drapes were made, seating arrangements were changed, and the school administration cooperated by repainting walls in colors to suit the esthetic desires of the children. Halls were covered with murals reflecting the children's interests and showing considerable merit in design and execution. And incidentally, as these children matured in their appreciation, steps were taken toward improving the youngster's homes esthetically. In many instances in this community, the child's room at home reflected his developing esthetic tastes.

IMPLICATIONS FOR TEACHERS

Implications for Mental Hygiene. One of the byproducts in a program for facilitating creative development is its beneficial influence on mental hygiene. Consequently the importance of instruction which provides for an emotional expression through creative activity is recognized more and more in mental hygiene therapy (8). Since leisure is being greatly increased by the shortening of work hours and since commercial recreation is becoming increasingly passive and receptive rather than active and creative, more and more normal individuals will need creative experience as a preventive measure. Our civilization undoubtedly lacks an educational program which provides training in the constructive use of leisure time.

The goal is not exclusively the prevention of idleness, unhappiness, restlessness, and mental breakdowns, but also the enrichment of living. When people form the habit of developing new interests and skills up through adulthood, time will be employed in a greatly enriched way. Consequently there will be less and less time for restless striving and continued seeking of empty, purposeless, momentarily entertaining utilization of recreational hours. Programs for creative development which explore arts, crafts, dancing, music, and numerous other creative media are considered helpful as a device for training children, youth, and adults for satisfaction in daily living.

Inhibitory Teaching. One of the points for teachers to contemplate is that the first step in the reorganization of a program for facilitating creative development is to stop doing some of the things that inhibit this development. Most conventional schools have given teaching, even in the arts, a vocational and disciplinary emphasis. In most instances, there has been complete teacher domination in selection of subjects, creation, and evaluation. The products under such teaching have followed a definite, preconceived pattern. Imagination has been largely discouraged, and appreciation has been insignificant and artificial because evaluation has been in terms of teachers' standards. Emphasis has been on production rather than creation.

Another inhibiting factor is the relationship between learning necessary skills and using them in a creative project. The conventional school has followed the sequence of teaching skills before permitting creative activity. This is exemplified by the art teacher who insists upon teaching the essentials of perspective, line, and color before allowing children the opportunity to exercise their native ability and curiosity sufficiently to become oriented to the need for certain of these skills. It must be remembered that nature has not designed the child's developmental pattern in accord with such an idea. The child's creative potentialities need to be developed simultaneously with his development in skill and utilization of media. The old idea that one skill must be mastered before another can be learned is contrary to our knowledge of how the child grows and develops. So, too, is the idea that creative activity can be delayed until the child learns certain skills. Both must develop together.

Creative Arts and the Regular Teacher. If creative development is to be affected by the school it will come about mainly through the efforts of those who do not directly teach the creative arts, since special art and music directors are rarely employed in the elementary schools. Until this teaching deficiency is corrected, it will be essential for home room teachers to carry the burden of the responsibility. And even when special teachers in the creative fields are available, the home room teacher must carry a greater responsibility than has been generally visualized. The following are some of the implications for these teachers:

1. Certain group activities related to the social studies are most effective in encouraging creative development. Lack of playground space can easily lead a group of children to an interesting study of their community, its assets and liabilities, its advantages and disadvantages. Many schools have made such an approach. In a reported experience of this kind children visited a certain city's planning commission with the city manager as guide (11). A survey was then made, and many plans were projected involving such creative activity as map making, plotting, and drawing. In this type of activity special skills involving creative activity can be nicely integrated with the general educational program. In such an integration the home room teacher has an opportunity which cannot be matched by a special teacher.

2. Activities selected for motivating creative development are most effective when they can interest children who represent a considerable range of experience and maturity. In respect to maturity the teacher may well ask two questions. Does the planned activity enrich the child's current life pattern and does it encourage expansion and further experience? To answer these questions the teacher must be aware of the maturity range of her children, their experiences, their breadth of potential appreciation, and their adequacy of expression. In order to sponsor creative activity, she must know much about the children with whom she deals. And interestingly enough, creative activity provides many leads toward understanding emotional and social development, the richness of the child's experiences, his imaginative powers, and many other aspects of development which are helpful in all phases of the instructional program.

3. Activities provided should be diversified enough to meet wide ranges in ability, interest, capacity for understanding, and appreciation. Many of the more familiar art media can be profitably introduced as meeting these criteria. Such materials allow for a variety of response from different children and provide broad

stimulation for exploring abilities and interests. Sketching, making murals, painting scenery, reproducing miniature buildings, constructing models, designing and making costumes, and dramatization are but a few of many possibilities.

4. Activities selected should promote the feeling of personal security which comes from continued self-direction, independent performance, and self-appraisal. No other school activity provides a better opportunity for the development of these traits. Realization may come through either individual or group activity. The creative arts supplement other activities provided for such development.

5. Activities selected should be sufficiently broad to provide variety, but sufficiently intense to offer a problem, to provide full opportunity for satisfactory solution, and to enrich meaning and understanding. Variety can be spread so thin as to result in ineffective and wasteful expenditure of time. The purpose of variety, in the main, is to satisfy a diversity of interests among a group of children and to broaden individual interests and outlooks. Except under unusual circumstances it should never be used merely to keep children from becoming bored and restless. When so-called creative activities become so superficial that new media are made available in a constantly flowing procession, it is evident that appreciation, understanding, and creative development are proceeding at a very low level.

Creative Arts and the Special Teacher. The best programs for developing the child creatively involve having special teachers available. Their availability does not mean that they take over the entire responsibility for realizing these goals. Rather they share responsibility with other teachers, provide expert instruction in the general program and specialized instruction in meeting individual needs. This point of view is implicit in much of the discussion of this chapter. Arts, crafts, music, the dance, and other creative activities are a resource in the child's development rather than a content of study in the elementary school years (11). Attempts to provide content rather than opportunities are the chief cause of the low esteem in which artistic activity is held by the average person.

Consequently, then, the utilization of specialists does not preclude the development of a broad integrated program of study, in which creative activity has a general, as well as a specific, responsibility. The complete program organized around the needs and capabilities of children must be based on this philosophy. Such special features as may be provided in the way of personnel, room, and media can provide maximum assistance in satisfying group needs as well as adequately broad and intense opportunity for a child to explore his personal creative abilities and interests.

Media are but part of what is needed for attaining the ultimate goal of the elementary school — the facilitation of growth and development toward well-rounded individuality characterized by maximum physical, mental, social, and emotional well-being. Although creative activities are usually a separate part of the curriculum, they are in reality supplementary agencies of general education.

The curriculum for creative development cannot be formalized by prescribing courses of study to be taught in specified ways at various grade levels. Instead, the curriculum for creative development should utilize all the child's worthwhile experiences both in and out of school. Some teachers fear that such elasticity may promote duplication and overlapping. While media may be duplicated in different grades, the standard of achievement will be progressively raised as the child proceeds through the elementary school. Children in both the first and sixth grades may be drawing landscapes, but on a different level of performance and expression.

To neglect the opportunity for developing creative abilities is to limit the opportunity for over-all development and deny children a part of their birthright.

SELECTED REFERENCES

1. BELL, JOHN ELDERKIN, "Perceptual Development and the Drawings of Children," *American Journal of Orthopsychiatry*, 22:386–393, 1952.
2. CANE, FLORENCE, *The Artist in Each of Us*. New York: Pantheon Books, Inc., 1951.
3. BRECKENRIDGE, M. E., AND VINCENT, E. L., *Child Development*. Philadelphia: Saunders, 1955.
4. BRUECKNER, L. J., "Language: The Development of Oral and Written Composition," *Child Development and the Curriculum, Thirty-eighth Yearbook of the National Society for the Study of Education*. Bloomington: Public School Publishing Co., 1939.

5. Davis, N., "Creative Activities for Gifted Pupils," *School Review,* 63:85–90, 1955.

6. Martin, William E., and Damrin, Dora E., "An Analysis of the Reliability and Factorial Composition of Ratings of Children's Drawings," *Child Development,* 22:133–144, 1951.

7. Mursell, James E., "How Children Learn Aesthetic Responses," *Learning and Instruction, Forty-ninth Yearbook of Society for the Study of Education,* Part I. Bloomington: Public School Publishing Co., 1950.

8. O'Brien, Mary A., Elder, Rachel A., Putnam, Polly, and Sewell, Miriam R., "Developing Creativity in Children's Use of Imagination: Nursery, Ages Two and Three," *Union College Studies in Character Research.* 1:35–42, 1954.

9. Olsen, Fred, "The Nature of Creative Thinking," *The Phi Delta Kappan,* Vol. 30, 1954.

10. Rudisell, Mabel, "Children's Preferences For Color versus Other Qualities in Illustrations," *Elementary School Journal,* 52:444–451, 1952.

11. Huggett, A. J., and Millard, C. V., *Growth and Learning in the Elementary School,* Boston: Heath, 1946.

12. Singleton, Doris, "Creative Writing in the Third Grade," *American Childhood,* Vol. 39: May, 1954.

13. Jersild, A. T., "Music," *Child Development and the Curriculum, Thirty-eighth Yearbook of the National Society for the Study of Education.* Bloomington: Public School Publishing Co., 1939.

14. Lowenfeld, Viktor, *Creative and Mental Growth.* New York: Macmillan, 1952.

15. Sister Jeanne Mary, "Creative Writing in the Middle Grades," *Catholic School Journal,* Vol. 55, April, 1955.

16. Patrick, C., "Creative Thought in Poets," *Archives of Psychology,* 178:30, 1935.

17. Rugg, H. O., *The Great Technology.* New York: Day, 1933.

18. Scheinfield, A., *You and Heredity.* New York: Stokes, 1939.

19. Wilson, Julie, "Rhythms and Dance in Creative Education, *Childhood Education,* Vol. 31, November, 1954.

20. Shaw, R. F., "Out of the Mouths of Babes: A New Way to Teach the Very Young," *Atlantic Monthly,* July, 1934.

21. Winslow, Leon L., "Stages of Growth and Development in Art," *Educational Administration and Supervision,* 38:18–24, 1952.

22. Wallas, Graham, *The Art of Thought.* New York: Harcourt, Brace, 1926.

9

PERSONAL–SOCIAL DEVELOPMENT

THE FUNCTION OF PERSONAL–SOCIAL BEHAVIOR

The expression *personal-social behavior* is used to describe that type of activity in relation to a group which furnishes the basis for social living and motivates activity leading to social progress.

At birth the child has no social concern. His first interests are egocentric (18). He demonstrates self-interest by sucking his thumb, pulling his toes, and exploring other parts of his body. As he gets a little older, he transfers these egocentric acts from body parts to body wants. He strives to satisfy, or to induce others to satisfy, his fundamental organic needs and desires. Thus for some time the child is not basically a social being. His whole early education has the function of transforming him from an ego-centered individual into a socially adjusted being.

Regardless of the kind of schooling or training provided, the total environment furnishes the stimulus for some kind of personal-social development. Where heritage is poor and the necessary conditions for promoting this development are not of the best, the individual may not be able to assume desirable social stature. A very poor heritage and environment may produce an individual who is not only uncooperative but whose actions are injurious.

Challenge to the School. The school and other developmental agencies seem unable to modify heredity to any great extent. However, they can aid in providing the proper environment for maximum development. This is the challenge that schools and teachers face, and it explains the importance of knowing when instructional activity is conducive to maximum development and when it is detrimental. Teachers must also understand the developing personal-social pattern so that they can appraise and evaluate conditions in terms of growth and status and organize for more effective instruction (19).

Survival Function. Man's mere existence depends upon social living. He has discovered that his greatest satisfactions are achieved through group contact. He has not only learned the benefits of working with others, but he has also discovered that one of his basic needs is best satisfied through the establishment of the security and feeling of belongingness that adequate group living provides. Nature has ordained that man cannot prosper in isolation. Social experience, with its companionship, its challenge, and its motivation assures an individual the opportunity for civilized living and the capacity for assuming social responsibility. The child must be oriented and inducted into this pattern of life. Acquisition of manners and morals, use of communication, utilization of institutions for his own welfare and the group welfare contribute to his developing personal-social relationships and responsibilities. By adopting the patterns of his group, the individual receives the approval of his fellows and thereby achieves a feeling of belongingness. These two are basic dynamic needs which can be achieved only through group living. The personal-social development of the individual at any given time reflects the extent to which these needs are being satisfied.

Basis of Progress. Society seems content to ignore the personal-social development of some of its members by failing to provide the facilities which they and their families cannot provide for themselves. The majority must have adequate developmental opportunity, however, if human society is not to degenerate to a mere animal level of life. Man would lose his power of speech, and communication would be possible only through low-level vocalization. Without developmental opportunity man would need to resort to improvising clothing from raw nature and contending with other animals for food and shelter. Human cultural qualities, therefore, are dependent upon the opportunity provided for personal-social development. Social living, with its opportunities for sharing and cooperating with others, is basic in human development and progress. It is the channel through which the child must learn to contribute to his peers and to receive in return a growing sense of personal worth (24).

THE IMPORTANCE TO THE CHILD OF PERSONAL–SOCIAL BEHAVIOR

Provides Belongingness. The point has already been made that one of the basic needs of the individual is to establish a feeling of belongingness within a group (31). In the child's early years, under normal circumstances, this need is satisfied by the family to which he belongs. In these years and throughout his stay in the family environment, it is essential for the child's well-being that he feel loved, wanted, and necessary for family unity. Gradually he feels the need of establishing other relationships. As he grows older he explores contacts with other boys and girls of his own age with whom he works and plays (5). It becomes increasingly important to him to attain a position of respect among other children while maintaining his family position. The contacts he has with other children during preschool, kindergarten, and elementary school years determine how he responds to other children and how he feels they react to him. A growing sense of belongingness will characterize his behavior if he is accepted by his peers. Achieving a sense of belongingness assures him that he is necessary to the group and that he has the ability to contribute what the group demands of him. By such identification, personal-social development is enhanced and the child adopts the characteristic behavior of the group with which he is identified (40).

Provides Peer Contacts. Of additional importance to the child is his need for establishing a confidential relationship with one or a few chosen individuals. Under normal circumstances, the child in infancy achieves such a bond of understanding with his mother. She is the person who cares for him, ministers to his wants, and provides the love that is so necessary for emotional security at this stage of development. As he matures, this need is manifested in the desire for intimate friendships with children of a similar age. Such a contact is assured when he finds an individual who accepts him as he is, without compromise, and in spite of personal idiosyncrasies. This need is deeprooted and real. The lack of such a stimulant for enjoyable comradeship leaves the individual dependent upon himself. Few individuals have adequate inner resources for self-sufficiency.

During the elementary and junior high school period children become increasingly conscious of these needs (31). Family security, so important in the preschool period, becomes secondary to the need of belonging to a group and having intimate friendships. In the junior high school years the problem is complicated by an emerging interest in the opposite sex. At adolescence the child spends a great deal of time and energy in the exploration of such potentially satisfying relationships. It is the responsibility of every elementary school teacher to assist her children in exploring a variety of social experiences and in forming satisfying individual and group friendships.

Challenge to the School. If elementary school teachers do not help the child to establish these contacts, the problem becomes acute at the secondary school level, when compensatory reactions to deficiencies are so harmful both to the individual and to society. It is obvious that if children do not begin to solve these persisting problems, they will grow into adulthood greatly handicapped in establishing satisfactory family and community relationships.

STRUCTURE OF PERSONAL–SOCIAL DEVELOPMENT

A. GENERAL FACTORS INFLUENCING FRIENDSHIPS

It is difficult to isolate the factors which contribute to satisfying personal-social contacts. Research has provided certain generally accepted clues to the problem.

Preschool Age. At the preschool stage of development, boys and girls of the same age, sociability, and physical development tend to seek each other out as companions. Young children pay little attention to intellectual differences, physical characteristics, or personality traits in forming friendships. Another characteristic of the early part of this period is the fact that these children are always ready to add another child to their little group, whereas at the later stage, from three to five years of age, they are more concerned with exploring friendships already formed.

Elementary School. In the elementary school grades other factors define the friendships formed. In addition to age, influential factors include being in the same school and grade and having comparable mental ability. In one study, seventy-five per cent of the friendship pairs were in the same grade or room (38). Another factor is the propinquity of a potential friend. For children of this age, close friendships are much more likely to be formed between children who live fairly close to one another.

During the elementary school years personal traits are much more important than in the preschool years. Seagoe found that athletic ability, cleanliness, courtesy, and similar traits are significant. In a study of large group relationships, the most popular children were those who were particularly able in motor skills, classroom behavior, and friendliness with playmates. These children were also the healthiest and best looking.

Junior High School. At the junior high school level, such factors as age, mutual interests, and intelligence are still operative. At this period of development the social background of parents first becomes meaningful. Among boys, intellectual ability is less important than size, motor ability, and age.

B. ANALYSIS OF SCHOOL GROUPINGS

Sociometric Techniques. One of the most popular and widely used techniques for studying the social cleavages of children is *sociometry,* developed by Moreno in 1934 (32). According to him the individual child can be appraised in terms of his relationships with other children, and the group can be interpreted on the basis of the characteristics of its members. In the evaluation of personal-social development the technique has great promise. It permits discovery of the characteristics of successful personal-social relationships among children as well as of factors that prevent some children from attaining them. It provides teachers with the nearest approach now available to a scientific analysis of the social forces operating in the classroom and the group attitude toward its individual members (26).

Definition of Terms. As in any new technique, a terminology has appeared to describe the characteristics of the cleavages found and it helps provide interpretations which may be understood by others. These terms and their meanings are:

  a. *Isolates:* Children who are unwanted and not attracted to other children.
  b. *Mutual Pairs:* Individual-to-individual cleavages; children who are inseparable; pals; intimate friends.
  c. *Chains:* A small group within a group but with some of these children maintaining friendships outside the "clan."
  d. *Triangles:* A small cleavage of three children.
  e. *Stars:* Children who are outstandingly popular among a considerable number of children.

There are three ways in which this technique may be used: (1) the status study of the child's developing personal-social pattern; (2) a study of these relationships in reference to selected factors such as chronological age, mental age, and the like; (3) a study at intervals of the same group of children.

Status Study. A good illustration of status study is one reported by Elliott (16). In this study the information was obtained by requesting the children to write down the names of not more than five, and preferably two or three, of their best friends. The graphical analysis of the results is shown in Figure 41. In this technique, a circle is drawn to represent an individual child. Each double line indicates a mutually recognized friendship, and each arrow from child to child represents a child named by the other child as a friend but not named in return. Elliott's analysis of these girls illustrates the typical use to be made of this technique (16).

According to him there are two main cliques represented. One group is rather small, the other much larger. The smaller group is represented by Lois (L), Mary (M), and Nancy (N). Olive (O) claims Mary as a friend, but the claim is not mutual. The observer is permitted to venture that Olive obtains but little security in this contact, since any issue between the two might cause Mary to cut her adrift. Interesting, but not unusual, is the fact that these four girls are quite isolated from the rest of the group. These four make no claims on other girls in the grade, nor do the other girls make contacts with them. It would seem then that they represent a small cleavage which is neither admired nor envied by the others.

Of the remaining children Alice (A) and Barbara (B) are the dominant personalities. Both boys and girls show a great deal of admiration for them. Among the boys Alice is mentioned by six, Barbara by five. Some other girls, of course, were mentioned by the remaining boys, but Elliott has not included them in the figure. Each of this pair has other close friends. Elizabeth (E) is a friend of Barbara's, but she also likes Alice. Most of the remaining girls seek the attention of Alice and Barbara and form an admir-

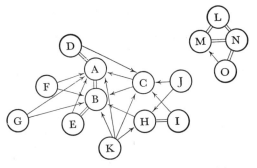

FIGURE 41. Friendship Pattern of Girls
in Classroom A

ing circle around them. Carol seems to have attracting qualities but is so busy maintaining her own contacts with the two dominant girls, Alice and Barbara, that she has little time to develop her own qualities of leadership. Of the remaining children, there is a rather close alliance between Helen (H) and Isuko (I), and there are the usual number of isolates. Among the latter are Joan (J), Katherine (K), and Gladys (G). These girls were not mentioned by any other girls as close friends.

Status in Relation to Achievement, Mental Age. An interesting scheme illustrated by Belden is the use of various standardized tests in connection with the usual sociometric technique of asking "Whom do you like to work with?" "Who is your best friend?" etc. (39). This makes possible the graphing of cleavages in respect to the items tested. In such an analysis each circle representing a child is placed on a graph according to the point of intersection of achievement-grade placement running upward on the chart with mental-age-grade placement running horizontally across the chart. In a representative illustration, Belden points out

that the only child in the graph below his mental-age-grade placement had contact with only one other child and this one a child
referred to as the dullest in the group (39). Significantly, the
"brightest" child in the group obtains very little attention and interest from the other children. In this particular instance, this
child would be classified as an isolate. The child receiving the
greatest attention of all rests midway in the group in his achieve-
ment-mental-age ratio. A study of the supplementary data presents
some interesting findings. 1. As has been indicated by other studies, boys and girls are likely to name as friends children who are
similar in chronological age, mental age, and school achievement.
There is some tendency for children to choose those who are
slightly higher as measured by the selected criterion. 2. Isolates
tend to be the children at either extreme, chronologically, scholas-
tically, mentally, and emotionally.

Other data indicate that the rejected children generally fall into
three main classifications: children with no significant expressed
interests, children who are socially unacceptable, shy, or passive,
and children who are more than normally rowdy, rebellious, and
boastful (1).

Study at Intervals. **An** approximation to the longitudinal approach is the sociometric study at intervals. Continuing study
makes it possible, first, to make a survey of the existing social situation in a classroom. The teacher may then plan a remedial program over a period of time and then retake the sociometric picture. This provides the opportunity for determining, to some
extent, the personal-social development of individual children in
the classroom. It also makes it possible to acquire added data for
the over-all study of the child. Some of the steps to be followed in
providing an improved environment for children at the extremes
are implicit in the following assumptions and suggestions:

Improving Status.

   1. It is likely that classroom seating more or less reflects the
      kind of cleavages indicated on a sociometric chart. It is
      certain that ability groupings do favor continued rejection
      of isolates.

      During the "remedial" attack on the problem, it is pos-
      sible to change seats and groupings and thereby place an

isolate within the borders of a distinct, small-group, social cleavage. With wise direction the teacher can do much for these children through this kind of environmental manipulation.

2. It is possible over a period of time for the teacher to render valuable assistance to children who are shy and retiring or noisy and "rowdyish." Sometimes these children merely do not know how to respond. Treatment following such a diagnosis should be based on this assumption.

3. Another technique is that of giving the child more opportunity to assume responsibility in the life of the group in school. Others need help in skills, and above all, assistance in acquiring a sense of competence and security.

Such suggestions have been made from time to time before this technique was known and available. Here is an opportunity to provide treatment and to appraise its effectiveness rather accurately.

C. FACTORS DETERMINING DEVELOPMENT

The period of personal-social development in the elementary school child is quite undramatic as compared with its development during his first few years and during his pubescent and adolescent years. Nevertheless, this stage of maturity should not be regarded as unimportant and unchallenging, for it is characterized by considerable change and shift. The early elementary school days represent the beginning of the preadolescent cycle, in which sex differences are at a minimum and programs for facilitating personal-social development need to differentiate least in this respect. As a matter of fact it is good practical advice to suggest that the less attention paid to sex differences at these ages, the better the program. During the middle elementary school years boys and girls participate socially, but their congeniality is disrupted somewhat by emerging sex interests. Boys become intrigued with games and girls develop more feminine interests. During the late elementary school years, particularly during the seventh and eighth grades, changing growth brings forth in full measure these developmental differences (35).

1. Effect of Physical Growth

The elementary school period is characterized by growth. The child has shed his baby characteristics and begins a rather intensive period of four to six years in which growth is the dominating factor in his whole pattern of behavior. Although he does not undergo any fundamental dynamic change in his body structure until about the seventh and eighth grades, growth is his outstanding trait. It is marked by the appearance of scholastic abilities, by the development of good motor coordination and movement, and by continuous physical progress. Motor and physical growth have important effects upon the child's personal-social development and its ensuing needs. Such changes as occur assume increasing importance as he matures.

Adolescence Aggravates Problems. Adolescence follows a slowing-down period in which children approach a maximum. During this stage the most dramatic growth since infancy occurs. As at the beginning of all new cycles of development, it is characterized by instability in performance. Some children show a disturbance in motor coordination; others tend to become fatigued. Girls reach this period on the average about one and a half years before boys. This discrepancy is most obvious in the seventh or eighth grades, where approximately two-thirds of the girls have reached the puberal cycle, whereas two-thirds of the boys are still preadolescent. Girls assume leadership, and boys are encouraged in forms of social activity for which they have little readiness. As a result of these changes among some children in the upper elementary grades, and among nearly all girls in the seventh and eighth grades, there develops a problem in the planning of activities for personal-social development. These changes are accompanied by new sensitivities concerning the body, an increased consciousness of self, increased emotional desire, wonderings, and daydreaming. Old adjustments with the home and with playmates whose rhythm of growth no longer runs parallel are upset, and new adjustments must be formed.

In regard to relations within the group, the physical maturity of children, due to individual differences in rate of growth or status, has a far-reaching effect. Physical growth status is a handicap for those who deviate markedly from the majority, particularly for those who are unusually small or slow in their growth pattern. Other things being equal, a certain amount of prestige accompanies more than average size. Loss of prestige due to unusual smallness does not necessarily involve a permanent emotional accompaniment. If current close friends follow a similar pattern of growth or if the child makes new contacts with children whose developmental status is similar, he does not necessarily become disturbed. On the other hand, extreme differences in physical growth do tend to motivate compensatory behavior.

Emotional Effects. At the upper elementary school level and during junior high school years, emotional accompaniments to changes and deviations in physical growth are much more common and serious. According to Meek, deviations in physical status regularly constitute an emotional hazard, and when status changes markedly such feelings of inferiority result that social relations are drastically affected (31). Particularly confusing to boys is deviation from characteristically masculine physical development. Boys who do not mature sexually as rapidly as others and boys who grow fat rather than muscular and strong are disturbed to such a degree that they feel, or fear, loss of status in the group. Consequently their attitudes and the attitudes of the others toward them are drastically affected. Such deviation is not exactly rare, occurring at some developmental stage to about ten per cent of normal boys.

Girls fear getting fat more than any other physical change. To them this is serious and is responsible for more emotional disturbance than any other physical growth change. Since a slender figure is the vogue it is the figure which most girls desire to approximate. Clothes favor the vogue, and plump girls are at a disadvantage when they wish to flatter their personalities with prevailing styles in dress. Plumpness does not bother the young girl, but when pubescence arrives it seems to become a distinct liability.

Certain other imperfections inhibit good social development during adolescence. In the earlier years these pass unnoticed and are regarded logically and without disturbance. At adolescence they assume a new meaning. The imperfections which most disturb both boys and girls are the necessity of wearing glasses, strabismus, and acne. There are others, but those which single out the individual as different are particularly detested and loathed.

2. Cultural Influences

The ideals, patterns of behavior, sanctions, and inhibitions of the community have most important effects upon the child's behavior. The environment of the elementary school boy or girl is a complex of conflicting influences with a multiplicity of pressures upon him to grow into a specific kind of person and to behave in a specific way.

Environment Defined. The environment is not made up of fixed, unchanging affective influences that operate according to scientific, determinable law. Rather, it consists of long-time, emerging patterns of action, mores, codes, speech, and feelings that guide and direct behavior. These result in designs for living for cross sections of the total population through which beliefs, superstitions, esthetic preferences, and biases are expressed. The emerging, over-all environmental pattern can continue only to the extent to which the current generation inculcates in its young its basic concepts and mores.

Environment is not entirely material. It is something within the individual as well, expressed in one's selective awareness, behavior, beliefs, religion, and ideas about man. It exists in the individual because the individual is a plastic organism capable of responding to his surroundings.

Family Influences. The most important factor in personal-social development is the family. This is true for four reasons: (1) it is within the family that the child first feels the impact of personal-social development; (2) its influence is felt over a longer period of time than any other; (3) family ideals, desires, and ambitions, frequently conflict with those of other influences; (4) the family group provides limitless opportunity for emotional behavior of one kind or another.

Personalization of Family Influence. Families are almost as personalized as individuals. Families always reflect the general culture or some aspect of it, perhaps the culture of another day, and it always reflects a high degree of specificity. It makes known to the child what it wants of him. It may be inconsistent in the processes by which it produces these desires. Nevertheless, there is considerable consistency in the accepted goal. This is the result of hopes, faiths, ideals, etc., some of which were acquired without modification from ancestors. Others result from life experiences, its frustrations, conflicts, and satisfactions.

Frequently, there is a complete lack of unanimity in the family goal for the child. Fathers and mothers often come from different backgrounds. It is not unusual to find that the father's ideals and desires for a daughter differ vastly from the mother's. Sometimes these conflicts are resolved or adjusted to the child's potentiality strictly in terms of what is good for him. Too often, however, there is open conflict, or else each parent, consciously or otherwise, adheres to his own standards. To a greater or less degree, this is true of every family. Each child thereby suffers a limitation of his own personal, temperamental individuality, since even the most well-meaning and "modern" parent is not entirely free from the need to exert his own standards.

Influence of Family. Parents, of course, are tremendously influential in orienting the child to the manners and general behavior patterns of the social group to which they belong. Of importance is the fact that the process or method used is as likely to produce acceptance or conflict as the goal or objective. The child is much more likely to accept and conform if he feels security and affection. He may rebel or show some other undesired behavior if the achievement of the parental goal is motivated through punishment and fear.

The way in which the child is introduced to family authority is also important to his future conduct. It is in the family that he first feels the meaning of authority. From his father and mother he first learns the significance of someone that must be respected and obeyed. How he responds to their restrictions depends greatly on the methods used. If his conflict with authority brings repression, frustration, and irritation, he will rebel openly or secretly and will show the same reaction to teachers or others in authority.

Use of Domination. Unquestionably parents must dominate a child during the early stages of maturity or he will not survive. Too frequently the adult finds the opportunity for dominance with his children which he has not found elsewhere. The adult so insecure as to need this outlet will never succeed in freeing the child from this influence. Repression or rebellion results, and the child may very well mature into an insecure person also. Domination should always project itself toward eventual freedom.

Influence of Brothers and Sisters. The influence of brothers and sisters is also very important and may condition and color relations with peers outside the family group. Because of the complexity of relationships involved, it is difficult to determine exactly how great this influence is. In these relationships there are evidences of conflict and rivalry as well as of affection and sympathy. This is brought out in a study by McFarland who studied sister-to-sister relationships (30). The study indicates that even in such a simple relationship there are many variations in the patterns of mutual response. No single factor can explain the relationship which exists. Variety rather than uniformity is the rule. Among these children, McFarland found many types of response. The pattern of behavior varied according to the attitudes of the children to one another, ar.d varied tremendously according to the immediate situation. One set of circumstances brought out a feeling of loyalty and mutual support, and a different situation brought out conflict and attack. Factors which were influential in calling forth contrasting reactions were the child's own physiological condition and the presence of other children and adults. Also important were each child's immediate objectives.

The advantage or disadvantage of brothers and sisters in one's personal-social development is not necessarily an automatic one. Brothers and sisters are available as playmates when other children are not, and they prevent a child from becoming an isolate. The great advantage is the opportunity for personal-social development, but this is realized only through mutual family planning and working together.

The family of several children held together merely by propinquity has little to offer in the way of advantages. Children must learn to live and work with brothers and sisters before the relationship has value.

Need for Security. There is abundant evidence that maintenance of security within the family grouping is one of the essentials for effective personal-social development. Without security emotional tensions arise to frustrate or color relations with schoolmates and friends. Where siblings interfere with a child's status in the affections of his parents, the basic fundamentals for adequate personal-social development both inside and outside family life are threatened.

Certain studies indicate that individuals who are admired as socially contributive are products of families that oriented them effectively in desirable mores, customs, and required patterns of behavior. And there is much more evidence that individuals whose behavior patterns are characterized by deviations, which we classify as crime, delinquency, and unapproved sex behavior, are products of families that have given them emotional conflict and repression.

During adolescence earlier problems become acute. The family becomes concerned with the child's activity in assuming adult patterns in his social relations, and pressure is likely to be increased. This is particularly true when family ideals are in conflict with the behavior of the gang with which the child becomes increasingly identified. Mothers question the "social status" of the children with whom their daughters associate. For a boy pressures are likely to take a vocational bent. Parents are ambitious about his future and frequently try to force him to accept their own vocational choice. School marks assume increasing importance, and a boy's success in ventures in and out of school takes on greater meaning.

Such conflicts are increased if the child's companionships are formed outside the social-cultural level of the home. For such children great conflict ensues. They are torn between loyalties to their families, with whom they have for so long been emotionally identified, and their wishes in respect to their own peer groups.

Influence of School. A third influential behavior factor is that of the school environment. Such an influence is found at all levels of the educational system. The school, assuming as one of its primary objectives the development of character and good citizenship, is important in the child's personal-social development. Conventionally, however, it is likely to reflect the aims and ideals of the adult social group which is dominant in its control. Children coming to school from this group receive the kind of pressure in

terms of objectives with which they are already familiar. Children
outside the social area in control may find entirely new pressures.

It is difficult to analyze the current environmental effect of the
school, since there is greater mobility in community life than a
generation or two ago. In the main the school reflects the objectives and ideals of groups in control and fails to supplement and
enrich them at the child's level. Change comes about slowly, and
parents and school officers feel that what was good enough for
them is good enough for "Junior." Change and experimentation,
therefore, are frowned upon. What these parents fail to see is that
the school must change as community life changes. The community influences which were dominant in a previous day no longer
exist. For the school to remain in its previous pattern while everything else changes is nonsensical.

Mores of Conventional Schools. In spite of some variation in what
they demand of the child in his personal-social behavior, certain
patterns seem to be characteristic of conventional schools. Although deplored by certain modern educators, "perfect" attendance is still rewarded. Promptness in school is cherished, as is
respect toward teachers and authority. Children must say "Excuse
me," when they pass in front of an adult, although little is said
when this response is lacking in respect to other children. Children
must also provide a chair for a visitor and loan him the book from
which the class is reciting.

The conventional school has also developed other patterns.
Children from "across the tracks" do not surprise anyone when
they seem to be guilty of petty stealing, and the child from a
"broken" home may be expected to exhibit innumerable kinds of
emotional instability.

Differences in School Demands. There are wide individual differences among schools and teachers. As the child goes from grade to
grade, he is faced by varying pressures, and lack of uniformity in
what is expected of him. Somewhat formal social behavior is the
pattern in one schoolroom, easy and friendly informality in another, and in a third, no rules are in force. Some children get the
opportunity in their teacher relationships to establish their own
rules in regard to room procedure and are allowed to judge their
behavior in terms of these rules. Most children, however, have only
the experience of living strictly according to the rule.

Influence of Teachers. The philosophy of teachers in teacher-child relationships determines to a considerable degree the extent of security achieved by children in school. Some children are pliable and adjust easily, since there is an over-all similarity to goals and conflicts to which they have already become accustomed. In other instances, real problems are formulated around conflicts in goal. Children affected by such conflicts exhibit rebellion, withdrawal, compensating activities, resentment, and uncertainty.

As the child grows older, peer influence becomes increasingly dominant. Throughout the elementary school years the child's behavior is increasingly colored by what other children think and do, how late they may stay up at night, what they spend their money for, and the like. Beginning with the middle elementary school grades, children develop what eventually becomes a behavior pattern almost completely dominated by peers. Although such identification is tremendously important to the child and should be desired by parents, it poses numerous problems. From the early middle through the upper elementary school grades, children are increasingly aloof to adult and school standards. It is difficult for parents and teachers to realize that such manifestation of peer identification is good for the child and indicative of desirable personal-social development.

Shifting of Influences. Such development is characterized by a shifting from parent and school influence to that of the group. For many boys, the special codes and standards of the group are more rigid than those of home and school. Group opinions are formulated for practically all ranges of personal-social behavior. Only slight deviation is allowed. In the upper elementary and junior high school stages of maturity, the child who ventures into eccentricity of behavior or deviation from accepted patterns, whether good or bad from the adult point of view, hazards his standing with the group unless he has already gained prestige.

Such a picture impresses one with the importance of gaining entrance into the "right" clique. It also shows that to understand a child's personal-social development it is essential to analyze the standards of his peers. Conflicts, potential and real, among the varying pressures of home, school, and group must be understood if the school and the home are to assure the child maximum development.

D. INNATE VERSUS ACQUIRED INFLUENCES

There is always a question as to the comparative effect of innate and environmental factors. It will seem strange to new students of child development that the great importance now placed on the environment as a factor is relatively recent. It was formerly assumed that heredity plus maturation determined growth and that social behavior developed principally as a byproduct of increasing chronological age.

Bühler, an exponent of this idea, noticed that children from six to twelve months of age showed considerable individual variation in social behavior. Since this occurred before environmental effects had much of an opportunity to operate, she concluded that the differentiation was mainly a matter of hereditary variation. As a result of this observation, she concluded that there were distinct types of social behavior. These were categorized as (1) the socially blind, (2) the socially dependent, and (3) the socially independent. The socially blind child was described as one who plays alone without paying attention to other children and their play. The socially dependent child is decidedly influenced by other children and their play, whereas the socially independent child, a type between these two extremes, shows awareness of other children and their play but is little influenced by them. Since her cases seemed representative of children in general, regardless of their home backgrounds, Bühler felt all the more that these categories represented clear-cut classifications. The more modern interpretation of these observations would place less emphasis on the hereditary background as an influence. Children undoubtedly demonstrate social tendencies at an early age. It is believed today that such differences are partially modified by training and environmental stimulation.

However, an imposing array of other investigations testifies to the importance of heredity in the child's social background (39). Piaget largely omits the social factor in reported studies of childhood thinking. Other studies mentioned by Thorpe are those of Gesell, McGraw, Bayley, and Shirley (39). Gesell emphasizes biological growth almost to the total neglect of cultural effect in his studies of child development (39). McGraw, likewise, in her famous twin studies, seems to conclude that learning is relatively ineffective as compared with the maturational factor. Bayley and Shirley in their studies conclude that innate factors are dominant in shaping the social sequence through which every child eventually passes. They report that crying in babies is fairly constant in amount during their first year and that talkative babies seem to become talkative children (39).

More recent research takes the opposite viewpoint. As a result of current findings, modern educators now conclude that social and general environmental factors are much more influential in the personal-social development of the child than was formerly believed. Assuming that the child is not born "that way," investigators have studied every aspect of the child's environmental pattern. The effects of family relationships, peer associations, community institutions such as the church, school, and clubs, the radio, comic books, and the community at large, are being studied and appraised. Results indicate that all of these are highly influential. Much is yet to be done, and little is known of the relative and the compounded influence of specified clusters of these environmental strands.

New Outlook in Research. Rather than continue on a controversial basis as to the relative effect of heredity versus environment, investigators are directing their research toward more practical and purposeful ends. Abandoning their concern with such factors as age, sex, race, and nationality, they recognize that behavior can occur only in a definite sociocultural setting. Consequently they are interested in detailed analysis and classification of such settings in reference to observed behavior, in making comparative studies of personality in contrasting cultures, and in using comprehensive, long-time studies with control groups. Similarly, other investigations are directed toward change and modification of social behavior, and toward the perfecting of devices and techniques for evaluating inner, personal organization and human relationships. In summary, it may be said that the new approach is directed toward understanding and helping the individual in whatever kind of environment he may be.

Such a tendency promises rich rewards in understanding the structure of the child's personal-social development. It will also provide increasing direction for the school in establishing the best kind of environment for facilitating maximum growth in this area (41).

THE EFFECT OF MATURATION

A. RELATION TO NEED

To be most meaningful, a child's educational experiences must be related to his individual purposes, drives, and motives. The problems of boys and girls are real at any period of maturity. Although it is true that they become more complex as the child grows older, it is nonsensical to assume that they are less troublesome or acute because they are only children's problems. Teachers must learn to understand these needs, drives, motives, and problems if they are to provide the best developmental environment for maximum achievement of desirable educational goals.

Growth Develops Needs. Teachers must realize that the needs and drives of children are not determined entirely by "development" and independent of enriching experiences. Needs, motives, and other personal-social drives are the product of continuous years of living in a particular environment. The mere routines of eating, sleeping, playing, going to school, going to church all have an impact. The kind of culture rising out of an environmental pattern determines significantly the growth of personality, the pattern of behavior, or what is referred to here as personal-social development.

Such a viewpoint results through realization of the interaction between an individual and his surroundings. At birth the infant has basic needs for the maintenance of life. He must have the proper food, warmth, and protection. The utilization of these is barely more important than the way in which they are provided. Where utilization and the manner of their provision is adequate, the child grows and develops. As growth proceeds, new needs and new demands arise. He must have more complex food, a wider range of action, broader contacts and relations with others.

Maturation a Product. It is a continuing and ever-widening growth of needs and their satisfaction that motivates development. In other words, the merging of intrinsic growth factors, entirely the result of heredity, with the extrinsic factors in the culture results in maturation or development. Needs are the product of the two. As the environment motivates behavior, new needs are created quite apart from those which are entirely the product of forces within the organism. The idea is not only interesting but challenging. If it is sound, it places praise or blame upon those who provide the child's educational environment. This would imply that the school influences growth and development, that its impact upon the child creates new needs, good or bad for him, and satisfies them, fully or partially, as they are created.

B. CHANGING PERSONAL-SOCIAL NEEDS

In reality there is no such entity as personal-social development and consequently no reality in the idea that there are distinct personal-social needs. These are the needs of the individual as an organic unit and are affected and colored by the intellectual, physical, and emotional phases of his development. Although it is essential to discuss them separately, one should always remember that each contributes to the growth of the others, and to the growth of the complete organism.

Effect of the Home. In infancy satisfying personal-social relations supply a sense of security. Such minor routine relations as the way in which the child is held by parents, the regularity and adequacy of feeding, and a loving attitude all contribute. Incidentally the infant seems passive in receiving them and does not at this time demonstrate pleasure or appreciation. It takes time for parent-child relationships to assume a dual tonal quality.

Growth does not permit such a simple relationship for long. Personal-social development reaches out and engulfs the child in new problems. It is important to know that in forming new relations, the old must change in certain aspects in order to prevent conflict between the two. Mere maintenance of family security is no longer entirely satisfying. The child needs to feel important to the happiness of others in his group.

The idea that the home is most influential in the early personal-social development cannot be overemphasized. Family relationships help to formulate patterns of behavior and serve as a point of departure (and return) in experiments with outside relationships. Each new contact, added to those the child has already made, presents both a threat and a challenge. Parents may not approve and consequently there is the chance that prestige gained at home may be hazarded or lost. On the other hand, there is the opportunity for compensating for conflict and lack of home security in the outside contacts.

Effect of Peer Relations. As the child progresses through school, his personal-social development passes far beyond the problems involved in establishing home security. In preadolescent growth his development is characterized by the problem of merging peer acceptance while retaining home and family security and satisfaction. During late elementary school years the problem of peer acceptance becomes more acute than formerly. Contacts with other boys and girls take on an emotional affect. Family security assumes only a secondary (but important) satisfaction and becomes a problem only when it is threatened. Incidentally, and in some instances unfortunately, the home provides less and less value as a compensatory base for frustration, conflict, and difficulty in adjusting to other children.

C. CHANGING BEHAVIOR PATTERNS

As children grow older they abandon certain specific types of behavior for newer, more socially approved means of adjustment. Young children normally outgrow tantrums and other contrary or negative forms of protest fairly rapidly. Fear and shyness in personal-social relations disappear as the child develops confidence in himself.

Exploratory Behavior Harmless. Personal-social development is often characterized by harmless, exploratory, transitory, negative acts. These should not be dealt with too severely, particularly when they occur at the beginning of new cycles of growth and are especially noticeable during the exploratory time of beginning adolescence. If they persist, they are bad and should be treated accordingly. In many ways personal-social development should be regarded as involving the abandonment of many types of behavior and activity as well as the development of more mature patterns of action. For teachers this implies patience and understanding.

Children should not be harried because of immature behavior. They must learn the futility of their own acts (8).

There is some evidence on the relation of specific types of behavior to chronological age. Blatz and his associates compared the frequency of certain traits, some found to increase, others to decrease, with age (6). As would be expected, evidences of timidity and fighting decrease, whereas impertinence and sulkiness increase in frequency throughout the elementary school years.

Decrease of Some Problems with Age. Other types of behavior problems which decrease with age include tantrums, restlessness, destructiveness, violence, and general attitudes and actions characterizing the "spoiled child." Traits that increase with age, merely hinted at during elementary school years but appearing early in adolescence, are depression, daydreaming, extreme laziness, inferiority, and sex deviations. Such byproducts of personal-social behavior as egocentricity, selfishness, sneakishness, sulking, and boastfulness show little relation to age.

THE SEQUENCE OF PERSONAL–SOCIAL RELATIONS

A. SOCIAL PERCEPTION

One of the first skills in the child's personal-social development is his rapidly increasing ability to interpret the attitudes and responses of adults in his environment. As this skill develops the child utilizes it very competently to adjust his own behavior.

First Perceptions. The child develops this ability early in infancy. First perceptions come from the voices and looks of the persons he sees frequently. As he matures he learns to distinguish between anger and friendliness and between animal and human sounds. The sequence in these early skills is generally thought to be as follows:

One Month: Develops ability to distinguish a human voice from other sounds.

Two Months: Reacts to parents and others seen about him by smiling and laughing.

Three Months: Has developed ability to discriminate between those seen about him, but cannot distinguish between adult expressions of friendliness and anger. May smile at either of these expressions.

Five Months: Reacts appropriately to friendliness or anger.

Six Months: Responds fully to facial expression of those around him.

Eight Months: Will withdraw from an angry face and advance to a friendly stranger.

These perceptions and variations of them may appear at widely differing ages. In studies conducted by Thompson and Gesell similar responses were found at successive ages up to fifty-four weeks (18). Response to smiling and talking is accomplished by nearly all children between four and eight weeks of age, whereas the ability to play "pat-a-cake" ranges from twenty-four to fifty-six weeks of age. Reactions to strangers are interesting: nearly all children between four and twelve weeks of age will accept strangers, but from this point on to approximately four and a half years this response gradually decreases.

B. PRESCHOOL PERSONAL-SOCIAL REACTIONS

Growth through infancy into the preschool years is accompanied by personal-social development in keeping with other aspects of progress. The child begins to lose his egocentric motives and is more willing to engage in group activity, in which he will demonstrate both aggressive and cooperative behavior. Quite normal response is represented by a range in social conflict from harmless verbal differences and physical interference to stormy quarrels and fighting.

Sister Relationships. From McFarland's study interesting relationships are discovered (30). Sisters were found to be more responsive to one another than unrelated girls. Older sisters showed more affection than younger ones. Physical condition and the presence of other children or adults influenced the kind of reaction shown.

Beginning of Sociability. In a study by Berne the influence of age is clearly shown (5). Three- and four-year-old children gave greater evidence than two-year-olds of sociability, understanding of property rights, freedom from jealousy, personal responsibility, and group conformity. Again the four-year-olds exceeded the younger children in cooperative activity.

Children of preschool age begin to give evidence of sympathy, a criterion of personal-social development. Indications of this are attempts to assist a child in distress or comfort another child, hitting or otherwise punishing an attacker, giving warning, reporting a child in difficulty, showing anxiety, and other sympathetic responses. Three-year-old children realize the significance of depriving someone in the group of toys or food. They also appear to appreciate a situation in which a child cannot play because he has to remain in bed, is being attacked by another child, is injured, or is crying.

Aggression and Sociability Develop Together. It is interesting to note that while children are developing social cooperation they also tend to develop such qualities as a sense of rivalry and aggressiveness. Teachers who feel that the school overemphasizes rivalry at the expense of cooperative activity will be interested in the developmental sequences of these traits. A study by Leuba rather generally indicates that children do not display rivalry until they are three years old (27). From four to six years old, children seemed motivated by the desire to excel. In regard to competition, Greenberg found about the same developmental sequence (20). Between two and three years of age children could not be motivated to try to excel others in making designs with blocks. Responding to group judgments regarding which made the prettiest designs, children between four and six years old showed an increasing amount of competitive interest. At the older ages some children not only made remarks indicating an affective competitive attitude but grabbed, quarreled, and generally interfered with those who were trying to outdo them. In the main, competitiveness is regarded as an acquired, rather than an inborn, characteristic of children.

Other negative aspects of personal-social development are found among preschool children. Stubbornness or resistance to adults appears at about eighteen months but fortunately reaches its maximum at approximately three years of age. From this point on it is less frequent. Jealousy is another negative trait which appears rather early and continues as long as the child feels that his security is threatened. Young children frequently show symptoms of jealousy with the arrival of a younger brother or sister. Most of

these traits tend to disappear in a home where there is some essence of cooperation and family unity in the solution of problems.

C. ELEMENTARY SCHOOL AGE RELATIONS

New Problems. When the young child first comes to school he
faces new and formidable problems. In a sense, however, his problems are similar to those of the preschool child, since security is
his basic need. His problem is new in that he has now reached a
stage of maturity where what he does is more important to others
and what others do is important to him. Therefore the problem
of belonging and maintaining status becomes exceedingly complex (34).

This is particularly true for the child entering the first grade.
If he has had nursery school and kindergarten experiences, he may
have developed a sense of security and a cooperative, willing attitude toward other children. Nursery school and kindergarten activities are almost universally in contrast to those of the typical
first grade. The gap between kindergarten and the first grade is
the greatest in the educational ladder. No one has explained this
to a child. What a shock it must be to him to be constantly har-
assed by the orders, "Sit down!" and "Be quiet!" The formality,
the necessity of beginning to read, to carry out orders, to walk in
a line all demonstrate the truth in the idea that entrance into the
first grade marks the first real threat in the actual structure of the
child's personal-social development. This problem, as well as that
of gaining status, occupies much of the child's attention in the
elementary school years.

Conflict Accompanies Social Development. Very interesting is the
fact that the more socially active a child is, the more conflict he
engages in. The forming of friendships is not all sweetness and
serenity. Quarrels are frequent among close companions. As a
matter of fact, quarreling appears to be a secondary characteristic
of the activity of winning friends. Apparently no child is wanted
as a friend unless he occasionally "stands up" for his rights and
ideas. Fighting, therefore, is sometimes required for the attainment of adequate status.

All in all, elementary school children show less hostility toward
each other than preschool children. Whether this is due to a

developmental stage or to more restriction and supervision by adults is an issue not fully explored. Bullying occurs most frequently as a result of difference in size. Such activity is definitely a symptom of maladjustment or insecurity and not characteristic of normal, personal-social development.

Evidence of Cooperation. In spite of the pressures of teachers for a child to work for the group or for the honor of the school, the child as a rule does better when he is striving for individual recognition. When rivalry is injected into a situation on a group basis, however, there is some evidence that he will work as hard for his "team" as he will for himself. This idea is not new to experienced teachers. If teacher-pupil relations are good, it is comparatively easy for a teacher to instil zest and interest in attacking relatively uninteresting school work through competitive activity. A total situation of this kind is conditioned by the composition of the group, the kind of individuals involved, and the nature of the task. There are many others factors, of course, including the extent to which pupil decision is permitted.

Gang Contacts. Between the middle and the upper elementary school grades children generally develop group relationships. As a result they begin to neglect home interests. At this time parents are first bothered by the inevitable request for permission to stay out and play longer in the evening. The child is driven by motives for group associations. He has now reached the beginning of the gang stage in which group loyalties compete with interest in family activities. In this connection it may be pertinent to define *gang*. One of the most interesting definitions is supplied by Thrasher (40). According to him, a gang represents a spontaneous grouping of individuals integrated through conflict. Its behavior is characterized by face-to-face contact, by a milling movement through space, and by planning and scheming in solving its problems (40). Through its over-all group behavior it develops traditions and codes, a group morale, group awareness and security, and interestingly, an attachment to a specific environment. Thus a gang can increase its numbers and expand its influence.

Gang activity among children is in reality a compensation for a gap left by society in its social structure. Gangs are not, as many people believe, necessarily antisocial and destructive. Actually, they represent immature attempts at cooperation and harmony in a given setting. The gang activity of children represents an effort to form a society of their own related to their personal interests and needs. Gangs and well-knit small social groups contribute to a sense of personal worth and give children the opportunity for satisfaction in managing their own affairs. In view of such developmental needs, the value of extracurricular activities can be questioned. Any organization real to the child must allow plenty of scope and elasticity in group management. It is likely that school-sponsored clubs and various groups developed around cultural and academic interests fail to meet these needs adequately.

Gangs may be good or bad in one respect according to the general social environment of the children concerned. This statement is based on the assumption that there is a fairly high correlation between a specific environment and the amount of security and affection provided by the homes within it. If this is true, the children who engage in desirable, socially approved gang activity are usually those who have achieved adequate security and affection and come from adequately motivating and stimulating homes. Conversely, children who feel rejected, frustrated, and in conflict with home and school are likely to form negative and harmful gang relations.

AN ANALYSIS OF IMPORTANT SOCIAL RELATIONSHIPS

A. POSITIVE AND CONSTRUCTIVE PERSONAL REACTIONS

Kinds of Positive Reactions. Maximum personal-social development includes the acquisition of three kinds of positive and constructive personal relations. These are:

1. Growth in ability to utilize social "niceties," as evidenced by courteous behavior in exploratory and orienting social activities.
2. Growth in ability to get along with children and adults in the peripheral social contacts of the individual, in school, in the dramatic club, etc.
3. Growth in ability to adjust to the demands of intimacy, in the person-to-person contacts, in the family, and in the gang or clique to which one belongs.

Children must begin early to learn the skills of the first type mentioned. Such skills lead to ease and poise in casual relations both during school days and again in later life. Specific abilities, generally recognized in all social climates, are such seemingly simple social skills as how to introduce people casually and easily but with a certain formality, how to meet social situations appropriate to the social levels of the home. If children receive natural and purposeful practice in such niceties they gain poise and ease of manner regardless of their social status.

In a sense the development of these skills is beyond the maturity level and the interests and needs of children. They may be acquired rather easily where the child has established security and freedom in his family relationships. His desire to maintain this relationship and to be approved by his parents makes the learning of the task rather easy. If the child is made the center of discussion, if parents make light and frivolous remarks about his achievements and misfortunes, or if the conversation is such as to make him self-conscious, the situation becomes unnatural and may hinder the development of a rather automatic, conditioned, easily acquired habit. If conversation about the child is entirely incidental or projected by himself there is nothing particularly unnatural about the whole situation.

Attitudes and Ideals Necessary. The second type of relationship is developed a little later, during the elementary school contacts. It is one which parents have but little opportunity to supervise and evaluate with the child. Teachers can play an important part in the development of this type of behavior. It is probably what teachers refer to conventionally as "good behavior," and perhaps "good citizenship." It is the kind of behavior which enables an individual to keep his temper day after day while in constant contact with friends who display irritating traits. To do this and to keep personal grievances to oneself is difficult but nevertheless a goal that can be achieved. The accomplishment of this to the highest possible degree depends upon developing desirable attitudes and ideals during the early school years. Punishment handled unfairly and without purpose, assignments and requirements made without consideration of the child's needs will accomplish little in this direction.

Experience Needed. Acquisition of the third type of personal-social relationship is more difficult. In intimate, personal relationships within the family, with chosen friends, and in the clique in which the individual is accepted, full play is given to deep-seated, emotionally affected response. This type of relationship reveals the total individual, his desires, interests, ambitions, frustrations, and egocentricities. The only preparation for effective, positive, cooperative expression of this kind is the overall life pattern of the individual. However, some of these desirable types of behavior can be ingrained through experience and the proper environmental stimuli. There is something more to such high-level response than the mere following of the "hereditary bent." The art of friendship and cooperation can be acquired and made the basis for desirable social development.

B. CONFLICT AND AGGRESSION

Conflict and aggression are singled out for discussion, since they are not clearly understood and stand somewhere between what have been called positive and negative behavior traits. Conflict and aggression in certain instances accompany the development of desired personal-social behavior and in certain other instances frustrate or negate such development.

Definition of Aggression. Aggression is not usually regarded by research workers in this field as a negative type of response adopted by children who wish to be contrary or difficult. This type of behavior is usually thought to be a reaction to some obstacle in the achievement of a goal. Such frustration may be caused by conflict with the desires of other children or adults. Included under aggression are also responses to planned and unplanned incidents that thwart the child and interfere with realization of his goals, however unimportantly. For instance, the child may show this response in a fit of anger engendered by breaking a toy, by getting his tricycle stuck in the mud, or similar happenings. Or, according to Caille, aggressive behavior may include failing to respond to an adult's command, failing to allow other children to take their turn with play equipment, and responding with retaliative measures (13).

Contrasting Theories. Prominent among other theories regarding the desirability of aggression in the maturing pattern of personal-social development is the "old-school" idea that aggression is primarily a means for attracting undesirable attention and therefore should be punished or otherwise repressed.

Another idea, not too prevalent, is that aggression has an instinctive basis and should not be repressed. Its advocates point out that aggression is the only natural outlet for a child completely dominated by his parents. Its appearance is considered by some a necessary element in desirable personal-social behavior.

Another group suggests the "avoid it" type of treatment. This group feels that the child can develop adequately without any such demonstration. Therefore satisfactory developmental motivation must bypass or exclude any frustrating factors in the child's environment. Such treatment comes from those who feel that the child is a frail, tender organism, easily deviated in his growth toward potential maximum development.

Probably the most sensible attitude toward aggression is based upon a viewpoint which emphasizes discovery of its causes and means of diverting it into more constructive expression. Or, stated more briefly, aggressiveness should neither be allowed to run rampant nor abruptly squelched, but directed into socially acceptable avenues of behavior. Available research tends to favor the latter viewpoint.

Discovering that aggression is caused by such physical factors as fatigue, hunger, or such psychological factors as unattained wants, investigators suggest that if the child is tired or hungry, these physical wants can be easily satisfied. If the problem is psychological and he desires things beyond his attainment, he must be helped to develop desires for wants more easily attained or taught patience in working toward goals outside his immediate possibility of achieving.

Psychiatric research also indicates the need for intelligently planned treatment (39) and demonstrates that aggression may result from emotional blocking and frustration. In such cases punishment only results in causing the problem and the motivation to become more deeply rooted and affective. Only a personal understanding of these causal factors can help the child.

Secondary Facts about Aggression. Certain other findings regarding aggression may have meaning for teachers. It has been demonstrated that some children who are aggressive are also the ones who are the most sympathetic toward other children. On the other hand, most children who show strongly structured, negative, aggressive behavior are found to be insecure in their relations with others.

In reference to sex differences, the evidence shows a lack of unanimity. Some investigators report that boys are more aggressive than girls; others find no such peculiar sex superiority. None however point out that girls are more aggressive than boys.

In the main all studies show that undesirable expressions of aggression lend themselves to treatment and redirection. Emotionally caused aggression, however, shows considerable resistance to correction.

C. TRENDS TOWARD DELINQUENCY

This chapter would not be complete without some discussion of personal-social manifestations that may lead to what is currently called "delinquency." A couple of generations ago it would have been difficult to interest teachers in the neurotic behavior of children. Boys and girls then, as now, showed variations of strong fears, anxieties, insecurities, hysteria, and tics of one kind or another. These were then regarded as evidence of a bad or naughty child, or at best a child whose behavior was no business of the school. Today the attitude is quite different. Educators feel that such children can and must be helped. However, there is still considerable confusion about what is so frequently called "delinquency." It is the purpose of this section to attempt to clarify some of the misunderstandings.

Pertinent Facts about Delinquency. Only about five per cent of all children who somehow have been classified as "delinquent" are really delinquent personalities. In connection with this statement which contradicts much current discussion, the following is pertinent (37):

> 1. The word "delinquent" in itself is practically meaningless unless we know first what we mean: *delinquent behavior of a child,* or *delinquent character and personality traits in a child.* . . .

2. Delinquent character and personality and personality traits in a *child need not cover the whole personality of the child.* In fact, they seldom do. . . .

3. Teachers cannot be offered a remedy as such . . . theoretically interesting, but practically of no avail to the teacher in practice. Teachers never deal with "delinquency." What they deal with is children who show "delinquent" behavior, some of which may be based upon delinquent traits, all of which must be understood and dealt with on the basis of the meaning which it assumes from case to case. It is important not to fall for patent medicine promises and not to count discouraging sweeping generalizations about the dangers and threats in regard to the decay of "present-day youth."

Redl lists four factors that contribute to deviations conventionally considered delinquent — (1) wrong handling and wrong setting, (2) growth confusion, (3) fear complexes — neurotic and otherwise, and (4) outlets for personality deficiencies.

Wrong Handling. All children need to be motivated by a desirable environment and by parents and teachers in order to establish the acceptance and security which is so essential for normal behavior. If these needs are not satisfied the best of children may develop neurotic or delinquent traits. So-called normal children without such aid may suddenly become rebellious, inattentive, hysterical, and careless of the property rights of others, or they may display unapproved sex behavior. Basically, such children are normal and are motivated by environmental deficiency or by ill-advised handling and treatment.

Growth Confusion. Children whose growth patterns are poorly integrated, whose timing characteristics in reference to beginning and end points of growth do not parallel each other, are inclined to show significant behavior deviations. A child, whose physical growth, for example, outstrips his mental growth, or whose social propensities are out of step with his growth in reading, may show disturbed behavior. Any unexpected shift in the growth pattern may itself produce the beginnings of delinquent behavior. This is particularly true at the start of the cycle related to the usual first- or second-grade maturity and at the beginning of growth in the adolescent cycle.

Although such factors may cause rebellious acts, stealing, or an outburst of sex emotion, these cases do not represent delinquent personalities. With intelligent guidance and understanding, neither psychiatric nor institutional treatment is necessary.

Fear Complexes. Supposed delinquent behavior is frequently the result of fear. The child may have fears regarding his status in a group. He may be unable to live up to the standards of his group, afraid of not being regarded as a "real guy," or he may be afraid to face a home situation or a relationship which seems to him intolerable. Again, only the form of behavior is indicative of delinquency, not the person himself.

Personality Quirks. So-called personality quirks are difficult to identify and treat. A child may develop some specific quirk, some compulsion for action, while his other motivations remain normal. Some of these children have abnormal drives or undeveloped consciences and codes of conduct. Some have both. Most interesting is the descriptive sketch by Redl regarding this type.

> I know many a thief I can easily trust with my wallet — so long as he likes me. He wouldn't steal from people who mean something to him. I know others I would trust with my wallet only if they hate me — for they have to take things from people they like as a symbolic token of getting more from them than those loved people are willing to surrender.

Environmental Inadequacies. Many children come from surroundings which are conducive to nothing but bad behavior. Specific weaknesses in the home which create various kinds of behavior deviations are too numerous to treat here. However, some of these will bear listing and discussion.

In some homes, sleeping arrangements force several children to sleep together, and in many instances adults sleep in the same room with children beyond the years of early infancy. This and other conditions force all aspects of adult life upon children, before they are ready. Insufficient rest, food, and toys, as well as lack of play space and equipment, are other contributive factors.

In certain other instances it is not physical factors which endanger normal behavior but rather emotional or intellectual ones. In many cases parents, teachers, and others who assume responsibility for children are at fault. These adults, and they are numerous at all social levels, have little insight into the real nature of a child. They frequently lack the patience to accept the challenge of growth and are guided by a very flexible and distorted concept of what a child "ought" to be. In such instances, rules and regulations, demands and taboos, rewards and punishments are entirely out of step with the child's real developmental needs.

Parent and Teacher Inadequacy. One universal fact confronts all those interested in preventing or curing delinquency. No matter how simple or serious the act may be, the love relations between the child and certain adults on whom he depends for help are almost always involved.

Unfortunate relations in this respect are many and varied. Some of the most significant involve a home in which the child is unwanted or basically rejected. Another, similar in its effect, is the home in which the child, originally greatly wanted and loved, is for certain reasons no longer so much loved. Probably the most difficult kind of child-parent relationship is that in which there is a great show of superficial love and affection with no real depth or sincerity. In such a situation, for example, parents may buy children all kinds of toys and playthings and express sentiment in a good many ways. In reality these parents love the child, not for himself but for what he does for them. Through what they give him they force the child to take on their own ideals and goals and use him to express or compensate for their own deficiencies and disappointments. From such a pattern neurotic and delinquent tendencies almost invariably develop.

Conditions Favoring Compensatory Behavior. Lack of love is not the only condition favoring delinquent tendencies. Many parents are sincere in their affections for their children but through ignorance, traditionalism, or distorted concepts of what constitutes a "good" boy or girl tend to force the child to compensatory behavior. Some of the "right" combinations for the development of conflicts are described by Redl as (37) :

> Parents very old and tradition-minded, youngster growing up in a rather "fast" neighborhood with behavior codes entirely unintelligible to the . . . adult.
> Parents blindly applying certain habitual techniques of

reward and punishment without any attempt to adapt those techniques to the nature of the children to whom they apply them.

Parents and teachers relying on punishment and reward as sole means of education so that the growth of a responsible personality is technically excluded from having a chance.

Exposure of children to cruel and unjust reproof or punishment, or to blind, undeserved criteria for praise, reward, and pampering.

Without real guidance, exposure of children who are growth-confused to punitive climates.

Frequent use of ridicule at the age where group prestige becomes a very much needed diet of a normal child.

Prolonged exposure to failure and discouragement without supplementary diet through personal guidance and positive experiences.

Exposure to delinquent experiences accompanied by an "I don't care what you do" attitude on the part of the . . . adult.

Seclusion from the learning process of community life and social behavior to the degree that social development is blocked.

Inequality of treatment as compared to that of sibling or classmate.

Exposure to violent outbursts of temper on the part of the adult or to other visible signs of mental disturbance and inefficiency, in spite of educational power of that same adult over the child.

SOME IMPLICATIONS FOR TEACHERS

A. GENERAL IMPLICATIONS

In addition to other goals the modern elementary school has the responsibility for providing experiences which will have meaning for children in terms of their purposes. This implies that it is the responsibility of the school to help children understand themselves in relation to the culture around them. This does not mean that personal-social development is the only goal of the elementary school. It should be evident, however, that the process of personal-social development greatly colors and affects scholastic achievement. In the light of this assumption it will be necessary to do more than most schools have done in reference to the total curriculum offering. Change in the experiential opportunity will proceed not so much in revised subject matter areas as in terms of opportunities for growth.

To a considerable degree the dominating objective in the revision of instructional programs should be that of providing environments which facilitate satisfying social relations. The key to determining the extent to which this has been done will be found in the general atmosphere of the school, in the informal relations between peers, in the friendships made, and lastly in improved teacher-pupil relations.

B. IMPROVED SOCIAL CLIMATE

If such goals are to be achieved, there must be a great change in the social climate of the school. There must be a shift from the cold, autocratic, teacher-dominated situation toward a greater friendliness and concern for personal relations. Each child should feel from his very first contacts that here is a fine place for him, that he is respected as an individual and liked for what he is rather than for what he should be. This is the affective relationship which should exist between teacher and pupil. It should be evident in the greetings exchanged between pupils and teachers, in the conversations, conferences, and in classroom relations. Further indications of friendliness would be opportunities both *during* and after school for satisfying social relations, and by the arrangement of the physical facilities provided for meeting such opportunities. At best, each school must provide the space for exploring and cementing person-to-person friendships, for small group activity, individual relaxation, and for large group activity. *Kind of Classroom Required.* A friendly, informal, natural classroom is the only kind in which the child's drive for self-assertion, for expanding individuality, and for free social intercourse with others can realize maximum goals. In the conventional room, teacher mandate, arbitrary assignments, marking which discriminates and puts children into undesired groupings make the child feel he is merely tolerated by his teacher or by other children. A child so threatened is a likely candidate for delinquent activity.

His personality is really threatened. It is not easy to improve the atmosphere throughout a given school. It requires teachers who like children and who are liked by them. An understanding teacher transfers some authority to children and occasionally overlooks momentary outbursts of undesirable behavior. This is not easy and requires study, knowledge, and understanding.

Need for Individual Attention. Most schools give some kind of lip service to the idea that children differ in capacity, in interests, and in rate of growth. As in other phases of development, the personal-social development of children is represented by wide variations. Some children require little assistance from the teacher or school in their social development. This is not to say, however, that these children do not need evidence over and over that they are respected individuals. Some fortunate children come from homes that provide maximum experiential opportunity. They have been able to make satisfactory adjustments from infancy on with playmates and adults in their environment. Others, probably more numerous, have not had such good luck. As a result many children are shy or aggressive, easily fatigued by strain, tense, or excitable, and some are rejected.

Each teacher must find a way to give these children sufficient attention to understand them and define their problems. Observation, day after day, is essential. This is one of the reasons that quite a few schools now recognize the need for longer contact with the child than can result from only one year with a given group. Many kinds of data should be collected and studied in order to supplement direct observations, which are the best and most indispensable clues for understanding child behavior.

C. IMPROVED HOME AND SCHOOL RELATIONS

In nursery school and in the early elementary grades, the relations of parents and teachers are fairly cooperative and profitable. The child rather easily accepts both in terms of authority and as guides and helpers. The child's development is of common interest to both of them, but each approaches this interest from varying points of view and background. The main distinction is the emotional connection between parent and child, which does not exist between teacher and child except under unusual circumstances. If the child appears to be doing well in school, is happy, and gets along well with other children, the relationship proceeds at a rather high level without problems or special influential action. On the other hand, if the child has difficulty — perhaps in reading, spelling, or arithmetic, or in his social relations with his schoolmates — the parent is disturbed and may react in a number of ways. He may attack the teacher and the school, he may become overly indulgent or protective, or display sympathy suitable only for infants. Or the mother may react by exerting pressure on the child to solve his own problems. He may be required to study during play hours or be punished in some other way. The parent's behavior, whatever form it assumes, indicates a feeling of responsibility for the child's actions. The teacher's concern is quite different. Although she shares the parent's interest in a boy or girl, each child is but one of many for whom she assumes instructional responsibility. She, of course, understands the child's problems, but unless some special relationship exists as the result of conflict or extreme annoyance, there is no emotional alliance. Anything personal in the teacher's behavior springs from achieving satisfaction in a professional way.

Need of Cooperation. Closer cooperation is essential for improved relations between home and school. A word of warning should be helpful here in regard to what is meant by cooperation. If schools think of cooperation as the docile acceptance by parents of orders issued by the school, nothing can be accomplished. Nor will anything be accomplished if parents regard school cooperation as the carrying out of their wishes. Real improvement is founded on a sharing of responsibility in decisions and mutual understanding of a child's problem. Parents must respect the professional knowledge of teachers and be ready to learn from them. Teachers must respect the integrity of the family and be ready to profit by a parent's knowledge of the child.

One of the best ways for parents and teachers to work together for mutual understanding is to undertake jointly a study of the problems relating to the child's stage of maturity. This should be the aim of conference periods between teacher and parent. At these times there is a pooling of interpretations with the purpose of understanding better the developing boy or girl.

For purposes of orientation to the problems common to all children within a given developmental range, more general programs for groups of parents can be held to supplement individual contacts. These meetings can be handled and led by the classroom teacher, the principal, or some outside consultant who has a special knowledge on the subject.

This kind of planning and working together furnishes good orientation and improves parent-teacher relations. Follow-up activity may consist of classroom observation by parents in small groups, all organized informally without special planning or show-off classroom activity. Utilizing a parent as a special consultant, for example, to help some children with weaving is a very good way to bring home and school into closer unity.

Need of Public Relations. If personal-social development is to be one of the school's primary goals, it is essential that parents have a better idea of what the school is trying to do. Teachers are so busy teaching that they find little time to help parents understand what they are attempting. They sometimes leave this job to the superintendent or principal. If schools are to reshift educational objectives, making the three R's secondary to the child's maximum development they must improve their public-relations programs. At best, such a concept of public relations does not mean a steady stream of convincing propaganda. Rather, it implies discussion of problems with parents. When parents have the opportunity to ask questions, give opinions, criticize and generally evaluate, the proper public-relations program is being stressed.

D. TEACHER-PUPIL RELATIONS

The harmony that exists between the child and classroom goals depends considerably on teacher effort. Children unquestionably work better with a teacher that they like than with one they dislike. Much of the attitude of teachers is reflected in their words and acts. Depending upon the specific relationship with each child, each of the teacher's actions affects children. For some it is satisfying, for others it may cause unhappiness, resentment, or frustration.

What is less known or realized is that the teacher too is responsive to stimuli. She is affected by the group as a whole and by individuals in particular. Because of group differences, one group may be much more stimulating and challenging than another. And each member of the group provides individual stimuli. Some groups are so united that they greatly challenge all their members. Others slow down creative, emotional, and personal impulses and motivations. Thus the entire group, along with the teacher, comprises a unique social situation representing the interaction of contrasting levels of maturity and the motivating influence of each individual upon every other.

Domination Inhibits Development. One of the best ways for the teacher to evaluate the kind of impact her personality has on the children is to ask herself, "Would I behave like this if these children were adults?" With children the teacher is able to develop autocratic relations without receiving much criticism if she is disrespectful, loses poise and dignity, or otherwise reverts to childish behavior. Adults would react strongly and aggressively in such situations, but children, though they may register silent conflict and aggression, generally accept such methods. Such situations cannot exist if personal-social development is adopted as a worthy educational goal. Children react unfavorably in terms of development to arbitrary domination, infantile behavior, lack of respect for children, and other types of demanding and coercive treatment.

Children learn better and respond more favorably, socially and emotionally to teachers who deal constructively with them. They like a well-organized classroom. They dislike the demanding, step-by-step mastery of essentials completely dominated (even though pleasantly) by teachers, as well as the laissez-faire, what-shall-we-do-today-children type of organization. According to Lippitt and others previously mentioned, they like best, do best, and respond developmentally to the mutually planned, cooperative type of organization.

Children, also, like to see each child engaged in some activity from which he profits and is interested. Nothing provides greater child-to-child motivation than a number of children working on problems, projects, or construction in which they display a high degree of interest and accomplishment.

In general children like teachers who like them. This becomes more and more obvious as one studies the research on the influence of teacher personality upon children. As someone has said, attitudes are contagious. This is undoubtedly true, since research clearly shows that peer and group relations are significantly improved by helpfulness and cooperation between teacher and pupil. It is unquestionably true that if teachers are aloof, dominating, or haphazard in their methods, irritating, or indifferent, similar relations begin to develop in the contacts between children. On the other hand, in rooms where teachers are friendly, interested, understanding, and cooperative, children tend to reflect these same attitudes toward each other.

The attitude of teachers is the result of their own developmental pattern. If teachers are socially and emotionally immature, their immaturity is frequently reflected in their behavior with children. This response is most likely to occur when they are faced with a like immaturity in the situations created by children.

Immature Traits. Two immature traits may characterize teachers' dealings with children. One is a lack of understanding of why children do certain things. This may result from the fact that some teachers may have had inadequate opportunities for realizing maximum personal-social development. Other teachers have experienced what seems to them a very happy early childhood. Perhaps because at adolescence or later they were blocked in achieving adult status, they continuously revert through their pupils to these childhood days. Both ways of acting and responding are to be condemned. Poise and emotional maturity are essential in handling children and in providing developmental opportunities for them. The past should serve only as a basis for understanding children, not as something to be relived through teaching and through contacts with children.

An effective way to establish rapport is through mutual acquaintance in out-of-school activities. It is undoubtedly true, if somewhat unfortunate, that the teacher has the opportunity to demonstrate personality traits here that are difficult to display in the classroom. Knowing pupils personally modifies the formality which characterizes too much of the teacher-pupil relationship in school. Incidentally, the child will discover that the teacher is really a human being.

E. CLASSROOM ACTIVITY FOR PERSONAL-SOCIAL DEVELOPMENT

It has been stressed throughout this chapter that the most desirable surroundings for children are those which inculcate security, personal relations, peer adjustment, group living, and individual opportunity for self-expression.

Requisites for a Good Classroom. The first requisite for a good classroom is one in which the child can establish belongingness. Such a goal cannot be achieved unless he can experience reasonable success in his undertakings, academic and social. It is probable that academic standards provide the greatest obstacle to the achievement of this goal. Schools and school systems, more often than not, make uniform demands on all children and then evaluate the products of such demands on a scale from "failure" to "excellent." The child who cannot satisfy fixed standards almost invariably suffers one way or another in his personal-social development. A child may daydream or scribble aimlessly. If he is to achieve belongingness, the situation needs to be improved. Some schools are experimenting with the practice of making assignments compatible with the child's level of ability. Another way of improving the climate for belongingness is to achieve widespread participation in group activity. Sometimes, however, a few aggressive children monopolize such types of class organization. This lessens the opportunity for others and frequently lulls the teacher into the belief that a good job is being done.

Another important personal-social motivation is the opportunity that some teachers utilize for helping children to become independent and self-motivated in their school work. Creating a situation for self-direction is not easy. It is, more often than not, less difficult to point out the exact place where a child has made an error than it is to emphasize habits of work and techniques by which the child can discover his own errors. This implies that there can be an overdose of guidance on the part of the helpful teacher. Proper direction should be given, but the teacher must be careful not to handicap initiative and independence. Pupils who require excessive attention and assistance are not achieving adequate personal growth, since the feeling of insecurity and unreliability is being nourished rather than cured.

SELECTED REFERENCES

1. AUSUBEL, DAVID P., SCHIFF, HERBERT M., AND GASSER, EDWARD B., "A Preliminary Study of Developmental Trends In Socioempathy: Accuracy of Perception of Own and Others Sociometric Status," *Child Development,* 23:111–128, 1952.

2. BEDOIAN, VAGHARSH H., "Social Acceptability and Social Rejection of the Underage, At-Age, and Overage Pupils in the Sixth Grade," *Journal of Educational Research,* 47:513–520, 1954.

3. BERENDA, R. W., *The Influence of the Group on the Judgments of Children — An Experimental Investigation.* New York: M. W. Drexler Book Co., 1950.

4. BIEHLER, ROBERT F., "Companion Choice Behavior in the Kindergarten," *Child Development,* 25:45–51, 1954.

5. BERNE, E. V. C., *An Experimental Investigation of Social Behavior Patterns in Young Children.* Iowa City: University of Iowa Studies in Child Welfare, Vol. 4, No. 3, 1930.

6. BLATZ, W. E., CHANT, S. N. F., AND SALTER, M. D., *Emotional Episodes in the Child of School Age,* Child Development Series, No. 9. Toronto: University of Toronto Press, 1937.

7. BONNEY, M. E., "Choosing Between the Sexes on a Sociometric Measurement," *Journal of Social Psychology,* 39:99–114, 1954.

8. ——, AND POWELL, JOHNNY, "Differences In Social Behavior Between Sociometrically High and Sociometrically Low Children," *Journal of Educational Research,* 46:481–495, 1953.

9. BUSWELL, MARGARET M., "The Relationship Between the Social Structure of the Classroom and the Academic Success of the Pupils," *Journal of Experimental Education,* 22:36–52, 1953.

10. CANNON, KENNETH L., STAPLES, RUTH, AND CARLSON, IRENE, "Personal Appearance as a Factor in Social Acceptance," *Home Economics,* 44:9:710–13, 1952.

11. CASSEL, RUSSELL N., AND SAUGSTAD, RANDOLPH, G., "Level of Aspiration and Sociometric Distance," *Sociometry,* 15:318–325, 1952.

12. COX, F. N., "Sociometric Status and Individual Adjustment before and after Play Therapy," *Journal of Abnormal and Social Psychology,* 48:354–356, 1953.

13. CAILLE, R. K., *Resistant Behavior of Preschool Children,* Child Development Monographs, No. 11. New York: Teachers College Bureau of Publications, Columbia University, 1933.

14. CUNNINGHAM, RUTH, ELZI, ANNA, FARRELL, MARIE, HALL, JAMES A., AND ROBERTS, MADELINE, *Understanding Group Behavior of Boys and Girls.* New York: Bureau of Publications, Teachers College, Columbia University, 1951.

15. DYMOND, ROSALIND F., HUGLES, ANNE S., AND RAABE, VIRGINIA, "Measur-

able Changes in Empathy With Age," *Journal of Consulting Psychology,* 16:202–206, 1952.

16. ELLIOTT, M. H., "Patterns of Friendship in the Classroom," *Progressive Education,* 18:383–390, 1941.

17. FINLEY, CECILE BOLTON, "The 'Social Opinion Inventory' as a Measure of Social Maturity," *Child Development,* 26: No. 1, 81–90, 1955.

18. GESELL, ARNOLD, AND THOMPSON, HELEN, *Infant Behavior: Its Genesis and Growth.* New York: McGraw-Hill, 1934.

19. GOODLAND, JOHN I., "Some Effects of Promotion and Non-Promotion upon the Social and Personal Adjustment of Children," *Journal of Exceptional Education,* 22:301–308, 1954.

20. GREENBERG, P. J., "Competition in Children: An Experimental Study," *American Journal of Psychology,* 44:221–248, 1932.

21. GRONLUND, NORMAN E., AND WHITNEY, ALGARD P., "Relations Between Pupil's Social Acceptability in the Classroom, in the School, and in the Neighborhood," *The School Review,* September, 1956, 267–271.

22. HORACE MANN-LINCOLN INSTITUTE OF SCHOOL EXPERIMENTATION, *How to Construct a Sociogram.* New York: Bureau of Publications, Teachers College, Columbia University, 1947.

23. GRONLUND, NORMAN E., "Generality of Sociometric Status over Criteria in Measurement of Social Acceptability," *Elementary School Journal,* 56:173–176, 1955.

24. HAVIGHURST, ROBERT J., "Research on the Developmental-Task Concept," *The School Review,* May, 1956: 215–223.

25. HORROCKS, JOHN, AND BUKER, MAE E., "A Study of the Friendship Fluctuations of Preadolescents," *Journal of Genetic Psychology,* 78:131–144, 1951.

26. LePERE, JEAN M., *Social Distance Ratings in Case Study Analysis* (unpublished master's thesis), Michigan State University, East Lansing, 1955.

27. LEUBA, C., "An Experimental Study of Rivalry in Young Children," *Journal of Cooperative Psychology,* 16:367–378, 1933.

28. MARTIN, WM. E., AND STENDLER, CELIA BURNS, *The Process of Growing Up in Society,* New York: Harcourt, Brace, 1953.

29. MASON, BEVERLY DERKSEN, "Leadership in the Fourth Grade," *Sociology and Social Research,* 36:239–243, 1952.

30. McFARLAND, M. B., *Relationships between Young Sisters as Revealed by Their Overt Responses,"* Child Development Monographs, No. 23. New York: Progressive Education Association, 1940.

31. MEEK, L. H., *The Personal-Social Development of Boys and Girls.* New York: Progressive Education Association, 1940.

32. MORENO, J. L., *Who Shall Survive? A New Approach to the Problem of Human Interrelations.* Washington: Nervous and Mental Disease Publishing Co., 1934.

33. MILLER, DANIEL R., AND STINE, MARGARET E., "The Prediction of Social

Acceptance by Means of Psychoanalytic Concepts," *Journal of Personality*, 20:162–174, 1951.

34. STENDLER, CELIA BURNS, AND YOUNG, NORMAN, "Impact of First Grade Entrance upon the Socialization of the Child: Changes after Eight Months of School," *Child Development*, 22:113–122, 1951.

35. TUDDENHAM, READ D., *Studies in Reputation: I. Sex and Grade Differences in School Children's Evaluations of Their Peers, II. The Diagnosis of Social Adjustment.* Psychological Monographs, No. 333, 1952, Washington: American Psychological Association, 1952.

36. ——, "Studies in Reputation. III. Correlates of Popularity among Elementary-School Children," *Journal of Educational Psychology*, 42:257–276, 1951.

37. REDL, FRITZ, "Deviations Tending toward Delinquency," *Child Growth in an Era of Conflict*, edited by C. V. Millard, Fifteenth Yearbook, Department of Elementary School Principals. Lansing: Michigan Education Association, 1944.

38. SEAGOE, M. V., "Factors Influencing the Selection of Associates," *Journal of Educational Research*, 27:32–40, 1934.

39. THORPE, L. P., *Child Psychology and Development.* New York: Ronald Press, 1946.

40. THRASHER, F. M., *The Gang.* Chicago: University of Chicago Press, 1927.

41. TYRON, CAROLINE, AND HENRY, WILLIAM, "How Children Learn Personal and Social Development," *Learning and Instruction, Forty-ninth Yearbook of the National Society for the Study of Education, Part I.* Bloomington: Public School Publishing Co., 1950.

42. WRIGHTSTONE, J. WAYNE, "Measuring the Social Climate of a Classroom," *Journal of Educational Research*, 44:341–351, September, 1950–May, 1951.

43. ZELENY, LESLIE D., "Status and Role among Fifth-Grade School Children," *Sociology and Social Research*, 35:425–427, 1951.

10

GROWTH AND THE ORGANIZATION
OF LEARNING

INTRODUCTION

In a book dealing with growth and development it is difficult to treat separately the subject of learning. This is particularly difficult when one's point of view is that growth and learning are but two phases of the same process of change. They represent two complementary aspects of a single whole. The maturing child grows and learns at the same time, and the process is so complex that we are unable to distinguish satisfactorily between the two. Nevertheless, previous discussions of educational processes have fixed the tradition of treating learning as a separate topic. The concession here is not entirely to tradition. Growth studies have made tremendous contributions to our knowledge of learning. In some instances they have caused an abandonment of practices based upon points of view which had not previously been fully explored and verified. In other instances these studies have confirmed early assumptions. We shall discuss learning separately but in relation to new data.

CURRENT CONCEPTIONS OF LEARNING

No other subject in educational psychology has been treated more extensively than the one designated by the term *learning*. Learning is important and demands much attention because it implies modification. If human nature could not be changed, or if individuality were a rigid entity, there would be no problem of learning. But this is not the case — the individual is constantly changing. It is therefore the responsibility of the school, and the teacher as an agent of the school, to facilitate desirable change. Consequently, the extensive literature and experimentation on learning are justified.

Definitions. Many specific definitions of learning have been given. At present the tendency is to define it in general terms. Powers, for example, describes learning as a behavior adaptation (29). A more elaborate definition has been proposed by Munn (24).

> Learning may be said to occur whenever behavior undergoes incremental modification of a more or less permanent nature as a result of activity, special training, or observation. To say that learning involves an incremental modification is to distinguish it from fatigue, which is also due to activity, but with which a performance decrement is associated. By indicating that the learning process involves a more or less *permanent* modification, we differentiate it from sensory adaptation, which disappears soon after removal of the stimulating circumstances. Finally, by including the statement that *learning* depends upon *activity, special training,* or *observation,* we point to the fact that it differs from modification which depends upon maturation *per se.*[1]

This definition is somewhat characteristic of the earlier concepts. His use of the word *incremental* gives the definition a quantitative meaning. Moreover, it tends to deny that sensory and motor change are a part of a learning situation and that learning is affected by maturation.

Such a view as Munn's is in contrast to Harmann's definition, that learning is a method for increasing mastery of experience, accompanied by improved adjustment to circumstances (14).

From the growth point of view, learning may be looked upon as a very general term, given specific meaning according to the experience of the individual. As viewed by most teachers, learning is mostly used to describe the academic progress of a child or group of children. This is too narrow a view. That the child learns arithmetic is true. On the other hand, he also learns to ride a bicycle, to throw a baseball, or to get along with other children.

[1] Reprinted by permission from *Manual of Child Psychology* by L. Carmichael, published by John Wiley & Sons, Inc., 1946, p. 370.

An Added Definition. The definitions which apply to all kinds of learning are more satisfactory. Let us add another to those already mentioned:

> Learning is that activity which results in quantitative or qualitative (or both) modification of the organism, resulting from reaction between the individual and his environment.

Such a definition would include learning to spell twenty new words as well as the kind of behavior modification which enables an individual to adjust to his peers. Learning in this sense may be temporary or permanent. The child may forget the twenty words learned, or he may learn new behavior which makes him unpopular with his group. Thus learning is not necessarily positive in reference to social behavior. From this point of view the adolescent may learn how to become a successful pickpocket, or he may learn how to become a leader in his community for positive moral good. It is the positive aspect, however, in which we are interested and to which attention will be given.

TYPES AND KINDS OF LEARNING

Research with children on learning followed the lead established by experimenters with animals. For example, Krasnogorski in 1909 adopted the techniques of Pavlov who had previously reported his now classical investigations on the conditioned salivary response in dogs (27). The early work of Thorndike and Small with animals and the studies of Bryan and Harter, Swift, and Book interested others in investigating the acquisition of certain skills. Studies in this area were also reported by Judd on dart throwing and by Hicks and Carr on maze learning. These studies are well known and are used even today for documentation purposes (24). The studies of Thorndike in particular were the source of our first well-known laws of learning.

Another experimenter, historically famous, was Ebbinghaus, who studied the process of learning nonsense syllables. A little later his memory-span test was developed and included in many of the first intelligence scales.

Problem solving, so called, did not get much attention until the work of Köhler became familiar during the 1920's. These investigations encouraged child study dealing with learning and the factors related to learning.

Recent Studies. More recent studies of considerable current significance to teachers include the findings reported by Smith and Tyler in the eight-year investigation by the Progressive Education Association, in which problem solving was broken down into specific behavior patterns (32), and the studies of Anderson on dominative-integrative activities of teachers (1). Other significant works are the studies of Levin (19) and Lippitt (20) dealing with the effect on child behavior of the learning "climate."

A. LEARNING BY CONDITIONING

Influence on Behaviorist School. Conditioning is a form of learning first explored by Pavlov (27), later by Watson and the school of psychology called *behaviorism* (34). Pavlov found that a dog produces a salivary response when the ringing of a bell, at first sounded repeatedly before and during feeding, is substituted for the feeding. The behaviorist group studied such reactions as those of a child when he has had a series of experiences in touching various objects at the same time that an unpleasant buzz is sounded.

In general, educators are indifferent to conditioning as an effective way of learning. Nevertheless, it does have certain values. It deserves discussion here because it has potential negative effects of which teachers should be aware.

Advantages of Conditioning. Conditioning occupies two places of importance in modern educational thinking. 1. It is of considerable importance during infancy. At this stage of development the child cannot communicate and consequently he cannot be given rational explanations or directions as a guide for his behavior. Although there is an argument against the idea, it is generally regarded as desirable, for example, to condition children by warnings, fear of consequences, etc., against the dangers of a hot stove, sharp knives, high places, and other similar menaces to the inexperienced infant. It is wiser, and in the long run more beneficial, to arrange the child's environment so that unrealized danger is at a minimum. As the child matures, rational analysis and explanation can be increasingly employed in his training program.

2. Conditioning can enhance the development of deeper and more significant learnings and attitudes. Desirable conditioning may be brought about through interesting room decoration, pleasant lighting, and soundproof features, all of which contribute to the development of favorable attitudes toward school. Unquestionably the value of such factors is greatest when utilized in a program which approaches learning through the child's intellectual, social, and emotional interests (19). And finally, to the extent that desirable habits are developed through conditioning, they increase efficiency through routinized or automatic fundamental action. Children may be conditioned toward desirable social attitudes and placed more quickly in a state of readiness for high-level learning. The teacher who understands the possibilities in desirable conditioning may also protect children against negative conditioning, such as the development of inhibitions, fears, and complexes. A teacher will be careful to avoid unfavorable influences and will attempt to promote desirable conditioning through use of proper sensory stimuli.

Undesirable Effects. Some educators consider conditioning only as a preliminary to high-level learning; some consider it a dangerous technique for use in the classroom, since the child is unaware of the meaning of the situation and has neither choice nor opportunity for creative or self-motivated activity. This is true because responses are produced by stimuli under the control of the teacher. Conditioning can be cultivated intentionally as a mode of learning, at the expense of learning which stimulates the growth of self-direction and self-evaluation. The prewar schools of Germany and Italy made such use of conditioning. Routinized and automatic response was the rule, and rationalization and analysis the exception. In this manner it was possible to mold a youth group blindly responsive to the direction of the few in control.

Through pure ignorance of conditioning and of the way it works, there is a further potential evil in its usage. Some teachers are unaware of the stimulus for which they are responsible and of the ensuing response in children. A harsh voice, the assignment of tasks impossible of accomplishment, dictatorial attitudes, sink or swim types of examinations are only a few illustrations.

Conditions for Desirable Conditioning. Life, however, would be very difficult without the benefits of conditioning. Desirable and effective habits provide the tools for profiting from earlier experiences. These tools are automatic reactions which enable us to meet similar new situations when they appear. This pattern of behavior is valuable only insofar as it can be modified to meet new needs, is subject to revision, and does not become fixed.

B. LEARNING OF MOTOR AND RELATED SKILLS

Work of Ebbinghaus. The closing years of the nineteenth century witnessed vigorous attention to the learning of motor and related skills. The problem was not that of discovering the best way to promote learning, but rather the problem of the nature of the learning curve. Ebbinghaus had demonstrated earlier that memorization tests provided a means for discovering the curve of learning. Skill in manipulation also demonstrated a method whereby the learning process could be analyzed in an experimental situation.

Work of Bryan and Harter. Bryan and Harter studied this problem as it applied to sending and receiving telegraphic messages (6). From recorded results they plotted curves representing a period of several months. The curves indicated that progress was much more rapid at the beginning than during the later periods and that in terms of the units of measurement expenditure of time and effort produced a gradually diminishing return as the curve approached its maximum.

Conclusions from Early Research. Three points of their conclusions received considerable attention and discussion. (1) The learning curve is characterized in its rise by jumps or irregularities rather than by a smooth, even progression. (2) There are periods of no progress, during which the learning curve is horizontal. These periods are called *plateaus.* (3) The curve for an individual reaches a point where no further gain is made. This point is called the *physiological limit.*

Work of Swift and Book. Similar experiments in the acquisition of skill were reported by Swift (33) and Book (4). Attention was directed primarily to a study of temporary plateaus, their cause, and techniques by which they could be eliminated.

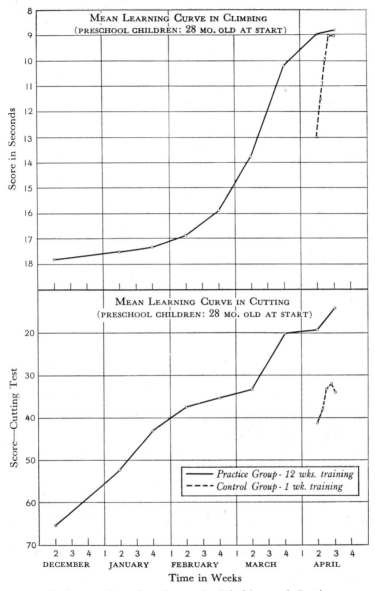

FIGURE 42. Learning Curves in Climbing and Cutting

Also of importance in this type of experimentation was the contribution of Book on *overlearning.* Ebbinghaus had demonstrated in his earlier findings that practice in memorizing beyond the point necessary for mastery slowed down the curve of forgetting. Book discovered also that overlearning resulted in more rapid relearning following an interval of nonpractice. The data seemed to demonstrate its value in the acquisition of skill.

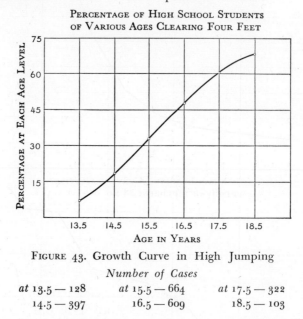

PERCENTAGE OF HIGH SCHOOL STUDENTS
OF VARIOUS AGES CLEARING FOUR FEET

FIGURE 43. Growth Curve in High Jumping

Number of Cases

at 13.5 — 128	*at* 15.5 — 664	*at* 17.5 — 322
14.5 — 397	16.5 — 609	18.5 — 103

As a result of the importance given to these early experiments, the pattern of the curve in various skills has been portrayed in nearly all books dealing with the psychology of learning. Because data in some instances, when graphed, showed a sharp initial rise, in contrast to other data which presented a slow beginning, the true shape of the learning curve has been debated (5). Only in recent years has it occurred to investigators of learning that maturity and age, as well as the difficulty of the task, were of prime importance in determining the picture of initial progress.

Well-known curves are those of Bryan and Harter (6) and of Book (4). More recent ones are those of Hilgard for climbing and for cutting (Fig. 42) and of Courtis for high jumping (Fig. 43 above).

Character of the Curve. In general, these curves are characterized by a slow beginning in the early stages of learning, a rapid rise during the middle stage, and deceleration as they approach their maximum. Occasionally, data do not follow this pattern. It is true that the particular character of the learning curve is affected by the developmental status, or maturity, of the learner (5). Nevertheless, the general nature of all learning curves is fundamentally the same. A rapid early rise is produced by data from a test that is too easy. In other words, curves that appear to begin without the typical slow start are probably constructed from data on tests that are relatively simple for the child at the period of maturity involved. The more mature children who begin to read early in the first grade show early rapid acceleration. Less mature children show the slow beginning first stage before demonstrating rapid acceleration.

In the cutting test of Hilgard (Fig. 43) and the receiving test of Bryan and Harter (6), there appears what conventionally has been called a plateau. The plateau is generally considered the result of a physiological limitation, or what Book calls the *critical stage* (4). It may, more than anything else, reflect a lessening of motivation or, in some instances, fatigue, or lack of interest in the task. The rise that follows it is conventionally regarded as the result of re-motivation.

Effect of Complexity. The growth explanation does not necessarily accept the idea of fatigue or lack of motivation but explains the result as an increase in the complexity of the task. The same type of effect would be produced if two lists of twenty-five words, one very easy and the other very difficult, were combined and given to children during the second, third, fourth, and fifth grades. During the early grades improvement would be continuous, since only the easier words would be learned, and the curve would appear to approach a maximum. In the later grades, as the more difficult words were learned, a new cycle of growth would appear (17).

Limitations in Early Generalizations. Curves of various skills merely reflect the nature and character of learning under specific conditions. They also point out how much more easily some skills are learned if they are adapted to the maturity of the child.

Faulty Implications of Early Studies. Studies of these curves have, however, led to faulty implications. Since the curves were usually based on short-time learnings they tended to influence curriculum makers to develop instructional programs in terms of short sequential skills. Spelling, for example, was measured each week in relation to the number of words assigned for the week. Short learning assignments implied drill, and the mastery "complex" became a fixture. Moreover, learning was attributed entirely to what went on in the classroom.

Longitudinal Studies Necessary. Exponents of the growth point of view regard learning in terms of an extended period of development and give credit to the general activity of the child, including of course what goes on in the classroom. The historically famous motor learning curves covering short learning periods have hinted as to the character of learning and its affective factors. Longitudinal and broad-learning data covering extensive periods of maturity of children give significant further assistance in understanding the way in which learning takes place and its relation to maturation. The later discussions will bring out these points.

C. MEMORIZATION

Characteristics of Memorization. Memorization is similar to learning by conditioning, in that time and repetition are common factors involved. It is unlike conditioning, in that such subjective aspects of individuality as goal, motivation, etc., are accorded greater freedom and are less under the control of the teacher, parent, society, or the person guiding the learner's behavior. The child may appear to react mechanically in learning to spell a word or in learning the multiplication tables. Nevertheless he is reacting with a total organization affected by purpose, amount of fatigue, interest, fear, and other subjective elements. And further, memorization is quite different from conditioning in that the child is aware of what he is attempting to learn.

Early Studies. The 1880's marked the first systematic studies of memory. Before this time the work done had been fragmentary. Some animal experimentation had been undertaken to determine whether such behavior was instinctive or learned, but in the main there was a dearth of material on general principles. Although psychologists were concerned with the problem of learning versus forgetting, there was no work in quantitative terms. The problem of "how much" or "how little" had not yet presented itself.

It was at this period that Ebbinghaus first published his findings. Naturally, his work received great attention. His results, probably, may be regarded as the first scientific contributions to a broad psychological problem which was not merely a part of a physiological study.

Influence of Ebbinghaus. The first aspect of his contribution was the adoption of statistical techniques. He applied these in measuring, by amount of variability from the mean, thereby giving meaning to his data. Utilizing such techniques, he may be credited as introducing in psychology that evaluative criteria which are expressed in terms of averages and probable errors. Another aspect of his contribution was the uniqueness of his selection of nonsense syllables as the means of experimentation. He thereby sidestepped the problem involved when words or phrases, which have meaning, are used.

Ebbinghaus undertook several problems all of which encouraged further similar study and research. One of the first was to determine the number of readings necessary for memorization when the length of the list of syllables was increased. He discovered that as many as seven or eight syllables could be learned in one reading, but when it was necessary to learn nine, ten, or eleven, a considerable number of additional readings were required. This experiment has frequently been described as the first systematic study of what we call *memory span.*

A second problem faced by Ebbinghaus was to ascertain the effect of repeated readings after the individual had mastered the list. This has already been referred to as *overlearning.* The technique was also responsible for new psychological terminology. In this instance, the term *savings method* was introduced. Ebbinghaus attempted to measure the number of additional readings required to rehabilitate what had once been mastered. Stated more specifically, if twenty repetitions are required to learn a given list of syllables, how many *more* repetitions would be required to retain the list for twenty-four hours? Briefly, he reported that the ratio approximated a straight-line relationship. Using nonsense material, the number of repetitions "saved" was roughly one third of the repetitions used in overlearning (24).

Of more interest to teachers was a third problem. This problem could be stated as whether a specific amount of time given to learning is more effectively used all at once, or whether it is more effective when broken into shorter periods with intervening rest periods. His results indicated that spaced learning periods were decidedly more effective and to be preferred.

In these experiments, both the early and the more recent (14), the general form of the curve of forgetting is consistently similar. It is characterized by a rapid loss at the beginning, followed by a slowing down of the loss rate, and finally culminating in a plateau representing the amount "permanently" learned. The various experiments dealing with learning verbal material, ideas, poetry, and motor skills, all demonstrate considerable uniformity. It is generally concluded that in every approach to learning something of the total amount learned is retained. Nevertheless, it is also true that because the rates of learning and the amounts retained all vary so much, the efficiency of any repetitive exercise must be determined under the conditions in which it takes place. Every teacher has had the experience of discovering that in learning certain materials, repetition is often desirable and necessary. In certain other situations, repetition and drill should be minimized.

General Principle for Effective Drill. In the main, teachers are more likely to overdrill than underdrill. Consequently certain dangers should be pointed out, particularly for this group. (1) It is not the act of repetition that produces learning. The primary purpose of drill is to provide a situation favorable to selecting the correct response. In many learning situations, review and drill make possible a filling in of detail which is incomplete at the time of a first response. And it must be remembered that relationships, meanings, and enrichment are the goals to be sought. Drill and repetition are a means to an end which is not mere verbalism but understanding. (2) Repetition and drill in many instances have been greatly overdone. Schools which emphasize drill may lose sight of the fact that mere memorization and retention of factual material is less important than understanding and applying what is learned. It must be remembered also that there is a point beyond which further practice brings boredom, loss of objective, and fatigue. A great improvement in the effectiveness of learning in the elementary school can be brought about through reduction of boresome drill and repetitive effort. Repetition, however, under favorable conditions can contribute much in the higher approaches to learning.

D. PROBLEM SOLVING

Research has been carried out on problem solving, but at the present time little is known about it or how it takes place (5). It must be admitted that much has been discovered about certain of its aspects, such as how children attack problems, the role of trial and error, the relation of insight to the solution of a problem, and the effect of chronological age and sex (35).

Knowledge of how it takes place has eluded investigators because of its complexity. Problem solving takes place at a much higher psychological level than learning by memorizing or by conditioning. In problem solving the climax is reached when a specific attainment or goal is achieved through the discovery of a relationship, the making of a generalization, the application of a principle, or what has been described by the Gestalt group of psychologists as achieving *insight*. All sorts of schemes and devices have been developed to investigate this problem. The earlier techniques and materials were similar to those of Thorndike and others who had studied the problem by using animals as subjects.

Trial and Error. In problem solving a typical method used is that of trial and error. In situations where the relations between elements in the solution are not readily apparent, the child uses trial and error, perhaps assisted by such devices as attempting to verbalize relationships (24). Children need more trials and make more errors than adults, but their reasoning and thinking processes are similar to those of adults. Reliance upon trial is justified, as are errors. However the solution to a problem will never be found through "blind" trial and error. It will be reached only if the individual knows what he is looking for and is mature and experienced enough to recognize it when it results.

Insight frequently occurs in problem solving, and the problem is immediately understood. Moriya reports on the ability of kindergarten children to achieve insight involving the use of a lever (23). It was discovered, however, that only the older children evidenced this trait. In an experiment with older children, Peterson reported that insight was demonstrated when the new situation contained some aspect of a problem which was already familiar to them (28).

Application of Principle. Another way of arriving at the solution of a problem is to discover and apply a principle. When a problem is solved in this manner it is conventionally referred to as *generalization.* Verbalization plays an important role in the solution of such problems. Pyles found in an experiment that verbalization is very helpful and also that the more familiar the material, the more rapidly the problem is solved (30). He found that when children were given names for unnamed forms which covered a few toys, learning was much quicker than when the molds were unnamed. Monroe similarly concluded that success is more readily achieved when problems are constructed in terms of the child's everyday life (22).

Problem solving apparently is not part and parcel of conventional classroom activity. In a review of the literature, Munn states that a large percentage of seventh-grade children failed to reason in solving problems in arithmetic. He claimed that problems were solved through use of patterned behavior rather than through reasoning. In a like investigation, where geometry was the subject involved, only thirty-two per cent of the college students in the experiment gave evidence of real insight into the problem. In the 285 test situations furnishing data for the study, responses of "Oh, I see" were very infrequent, occurring but seventeen times in all (24). Munn reports like results in a social science class in which learning curves were plotted in terms of the various elements learned. High school seniors showed a very slow rise. It was thought that the tests emphasized the solution of logical problems and were designed to measure development and application of principle. Nevertheless, there was little evidence of utilization of thought processes higher than pure memorizing.

Such a condition is probably due to the traditional organization of subject matter and the method by which it has been taught. A serious question can be raised regarding whether such subject-

matter experiences in mathematics, language, and science train
the mind in clear and precise thinking. There appears to be little
evidence that the simple-to-complex order of teaching science and
mathematics has any true similarity to the thinking processes used
in the attempt to solve a life problem. Scientists and others have
pointed out that their own thought processes in the solution of a
problem are disorderly and unsystematic and at times utterly out
of harmony with what we have called logical thinking.

Characteristics of Problem Solving. In the first place, thinking or
problem solving must be considered an instrument for promoting
action at all levels of maturity. In such a concept, thinking is a universal activity. Thinking so considered is a means to an end rather
than an end in itself. One may stop to think when making a decision between two alternatives, when faced by an obstacle, or when
solving a financial problem. Real problem solving is not produced
in a vacuum. It cannot be taught without the opportunity for action. This leads one to conclude that the effectiveness of learning
parallels the realness of the situation faced by the learner.

Part of Total Organismic Action. The second characteristic of
problem solving is its relationship to other approaches to learning.
Thinking does not occur without memory learning, motor learning, or conditioning. Nor is it an accomplishment of only one aspect of individuality. Thinking is a part of the total behavior of
the individual. In other words, problem solving is an aspect of the
total process of adjustment to life's various situations.

The relationship of thinking to the "whole child" is demonstrated by the evidence regarding the bodily change that takes
place during the process. Such evidence includes changes in pulse,
respiration, psychogalvanic reflex,[2] and other physiological accompaniments to thinking. Evidence is also available that speech
and expressive movements, mainly among children, accompany
the solution of a problem.

Problems, both simple and complex, present themselves at all
stages of the individual's maturity. In the lives of young children
thinking accompanies simple play, construction, and creative activity. Individuals acting alone and groups working or playing

---

[2] A momentary decrease in the apparent electrical resistance of the skin, resulting
from activity of the sweat glands in response to exciting stimuli.

together have problems to solve. In the later childhood years, language and symbols become dominant and to a considerable extent replace the earlier motor accompaniments. During these years children use generalizations in arriving at solutions. During and after adolescence problems become more definitive and more complex. Suggestions, experimentation, inference, and generalization play an expanding role as the individual matures. The culmination of problem solving is prediction with verification, as far as circumstances permit, through actual trial.

Certain implications of the research have considerable meaning for teachers. These points have been touched in the discussion but need further emphasis.

1. Thinking does not take place in a vacuum, nor does it function effectively apart from the needs of the individual. Neither does it operate mechanically under general rules which enable the individual to think clearly in all kinds of situations and problems. Each situation has its own peculiar aspects and requires a specific type of attack. It must be remembered that beyond certain habits of action, children do not learn to generalize. The social and physical sciences may have the common objective of teaching children to interpret data and to draw generalizations, but they provide different approaches. Consequently, sufficient diversity in the curriculum is essential in solving varied and multiple problems.

2. Thinking, or problem solving of a particular kind, requires a background of information related to the problem at hand. Readiness in solving a problem depends considerably on such a background. Here is found the aspect of transfer of identical elements. This should not be interpreted to mean that familiarizing the child with the elements of successful problem solving can come about through memorizing or learning discrete aspects of the situation. Success in problem solving depends on previous successes in problem solving.

3. Problem solving must, to a considerable degree, be based on a real and felt problem. Thinking is rare in the conventional disciplinary type of classroom because most of the problems are but the *materials* of problem solving. The successful teacher will adjust the curriculum to meet the needs, interests, and maturities of

the children. Adult or hypothetical problems create much boredom, particularly when combined with overemphasis on rote learning. Getting or learning the facts is not enough. Facts are only the means to the end.

TEACHING VERSUS MATURATION

Up to this point there has been little emphasis on the role played by the teacher in the learning situation. It is the purpose of this section to point out certain relationships implied in the foregoing discussion.

A. THE EFFECT OF PRESSURE TEACHING

Many people believe that better learning results when a certain amount of "pressure" is applied and children are induced to spend more time on their school work. It is true that learning curves respond to efforts of this kind. In a situation where longitudinal data were maintained overlearning and incidental learning were organized. One of the most interesting was conducted in the fifth grade in spelling. Available data provided group learning curves covering grades one, two, three, and four, and data were collected during and in the years following the experiment (Fig. 44).

The experiment lasted for about four months mainly during the winter. Contests, games, rewards, holidays were utilized. The scores of the children continued to rise until they reached ninth-grade standards. After each testing, results were announced and the children were encouraged to better their scores for the next testing. No child was punished in any way nor made to feel badly if other children had higher scores. Each child was assured that he contributed his share if his score was better than his last score. Improvement alone was the basis on which the teacher gave rewards.

After the time prescribed for the experiment had passed, the children reverted to their regular spelling period three times a week. Fifth-grade lists were resumed, and the program went on as it had before the experiment. The nature of the curve following the experiment is highly significant. Within two months much of the excess gain had been lost and in the year following the pattern of emerging growth was almost exactly an extension of the pattern established before the experiment.

The curve dropped rapidly because the children were merely memorizing. The words that they memorized in reality had little meaning. They were not necessarily used in the child's daily

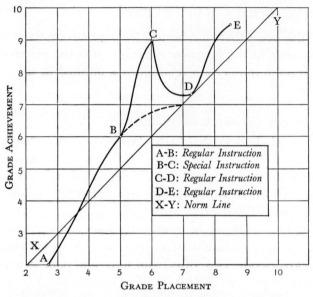

FIGURE 44. The Effect of Overlearning in Spelling

This figure shows:
  1. The loss following special instruction (C–D)
  2. No carry-over of special instructional effects
  3. Resumption of initial pattern of growth (D–E)

speech and they were not a part of his reading vocabulary. Of significance also is the fact that the growth pattern previously established was again picked up when the extra pressure, rewards, and other extraneous motivations were withdrawn.

B. INCIDENTAL LEARNING

In an accompanying experiment in spelling, a procedure somewhat in reverse was instituted for a group of children in the fourth grade. A curve was constructed from longitudinal data gathered while these children were in grades one, two, and three. Through-

out the course of the fourth grade the "three-days-a-week" sequence in spelling was entirely eliminated. Tests were given during the experiment, and records were graphed.

No attempt was made to teach spelling in other classes. The
time previously used was given over to other subjects, but no fur-

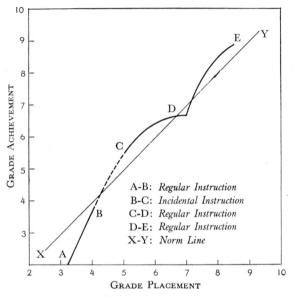

FIGURE 45. The Effect of Incidental Instruction on
the Growth Curve in Spelling

This figure shows:
   1. Continuation of learning curve without formal
      instruction (B–C)
   2. Continuation of initial pattern after formal in-
      struction is resumed (C–D)

ther changes were made in the school program. The results were
most astonishing (Fig. 45). The curve maintained its previous
progress. No loss whatever was discovered.

The explanation for such a happening might be that the instruction was so poor in the first place that its elimination caused
no particular handicap. The kind of teaching certainly differed
from that used in the earlier experiment, where children were induced to make gains beyond normal expectations. To direct efforts toward spelling goals that lack adaptations for use and mean-

ing, which was done in the first experiment, would certainly not be recommended by anyone interested in the welfare of children. On the other hand, to eliminate spelling as such would perhaps require more courage and confidence than could be inspired by the results described. While the results of the experiment do not suggest that spelling should be eliminated, they do suggest that the kind of teaching procedure conventionally used is probably wasteful and inefficient. Of even greater significance is the suggestion that what the child learns is a product of much more than what happens in the specific teacher-pupil contact devoted to a given teaching period. Children learn to spell through their school reading activities, through their home reading activities, through their developing vocabularies, written and spoken, and through their increasing knowledge of the meaning of words.

As in spelling, it is probable that similar relationships exist between instruction and other growth-learning curves. Such a concept forms the psychological basis for the idea of the community school. Learning is a full-time activity of the child. It is likely that as this thought is fully explored and implemented in school curricula, instruction will become more and more of an activity toward enriching the environment which provides the motivation for learning, and less and less of a teacher-motivated activity toward developing skills in narrow, specific learning areas (3).

C. SPECIAL EFFECTS

The most marked permanent effect on a learning curve that extends throughout the school years is the effect of adolescence, which produces a permanent shift in the pattern of learning. Where data are collected from test results which impose no restriction on the maximum,[3] a rate of learning emerges which is considerably increased over the preadolescent rate. The teacher should be warned that longitudinal data with certain standardized tests do not demonstrate this point. These tests limit the more competent children in their adolescent maxima to a mere token expression of their full potentialities. Where adequate tests are used longitudinally, the effect of adolescence is most marked.

The implication of such an effect is almost completely ignored

---

[3] Some standardized tests are so easy for certain children that they are unable to demonstrate their maximum capacity and ability.

or misunderstood. Where teaching is looked upon as effective causation, the situation develops about as follows. In the sixth grade, achievement scores frequently show no gain; they sometimes show losses. Supervisors and administrators are critical and may feel that the teaching during this period has been ineffective or poor. The teacher accepts responsibility and is also concerned about the matter. In the seventh grade the same child shows considerable gain. The teacher is happy over the results, is envied by the sixth-grade teacher, and receives the commendations of her principal and supervisors.

Actually, teaching has had but little direct effect in either instance. The child in the sixth grade is normally approaching a maximum and at this time will show little or no gain. Since this is the time of instability in performance, he is just as likely to show a loss. If his maturity is average, his seventh-grade efforts will gain him much favor. Scores will increase and he will proceed toward a second maximum simply because of his maturity status. *Adolescence with its organic changes, other factors being constant, will, in and by itself, produce desirable changes in the learning curve.*

D. REMEDIAL INSTRUCTION

In view of the relationship between learning and maturation, one may well question the importance of remedial instruction. Will special remedial attention help the child who is progressing slowly? Most teachers believe that it will. Nevertheless, there is evidence that much remedial instruction is needless, most of it ineffective, and some of it harmful.

Early Cross-sectional Studies. Much of the evidence in favor of remedial instruction is based on cross-sectional data. As has been pointed out previously, data so handled obscure many important facts about child development. In general educators have believed that a year of gain should be made in a given chronological year. If growth follows a curvilinear pattern, it is obvious that individual children deviate considerably from such a standard. In Figure 46 several types of reading growth are illustrated. What produces such differences? Certainly not the kind of instruction received. If there were any differentiation in terms of time and effort, it would favor those who performed at the lower levels.

The differences among these children dramatically underline

the instructional problem which the teacher must solve. Cases 25
and 28 at nine years of age are capable of handling materials several years beyond their grade placement (Fig. 46). Cases 16 and 14
represent the reverse situation. They need materials considerably

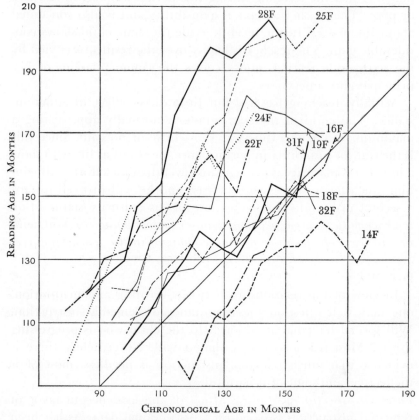

FIGURE 46. Differences in Reading Achievement (Girls)

below their current grade level. In such a situation a teacher who
is forced to utilize a specific grade-level course of study, books, or
curriculum, is totally unequipped to meet the needs of these four
pupils.

Solving the problem by promoting some and holding the others
back might appear to be a logical solution, but it is not.

In the cases shown in Figure 47, two children are progressing by
quite different routes and with varying grade-level achievements

toward equivalent maxima. Shuttling these two children back and forth in reference to grades would cause constant disruption. Assuming that thirty to forty children comprise the usual number in a grade there would be many instances where children would be promoted or would skip a grade and in some one grade year would be held back or even sent back a grade or two.

The assumption that a single standard rigidly applied eliminates differences is entirely a matter of wishful thinking. If status grouping in a given learning area were the only problem to be

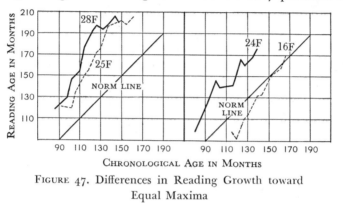

FIGURE 47. Differences in Reading Growth toward Equal Maxima

solved, it might be accomplished in spite of the difficulties enumerated. What complicates the problem beyond any conceivable solution of this kind is the fact that high achievement in one learning area may be accompanied by low achievement in some other. Moreover, there is the matter of social, emotional, and physical maturity as well as other kinds of differences.

Attempts have been made to solve the problem through remedial instruction. Many claims have been made and much data offered in validation. This writer agrees with general claims as to the immediate effect. It is possible to raise the scores of individuals under the special circumstances usually instituted under remedial conditions. He doubts, however, the permanence of such gains and questions whether they carry over into the period after remedial treatment is relinquished. Olson, too, states that he has been "unable to find trustworthy reports of durable gains in reading comprehension attributable to special approaches" (26).

An interesting study in reading, quite unlike the usual procedure, was made by Dunklin (10). In this experiment with first-grade children experimental and control groups were selected from the lowest third of scores on a learning-to-read test. Scores, age, sex, and school experience were taken into consideration, and on this basis the two groups were matched. The control group proceeded in the conventional manner, but the experimental group was handled quite differently. Each child was taught individually in respect to reading, and every effort was made to give each child a successful experience. No pressure was used, and each child literally progressed at his own rate. This group was approximately a grade ahead of the control group after a period of seven months. Whether this rate could be maintained was not answered, nor was there any study of the permanent effects. This study should be questioned as should the more conventional approaches to the problem. Dunklin reports change in score but does not report changes in the growth pattern of the children involved.

There is much literature filled with the records of remedial experiments, all tending to show the advantage of special attention. Olson challenges such data and points out that this kind of evidence is *not acceptable from the scientific point of view* (26) : His arguments are as follows:

1. The gains in beginning reading in a group of high readiness, select social status, and somewhat superior intelligence are compared with the gains of groups of average children as reported in norms.

2. The results obtained with children in experimental groups are compared directly with norms without regard to differences in the policy of classifying children. A group is obviously comparable to the norm only when random samples of children of the same age are being compared. Classification and promotion policies arbitrarily affect the composition of grades.

3. The percentage of boys and girls has been ignored. The writer recently visited a series of reading classes in the same room in a second grade in which the top group consisted of nine girls and two boys and the fourth or bottom group consisted of six boys. If the school had decided to keep those six boys back in the first grade, the average achievement would have been much changed.

The above statements imply that the claims regarding the effectiveness of remedial instruction may or may not be true. There is a great need for the development of special methods to ascertain whether such changes as are noted are permanent. In this connection it is safe to say that only to the extent that special learning effects are related to maturity, environmental motivation, and the needs of the organism, can they result in permanently improved rates of learning and growing.

A second criticism of remedial instruction and one most frequently pertinent is the lack of necessity for much of what is done. In the elementary school a higher percentage of remedial attention is given to children who are hovering around the beginning point of a curve of learning. The result of efforts regarded as successful cannot be differentiated from learning which *might* have occurred without the benefit of special attention. Wide differences in the ages at which children begin to learn the various skills are a challenge to action. Such differences are regarded as an unnatural phenomenon, and the children who are late in beginning to learn are considered proper subjects for remedial attention. When given special help these children may respond satisfactorily enough to present rather convincing results. Because some of them were about ready to react anyway without extra consideration, conclusions are exaggerated. In many instances the results attributed to special methods would have occurred without the use of such methods.

This kind of error is frequently made, and its solution is not simple. There is no method of determining whether remedial attention is effective, except in terms of the child's own growth pattern. Where rate is changed and stays changed, the difference in rate may be attributed to the special effect which was utilized. Where remedial attention is directed toward change in cases where growth has not yet occurred, it is wasteful and harmful. Remedial attention can correctly be applied only where growth has already started. Attention previous to this stage of maturation should be of an experiencing and enriching nature and should not be regarded as a special remedial effort or procedure. Such a thought challenges the whole concept of remedial attention as it is conventionally regarded. It would appear that even where the learning curve has been fairly well established, if special attention is to be given, it should have as its objective enriching experiences in the total situation rather than a spurious, temporary, specific change unrelated to social, environmental, and other stimuli. Broad-area learning as described so frequently of late seems justified and able to handle the problem of diversified abilities (8) .

Treats Symptom Rather than Cause. A third criticism may be directed toward the practice of treating the symptom, rather than the cause, of a given disability or retardation. This is the case particularly where children are clearly overdue in reference to reasonable expectations. Children in the fourth, fifth, and sixth grades who are intelligent enough but read or achieve otherwise at first- or second-grade levels are representative of this group. Such children usually do not need remedial instruction. Their reading incapacity is usually only a symptom of their real difficulty. Robinson reports that children seriously retarded show significantly more than the normal emotional, social, physical, and mental difficulties, and perhaps of even greater significance, a slower pattern of maturation (31) .

THE SOCIAL CLIMATE IN RELATION TO LEARNING

Lippitt's Study. Comenius, Pestalozzi, Kilpatrick, Dewey, and hosts of others have stressed the value of the proper social climate in learning. It has remained, however, for Lewin, Lippitt, and a few others, working at the University of Iowa, to demonstrate convincingly the relation between various types of social organization and broad fundamental learnings carried in one of their studies with a group of ten- and eleven-year-old children (20) . The purpose of the study was to compare the effect of various types of social relationships upon the behavior of these children. After considerable deliberation the three types of social settings selected were categorized as (1) autocratic, (2) *laissez-faire,* and (3) democratic. The study was organized so that all the children had six weeks of experiences under each of the three types, the teachers changing their roles according to the kind of situation under which they were working. In the main, the learning activities consisted of construction tasks and involved little of the so-called achievement learnings.

The role of the teachers under each of the categories may be described summarily as follows:

Autocratic: The teachers in this instance were not of the extreme kind. They made assignments, gave directions, and assumed full control of the activity. Praise and blame were distributed as they saw fit. They were not unfriendly.

Democratic: The teachers in this category became participating members of the group. The group was fully cooperative, accepting the teachers' suggestions or feeling free to reject them. The teachers did make suggestions in an objective and impersonal way as the project progressed. Planning, generalizing, and judging was a group responsibility and was so carried out.

Laissez-faire: In this instance the teachers were not members of the group, nor did they direct the project. The children did as they pleased, with assistance from the teachers only as it was requested.

Records were carefully kept of the entire experiment. Attitudes of the children toward each other and toward the teachers were carefully observed. Aggressions of the children toward each other were also recorded, as were indications of striving for social status, striving for teacher preference, and other behavior characteristics. *Democratic Climate Best.* In the main, the results were greatest in the democratic-cooperative setting (Fig. 48) . The children worked more carefully, had the greatest interest, made more suggestions, and in greater numbers finished the jobs they had started. In the autocratic setting the children reacted with resentment toward the "drive" furnished by the teachers to get work done according to schedule. Children made complaints against the *laissez-faire* teachers because of lack of direction and suggestions, and easy-goingness which allowed friction to develop among the group.

More Aggression under Autocratic Teachers. One of the outstanding results of this experiment is the evidence it produces that relations among the children parallel the relations of teachers to pupils. In the autocratic teacher-directed activity the children reacted in an aggressive way toward certain few members of the group. This is explained as the need for the children to vent expression on some inferior child because of the feeling of repression and aggression developed under this type of teaching.

Teachers who wonder if they have "pets" among the children

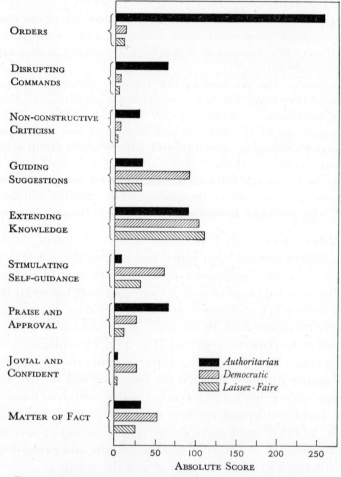

ORDERS

DISRUPTING
COMMANDS

NON-CONSTRUCTIVE
CRITICISM

GUIDING
SUGGESTIONS

EXTENDING
KNOWLEDGE

STIMULATING
SELF-GUIDANCE

PRAISE AND
APPROVAL

JOVIAL AND
CONFIDENT

MATTER OF FACT

■ *Authoritarian*
▨ *Democratic*
▧ *Laissez-Faire*

0   50   100   150   200   250
ABSOLUTE SCORE

FIGURE 48. Comparison of Behavior of Average Authoritarian, Democratic, and Laissez-Faire Leader

they teach will be interested in the contrasting ways in which the children in the experiment manifested their struggle for status. In the autocratic group more children definitely humbled themselves and became submissive in order to gain favor. More children also struggled for status by picking on other children. In the democratic groups there was much less of this kind of striving and there were more attempts to do the kind of job that pleased the entire group. Consequently, the cooperative activity fostered the most effective work and, undoubtedly, the greater security in the kind of social status achieved.

Further results of the *laissez-faire* teaching are likewise interesting, particularly for those who have considered "progressive education" as something similar to this kind of a teaching situation. In the first place, considerable tension was invoked by the absence of a plan. Children literally fell over each other. They interfered with each other, and consequently there was more aggressive activity when the children were in this group than in either of the other two. It is pointed out in the experiment, however, that when the autocratic teacher left the room the number of aggressive actions occurring was on a par with or greater than in the *laissez-faire* situation.

Social Climate Contrasts. For a long time, learning has been considered an acquisitional activity. The farther back we go in history, the stronger the acceptance of this point of view. In early days, learning and acquisition were entirely synonymous.

This point of view has become entrenched as a result of the concept that the goal of learning is the transmission of the social inheritance. In the early days this meant handing down to the younger generation the prejudices, feuds, and, on a more cultural level, the accumulated knowledge of the tribe. As civilization began to develop, responsibility for learning had to be given over to teachers. Parents became too busy with other duties, and teachers were obtained to impart the knowledge, skills, habits, customs, and ideals that the older generation regarded as essential. Through learning, then, the social heritage was "acquired" by the new generation.

Through the years cultural learnings emerged. These were given precedence in the teaching program over the skills of self-protection, knowledge of fighting, and preservation of the family, clan, or tribe. Since that time evaluative activities have directed curriculum programs away from personal and physical needs toward performance of a mental or intellectual nature. Because of the developing emphasis on intellectual tasks, learning in school became more and more of an activity deliberately severed from any connection with practical life activities. The school was given this function; the home, the church, etc., the others. As a result, learning in the conventional sense required evidence of memorizing and knowing. The criterion of the educated man became that of possessing certain information.

Learning as Acquisition. Some of the characteristics of such a point of view, when applied in the classroom, have emerged with considerable clarity. The following outline includes most of them (7) :

> *First:* Learning is classified as acquisition when
>   a. There is subject matter set out in advance of teaching as material to be learned.
>   b. The teacher's efforts are directed toward bringing children to a predetermined goal.
>   c. The emphasis is upon an outcome of possession, achievement, conformity.
>
> *Second:* Learning is to be classified as acquisition when the activities of the teacher consist of
>   a. Setting tasks
>   b. Giving reasons for the tasks set
>   c. Offering rewards for effort, and setting and administering penalties for lack of effort.
>
> *Third:* Other activities of the "acquisitional teacher" may be
>   a. Expressing sympathy or interest
>   b. Controlling order by issuing rules and disciplining offenders
>   c. Directing activity by commands or questions
>   d. Explaining points not understood
>   e. Setting models to be copied or followed
>   f. Doing things for pupils they cannot do for themselves
>   g. Hearing recitations based on repetitions of memorized materials
>   h. Drilling, reviewing, inspecting, and perfecting for no other obvious purpose than for perfection
>   i. Making and recording judgments of performance in relation to predetermined standards.

Depends on Autocratic Control. In this situation there is complete, or almost complete, domination by the teacher. The responsibility for what is learned, what is to be done in order to learn, how and when it is to be done, and whether or not it is done satisfactorily rests with the teacher alone. And teaching and its results are determined by subject-matter tests of knowledge and skill.

As a result of the progress of experimentation in learning, a reaction has been arising. This new view looks upon the child as a developing organism with inherent potentialities and looks upon his environment as the main base for the motivation of development toward those potentialities.

Learning as Growth. Teaching in relation to learning takes on a new role. It aims not at forcing the child to grow but at providing the conditions favorable for growth. Learning in the conventional sense is not disregarded. It shifts its position, however, to that of a means to an end rather than an end in itself. It is looked upon not as a passive or isolated activity but as something acquired from experiences which have meaning and value for the child. Teaching from this point of view should be evaluated not by what the child *knows* but rather by what he *becomes*. The following points are characteristic of the teacher in this kind of situation:

> *First:* Learning of academic facts is not a major outcome. The accumulation of knowledge is incidental to experience. This means that learning itself is a byproduct of experience, something growing "out of" rather than something "added to."
>
> *Second:* Learning is given a growth emphasis when the teacher's efforts are directed toward helping children either to have experiences or to profit from their experiences.
>
> *Third:* Subject matter is determined by the needs of the child as brought out and made clear through experience.
>
> *Fourth:* The teacher stimulates realization of purposes by presentation of objects, situations, or opportunities.
>
> *Fifth:* The activity of the teacher includes guiding purposes to higher levels which will result in action and changed behavior.
>
> *Sixth:* Other activities of the teacher are those which:
> a. Provide restimulation and guidance
> b. Overcome fears and inhibitions
> c. Express sympathy and interest
> d. Point out successes
> e. Explain difficulties

f. Aid in solving conflicts, disputes, etc.

g. Call attention to unnoticed problems, supply materials, references, etc.

The contrast between the two viewpoints implies that a teacher may be representative of one group but not of the other in his conduct of the learning situation. Teachers would be less con-

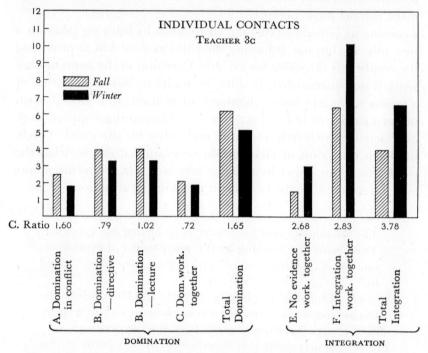

FIGURE 49. Illustration of Shift in Teaching Activity from Dominative to Integrative Relationship

fused by this contrast, when they try to identify their own practices or attempt to reflect the growth point of view exclusively, if they would realize that nearly all teaching includes both kinds of activity. Good teaching merely requires a gradual, constant shift toward the growth viewpoint.

No one has illustrated this point any better than Anderson in his study of dominative versus integrative classroom climates (Fig. 49).

This figure illustrates a shifting from dominative to integrative contacts with children. Such a shift is interpreted by Anderson as follows (1):

> . . . the changes can be said to be consistently in the direction of improvement from the standpoint of the mental-hygiene assumptions: (a) Significantly more total integrative contacts in the winter sampling, (b) Consistently lower frequencies of total domination and of each of the types of individual domination, (c) Decrease in A contacts and increase in F contacts. The mental-hygiene quotient for individual contacts rose from 2.56 in the fall sampling to 5.63 in the winter. (d) Higher frequencies of F than of E or of A, (e) Change from D–I [4] ratios from 1.59 in the fall to 0.78 for the winter.[5]

The point to be made is that the *growth* concept of Courtis, the *democratic* concept of Lippitt, and the *integrative* definition of Anderson agree to a large extent on the implications for effective learning. Whereas one points out the improvement in mental hygiene, the other emphasizes more natural learning, and the third underlines the development of freedom and self-direction. All of these are factors related to good learning.

From these points of view, attention is shifted from the teacher as a drill master to the child as a living, purposive, growing organism. The teacher is a counselor rather than a person who sets tasks and maintains order. Instead of being a passive listener the child is an active participant in planning, executing, and evaluating. Such is the modern concept of the classroom as a place for effective learning.

Education based on a continuing reconstruction of the total social and individual experience through purposeful activity cannot ignore the kind of learning that is most helpful in developing the child in something other than academic matters. According to this point of view, the nature and sequence of learning activities are those which best adapt the individual to meet the needs of his sociocultural environment.

[4] Key to letters:
    A — domination
    F — integration with working together
    E — integration with no working together
    D–I — dominative-integrative
[5] From *Child Behavior and Development,* edited by Barker, Kounin, and Wright, 1943. Courtesy of McGraw-Hill Book Company.

SELECTED REFERENCES

1. ANDERSON, H. H., "Dominative and Socially Integrative Behavior," *Child Behavior and Development,* edited by R. G. Barker, J. S. Kounin, and H. F. Wright: McGraw-Hill, 1943, p. 477.

2. BAHRICK, H. P., "Incidental Learning under Two Incentive Conditions," *Journal of Experimental Psychology,* 47:170–172, March, 1954.

3. BROWN, GEORGE, "Factors Influencing Incidental Learning," *Journal of Experimental Psychology,* 47:163–169, March, 1954.

4. BOOK, W. F., *The Psychology of Skill.* New York: Gregg, 1925.

5. BRUCE, W. F., AND FREEMAN, F. S., *Development and Learning.* Boston: Houghton Mifflin, 1942.

6. BRYAN, W. L., AND HARTER, N., "Studies in the Psychology of the Telegraphic Language," *Psychological Review,* 4:27–53, 1897.

7. COURTIS, S. A. (from unpublished material)

8. BRUNER, J. S., MATTER, JEAN, AND PAPANEK, M. L., "Breadth of Learning as a Function of Drive Level and Mechanization," *Psychological Review,* 62:1–10, January, 1955.

9. BURTON, W. H., *The Guidance of Learning Activities: A Summary of the Principles of Teaching Based Upon the Growth of the Learner.* New York: Appleton-Century-Crofts, 1953.

10. DUNKLIN, H. T., *The Prevention of Failure in First-Grade Reading.* New York: Teachers College, Columbia University, 1940.

11. BUSWELL, M. M., "The Relationship between the Social Structure of the Classroom and the Academic Success of the Pupils," *Journal of Experimental Education,* 22:37–52, September, 1953.

12. CALVIN, A. D., "The Growth of Learning During Non-Differential Reinforcement," *Journal of Experimental Psychology,* 46:254–284, October, 1953.

13. DEUTSCH, MORTON, "Social Relations in the Classroom and Grading Procedures," *Journal of Educational Research,* 45:145–152, 1951.

14. HARTMANN, G. W., *Educational Psychology.* New York: American Book Company, 1941.

15. GIBSON, J. J. AND E. J., "Perceptual Learning: Differentiation or Enrichment?", *Psychological Review,* 62:32–41, January, 1955.

16. MIEL, ALICE, *Co-operative Procedures In Learning,* New York: Teachers College, Columbia University, Bureau of Publications, 1952.

17. SALTZMAN, I. J., "The Orienting Task in Incidental and Intentional Learning," *American Journal of Psychology,* 66:593–597, October, 1953.

18. SCHUESSLER, KARL, AND STRAUSS, ANSELM, "A Study of Concept Learning by Scale Analysis," *American Sociological Review,* 15:752–762, 1950.

19. LEWIN, K., "Field Theory and Experiment in Social Psychology: Concepts and Methods," *American Journal of Sociology,* 44:868–896, 1939.

20. LIPPITT, R., *An Experimental Study of the Effect of Democratic and*

Authoritarian Group Atmospheres. Iowa City: University of Iowa Studies on Child Welfare, Vol. 16, No. 3, 1940.

21. SIGEL, I. E., "Developmental Trends in the Abstraction Ability of Children," *Child Development,* 24:131–144, June, 1953.

22. MONROE, W. S., "How Pupils Solve Problems in Arithmetic," *University of Illinois Bulletin,* 26:438–442.

23. MORIYA, M., "An Observation of Problem-Solving Behavior in Pre-School Children, Application of the Principle of a Lever," *Japanese Journal of Experimental Psychology,* 4:63–81, 1937.

24. MUNN, L. N., "Learning in Children," *Manual of Child Psychology,* edited by Leonard Carmichael. New York: Wiley, 1946.

25. STRAUSS, ANSELM, AND SCHUESSLER, KARL, "Socialization, Logical Reasoning, and Concept Development In the Child," *American Sociological Review,* 16:514–523, 1951.

26. OLSON, W. C., "How Children Grow," *Journal of the National Education Association,* 36:436–437, 1947.

27. PAVLOV, I. P., "Innervation der Magendrüsen beim Hunde," *Centrabl. Physiol.,* 3:113–114, 1890.

28. PETERSON, G. M., "An Empirical Study of the Ability to Generalize," *Journal of Genetic Psychology,* 6:90–114, 1932.

29. POWERS, F. P., "General Aspects of Learning," *Elementary Educational Psychology,* edited by C. E. Skinner. Prentice-Hall, 1945.

30. PYLES, M. K., "Verbalization as a Factor in Learning," *Child Development,* 3:108–113, 1932.

31. ROBINSON, HELEN M., *Why Pupils Fail in Reading.* Chicago: University of Chicago Press, 1946.

32. SMITH, E. R., AND TYLER, R. W., *Appraising and Recording Student Progress.* New York: Harper, 1942.

33. SWIFT, E. J., "Studies in the Psychology and Physiology of Learning," *American Journal of Psychology,* 14:201–251, 1903.

34. WATSON, J. B., AND RAYNER, R., "Conditioned Emotional Reactions," *Journal of Experimental Psychology,* 3:1–14, 1920.

35. THORNDIKE, ROBERT L., "How Children Learn the Principles and Techniques of Problem-Solving," *Learning and Instruction, Forty-ninth Yearbook of the National Society for the Study of Education.* Part I, Chapter VIII, 1950.

36. THORPE, L. P., AND SCHMULLER, A. M., *Contemporary Theories of Learning: With Application to Education and Psychology.* New York: Ronald Press, 1954.

PART III:

CONCOMITANTS OF GROWTH AND LEARNING

11

THE ROLE OF EMOTION IN
CHILD DEVELOPMENT

JUSTIFICATION FOR STUDY

The role of emotion in child development is much more complex than, for example, the normal physical growth of a child, his growing motor coordination, or even mental development or language growth. Both teacher and parent are able to observe clearly growth in height or weight, or to see that a child is becoming more competent in his play, or that his language and sentence structure are developing normally. Emotional characteristics are harder to understand. Feelings of pleasure or displeasure, the reasons for excitement and joy, fears, and sullen attitudes are frequently a cause for great concern. Feelings and emotions exhibit no standard maturational pattern. They are entirely inner and personal, but not thereby better understood by the individual. It is true that there are observable signs of emotional feelings. Facial expressions, laughter, crying, and other physical and physiological manifestations are noticeable. However, they provide little in the way of clues to their cause and their structure. Teachers frequently wonder whether affective feeling is primarily induced by inherited patterns of growth or by the cultural surroundings of the child (44). It shall be the purpose of this chapter to discuss these important questions.

A. THE JOB OF THE TEACHER

The emotional behavior manifested by children in any classroom is quite as important as their achievement in reading, their spelling ability, and their scores on standardized tests. Children show any number and variety of ways of behaving in order to relieve tensions. All teachers are familiar with such demonstrations as temper tantrums, fighting, aggressive action, daydreaming, shyness, and withdrawal. There is a growing belief that it is the responsibility of the teacher to recognize the significance of these, to trace out their causes, to determine what produces such behavior, how it is learned, and to teach children to find more mature and more appropriate avenues of expression (30). This is, of course, a difficult problem and one that will exhaust all possible facilities in its solution.

In the past, teachers and school officials have been concerned primarily with helping children acquire knowledge and skill in fundamental school subjects. There is a trend today toward recognizing as equally important the job of diagnosing and treating inappropriate patterns of emotional behavior. According to this concept, the teacher has not completely fulfilled her responsibility if her motive is merely that of making learning more effective. One of her basic goals must be a more effective realization of personal needs. In this sense guidance takes priority over instructional demands. Properly handled the two do not necessarily conflict. Learning what is needed is not necessarily difficult when children are given the proper motivation and the correct orientation (45). And further, learning is facilitated rather than handicapped when the child's emotional needs are given consideration as they arise in the learning situation. Emotions may enhance or weaken the opportunity for learning. In this sense the two functions go hand in hand. Trying to understand emotional behavior does not necessarily mean that the teacher is taking time away from instructional activity. Rather, it is the base and the beginning point for the most effective teaching.

The study of the child's emotional behavior is an important consideration in evaluating his total life pattern. Schools rather commonly check on physical defects, dental caries, and other products of faulty backgrounds. They should also look into the emerging patterns of children's emotional behavior (7).

Cannot Be Attacked Directly. The problem of identification and treatment is much more difficult than it is in some of the more familiar areas (6). The task is not approached directly, for instance. One cannot force an individual child or adult to abandon consciously one mode of behavior for another. Emotional affectation is frequently the product of a reaction long since forgotten. The individual does not know why he responds as he does. Forcing merely diverts the reaction into other avenues of expression. In such instances, new outlets are found and new behavior anomalies appear. Effective treatment requires a much more subtle approach. Much knowledge of the child's background and orientation to his total behavior is required. What personality needs are being blocked? How can needs be met? How can new, more appropriate patterns be encouraged? These questions and many others must be answered by those who assume responsibility for the child.

B. STUDY NECESSARY FOR COMPLETE UNDERSTANDING OF THE CHILD

A final argument for studying the emotions can be based on the fact that the child as an individual cannot be completely understood without some knowledge of his emotional behavior patterns (34). Emotion affects performances of all kinds. It is closely related to the quality of personal-social development, as well as to language development and to the continuity of the academic learning curve. Its effect on mental growth and on motor coordination has likewise been demonstrated.

Poor performance in school is usually blamed on ineffective teaching or on defective mental capacity. Studies of children's emotional behavior are beginning to show that poor performance is often tied up with emotional problems. Sound educational diagnosis today demands as much attention to the child's emotional reactions as it does to the mental and the academic (2).

DEFINITION

A. MANY CONCEPTS EXIST

An illustration of the complexity of emotion may be found in the fact that there is no great unanimity as to its meaning nor much agreement as to its role in the dynamic aspects of child development. Emotion is used almost synonymously with such concepts as feelings, needs, prejudices, and impulses. Confusion results from the fact that the various emotions do not present separate and distinguishing reaction patterns that would make them readily observable and open to study.

A current definition describes emotion as that feeling which goes beyond the general mild level of pleasantness or unpleasantness and which involves sensory perceptions and visceral change (42). Feelings are generally elicited by inner or outer stimuli, but they in turn may form a future pattern which encourages persistent response. As a result, there is some tendency to regard emotion as the cause of behavior, the driving force for the dynamics of personality (53).

The acceptance of the definition stated above implies that emotion represents a complex interaction between the child's physical-social environment and his organic being. This viewpoint does not accept emotion as innate nor as a reaction produced by maturation alone.

Emotion at one time was considered in the same general category as instinct and mind. Such a classification gave it a generic background. This is a faulty view and represents a tendency to forego research on its actual source and structure. Such investigators as McDougall, Watson, Allport, and Gates felt that the real meaning of emotion could be established only by ascertaining its characteristics before environmental pressures had the opportunity to condition it or divert it from its original tendencies. McDougall, who believed that instincts were inborn attempted to relate emotions to them. He advocated the idea that each instinct has an emotional counterpart. For example, he claimed that combat, which was one of his specified instincts, was accompanied by anger (37).

Watson's Categories. Also in considerable disagreement with more recent thinking, is the concept of Watson (56). He listed all emotions under three categories — fear, rage, and love. Watson believed that all emotions not only fell within these three categories but that they were all congenital. This idea is not generally accepted by other investigators. Regsdale, for instance, points out that such clear-cut differentiation cannot be seen in children's behavior (47). According to his observations, the response of the individual to fear is miscellaneous rather than specific and is characterized by avoidance. The response to rage is characterized by violence, which later shifts into what he calls an approach reaction. Love is explained as a merely passive attitude or mild approach to the source of stimulation. Bridges, also, disagrees with Watson as the result of experimentation which failed to reveal well-defined specific patterns (7). The Shermans also attack the view from the standpoint of Watson's proposed inherited dispositions (51). According to their research, infants do not exhibit innate, differentiated, emotional response. Reactions at first are of a more generalized type, such as "accepting" or "rejecting" stimulating conditions. Viewpoints like those of Bridges and the Shermans are more consistent with current concepts. General and undifferentiated at first, these emotions later, as the result of maturation and environmental stimulation, are expressed by specific types of behavior.

More nearly allied to the current view are the theories of Allport and Gates. Allport classed all emotions as showing only an affective state of pleasantness or unpleasantness. Gates, in contrast, provided several categories (20). He did not recognize these as having an innate pattern but rather as having an organic basis for their appearance. He listed (1) the strong "emergency" emotions, considered dependent on the sympathetic divisions of the autonomic system; (2) the milder elational types, regarded as having their basis and origin in the activities of the sacral and cranial divisions; (3) the sex emotions, whose origin and affective reaction Gates attributed to the neural system.

Dumas' Classification. An interesting explanation is one offered by Dumas (16), who described emotion as being typified by three levels of behavior, *mild, strong,* and *disintegrative.*

Mild Emotion. Mild emotional response results in increased gastric and salivary secretions, stomach peristalsis, bladder contraction, increased pulse and blood pressure, as well as increased breathing. Examples provided by Dumas of this level are such negative or unpleasant experiences as the threat of being pricked by a pin, the sight of broken glass, or the stimulation from reading erotic literature. On the positive side there are the effects of listening to a musical composition which has associated meanings, real appreciation of art and other esthetic productions, and the accomplishment of a self-motivated, self-planned task in school. All of these are considered good for the individual in that they are thought to have a tonic effect on the physiological processes in particular and on the general well-being of the child (19). Other illustrations might include the established habits of certain groups who habitually enjoy soft music during a meal, attractive decorations, and interesting conversation. At the child's level also a feeling of well-being may accompany dancing, participating in and observing games and sports, observing beautiful scenery, and enjoying other esthetic experiences (45).

Strong Emotion. Strong emotions differ from the mild mainly in that they take on the nature of crisis. They are also characterized by violent visceral and generalized physiological change (50). Strong anger, joy, and fear are paralleled by vivid sensations and demanding courses of action. Action is essential to reduce the bodily stress which is produced. In order to accomplish such action, organic functioning must be raised to a higher level of capability in which all the resources of the individual are mobilized (8). On the other hand, this level of emotion may accompany quite contrasting motivations. Deep sorrow, grief, and despair are of this type. In these kinds of emotions body functioning is of the inactive, depressing, or conserving kind (53). Constant frustration of fundamental personal needs is one environmental influence which produces this effect. Sometimes the emotional response is serious enough to produce skin disorders, organic malfunctioning, and loss or lessening of the powers of the sense organs. In the main the distinction between "action" emotions and "depressing" emotions lies in the comparative physiological changes which accompany the emotion involved. In an action emotion there are increased heartbeat, increased respiration, etc., all leading to increased potential strength. In the depressing type of emotion quite the contrary is true. Pulse rate and blood pressure decrease, and breathing becomes slow and irregular.

It has been pointed out that mild emotional affect has value for the individual. This is not true for strong emotional states. Cannon, who has studied the problem intensively, attributes many kinds of organic malfunctioning to continued emotional reaction.

Some disturbances have been mentioned. Others include heart disease, circulatory disorders, and derangement of glandular function (9).

Either the manic or the depressive type is of serious consequence to an elementary school child. The foregoing statements might imply that the physiological disturbance represents the most harmful effect on the child. Though undoubtedly bad, this is merely an accompaniment and an indication that the child is in difficulty. The real harm is the effect on the child's personality and social development, if the appearance becomes frequent.

Unfortunately, in many cases, behavior anomalies resist identification and observation. Children in the public schools are not generally given the health checks which would point out that undesirable affective behavior is frequent. And quite often behavior manifestations follow a mild, unnoticeable, and generally approved pattern. Thus teachers are often guilty of encouraging what is for the child a very bad behavior sequence. In the main, cases at this level may be found among the very mild who pass unnoticed and the very aggressive as with persistent fighters, bullies, and children with very negative attitudes.

Undoubtedly the identification of children who are potentially capable of harmful emotional reactions will require great care and exacting observation. And likewise, once they are properly identified, great care and exhaustive planning are necessary in setting up for them the proper environmental stimuli for improved emotional expression. In the main this means a setting in which personal and social needs are adequately satisfied.

Disintegrative Emotions. Although it is not likely that elementary school children will show evidences of the advanced effect of disintegrative emotions, it is necessary to present the picture of this extreme type, since emotional behavior may progress from one level of intensity to another as the individual matures. Types of behavior illustrative of this level are represented by cases of serious physical and mental pathology in which intense stresses and conflicts of long duration, rather than organic causes, lie at the root of the difficulty (27). Individuals with such conflicts are patients of psychiatrists, occupants of mental hospitals, and others equally maladjusted who have not submitted to treatment. They may show one or more patterns of emotional reaction as hysteria manifested in simulated physical disorders of a functional nature, delusions, or hallucinations (52). Others include loss of coordination, uncontrollable trembling, loss of control of bladder and colon muscles, or even a complete paralysis.

For teachers the main point of the idea of levels of affective emotional behavior is to realize that the three levels cannot always be clearly distinguished. Borderline cases are difficult to recognize, and emotional behavior may continue, if permitted, on a gradient from the mild to the most devastating type. Although elementary school teachers are not likely to be concerned with the extreme cases, they must be reminded that these latter have their beginnings in the milder forms which first appear during childhood and elementary school days. Therefore, for preventive purposes, all teachers when dealing with emotional behavior should attempt not only to identify the level of its affectiveness but to foresee trends which it may take in the future. Visualizing the ultimate pattern should provide motivation for giving assistance at the period of maturity where treatment mainly involves prevention and redirection (57).

B. RELATION TO FEELINGS

After reading the preceding discussion teachers will naturally ask, "What is the difference between feelings and emotions?" Investigators have also raised this question. According to one group feeling and emotion are not clearly separated, both being simply relative degrees of the same type of affective experience. This would imply that feelings are more closely associated with what has previously been called mild emotions.

Their similarity lies in the fact that both seem to cause the same type of affective physiological response. As Meyer has pointed out, vascular-muscle, skeletal-muscle, and glandular response accompany both so-called feelings and emotions (38).

Though alike in some ways, they are different in others. In a sense feelings come closer to representing an intellectual or appreciative activity. This is particularly true when they reflect a rationalization or an appraisal of creative art. At times feelings and emotions are complementary to each other, particularly in stages of behavior where strong emotions are involved. Interestingly enough, the feeling accompaniment to emotion is more characteristic of humans than of animals and more characteristic of bright than of dull children. Consequently, because of such accompaniment, diagnosis proceeds toward an understanding of emotional behavior through analysis of the more approachable feelings.

C. RELATION TO NEED AND DESIRE

The first point to be brought out is the fact that emotions themselves are not needs, nor are they drives to action as thought earlier. They are thought to be an effect and not primarily a cause. This point of view has not been too generally understood. Perrin, for example, claimed that all emotions are motives and drives for actions. In his statement that "just as hunger impels the organism to obtain and to devour food, so fear prompts it to flee from danger, and anger spurs it to belligerent activity," he overgeneralizes (43). Hunger is truly representative of a state of inner organic imbalance, but fear is a learned reaction brought on by experience, with some external, inciting stimulus. Thorpe likewise disagrees with Perrin's statement in his analysis of the comparison when he states that whereas the visceral stresses representative of hunger are initial drives, the emotional affectation of fear is caused by a specific, meaningful outside situation (53).

Secondly, although emotions and drives are not of the same cloth in terms of their motivation possibilities, they are however closely identified in other ways. In many instances a personal need is the cause that produces emotion.

This relationship, although generally recognized, has been given one-sided treatment. As a result there has been the tendency to imply that emotion is an undesirable affectation resulting from a frustrated need of the organism. Emotion, of course, does result when such is the case. The reader is undoubtedly familiar with statements which suggest that emotional stress is inversely proportional to the degree of frustration in the fulfillment of needs. Or as Trow has stated, the intensity of the emotional effect varies with the strength of the thwarted need (55). On the other hand emotional expression results through the satisfaction of needs. To a considerable extent this kind of relationship is desirable and should be given attention and emphasis as well as the more negative aspects of the relationship.

THEORIES REGARDING EMOTION

A. EARLY BELIEFS

Since the middle of the nineteenth century there has been considerable effort expended in attempts to determine the nature of emotion and its functions. This is not to say that this subject was not studied in the early days of man's civilized state. As far back as the first Greek period it was generally believed that there were physical accompaniments to emotional behavior. Although understanding of its relation to various physiological systems such as the glandular, the nervous, and the circulatory, are products of more recent research, the Greeks did identify emotions with certain organs. These parallels are sufficiently interesting to record here, since many of these ideas are held today by the uninformed, and the parallels are implied in lay language in which such description of behavior is commonly used as, "it breaks my heart." In general, sorrow was expressed from the heart, jealousy was associated with the liver, hate with the gall bladder, and anger with the spleen.

Puritanical Concept. Up to the nineteenth century, emotions were primarily considered as psychic or conscious mental states. This explains the puritanical concept of disciplining the emotions. It was thought that emotional behavior could be consciously directed by the individual. Exhortation for control, however, applied only to the "baser" emotions. Those which reflected high social and moral principles, of course, should be encouraged, while those of a more erotic or "immoral" nature should be "cast out."

Darwinian Theory. One of the first scientific and objective approaches came from Darwin (12). Taking the evolutionary approach to the problem, he postulated the idea that emotions were the vestigial remains of what were in the remote past among the most important responses in primitive man. Darwin's study gave emphasis to the significance of the bodily structures of the human being in the expression of his emotional behavior.

B. JAMES-LANGE THEORY

Darwin's generalizations undoubtedly led to an idea which has become well known as the James-Lange theory. The general thought regarding the sequence of affectional behavior was that emotion, resulting from a confused conscious state of mind, immediately followed the inciting stimulus, which in turn produced the ensuing physiological disturbance.

William James concluded from his experimental studies that emotions as conscious states were induced by a widely differentiated group of sensations circulating in the visceral and body musculature. Lange, a Danish physician, came to similar conclusions a short time later, but emphasized the circulatory or the vasomotor system as the motivating source. Both James and Lange defined emotion as the feeling of the bodily changes that take place directly after perception of an exciting fact. Thus emerged the James-Lange theory, as it came to be known (33).

James-Lange Sequence. In effect, the theory motivated renewed attacks on the problem through its reversal of the old order and its new connotations. The components of emotional behavior as suggested by the theory were generally accepted, but their order was universally challenged in the research that followed. An interesting hypothesis, had this theory been substantiated, was its implication for possible treatment of emotional response. According to James, all that was necessary was a rationalization in the matter. Deleting from consciousness all the feelings of the bodily symptoms would resolve the difficulty and return the individual to a normal state. Rational analysis of the meaning of the effect and the situation itself would alleviate tension. This thought is almost entirely abandoned today, and the idea that the conscious state itself is the emotion has been almost completely repudiated.

C. CANNON'S EMERGENCY THEORY

Cannon postulated the idea that the emotions play an important part in behavior in that they prepare the organism to meet emergencies. The relationship between an emotion and its physiological effects makes such a theory plausible. Under conditions of great stress the organism prepares for vigorous action. It quickly adapts itself through physiological change by developing increased strength, by banishing every trace of fatigue, by increasing the speed of its reaction time and by intensifying every other process needed to ensure efficient bodily response. This provides it with a natural tendency for survival.

In developing this idea numerous facts have been brought to light concerning the relationship of emotion to the autonomic nervous system. This system, comprising a complex series of ganglia attached by connecting fibers to the spinal cord and parallel to it, has three main divisions: the upper or cranial section; the middle section, called the sympathetic or thoracolumbar; and the lower, or sacral, part (9). This system in its entirety controls heart action, respiration, digestion, and blood distribution.

Cannon has pointed out that whereas all glands and organs of the viscera are connected with one or more of the three parts of the autonomic section mentioned, the sympathetic becomes dominant during intense emotional stress and excitement. Under such conditions the organism is stimulated by the sympathetic section toward hyperactive behavior. This is most clearly demonstrated by increased heart action, higher blood pressure, and increased breathing. Other organs, of course, are affected which also depend upon this region for innervation. As a result the normal picture of emotional behavior is seen. The adrenal glands release increased amounts of adrenalin into the blood, and sugar is released by the liver into the blood stream. Respiration speeds up, the face becomes flushed, excessive perspiration appears, all with the result that the entire organism becomes ready to respond to unusual demands.

The logic of this viewpoint lies in the generalization that primitive man needed such incentives for physical action when faced with an emergency. Its weakness may be found in the lack of explanation as to why modern man should be so well equipped for the kind of situation in which he only infrequently finds himself. Such potentialities as obviously exist represent a problem for him rather than a means for existence. When uncontrolled, emotions of this kind are harmful both to the individual and to his social culture.

D. CURRENT ATTITUDES

There is less theorizing today regarding the question of innateness, of whether emotions are merely conditioned responses, of whether they are only a part of a general organismic reaction to certain situations. Duffy, representative of the current investigators, raises the question "whether there is an important difference in kind between emotional and other responses" (14). Other investigators are also beginning to question whether emotions differ from other forms of reaction except in intensity or degree (53). The idea that they do not receives some substantiation from the fact that various physiological functions accompany all kinds of organismic response and that emotions, while representative of a peculiar kind of reaction, are necessarily a part of the total behavior of the individual. Emotions as aspects of total behavior give color and a means for variation in action which at best provides the highest level of satisfaction to the individual in his personal and social contacts.

It is altogether possible that at some future date the idea of emotion as a discrete response will be abandoned and regarded as a component of general organismic reaction, differentiated only in terms of its intensity. In such a case all behavior could then be described in reference to physiological or psychological processes and effects rather than in reference to designated behavior categories.

Emotions as Clues to Behavior. Although such a trend may be desirable it should not cause one to disregard entirely what is now referred to as emotional behavior. Theoretical considerations of whether emotions exist discretely or not are relatively unimportant to the teacher. And equally unimportant is the question as to which theory one should accept in dealing with emotional behavior. Emotions, as we recognize them today, are important clues to response and present focal points for understanding the child. As such, they represent "peaks" in the expressed feeling tone of the child as he faces the problem of adjustment in his daily life. From the various theories described one can gain considerable knowledge of the complexity of emotional behavior. All these theories contain common elements and much vital truth.

THE EFFECT OF MATURATION AND PRACTICE

It has been argued that specific patterns of emotional response are not manifested in the behavior of the newborn infant but appear from time to time throughout the life of the individual (19). This poses the problem of the effect of maturation and practice in their appearance. Does the process of maturation give rise to specific innate potentialities, or is the appearance of emotional response largely the result of experience and practice?

A. MATURATION

Investigators of the role of emotion in the behavior of the individual have given little attention to the effect of maturation. Early investigators attempted to relate emotion to inherited ways of behaving and acting, and the more recent investigators tend to emphasize environmental causes. One investigator who deplores this tendency and feels that emotion is not thereby fully understood is Gesell (22). In illustrating his point, Gesell points out that fear may be resolved through maturation as well as through change in environment.

Maturation is essential in the physiological growth of the child. It is essential in his mental growth, in his creative growth, and in all phases of growth that follow a natural pattern of development. Emotion, however, is not a demonstrable phase of development but rather a growth accompaniment or growth effect. Therefore maturation, although significant, has a more indirect relationship. Maturation, for example, plays a part in emotional behavior through the influence of the developing intelligence of the child. Maturation may also be influential through its effect on the developing physical organism, height, weight, increased motor coordination, glandular growth, and the like. From this viewpoint, maturation may be seen to be effective in emotional expression through its indirect influence in developing the capacity for emotional behavior. A similar reasoning is expressed by the Joneses in their discussion of this particular effect on emotional behavior (29). Utilizing fear as an illustration they point out that this emotion may be regarded as a response to a change in the total situation. As new elements appear they require a revised adjustment. The kind of fear produced depends to a considerable degree upon the child's stage of maturation. The infant responds with fear to unfamiliar noises (under certain circumstances), to pain, or to bodily discomfort. Some fears suffered by the infant are resolved by overcoming the situation — helping himself or seeking assistance in a rational manner. As he becomes older the mere use of increased intelligence may resolve his fear.

B. PRACTICE

Teachers will be interested in the part that practice plays in emotional response. Most of the experiments in this field have employed the conditioning technique (6). The experiments contribute little to our knowledge of the actual pattern of emotional behavior. They do, however, present encouraging evidence of the practicality of re-educating children whose emotional reactions are undesirable (34).

Interesting as the fact may be that children and adults can be reconditioned toward desirable patterns of behavior, of more interest is the substantiation provided by research of the idea that emotional behavior is a product of environmental circumstances. This would seem to indicate that what is needed in the first place is a proper ordering of events so that treatment and redirection later would become unnecessary.

The parent, as the first person in contact with the child, must accept responsibilities which are of great importance in determining future behavior. As the child widens his contacts, other individuals become important and effective in shaping his developing emotional pattern. This does not imply that the organism is entirely elastic, without some foundation, without structure of its own, and without some ability to withstand pressures to act one way or another. Longitudinal case studies indicate the following general principles in relation to practice.

(1) At an early age the child begins a way of behaving which assumes more and more individuality as he matures. Change is resisted and is more easily pushed aside as he becomes older. Many people, perhaps the great majority, follow from infancy to adulthood a path which may seem varied and without design at times but which in its general nature has been outlined in the individual's early years.

(2) That kind of emotional behavior evolves which gives the

individual the greatest satisfactions, and he tends to repeat the acts which give him greatest satisfaction. In so doing he adjusts himself to various levels of action and social opportunity.

(3) The individual gives himself considerable opportunity to practice the evolving pattern. The child at a very early age develops competence in selecting situations where his emotional expression is satisfying and where he may avoid annoying and deviational distractions. To overcome this characteristic, practice on a new design must be extensive and must be applied over a considerable period of time.

(4) If parents or teachers are to alter the original design so as to produce deviations in the direction of more desirable behavior and greater satisfaction to the individual in the long run, they must obtain the indorsement of the individual concerned. Teachers often gain momentary or artificial cooperation when the goal seems reasonable but is too far removed from existing satisfying behavior.

(5) All behavior and growth, although individual in pattern, is somewhat deviational in nature. This probably applies more to emotional reactions that to any other kind of development. This is to say that for no individual is there an exact design for maturing. It is true that certain individuals seem to be moving directly toward a well-defined fate. Were one to have complete insight into all the motivating factors of a life, it is likely that one would find certain critical periods when a given event had effects that it would not have at any other time. Therefore, while each individual is following a general design in his emotional life, there are deviations from the pattern. It is this latter principle that makes guidance and redirection possible.

PATTERNS AND DEVELOPMENTAL ASPECTS OF EMOTION

A. EARLY INDICATIONS

Emotion in Infancy. From birth the human infant shows a relation between emotional states and personal organismic needs (19). Needs are simple at birth, and the corresponding emotional behavior related to their fulfillment is likewise simple. If the child is startled by a loud noise or by an abrupt movement, he stirs, moves his whole body, or cries. As long as he remains quiet and undisturbed, he is relaxed and contented.

One of the first steps beyond such a simple manifestation is his ability to differentiate between pleasant and unpleasant conditions. As has been indicated above, the first differentiation between these is shown only in the reaction of movement or withdrawal or non-

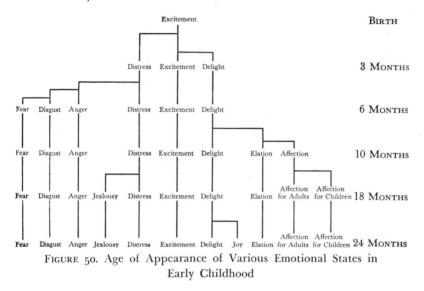

FIGURE 50. Age of Appearance of Various Emotional States in Early Childhood

activity and relaxation. By the time the child is one year old he shows vastly greater response to both pleasant and unpleasant stimuli (25). For example, he shows pleasurable reactions to the visual stimulus of his bottle or to a parent who is ready to play with him. Such growth in affective expression is contingent upon increasing ability to distinguish objects and in learning the meaning of people and things. Between five and six months he begins to differentiate between family and strangers. At this age he withdraws from an unfamiliar person, whereas previously he has accepted strangers and family alike. At about this time also he has learned to distinguish facial expressions, especially when they are associated with distinctive verbal aspects such as a friendly or threatening voice. This beginning in maturity of response illustrates a principle which continues throughout the life of the child.

With the increase in ability to make discriminations, specific desires and needs arise which produce emotional patterns differentiated according to the amount of frustration or satisfaction experienced in their attainment.

The various, simple affective reactions of infants to adults and others have been portrayed by Bridges in relation to their first appearance and continuance up to two years of age (Figure 50). Such a representation should not necessarily be accepted as a norm for the appearance of these traits in all children.

B. THE THREE-YEAR-OLD

Interesting is the fact that certain aspects of the growing child's emotional responses are closely tied in with his developing personal-social experiences. Jealousy is an example of emotional behavior so related. This may occur when the youngster is suddenly confronted with a new brother or sister. Especially is this the case when parents unwittingly transfer a great deal of affection from the youngster to the new baby. The wise parent, however, alleviates such a conflict by transforming the situation into one which provides the child with the opportunity for the expression of sympathy and love and consequently a broader opportunity for personal-social development.

Relations outside Home. The three-year-old begins to develop affective relationships outside the family (25). He forms new friends both with adults and with other children. His emotional behavior, therefore, has a wider range of expressive opportunity. As security is established, he shows confidence in his relationships with others. If security and satisfying relationships are difficult to attain, his emotional responses take on a negative coloring. The development of sensitivity to sound, color, and rhythm lays the foundation for present and future esthetic appreciation with its desirable emotional accompaniments. At this age he has advanced far in the direction of extensive and diverse potential organization of emotional expression (54).

Maturity of Nonsocial Response. In reference to emotional traits which have less dependence on personal-social development he shows considerable maturity. The three-year-old may still be somewhat afraid in the dark, but he begins to show an emergence from this pattern, particularly when aided and abetted by intelligently planned action by his parents. He has learned caution with animals and has abandoned his earlier, reckless fearlessness in regard to them. He can distinguish clearly between persons and reacts differently to individuals. He knows that automobiles are dangerous and that he must not thoughtlessly rush into the street. His total reaction to his experiences indicates considerable maturity in the human quality of adjustment between fear and reckless action.

This complete pattern of development is related to increased motor skills, developing language, and developing personal-social growth. It is particularly influenced by a satisfactory compromise between fear and recklessness, a growing sense of security, and the broader aspects of personal-social development.

C. CRITERION OF MATURITY

Teachers and others often speak of *emotional maturity,* or they say that such and such a person is "emotionally immature." What is emotional maturity? How can it be developed? Such questions cannot be answered fully, nor can emotional maturity be measured like physical or mental maturity (11). The complexity of emotions themselves, their physiological accompaniments, their relation to needs and drives, and their accompanying feeling tone has provided a task for measurement, which is as yet very incomplete. Nevertheless, the task has been defined, some interrelations discovered, and considerable progress achieved in ability to answer some of the questions raised. In order to understand fully the growing child, it is essential that much progress be made in evaluating the affective aspects of his development. In this connection, Prescott's statement of necessary work still to be done and the appraisal of work already done is enlightening. It provides both a challenge and a warning to teachers and others interested in interpreting growth and development (45). Prescott makes a plea for a description of normal behavior ranges. He would include relationships between an individual and members of his family, relationships in a succession of social groupings on an expanding social adaptation, manner of meeting various kinds of frustration, forms of expression of sex-motivated activity, manner of meeting fear and success situations, emotional level involved in esthetic situations, the relation of emotion to loyalty, sensitiveness to sympathy, and affective behavior following the reading of various types of literature. In such research Prescott proposes that data be organized so as to provide normal behavior ranges at various age levels and studied so as to give sequences of behavior for normal adjusted maturity. He suggests that such information be made available in descriptive rather than in mathematical terms. To the extent that measurement data can be validated, he proposes factor analysis treatment, but only where there is no question of the elements evaluated. Obviously, Prescott suggests that there is a great need for a clinical or longitudinal approach to the problem with less dependence upon correlational studies from mass data.

There are other limitations in procedure than those implied by Prescott which make it impossible to answer all the questions needed for interpreting child development. Psychologists and psychiatrists are not now ready to give a complete description of the kind of behavior, at progressive stages of maturity, that can satisfy needs in the social structure. Such evidence as is available is predominantly clinical, is not based on the problems of normal individuals, and is somewhat haphazard and unsystematized. A further weakness is the lack of a common terminology which would aid in organizing a body of scientific knowledge. We have evolved certain ideas about mature emotional behavior (24). For example, we consider that maturity is indicated by a certain amount of restraint of the overt expression of emotion. Maturity is also characterized by an ability to sublimate drives and their accompanying emotional behavior. In regard to our knowledge of ranges of normal behavior at various stages of maturity, only a beginning has been made.

Indirectly, emotional maturity may be determined by ascertaining the ability of individuals to respond satisfactorily in natural social-personal situations. This criterion implies adequacy in broad life areas and in many diversified situations. In other words the individual who responds to anger in a controlled, socially approved way, but who does not express desirable affective response to esthetic situations and who ignores situations in which such responses might develop, is emotionally immature to a certain degree. Complete emotional maturity then not only involves appropriate response but appropriate and widely stimulating experiences for broader response. In this sense, also, emotional maturity is marked by behavior which is a function of the dynamic relationships between immediate needs and situations experienced as well as between needs and situations which can be developed only through wide experiencing.

Prescott quotes Sherman as giving a similar criterion of emotional maturity. According to Sherman's definition, it implies a readiness for making proper emotional choices independently of the persons who are normally responsible for the individual (45). Such a definition probably implies that choice or control of expression must be freed from the influence of people about the individual. This suggests the same high level of response already mentioned but considers such response to be mature only when it reaches such a high level without social approval or condemnation. Or perhaps it implies as a satisfactory criterion the choice which satisfies only the immediate needs of the individual.

No General Scale Likely. There is as yet no general scale by which emotional maturity can be measured. Affective behavior is so diversified that it eludes successful evaluation. Measurement specialists are not able today to measure accurately general affective maturity, and it is unlikely that at any time in the near future they will be able to do so. It must be admitted, however, that eventually someone will develop a concept of emotional age similar to Olson's "organismic age" in which various components of emotional behavior may be reduced to a normative basis. Such an attempt may incur the weaknesses inherent in all practices which reduce or hide extreme variations of behavior through "averages." In reference to specific emotional reactions, however, one may be more optimistic.

EMOTIONAL EFFECTS

There is no one answer to the question whether emotions are harmful or helpful. In some instances emotions are harmful; in certain others they are very helpful. If emotion is regarded as resulting from a confused state of equilibrium, or what Dumas has referred to as "strong emotion," there is little doubt as to its harmful effects. Fear and anger have been universally experienced as dissipating and inhibiting verbal, artistic, and neuromuscular skills.

Mild Emotion Helpful. On the other hand the beneficial result of mild emotion has been pointed out. Undoubtedly there are well-defined limits for emotional behavior for each individual which determine whether its effect is harmful or helpful. Thus it may be concluded that up to a certain point, some reactions are beneficial and beyond this point inhibiting. It is also obvious that a certain type of response is helpful for one person, harmful for another.

Causes of Conflict. No one questions the fact that certain kinds of emotional behavior lead to serious illnesses. This is the result of competition within the individual between personal and social demands — a problem peculiar to a civilized society. Thereby it might be assumed that emotions have to a great degree outgrown their usefulness in modern society. This is probably an over-simplification of the facts. Man undoubtedly utilized his emotional reactions in a different way during primitive days. There is much to indicate, however, that it is his finer emotional accompaniments which have made possible a higher cultural and ethical concept of life.

Such a consideration does not minimize the problem. Faulty conditioning or other contributing forces create the problem of handling extreme emotional behavior. The solution hinges on finding ways and means of releasing generated energy while still receiving the endorsement of the culture in which the individual finds himself.

Effect of Restraint. The tendency of some, in responding under such conditions, is to bottle up or restrain all emotional feeling. This, of course, leads to a psychopathic condition which may eventually cause the individual to do great harm to himself or others. Continuous blocking of the tendency to become angry may lead to traits of moodiness and introversion, whereas necessary and continued frustration of the love motive may result in certain forms of autoeroticism, erotic daydreaming, and perhaps even complete disorganization of personality. Society and innate drives furnish motives for action, but according to many writers do not provide adequately for the relief of emotionally created tensions. The compelling erotic and other personal-social drives on the one hand

and the inhibiting group sanctions, ideals, and mores on the other provide for some enduring and continued conflict.

Effect on Learning. In the chapter on learning, the effects of contrasting types of social climate on the learning situation have been discussed. The evidence presented on the effect of teacher attitudes and social organization in the classroom dealt mainly with general attitudes and procedures (34). This evidence leads one to conclude that where satisfaction is available in the way of self-direction and self-evaluation, results are at a desired maximum. Other experiments have been developed to test the effect of praise, blame, frustrating conditions, and of many other conditions under which learning might be carried on (54). Reward versus punishment, for example, has been a frequent area of research. In the main these studies have been quite disappointing. Lack of uniformity in findings is the rule rather than the exception. One may examine this literature and select evidence to support a preconceived point of view. In the main only one generalization can be made in which there is considerable unanimity of opinion — that children and adults tend to avoid behavior that leads to unpleasant reactions. Unpleasant consequences inhibit learning, whereas pleasant consequences promote it.

CONTROLLING EMOTIONAL BEHAVIOR

A. CONTROL AND REDIRECTION POSSIBLE

Basis of Idea of Trainability. General research strongly supports the idea that emotional behavior may be controlled under certain conditions and that it is distinctly trainable. Schools are therefore beginning to become interested in their responsibility to this problem, and teachers may find in the idea both a warning and a challenge.

The idea is based upon a series of generalizations which have been presented throughout this chapter. (1) Emotional behavior does not spring from innate specific patterns common to all individuals and consistent within a given individual. (2) Emotional behavior changes with increasing age and experience. (3) Emotional behavior tends toward manifestations which are socially acceptable, and all circumstances considered, more satisfying to the needs of the individual. Consequently, one may be optimistic concerning its trainability and potential plasticity.

Most of the studies which have dealt with the role of training in emotional behavior have utilized various aspects of conditioning. Retraining in this instance has involved the procedure of developing a secondary (more desired) response to a given stimulus. The work of the Joneses in this connection has been frequently cited (29,30). They clearly indicate success in establishing conditioned emotional responses as well as in substantiating previous evidence that more desirable secondary responses may be learned. These experiments are important, not necessarily because of their contribution to our knowledge of the actual pattern of emotional behavior, but because they fully establish the feasibility of retraining where emotional reactions are harmful and detrimental to positive, desirable development.

B. CONTROL BY AVOIDANCE

There should be no question in the minds of teachers of the devastating effects of unrestrained emotional behavior. As previously mentioned, such untrammeled display throughout childhood and school years can eventually result in serious physical or mental derangement. The simplest means of controlling undesirable emotional behavior is through avoidance of the stimulus or situation which produces it. This is not to imply that retraining or correction should not be employed with those who need assistance. Nor does it imply that the instructional situation should not be organized so as to provide the proper contacts which direct emotional expression into desired channels of expression. What is implied here is the desirability of avoiding low-level emotional stimuli which result in conflict or frustration and thereby minimize the opportunity to achieve desirable social purposes.

C. CONTROL BY DISCIPLINE

In a good many instances self-control and discipline must be learned. This is a problem of development and may result efficiently and satisfyingly in accordance with the maturity achieved by the individual. Overdiscipline in the way of completely frustrating the response should be avoided, since the reaction to this stimulus itself can result in undesired emotional expression. Discipline, gradually self-imposed and self-rationalized with growing maturity, should be encouraged in the classroom. Thwarting and conflict, however, cannot be entirely avoided. Emotional maturing, or the problem of adjusting more effectively, requires problem solving of this nature. An increasing number of investigators warn against the purely automatic guided response, or what might be called too much smoothing of the path of adjustment.

D. CONTROL BY RELAXATION

One of the promising new methods of getting at the problem of training, directing, and controlling emotional behavior is the technique of relaxation. The argument as to the validity of this method is based upon the idea that since nervousness and emotional tension are accompanied by various muscular tensions, a relaxation of these muscles tends to reduce the intensity of the emotion. Jacobsen reports that it often takes months for the patient to learn the technique (25). One muscle group after another is relaxed until the whole body has been covered. In practice with any one muscle group the patient is encouraged to go beyond the point where he thinks relaxation has occurred. Of interest are the stages of treatment which begin in a prone position, then sitting, and finally standing.

Little has been done in the way of determining whether young children of elementary school age can be taught such methods. Such suggestions, however, have implications for a "relaxed" social climate in learning and likewise in recreational programs which result in relaxation rather than in fatigue and emotional stress.

E. CONTROL BY CONDITIONING

In the preceding chapter conditioning was discussed as a technique influencing learning at a somewhat low level. As a technique for developing automatic, desirable, emotional response it has a reverse high-level desirability. The faith vested in its effectiveness rests in the belief that emotional behavior has little of an inherited nature but much in the way of conditioned response. In other words, if much of undesired emotional response is the result of conditioning, it is reasoned that desirable behavior can be produced in a similar manner.

The early conditioning experiments have been previously discussed. Some of the later are sufficiently significant for further attention. This experimentation can be divided into two groups in the way of findings. The one group experimented intensively with techniques for facilitating conditioned responses, whereas the other, mainly represented by the behaviorists, dealt directly with motivating secondary responses to given stimuli.

Early Experiments. Krasnogorski was among the first to apply Pavlov's conditioning technique to the study of children (32). One of his experiments consisted of giving children chocolate to eat during the ringing of a bell. He soon found that opening and swallowing movements were easily developed when the bell rang even if the children received no chocolate. Thus the simple generalization was made that human beings as well as animals could develop new responses to stimuli. Of incidental importance was his finding that the more intelligent the child, the more readily the conditioned response was learned. Perhaps of more importance, but incidental to Krasnogorski's experiments, was a difference between so-called stable and unstable children. The stable were found to adjust more readily to changes and fluctuations of inhibiting and irritating stimuli, whereas the unstable showed less flexibility of adjustment.

Behaviorist Experiments. Mateer also produced like information relative to conditioning processes (36). Utilizing intelligence test results on children in her conditioning experiments, she also concluded that the more intelligent responded with greater facility than did the others. Although Watson's experiments raised great debate and controversy concerning the so-called innate emotions, his incidental generalizations concerning the effect of conditioning have been generally accepted. Watson formulated his problem around the idea that hundreds of children fear the dark, women are afraid of mice, and emotions seem to be associated with certain people, places, and situations such as the woods, water, etc. (56). How can objects which at first have no such significance later call out emotions and highly affective feeling? Such were the questions which he attempted to answer.

Following extensive investigation, Watson finally concluded that aside from what he called the innate emotions of fear, love, and rage, all emotional responses of any intensity or stress are conditioned through experiences in one's environment. The reader is probably familiar with much of the detail of his experiments in inducing fear on the part of children. These experiments convinced him that many fears which have no basis in original nature are developed without one's knowledge of their exact origin. Being unable to identify its origin the fear cannot be explained and consequently becomes an ingrained pattern reaction.

An outgrowth of conditioning has resulted in experiments in what has been called *unconditioning*. Unconditioning differed from conditioning in that retraining is directed toward the visceral reaction rather than toward forming a new emotional outlet. This method seems too complicated for discussion here, and the assumption on which the technique is based — the trainability of the visceral reaction involved — is highly controversial (53).

Watson's Contribution. Although greatly debated, the work of Watson has contributed much to our knowledge of emotion and has developed considerable optimism concerning the potential effectiveness of the school in producing desirable behavior. The experiments of Watson and the others have encouraged acceptance of the idea that many personal qualities and limitations which are ordinarily considered innate and fixed are in reality conditioned and pliable. Such a view places a great responsibility upon the school and provides an optimistic attitude concerning its function in the development of the individual.

F. CONTROL BY ATTITUDES

How Attitudes Are Built. It is generally recognized that attitudes or feelings are related to emotional response and that they represent dispositions to act in characteristic ways. An attitude may produce emotional behavior, as well as affect its mode of expression. In this sense, it represents a kind of readiness which exerts a tremendous influence upon the individual's life. Allport has classified the channels through which attitudes are built as (1) the process of the accretion and integration of numerous and varied experiences; (2) the individuation of specific action patterns from early, exploratory, mass action behavior; (3) the result of traumatic incidents, particularly those that produce shock; and (4) the result of imitating and absorbing the attitudes of parents, other adults, and peers (3). This classification seems to imply that control of emotions can most easily be effected by building desirable attitudes at an early age. Undoubtedly this is true, but many conflicting and inhibiting factors make the task difficult even at this age (58).

Nevertheless it is the responsibility of those who direct child development to take into consideration all the factors and direct all possible energies toward solution of the problem.

Attitudes Become Fixed. In working toward the development of desired attitudes or in attempting redirection, it must be kept in mind that attitudes may remain fixed over a long period of time. This would indicate that redirection is difficult and takes a long period of time, particularly when the influence first operative in its development consistently remains in a directive relationship.

Role of the School. It is quite likely that such a relationship between cause and effect, in attitude development, exists during the school life of the child. The child's home, his playmates, the social groups among which he lives, his economic circumstances, his racial heritage constantly influence his development. The role of the school in comparison with other influences as a potentially more objective, more analytical agent is a matter of question. The discussion up to this point has been clearly optimistic concerning opportunities for guiding, directing, and retraining emotional behavior. Although the potentially important role that the teachers and the school can play in directing child behavior should not be minimized, teachers must guard against any naïveté regarding the complexity of the task, and they must realize that success is greatly to be prized as a significant and important outcome of educational goal. The school, in terms of time of contact with the child, is decidedly a minor influence. The family, the child's brothers and sisters and his playmates, the social circumstances of the family in which the child lives, its unemployment, disasters, fears, and hates — all are closer to the child than either the school or the teacher. Nevertheless the school remains highly important. Parents do not agree, or newly formed playmates present new and conflicting ideas. The child learns and has experiences which parents have not had, and has ideas which are in conflict with those of his parents. If elements in the basic environment in the development of attitudes reach a deadlock or conflict, the school then assumes a more dominating role. Frequently it develops such a role through intelligent utilization of its own resources, such as community study projects, paper drives, etc., which it can direct out and into the environment itself. Thus the most effective work is done when the school in its program makes a dual attack both on the child and on his environment. Such is the concept and the basis of action of the community school.

With the approach defined and the position and problems admitted, many specific things can be done as a counterattacking force in the development of attitudes. These have been nicely summarized by Prescott (45). A majority of these have been mentioned previously but bear repeating. First, according to Prescott, is the child's need to explore a great variety and diversity of factual knowledge. The purpose of this is to eliminate bias and to diminish the opportunity for developing attitudes on inaccurate or incomplete information. Prescott does not imply conventional school organization in such an exploration but rather a problem-solving approach based upon needs and interests. Secondly, he points out that a primary purpose of the school is to help children understand the dynamic nature of life and the social processes which it requires. In this connection he recommends beginning with the present as a point of reference and proceeding to the physical, social, and spiritual evaluation of mankind. The conventional school with its program of well-ordered curriculum capsules is quite unprepared to follow this suggestion. More appropriate are the emerging community schools in which curriculum in larger blocs ties in more directly with the problems of community living. With this frame of reference schools may arrive at a point of understanding and expectation of further problems which they themselves will need to solve in the area of curriculum selection. Prescott's third point in outlining the responsibility of the school is that successful efforts demand a cooperative venture between pupils and teachers in determining those values that are most important. It is his thought that once these are understood, they form the basis for the development of attitudes necessary in a period of social change.

IMPLICATIONS FOR TEACHERS

Cues to Behavior. Certain aspects of emotional behavior need re-iteration and emphasis and more specific comment as to their implication for instruction. One of these is that observance of his emotional behavior represents a point of departure for intelligent understanding and handling of a child. Insight into the part played by attitudes and emotions should stimulate a great deal of scientific curriculum research. Knowledge of the possibilities for enriching life by wholesome affective experience should challenge all teachers to consider their programs for developing esthetic experiences. Strong emotions should not be regarded necessarily as something to be feared and repressed but rather as basic biological phenomena which need some kind of outlet. As such, strong emotions expressed in harmful or antisocial ways indicate the need for treatment or redirection toward social satisfactions (18).

Some Needs of Children. In meeting the emotional needs of the child, the teacher should be impressed by the necessity of helping children, not only by manipulating the environment so that its pressures are not too great, but also by helping the child to learn how to face some of the world's pressures. In this connection the problem of the introverted versus the extroverted child comes to mind. The emphasis upon the problem of the child who spends considerable time alone, who daydreams, or who occasionally wants to get away from the group has worried many teachers and parents. The child's tendency to be seclusive may be in part the result of an overcrowded schedule. Parents and teachers become anxious unless children develop many social skills and extrovertive interests. Part of the trouble is the parents themselves who, under the guise of helping children develop naturally, are merely exploiting them in their own drive for social status. Tap dancing, dramatics, art lessons are frequently a far cry from activities engaged in to develop natural creative ability and may be only an attempt to gain social approval. Some of the more sensible agencies which promote outside-school activities are showing marked reform, as indicated by programs which have moved from the highly scheduled, adult-dominated affair to the more informal creative situation. Although many children need more time to play freely, to develop initiative in their own planning and thinking with others, some need time to be alone with their thoughts. The child who dislikes to spend any appreciable time by himself is in just as bad a condition as the child who is uneasy with the group and who continuously wants to be alone. There is no doubt that we have erred considerably in making available so little time for quiet, peaceful, and recreative pursuits. This point is emphasized by Plant who points out that children frequently need to be alone to think or to "ripen." His argument rests on the idea that they need strong inner, personal resources, a strong philosophy of life, so that when things go badly for them in a social way, they can still spend some time with themselves (44). Such a balance must be achieved by the child if his emotional reactions are to be normal and desirable.

Need for Security. Adequate emotional expression likewise demands emotional security. The child's need for love has been discussed in a previous chapter. Regardless of his deficiencies and handicaps, he needs to know that the love he receives is meant especially for him and that no other child can quite take his place. A similar affection shown in his classroom is helpful. This will preclude jealousy of other children and prevent drives toward undesirable emotional response in order to obtain attention (23).

Importance to Education. It is probably wise to reiterate that the various affective phenomena discussed throughout this chapter have other significant implications for classroom teachers. No one will question the fact that the social climate of any classroom promotes or inhibits desirable emotional expression. Nor will anyone question the fact that each schoolroom is comprised of individuals, each with varying feelings and attitudes. Recognition of these in the study of the child is a primary condition for the establishment of understanding and desirable diagnostic-remedial relationships. In directing emotional response and training, teachers should see that schoolrooms have a desirably affective, tonal quality in seating, lighting, and other appurtenances.

Teachers must be warned to treat strong emotions with a great deal of care because of their potential, critical nature and their great affective possibilities. Discipline in this connection demands good judgment with due regard to emotional and feeling affects. Children undergoing strong emotional experiences outside the school should be handled with a great deal of care. Tasks and assignments need to be modified frequently for such children and at times entirely abandoned.

The responsibility of the school in the development of attitudes has been touched upon in several parts of this chapter. Nevertheless, it should again be emphasized that this responsibility is fundamental and basic. Many experiments indicate that specific academic teaching differences have but little significance on children's permanent learnings. No evidence, however, minimizes the importance of the teacher's role in attitude formation and in other kinds of affective response.

Need for Experimentation. There is still much to be done in discovering the normal developmental sequence of affective behavior. Available genetic studies are based on cumulative observation of the same children and in that respect they are significant. However, they are deficient in that in the main they are concerned with preschool children. Studies now under way with other levels of maturity may be expected to make great contributions and to uncover other significant problems (17, 35).

For complete understanding it is absolutely necessary to develop techniques whereby the total development of the child can be evaluated. Some of the problems which need to be solved are:

    a. Development of devices for determining stages of maturity of various aspects of affective behavior
    b. The determination of their interrelations
    c. The relation of variability in the currently more valid measurable aspects of development to emotional instability and to emotional expression

From the viewpoint of measurement no device is more needed at the present time than one which would permit calculation of emotional maturity. As has been stated previously, it is likely that no single scale will do the job, since emotional expression covers such a wide variety of response. Scales measuring various aspects of progressive change in affective behavior are more feasible. Such devices would enable one to measure the effect of a given strong emotional response upon a contrasting one or, in other words, to determine their respective interrelationship.

How New Techniques Could Be Used. The development of such measurement devices would also help one discover whether a wide range of developmental maturity reflects a desirable or undesirable educational environment and might reveal common factors underlying various affective phenomena. Such devices would also indicate whether a child showing widely divergent growth attainments at a given time is emotionally more mature and stable or less so.

One current hypothesis is that marked variations in performance or in growth achievements represent a type of emotional insecurity and, conversely, that minimum variations in the growth curve indicate more stability and undifferentiated emotional response. This also raises the question as to how much variability is permissible in the normal range of stability and what factors, such as age, sex, maturational status, etc., are influential in its manifestation. All of these and similar problems can be solved only by devices which will accurately measure and appraise emotional behavior.

Case studies based upon systematic observations and records of the behavior of the same children are entirely essential in the solution of such problems. Studies such as those employed by Lewin in determining the results of affective social climates, the studies of Jones on adolescence, the studies of Anderson on integrative versus dominative behavior of teachers are all outstanding and significant. Before such problems as have been mentioned can be solved, there must be added to the methods of these men some of the techniques of biologists and others, particularly scaling devices which would make possible the determination of relative maturity as the child grows older or, as we might say, would show maturity longitudinally or in terms of degrees of growth, rather than horizontally or in aspects of comparative status with other children.

Along with such an approach to the problem, there must be a broadening of our knowledge of affective behavior. We must discover not only the changes in behavior which develop with increasing age, the change (or lack of change) which underlies increased maturity of response, but also the experiences that influence individual affective behavior. This is a large order, but it is the task ahead.

SELECTED REFERENCES

1. ALLEN, R. M., "An Analysis of Twelve Longitudinal Rorschach Records of One Child," *Journal of Projective Techniques,* 19:111–116, June, 1955.
2. ALMY, MILLIE, *Child Development.* New York: Holt, 1955, 336–360.
3. ALLPORT, G. W., "Attitudes," *Handbook of Social Psychology,* edited by Carl Murchison, Worcester: Clark University Press, 1935.
4. AMES, LOUISE BATES, LEARNED, JANET, METRAUX, RUTH W., AND WALKER, RICHARD N., *Child Rorschach Responses: Developmental Trends from Two to Ten Years.* New York: Paul B. Hoeber, 1952.
5. BARUCH, DOROTHY W., "One Little Boy," *Pastoral Psychology,* 2:42–46, 1952.
6. BREGMAN, E. O., "An Attempt to Modify the Emotional Attitudes of Infants by the Conditioned Response Technique," *Journal of Genetic Psychology,* 45:169–198, 1934.
7. BRIDGES, K. M. B., "Emotional Development in Early Infancy," *Child Development,* 3:324–334, 1932.
8. BRUCE, W. F., AND FREEMAN, F. S., *Development and Learning,* Boston: Houghton Mifflin, 1942.
9. CANNON, W. B., *Bodily Changes in Pain, Hunger, Fear, and Rage,* New York: Appleton-Century, 1929.
10. BOUSFIELD, W. A., AND ORBISON, W. D., "Ontogenesis of Emotional Behavior," *Psychological Review,* 59:1–7, 1952.
11. CHAMBERS, O. R., "A Method for Measuring the Emotional Maturity of Children," *Journal of Genetic Psychology,* 32:637–647, 1925.
12. DARWIN, C. R., *The Expression of Emotions in Man and Animals,* London: Appleton-Century, 1872.
13. BULLOCK, BURLEEN J., AND BROWN, WILLIAM H., "Screening a Fourth Grade Class for Emotional Needs," *Understanding the Child,* 22:116–120, 1953.
14. DUFFY, E., "The Measurement of Muscular Tensions as a Technique for the Study of Emotional Tendencies," *American Journal of Psychology,* 44:146–162, 1932.
15. BURLINGHAM, DOROTHY, *Twins: A Study of Three Pairs of Identical Twins.* New York: International Universities Press, 1952.

16. DUMAS, GEORGES, *Nouveau Traité de Psychologie,* Vols. I–III, Paris, Felix Alcan, 1932.

17. DAVIDSON, HELEN H., AND GOTTLIEB, LUCILLE S., "The Emotional Maturity of Pre- and Post-Menarcheal Girls," *Journal of Genetic Psychology,* 86:261–266, 1955.

18. DUNBAR, H. FLANDERS, *Emotions and Bodily Changes.* New York: Columbia University Press, 1954.

19. FRANK, L. K., "The Newborn as a Young Mammal with Organic Capacities, Needs and Feelings," *Psychosomatic Medicine,* 7:169–173, 1945.

20. GATES, A. I., *Psychology for Students of Education,* New York: Macmillan, 1930.

21. FRIED, RALPH I., "Socio-Emotional Factors Accounting for Growth Failure in Children as Measured by the Wetzel Grid," *Proceedings of the Association for Research in Nervous and Mental Disease,* 29:317–325, 1949.

22. GESELL, ARNOLD, *The Guidance of Mental Growth in Infant and Child,* New York: Macmillan, 1930.

23. GEWIRTZ, JACOB L., "A Program of Research on the Dimensions and Antecedents of Emotional Dependence," *Child Development,* 27:205–221, 1956.

24. HERSEY, R. B., "Emotional Cycles in Man," *Journal of Mental Science,* 77:151–169, 1931.

25. JACOBSEN, E., *The Child's Emotions,* Chicago: University of Chicago Press, 1930.

26. JAMES, WILLIAM, "The Physical Basis of Emotion," *Psychological Review,* 1:516–529, 1894.

27. JERSILD, A. T., GOLDMAN, B., AND LOFTUS, J. J., "A Comparative Study of the Worries of Children in Two School Situations," *Journal of Experimental Education,* 4:323–326, 1941.

28. HEATHERS, GLEN, "Emotional Dependence and Independence in Nursery School Play," *Journal of Genetic Psychology,* 87:37–57, 1955.

29. JONES, H. E., "Conditioning of Overt Emotional Responses," *Journal of Educational Psychology,* 22:127–130, 1931.

30. ———, AND JONES, M. C., "A Study of Fear," *Childhood Education,* 5:136–143, 1928.

31. HOLMES, CARLOTTA R., AND BROWN, WM. H., "Persistence of Emotional Needs In Young Children," *Understanding the Child,* 23:120–125, 1954.

32. KRASNOGORSKI, N. I., "The Conditioned Reflexes and Children's Neuroses," *American Journal of Diseases of Children,* 30:753–768, 1925.

33. LANGE, C. G., AND JAMES, WILLIAM, *The Emotions,* New York: Williams and Wilkins, 1922.

34. LEWIN, KURT, LIPPITT, R., AND WHITE, R. K., "Patterns of Aggressive Behavior in Experimentally Created Social Climates," *Journal of Social Psychology,* 10:271–299, 1939.

35. HOWARD, P. J., AND WORRELL, C. H., "Premature Infants in Later Life: Study of Intelligence and Personality of Twenty-two Premature Infants at Ages 8 to 19 Years," *Pediatrics*, 9:577–584, May, 1952.

36. MATEER, FLORENCE, *Child Behavior*, New York: Badger, 1918.

37. McDOUGALL, WILLIAM, *An Introduction to Social Psychology*, Revised Edition, Boston: Luce, 1926.

38. MEYER, M. F., "The Whale Among the Fishes—The Theory of Emotions," *Psychological Review*, 40:292–300, 1933.

39. JENKINS, DAVID H., "Interdependence in the Classroom," *Journal of Educational Research*, 45:137–144, 1951.

40. JERSILD, A. T., "Emotional Development," *Manual of Child Psychology, Second Edition*. Edited by Leonard Carmichael. New York: Wiley, 833–917, 1954.

41. PODOLSKY, EDWARD, "The Father's Occupation and the Child's Emotions," *Understanding the Child*, 23:77–85, 1954.

42. OLSON, W. C., *Child Development*, Boston: Heath, 1949.

43. PERRIN, F. A. C., *Psychology: Its Methods and Principles*, New York: Holt, 1932.

44. PLANT, J. S., *Personality and the Cultural Pattern*, New York: The Commonwealth Fund, 1937.

45. PRESCOTT, D. A., *Emotion and the Educative Process*, Washington: American Council on Education, 1938.

46. RECTOR, BESSIE M., "An Approach to Emotional Growth In the Classroom," *Understanding the Child*, 23:77–85, 1954.

47. RAGSDALE, C. E., *Modern Psychologies and Education*, New York: Macmillan, 1932.

48. REYMERT, M. L., *Feelings and Emotion*. New York: McGraw-Hill, 1950.

49. SHEPPARD, D., AND SHEPPARD, E. U., "Color Association," *Psychological Newsletter*, 5 (3):77–95, 1954.

50. SAUL, L. J., "Physiological Effects of Emotional Tension," *Personality and the Behavior Disorders, Vol. I*, edited by S. McV. Hunt, New York: Ronald Press, 1944.

51. SHERMAN, W. AND I. C., "Sensory-Motor Responses in Infants," *Journal of Comparative Psychology*, 5:53–68, 1925.

52. SYMONDS, P. M., *The Dynamics of Human Adjustment*, New York: Appleton-Century, 1946.

53. THORPE, L. P., *Psychological Foundations of Personality*, New York: McGraw-Hill, 1938.

54. ——, *Child Psychology and Development*, New York: Ronald Press, 1946.

55. TROW, W. C., *Educational Psychology*, Boston: Houghton Mifflin, 1931.

56. WATSON, J. B., *Behaviorism*, New York: Norton, 1930.

57. TOPP, ROBERT E., "Preadolescent Behavior Patterns Suggestive of Emotional Malfunctioning," *Elementary School Journal*, 52:340–343, 1952.

58. WINKLEY, RUTH, JACKSON, KATHERINE, FAUST, OTTO A., MURRAY, MARJORIE F., AND CERMAK, ETHEL G., "Emotional Reactions and Behavior of Children In the Home: A Method of Study," *Journal of Pediatrics,* 38:476–481, 1951.
59. ZULLINGER, HANS, "The Case of Franz and Lotti," *Journal of Projective Techniques,* 17:61–65, 1953.

12

THE DEVELOPMENT OF MORAL
AND ETHICAL BEHAVIOR

INTRODUCTION – A CHALLENGE

There exists a great need for teachers to assume more responsibility in aiding children in the development of desirable moral and ethical behavior. Such a point of view is based mainly upon three seldom recognized facts. First, because of the changes now taking place in home and community life, there is a lessening of the influences that in the past have molded and facilitated desirable moral and ethical behavior. Today the family is more far-flung in its activities. Fathers seem to have less contact with their children, and mothers are working or spending more of their time outside the home. In the past children were part of the economic background. They were necessary for work that made the home economically sound. They labored in and around the home with parents. The development of desirable moral and ethical behavior evolved as a part of daily life. Today the development of these traits is contingent upon a greater variety of influences. Parents seem less inclined to include children in such talk as adults may have on moral and ethical problems. There is less opportunity for children to become a part of family functioning in which moral and ethical attitudes evolve through the pattern of daily living. The absence of child participation in family life has forced parents, in training children, to rely on moralizing and to set rules of behavior. Quite frequently, since moralizing is merely rationalizing and does not necessarily reflect the actual parental ideals in practice, children become confused. Parents set for their children codes of behavior which they themselves do not practice. Because of such insincerity and the lack of opportunity for integrating the development of standards with the activities of family life, other influences assume increasing importance.

An Opportunity for the Schools. As a result, teachers and schools have a greater opportunity than ever before. Teachers, in their own drive for expression and in their attempt to free themselves from the inhibiting influences of "small-town" demands made on them, are reluctant to assume any kind of role that requires being a model of exemplary behavior. For too long they have resented the artificial restraints imposed on them. We do not advocate a continuation of this point of view. The development of moral and ethical behavior requires much more than artificial or real teacher models. If modeling is to be a factor, it should be based on such qualities as consideration, understanding, and fair dealing with children rather than on the kind of hats one wears, the church attended, or the kind of company kept (48) .

Part of Total Growth. Secondly, the development of desirable moral and ethical character is a part of the total growth process. Physical growth, mental growth, and emotional response are all related to this phase of development. Maturity is likewise a factor. As the child grows and matures, old ideals shift or are reinterpreted in terms of new needs and demands. Or, if shifting and reinterpretation do not aid in the adjustments of the child, he adopts new ideals and standards. The school should assume some responsibility for assisting the child in his behavior motivations, aspirations, and other psychological activities related to goal-setting.

Perhaps the best argument for encouraging teachers to become interested is that they should be concerned in the matter of attitudes with helping the child to do better what he is going to do anyway. There is no denying that the activities of the school contribute to the development of moral and ethical behavior. The law of practice, in learning, substantiates this view. If the child has developed petty cheating in his social relations with other children, the school is not helping him any if it encourages, through pressure tactics, petty cheating on tests. And certainly, on the other hand, when the child has certain wholesome ideals and behavior traits, these should not be undermined by such practices but protected and encouraged through cooperative and group achievement as well as through personal accomplishment evaluated in terms of the ability, capacity, and growth status of the child.

Evidence shows that as the child gets older and more mature, he turns more and more to the social codes, modes, biases, and prejudices of his family (5). Such evidence might be taken as an indictment of the conventional school program in which its activities for improving ethical and moral behavior tend to solidify status already achieved. If the child is honest, he is singled out and made a hero. If he has indulged in petty thefts, all perhaps the result of an impoverished background, faulty family relations, or poor peer adjustment, the conventional school is likely to foster or entrench these traits. The school develops heroes by having culprits available. By contrast, or by its concept of the "normal curve," one child is good and another is bad. The growth point of view considers such notions products of a discarded and invalid psychology. All children are plastic and amenable to environmental stimuli. From this point of view, growth in any aspect of development is possible. Consequently, the school should assume some responsibility for this phase of its culture.

DEFINITION

There is some substantiation of the idea that moral and ethical behavior reflects the character of an individual. Hartmann agrees with this view as evidenced by his statement that ". . . a moral quality surrounds the word character . . ." (17). Jones is inclined to be more specific in pointing out the differences between ethical behavior and character, but does not deny the relationship between the two (29). According to him character is not coextensive with ethical or moral behavior. Morality implies conformity with, and acceptance of, existing standards, whereas character may imply quite the contrast. From this point of view nonconformists may show the greatest depth of character in contrast to character which meekly accepts the status quo. On the other hand, Jones does not imply that character has no relation to morality. Character is regarded as more dynamic and is the more inclusive quality, of which morality is only a part. Adding to morality the ability to select goals and values and to direct behavior toward their achievement is what he seems to mean by character.

Taking this as our definition of moral and ethical character, we see that morality is a broader aspect of behavior and does not necessarily imply conformity but rather the problem of conformity. Conformity frequently involves a very difficult decision. Thus moral behavior may be positive or negative in reference to codes or mores. This meaning is very similar to the viewpoint expressed by Breckenridge and Vincent, who describe it as mature judgment which assesses properly the balance between individual and group rights in evaluating behavior. It includes self-control, awareness of one's rights, reaction to authority, and skill and insight into group relations (6).

STAGES OF MATURITY

Gradual acceptance of group codes and the ability to weigh these against personal, impulsive, willful behavior is brought about through maturity as a product of the reaction of the individual to his broad social experiences. Piaget has outlined three stages in its development (27, 34).

First Stage, Blind Obedience. In the first stage, the child's concept of what is right or wrong is based simply on what his parents permit or forbid. This is what Piaget has called "moral realism." In this stage no concept is involved. No shading of behavior is possible. The act performed is right or wrong. Children regard justice in punishment not in the implications of rightness or wrongness of the act but in terms of the seriousness of the damage done. This stage lasts for several years (30).

Second Stage, Interprets Rules. As the child gains experience and some understanding of the implications of his acts for himself and for others, he advances to the second stage. He gradually learns that a rule which applies at one time does not always apply at another. He begins to see that rules are not necessarily fixed and that parents and others modify them under given circumstances. Teachers are well acquainted with the situation in which kindergarten children who have been told by parents to come home as soon as school is dismissed show concern if an unexpected shower causes them to remain at school until the storm is over. And teachers are well aware that some children arrive promptly at school during bad weather because they have been encouraged to believe that it is wrong to be late. Such children have not reached the second stage in which the spirit rather than the letter of the rule is the important idea. Children generally begin to understand elasticity in authority of this kind at nine or ten years of age.

Third Stage, Interprets the Act. In the third stage, the full implications of an act are understood. This level of understanding includes an appreciation of the necessity for punishment or atonement. Reaching this level of maturity requires experience, understanding, good treatment, and considerable intelligence. The moral judgment of adolescent children, though more mature, is frequently less in harmony with the codes of adults than the judgments of elementary school children. Whereas maturity makes it possible for the individual to grow out of the more childish, dependent outlook on right and wrong, it also offers the opportunity to develop codes of behavior quite contrary to those of the adult society. In some ways the young adolescent is an outcast. He is mature enough to desire independence and to feel many of the basic needs and drives of adults, but immature enough to be considered unimportant in his potential contributions to adult life. Consequently, it is often difficult for the adolescent to accept the codes given him by adults. As the child's capacity for identifying himself with others increases, his acceptance of adult standards begins.

Nine to Twelve Good Learning Years. In spite of the difficulties mentioned, which are exaggerated by poor guidance from parents or teachers, the child from nine to twelve years of age can develop considerable ethical and moral independence. Concepts of fairness, truthfulness, honesty, and justice come to have deeper and broader meanings. At this age, the generalizations and supporting rules and regulations begin to be understood as participation includes broader social experiences. The child who has a background of affection and has achieved belongingness is ready to assume increasing personal responsibility, a greater interest in school demands, and a desire to cooperate in school and group affairs.

Adolescence Brings Conflicts. Adolescence is normally the period when opposition between peer codes and adult standards must begin to be resolved. Learning to cooperate harmoniously with others, to appreciate fairness and loyalty to associates contributes to a necessary state of readiness. This, of course, is the period of absorption with new personal and social needs and the resultant potential conflict between peer and adult codes of acceptable behavior. Whereas society provides a challenge and innumerable difficulties, nature provides an equalizing force. The adolescent, typically, is endowed with the power of developing an intense idealism. Thus, for most adolescents improvement and understanding rapidly move in the direction of the finer and more idealized thoughts and standards. On the other hand, the great natural drive and need for expression requires careful nourishment. If denied proper outlets, or if forced to accept immobility of expression, there comes a time when this need finds unapproved satisfactions in socially destructive action.

PROBLEMS AND DIFFICULTIES

Child an Egocentric. One of the basic difficulties in developing satisfying moral and ethical traits is the opposition offered by the child's own personal egocentric drives. The very young child is primarily selfish and impulsive. Fortunately, as he matures his egocentric interests are replaced by more social motives. He learns self-control and consideration by eventually realizing that he is happier and his needs are better met if he is living harmoniously with others. Such conflict as he finds between his own personal wishes and the wishes of the group is most satisfactorily resolved by learning to determine the proper balance between what one owes to oneself and what one owes to others. The goal is sufficient control over one's primitive and selfish impulses to enable one to live happily within a group. This is not brought about through simple repression. The goal can be achieved only through the projection of emotional energy into channels which are mutually satisfying (11).

Background Differences. Another factor which makes group teaching of ethical and moral behavior difficult is the variation in home and social backgrounds. At the two extremes are the underprivileged and the overprivileged. Those with the strongest pressures toward deviational behavior are often found at either of these two extremes. Whether it is stealing, lying, or sex misbehavior, these two groups produce many instances of deviational behavior.

The child from the underprivileged home has pressure to steal, to attract attention, etc., because he has fewer of these things in his own environment. Children in such circumstances have very little opportunity to learn the meaning of property rights. Since they have but little opportunity to possess, they learn little about what it means to cherish something. Because they don't know how it feels to have possessions stolen, lost, or damaged, they think but little of stealing things from other children (6). Added to this is their background of using everything in their environment within reach. Together the total situation tends to make them feel that they may rightfully use whatever is at hand. In their environment they take an orange from a fruit stand without any compunction and similarly take a pencil from a classmate. Taking a pocketbook is an easy step when the environment has helped promote the habit of petty stealing.

The overprivileged have difficulty in learning desired behavior in regard to property rights for exactly the opposite reason. So many things have been given to them that they have had no opportunity to learn values. Consequently the appreciation of another child's property has no significance. Like the underprivileged chidren, they have but little chance to develop a feeling of guilt or wrongdoing when, without purpose or to satisfy a passing need, they take something from another.

Individual Differences. Probably the greatest difficulty one meets in attempting to help children develop desirable moral and ethical patterns is the wide range of individual differences in behavior already established.

Children Cannot Be Definitely Classified. What strikes the teacher first after becoming acquainted with her group is the fact that children cannot be classified as honest and dishonest, as morally strong and morally weak. Individual differences in ideals, in moral character, in ethical behavior are as widespread as differences in reading, in height, or in general intelligence (Fig. 51). The distribution shown should prove interesting because it represents a spread based on tests of honesty-dishonesty in play and in regular school situations. It does not represent a distribution from a test in which pupils indicated that they would act in a certain way, or on knowl-

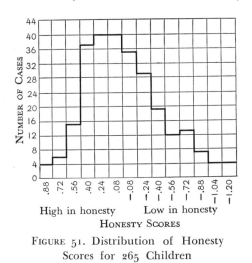

FIGURE 51. Distribution of Honesty
Scores for 265 Children

edge of how to act, but on actual test situations ingeniously devised so that cheating efforts were recorded and children did not realize the purpose of the tests.

The wide range of behavior observed in these children is similar to the distribution of performances in reading, or height gain, and resembles many other performance distributions. Of even greater importance and a fact that further complicates the situation is the elusiveness of the honesty-dishonesty pattern in the same child. A child may be honest in one kind of situation and dishonest in another. The difference, of course, is largely the result of differences in the power of the motivating force. A child may cheat to get a good mark or to obtain the approval of his parents but refrain from stealing a single penny or pencil. Another child may steal the pennies but show considerable resistance toward cheating on a school test.

Problem of Trait Conflict. Related to this same problem, in the way of difficulty in understanding and guiding development, is the fact that occasionally one desirable trait sometimes conflicts with another equally desirable. For example, in order to retain the loyalty and trust of a peer group, a child may be forced to lie to a teacher or parent. To ask a child to "tell on" other children places him in a most difficult situation, particularly if the search for truth is being conducted by a teacher or parent who is liked or loved. In keeping with the hypothesis regarding delinquency, that the child does not necessarily show delinquent trends, but rather demonstrates delinquent behavior in a specific kind of situation, the child may be regarded as differing in degrees of honesty according to the situation and the nature of the motivation involved.

FACTORS AFFECTING BEHAVIOR

A. BIOLOGICAL DETERMINANTS

There are many biological factors which are operative one way or another in determining moral and ethical behavior. From infancy to adulthood, such factors as the individual's energy output and his general vivacity affect the kind of attitudes and ideals displayed. Health and general physical well-being are therefore important. The vigorous, active child, other factors being equal, rather easily learns desirable behavior. The sickly child who is phlegmatic, shrinking, or withdrawn will learn with greater difficulty. One child may be cheerful and another fretful, easily hurt, and irritable. Other factors which influence the development of ideals and attitudes are motor coordination, strength, attractiveness, racial background, and sex. Such constitutional sex differences as exist are further exaggerated through differences in codes and ideals held for them by society.

Intelligence when considered as a hereditary influence may also be called a biological determinant. Bright and dull children vary considerably in their ideals, attitudes, and responses to various motivations. Bright children are much more likely to be liberal in viewpoint, for example, than dull children.

B. SOCIOECONOMIC BACKGROUND

Socioeconomic factors influencing moral and ethical development are too numerous to mention in detail (5). Consequently, the whole group will be treated under certain general headings or categories. It must be kept in mind, however, that behavior is rarely the result of one single grouping of influences. Behavior is the product of many influences acting in a determinant combination.

1. The Home Influence

The importance of the home has already been mentioned. Its importance has been noted particularly in the chapter dealing with personal-social development and in the role of emotion in the child's development. As in these other aspects, the home is also the strongest potential influence, although it is but one of several institutions and agencies that contribute to the child's development. Frequently its power derives not from what it is but from what it is not. On the other hand, a real home makes a strong positive contribution to the child's behavior (7).

Type of Research. Evidence of the home's influence has been obtained in two ways: (1) by observing the behavior of children from poor environments and (2) by attempting to determine the effects of positive teaching efforts. Unfortunately, there is more of the negative kind of data, but it is nevertheless of great value. Children who develop deviational behavior through faulty attitudes or misdirected drives land in institutions where they can be intensively studied. Quite typical of the kind of data presented is that of Pressey (35). In comparing boys in institutions for delinquent children with children in the public school, Pressey points out that fifty-five per cent of the parents of delinquent children were living together as compared with eighty-one per cent of the parents of typical school children. Further comparisons show that thirty-two per cent of the delinquents had only one living parent as compared to fifteen per cent for normal children, and the parents of ten per cent of the delinquents were divorced in contrast with three per cent of the others. Similar to the above information which points out the influence of a faulty home, Paynter and

Blanchard attempt to rate the characteristics which contribute most to undesirable behavior and least to desirable moral and ethical attitudes (33). Some three hundred children were observed through child study clinics. According to these investigators lack of discipline and training was considered the greatest contributing influence in ninety per cent of the cases.

The attitudes of parents on moral and ethical issues are also significant. In this connection Hartshorne and May studied the similarity of viewpoints of the child with others in his environment (19). This study reports correlations of scores of children with scores of parents to be .54, with friends .35, with club leaders .14, with teachers .06, and 0.00 with Sunday-school teachers. These findings relate to specific beliefs and attitudes and do not negate the fact that teachers reflect the general point of view of parents who hold status in the ruling social grouping of a given community. It also reports the influence of peers as follows: with friends in different classrooms .23, but with friends in the same classrooms .66. This would indicate that such influence as the teacher has should be directed toward group change rather than toward influencing the individual child. These data also indicate the dominant position of parental influence.

Variation of Influence in the Home. Within the home itself there is a variation of effectiveness of factors influencing behavior. The child almost invariably shows a closer relationship with the mother than with the father. Size of family probably plays a part but to date no clear conclusions have been formulated. The amount of security achieved by the child is often mentioned as an important factor. There is much evidence that if a child is rejected by either or both parents he becomes aggressive in his behavior and through the action involved can easily develop antisocial ideals. Teachers should keep in mind that their rejection of a given child can easily lead to compensating oversolicitude on the part of parents with possible ensuing evils, or it may add to the pressure already felt through rejection by parents.

Although low economic background is generally regarded as having a great influence on the child's moral outlook, it is likely that its effect has been overrated, since it accompanies so many other affective forces. Jones in summarizing the work of Healy and

Bronner brings out a similar conclusion (29). In this study delinquent and nondelinquent children in the same family were paired. Equating home background decreased the seeming influence of formal sociological factors, but it did not eliminate psychological factors. In the same home it was found that the delinquent child rather than the nondelinquent felt discriminated against or frustrated. Such children reported a lack of parental affection and general emotional stress.

2. Influences of Associates

As indicated by the high correlations between scores on tests dealing with concepts of right and wrong, few factors have greater influence than intimate companions. It is evidently the small group intimacies within a gang, rather than the gang itself, which are important. This does not negate the general influence of the gang. Within the gang there are small cliques, intimate friendships, and loyalties, as well as counter loyalties and antagonistic groups.

3. The Church Influence

In the main, the evidence regarding the role of the church in guiding moral and ethical behavior is encouraging (42). The problem has been attacked from two different angles. First, considerable testing has been carried out to determine the relation between Sunday-school and church attendance and scores on certain types of honesty measures. And secondly, correlations have been computed between character ratings by teachers and scores on tests of Biblical knowledge (24).

One of the most outstanding series of studies has been made by Hartshorne and May (18). Utilizing a test which provided an opportunity for cheating as well as recording such incidence, Hartshorne and May in one study compared the honesty scores of children attending Sunday school with those who did not attend. In two samplings, with a large number of public school children used as cases, the results showed a slight but scarcely significant superiority in favor of those attending Sunday school. In one sampling the percentage of cheating for those attending Sunday school was 31 as compared with 40 for the nonattending group. In a second sampling, the comparative percentages ranged from 38 to 43. In another test purporting to measure helpfulness, children who attended church schools obtained slightly higher scores than those who did not attend, and those who attended regularly received higher scores than those who were irregular in attendance. Further evidence of the effect of church affiliation has been presented by Maller who showed, on the basis of his honesty tests, that a group of Jewish children obtained an increase in score during a period of attendance at religious classes (31).

On the question whether Biblical knowledge has a moral influence, the data also shows some significance. Taylor and Powers obtained correlations of .50 between the teachers' character ratings of the children and their scores on the Laycock Bible Test, whereas correlations between the character ratings and intelligence test scores were found to be only .24 (42). This is believed to indicate that the relation between the character ratings and the Bible test scores was something other than the result of intelligence. Hightower found less convincing results. Little or no relationship between the various phases of moral behavior and Biblical knowledge was detected. In this study, correlations were computed between Biblical knowledge scores and scores on tests of lying and cheating, as well as between Biblical knowledge scores and teachers' ratings of character.

It has been argued that the slight differences generally favoring church and religious activity are really the result of background and home factors rather than the result of church and religious affiliation. Unfortunately, the complexity of the various relationships has been so great that it has been almost impossible to measure one of these effects isolated from the others.

Effect of Moral Knowledge on Behavior. Closely related to the effect of church attendance and Biblical knowledge is the question of the extent to which knowledge of desirable behavior actually leads to the kind of behavior desired. Character education has universally been based upon the principle that knowledge of proper behavior leads to good conduct. This idea has been virtually abandoned at the present time, but because it is still held by some lay leaders it demands further attention. A discussion is particularly pertinent at the present time, when not only unethical behavior is deplored but the teaching of citizenship, American idealism, democracy, etc., is quite generally challenged. In the main, the idea that better citizenship will result primarily from better and more complete knowledge of history and government and that ethical behavior will result from knowledge of desirable behavior, can be dispelled by anyone who accepts objective evidence in regard to the situation. Generally accepted findings are about as follows: character training has generally been based on the idea that if one rationally accepts an ideal or value, he will act in accordance with the precept held. Acceptance of such a view was motivated by the Herbartian psychophysical theorists who maintained that dominant psychic ideas controlled overt behavior. This idea is dispelled by a whole series of psychological developments regarding the matter. Outstanding among these are Dewey's concept of learning, the Thorndike bond theory, and lastly and most important, the principle of specificity as portrayed in the experiments of Hartshorne and May.[1]

The research seemingly verifies such a generalization. Early studies showed almost no relationship between knowing and doing. The more intensive character education research of the 1930's indicated some relationships but scarcely enough to justify the many current traditional schemes for improving citizenship and for developing desirable ethical and moral behavior.

Healy and Fernald were among the first of the modern group to investigate this problem (20). Comparing moral judgments and moral nature in general they discovered no tangible connections. In the same decade Haines failed to find any significant differences between the moral judgments of normal and delinquent girls (16). Raubenheimer (36), Weber (45), and the Chassels (10), all arrived at similar conclusions from experiments conducted in the following decade. Raubenheimer obtained correlations from — .11 to .31 in attempting to discover the extent to which offense ratings would differentiate between delinquents and nondelinquents. Weber obtained approximately the same results in a study prepared to distinguish between normal and delinquent women by

1 Briefly, Dewey's learning by doing, Thorndike's theory that behavior involves specific neural connections, and the Hartshorne-May concept that an individual may demonstrate both ethical and unethical behavior depending on the situation, rule against the idea that ethical behavior is general.

their judgments of the seriousness of certain specified offenses. The Chassels obtained low positive correlations .17, with their data on judgments of consequences of acts and the quality of actual conduct. Such evidence seems to indicate that where knowledge is completely isolated from experiences in learning attitudes, it is quite unrelated to conduct. Those who are interested in improving character training programs must conclude from such data that desirable behavior can only result through generalization based upon satisfying experience in the specific trait desired.

Whereas the data just reviewed dealt with isolated groups of individuals, some considered normal and others delinquent, the character education studies of Hartshorne and May used as subjects children whom they found in various school situations (19). The work of these men differed considerably from that of the earlier investigators. A large number of knowledge and attitude questionnaires were devised and used to obtain data. In many instances the same children were observed in a series of ingenious conduct situations. Here no child was labeled normal or delinquent through some chance or inadvertent legal characterization. The conduct situations included behavior on tests, games, athletics, and many other activities which were a normal part of regular school life. Correlations generally were positive but low. Although low, these correlations suggest some kind of a relationship between knowledge of right behavior and the conduct of the individual displaying such knowledge. The conclusion to be drawn may be taken from the authors themselves who say, "When pupils are led to think efficiently about conduct, genuine changes in conduct may be expected." The reader should not be misled into believing that this is a simple matter, however. Mere moralizing or vague readings will not bring satisfactory results. "Thinking efficiently" involves action, judgment, and generalization with all its implications (22).

4. Peer Influence

The point scarcely needs repeating that a child's associates greatly influence his behavior. A very interesting finding which explains that the behavior of a child while with the gang may be quite different under other circumstances is one brought out in the 1928 study of Hartshorne and May (18). In this survey it was found that correlations between children's standings on tests of deception were much higher when compared with scores of friends in the same home room than when compared with those obtained between friends in different home rooms. The correlations obtained were .66 and .23 respectively. Such a difference would indicate the greater influence of companions in close proximity, where encouragement, suggestion, "dares," and other aspects of close association are most effective.

Specificity of Group Behavior. This same idea is borne out by observers who testify to the effectiveness of group morale. As has been previously indicated, the character traits exhibited by a child or by groups of children are very specific in nature. While it is possible that habits of neatness, honesty, and courtesy may be encouraged in the whole group, it is also possible for the same group to be snobbish and to present closely knit exclusive social boundaries. This characteristic of specificity may be demonstrated by a group which shows a high degree of courtesy, honesty, and cooperation in relations with one teacher, and with another teacher a half hour later demonstrates almost exactly the opposite behavior.

An experiment by Jones presents some very interesting facts regarding the permanence of learning of this kind. In brief, in an experiment involving seventh- and eighth-grade children, projects were developed which had for their goal improved character and good citizenship (28). Jones' procedure involved testing during the course of the project and again later after the experimental groupings had been dissolved. As might be expected from the facts previously noted, the groups with the best morale made the greatest gain. However, on the later testings, when the groups had been dissolved, it was found that the greatest retention was shown by those children of the poor morale groups who had showed gains. Conversely, the original gains were retained most poorly by the children of the high morale groups.

Implications for Teachers. Although at first this seems discouraging, there are implications here for teachers. What Jones refers to as *group-linked* gains are dependent for their effect upon the total group and the general morale which it reflects. For example, a group which is retrogressive in respect to desirable behavior may influence a child to act in a way which is not customary for him. The influence, although bad, is only temporary. On the other hand, when a child demonstrates behavior characteristics which are acceptably superior to his usual mode of action, the observer, teacher, or experimenter must not expect such desirable behavior to continue when the contact has been brief. In other words, the influence of group morale, either good or bad, must continue for a considerable period of time. The first offense, then, of a child under group influence should not be considered too serious, if the child can be quickly removed and placed with other children. And further, remedial treatment which is dependent on placing a child in a desirable social setting must guarantee a lengthy continuance of the contact.

5. Extracurricular Influences

Factors of this kind which have been studied, in regard to their effect on moral and ethical behavior traits, are many in number. Perhaps the most important of these are clubs, motion pictures, the radio, and reading activities.

Much is made today of clubs and club activity in combating delinquency among young adolescents. To the lay person such activities carry inherent values for improving behavior, although the evidence is not too conclusive in their favor. Undoubtedly the meager advantages found are the result of difficulty in dissociating the effect of these organizations from the behavior influences of the gang, the church, the home, and the school (41).

Effect of Club Membership. Regardless of whether there are complementary effects or not, the evidence points to some beneficial results. Voelker's study, although based on too few cases to justify unqualified conclusions, indicates certain values to be derived from participation in such activities as the Boy Scouts (44). Numerous other studies point out the striking results of good club programs under competent leadership. It is generally conceded, however, that the development of desirable traits must be clearly and intensively directed toward specific desired ends. And although the results seem to be specific, there is a general belief that the causal factors are rather general.

Influence of Movies. Much interest has been displayed in the effect of movies on child behavior. Recently popular magazines have devoted considerable space to this problem, and nearly everyone has seen the photographs in the picture weeklies of the facial expressions of children while watching movies. There has been considerable debate on the topic, and parents and teachers have been greatly interested.

Lay and near-scientific consideration of the problem does not represent exclusively the extent of attention paid. There has been a considerable amount of well-planned research on this topic. One of the most disturbing facts revealed by this type of study has been the data dealing with frequency of movie attendance by young children. Although there are wide variations in different parts of the country, it is generally agreed that urban children attend the movies frequently. And most significant is the fact that in urban areas the children who live in the most overcrowded parts of the city attend most frequently. In the areas where attendance is the most regular it was found that children begin to go to movies at about eight years of age and attend on the average as often as four or five times a week. If movies are bad for children, the findings of Dale are certainly distressing. He has reported that in a certain section of New York seventeen per cent of the movie audience was comprised of children under seven years of age (13). Equally distressing is his finding that over fifty per cent of the audiences were under twenty years of age. Incidentally, it is believed that during the war years, with increased means and an increase in the number of working mothers, these percentages were considerably greater.

Most significant is the analysis made of the picture themes viewed by children. Outstanding was the great frequency of crime, the overemphasis on love scenes, and the lack of relation between the clothes worn by the actors and the work of the characters they portrayed. As Dale points out, most of them had no visible means of earning a living and yet about seventy-five per cent of them appeared at one time or another in evening clothes.

Related to the lack of work habits is the easy success achieved in many of the stories portrayed. Economic background is also exaggerated. Average people — their problems, loves, interests, successes — are generally ignored. The very rich and the very poor are the chief subjects of these films. And equally exaggerated are luck and physical attributes. There is no question that such characterization and unreality is quite incompatible with the growth needs of young children and furnishes little in the way of positive good.

Evidence of Effect. The question whether such influences are bad is not decisively answered. Some investigators have concluded that they contribute to delinquency and to the development of bad habits because they are too mature for the child's stage of development at the time he sees them. Certain results obtained from questioning delinquents point clearly to such effects. In general, these investigations indicate that undesirable movies are direct causal factors in delinquency in from ten to twenty per cent of the cases. Blumer and Hauser (4), as well as Cressey and Thrasher (12), present such evidence. Other investigators feel that delinquents are incapable of diagnosing their own difficulties and that the results obtained by questionnaires and interviews are quite invalid. Healy and Bronner (22) and Burt (8), for instance, are among this group. Burt points out that the actual influence is small, and Healy and Bronner consider that only about one per cent of their delinquent cases have been so influenced.

General Conclusion on Movies. All in all it would appear that some movies have undesirable effects and others have good effects. It is reasonable to assume that effects, good or bad, more likely result when the attitude pictured is not too far from the life problems of the child. The child with delinquent tendencies may receive just the stimulus he needs for overt delinquent behavior when what he sees strikes a sympathetic chord with his own pent-up emotions. The child on the borderline of more desirable behavior will also receive motivation in the right direction by seeing movies of the better kind. In regard to pairing "bad" children with good pictures and "good" children with bad pictures, results would probably be negative in both instances. At least a considerably lengthy interaction in either case would be necessary to produce significant changes in behavior. Movies, to a considerable degree, are a part of the child's total environment. To the extent to which they reflect good or bad environments they influence his behavior.

Radio Influence. The influence of the radio on the development of moral and ethical behavior is similar to that of the movies (47).

Most children spend a great deal of time listening to radio programs which seem to have little effect one way or the other on their behavior. And on the other hand, a smaller number listen to programs that are either good or bad. Such influence as is exerted is usually the kind which arouses emotional response. Children show emotional reactions in listening to exciting, and for them, frightening programs. In some instances such programs can contribute to persisting emotional disturbance. In other instances, less harmful but definitely not good for the child, radio provides an escape. For the child who is unsocial and shy and has a tendency to withdraw from group life, programs of this sort are especially harmful.

On the good side, the contribution of the radio is more educational than behavioral. Of course it must be admitted that learning can lead to the development of attitudes which in themselves influence and color behavior. The influence of radio as a factor in enhancing learning and desirable development has evaded acceptable research and scrutiny. This is probably due to the fact that most programs are either mediocre or bad and that the problem of relating radio to children's needs and to basic curriculum problems has not been solved. Radio has been dragged into the situation rather than used as an outgrowth of an experience.

Effect of Books and Magazines. Much can be said about the effect of reading material. Since reading represents such a broad problem and has been given great attention by educators and others, it need be discussed here only as it bears upon moral and ethical development.

For many years reading has been looked upon as a positive means for promoting desirable character. Such a point of view undoubtedly goes back to the early colonial days when the purpose of teaching reading was to enable the young to learn to read the Bible. Since that time there have been numerous schemes utilizing the reading of certain selected stories and anecdotes as an aid in character development. Recent research can find no significant differences between groups where one was used as a control and the other was subjected to readings prescribed for improving moral knowledge and behavior. In reference to its negative effects, there is more evidence. Healy in 1915 (21) and again in 1936

with Bronner (22) gave evidence to support his belief in the perni-
cious effect of certain reading matter.

To the reader, this discussion of the effects of the movies, the
radio, and of reading matter may seem inconclusive. It is. On the
basis of the research, one can only say that in some instances these
aids to learning seem beneficial, in others they are detrimental in
that they waste time which might be given over to more profitable
activities. They may even disseminate knowledge which leads toward individual or group harm. The difficulty in arriving at definite and specific answers to the problem is the fact that these three
factors are not only interrelated in a highly complex way but are
closely related to many other environmental effects. In fact they
are so closely related that there seems to be no known way of
isolating one from the other so that individual influences can be
studied. Results, however, are clear enough in regard to both
beneficial or harmful tendencies to merit a few broad generalizations.

1. There are good movies, books, and radio programs which
children should see, read, and hear, respectively, and there are
poor movies, poor books, and poor radio programs. Obviously,
teachers are interested in introducing children to the good and
shielding them from the bad. In doing this, or perhaps we should
say in doing this with beneficial results, certain safeguards must
be established. It would be a waste of time, for example, to introduce a group of borderline delinquents to good movies, good
books, or good radio programs in isolation from certain other influences. Wise use of these aids demands that they be part of a
general program to improve the total environment. Better hous-
ing, better recreation, better health facilities, and fair treatment
are probably essential in such a program. In other words, there is
the necessity for relating what is being seen in a picture — characterization, attitude, broad-mindedness, fairness, sympathy and
understanding, kindness to animals — with group needs and problems and motivations which are basically important to the group
or to the individual.

2. There is a middle classification between the extremes of good
and bad which can be subdivided into two parts. In this area
would be the books and programs that waste time and those that

have a mildly stimulating effect on the emotions. Some books and movies can be considered a waste of time because they seem to have neither positive nor negative effects on the child. The books and programs that have a mildly stimulating effect on the emotions may or may not be desirable. Their effect may be good or bad depending upon the child. Some children may need the kind of emotional release provided by viewing or listening to pictures or programs whose value can be questioned because they are exciting. And other children may be overstimulated, develop fears, become afraid of the dark, or manifest such other undesirable behavior traits.

3. Whether the result be good or bad it must continue over a period of time to be effective. Learning does not take place at once, nor does it take place over short specified periods of time such as a day, month, semester, or year. Since learning is a continuous process paralleling the development of the child, the use of learning aids must be continuous and repetitive to be most effective.

INNER FACTORS AFFECTING BEHAVIOR

A. THEORIES OF MOTIVATION

Conventional psychology has presented several viewpoints which purport to explain the inner dynamics of behavior. One of the most interesting explanations is that of psychoanalysis, which developed originally from the doctrines of Freud. Another, quite generally discarded today, is the explanation for which William McDougall is generally regarded as responsible. More recent is the behaviorist explanation suggested by John Watson in this country but which many think to have sprung from the early German school of thought [2] which discarded the psychological for the physiological interpretation of behavior. This viewpoint is probably responsible for the oversimplified explanation of all behavior as a complex of conditioned reflexes, thereby taking its cue from the work of Pavlov. A further viewpoint is Sherrington's, which attempts to explain behavior as a result of neuromuscular action.

[2] A. Bethe, Th. Beer, and J. von Uexküll proposed to eliminate all psychological conceptions from the study of behavior.

Freud's Theory. Freud's analysis of motivation rested upon the idea that in addition to the conscious mind, there is also a subconscious or unconscious mind which is influential as an organized and dominant behavior control in all human beings (15). Thus Freud saw the mind as having two clearly separate compartments, the conscious and the unconscious, respectively. Difficulties in interpreting behavior which cannot be explained as conscious can be solved by exploring the unconscious. Individuals frequently behave in a way contrary to conscious desires or wants because they are motivated by a subconscious unknown desire to act in a manner deplored by the conscious mind. As Freud explains it, the act is performed in spite of the objections of the conscious mind because of the dominance of the unconscious in relation to the particular act. Ideas or desires which are objectionable to the conscious mind are repressed. Repression does not obliterate them but forces them into the unconscious, where they operate according to their strength of drive or dominance in given situations. The development of the unconscious mind results through either voluntary repression or expulsion from the conscious mind as the result of injury or accident of an unpleasant nature or some sort of shock (43). Unconscious drives repressed through either means develop in relation to the meaning of the individual's social experiences and operate and influence behavior in a purposeful manner. Even more sensational is Freud's theory that the sex motive is the basis for all psychic energy and motivation. This concept is probably necessary to Freud's theory, since generally in the ordinary social situation the sex motive is substantially repressed and in the attempt to become freed does so in various types of camouflaged ways. Thus, types of abnormality and deviational behavior occur. Since other theories devote much attention to the physiological accompaniments of motivation, it is pertinent to point out that Freud virtually dismisses physiological accompaniments and devotes full attention to psychological activity.

Adlerian Theory. Also holding considerable prestige is Adler's concept of the inferiority influence. Adler rejected the idea that motivation is dominated only by repressed sex drives and claimed that an equally dominant factor is the motive to compensate for some real or felt functional or organic deficiency. The idea of repression was accepted by Adler, who believed that it explains deviational behavior through the unconscious drive to convince oneself and others of superiority. The basic force for motivation is the will to power or what might be called the desire for supremacy.

The Instinct Theory. According to McDougall, the human mind has specific innate tendencies which represent the basic motivations of all thought and action. Consequently they are regarded as representing the bases from which character and will are gradually developed under the influence of intelligence (32). To these he gave the name *instinct.* In a general way, an instinct may be defined as an inherited tendency to action of a specific kind. The action itself is motivated by a definite range of stimuli. Each relationship between instinct and motivation for action is regarded as having congenital value. In the main, the concept of instinct motivation is wholly physiological. McDougall, however, regarded instincts as having a purposive force with some selectivity of possible motor expression. Historically it is important to note that James also generally accepted the theory. He lists as instincts what today would be looked upon as mere reflexes — biting, chewing, clasping, crying, grimacing, licking, smiling, and the more complex behavior like curiosity, imitation, pugnacity, sympathy, self-assertion, and acquisition. The instinct view is quite outmoded today for two reasons: (1) the lack of agreement on the part of those who have proposed such views and their inability to differentiate between inherited and acquired aspects; (2) advances in research on conditioning and the growing belief in the organismic concept of behavior.

Mechanistic Explanations. During the latter part of the nineteenth century, the idea that animals were provided with a response system called *tropism* led to a great deal of experimentation. The idea gave rise in Germany to what might be called the physiological school of thought. The basic mechanism for motivation was to be discovered entirely in an individual's physiological equipment. This group, in its attempt to explain behavior entirely ignored all psychological phenomena. It made no important contribution to the problem of motivation but provided a link in the chain of experimentation which led eventually to what we call today *behaviorism.*

Most prominent, and accepted in part by many as an explanation for behavior, is the idea of the conditioned reflex. Probably the greatest contribution of the group holding this theory is in their demonstration that the relation between stimulus and response is dependent upon both physiological and psychological processes.

B. PRINCIPLES OF MOTIVATION

Two rather recent outstanding attempts have been made to reconcile the various theories of motivation. The first attempt was made by Troland in 1928 (43), the second by Jones in 1946 (29). Troland, leaning somewhat on the Freudian and the conditioning concepts, developed what he considered a new viewpoint but actually a synthesis of many features of the various earlier theories, all of which have some overlapping aspects. Jones fails to come out with any new combination of ideas organized into a unified theory. He also seems to depend much on the idea of conditioning as an explanation of motivation but adds points from the other theories which seem to him relevant and logical. A survey of the proposals and problems as discussed by these two investigators examined against the principles of growth and development would lead to the following conclusions.

Principle of Multiplicity and Modification. The organismic point of view would indicate that the individual is born with a multiplicity of potential actions. The tendencies to action, depending on varying individual receptiveness to stimuli, become integrated through experience-producing stimuli and usage in different ways. This viewpoint harmonizes and explains differences in behavior where all other factors seem equated or accounted for. To be more elaborate, potentiality is contingent upon the idea of the existence of the single cell or neurone. As a biological unit the neurone is differentiated within the individual so as to function under conditions of excitation and conduction. In the organism itself neurones merge to form various reacting combinations. The simpler of these are the reflexes; the more complicated are the pattern reactions. The important point to be made is that circumstances may modify the expected reflex or even bring a shift in the organized broad pattern.

Principle of Need. Supplanting the earlier idea of instinct is the more recent concept of need or want. In contrast to the specificity of the idea of instinct and its appearance as almost entirely contingent upon heredity, the idea of want or need is more developmental. The idea of a dynamic organism existing without a drive or tendency to action is untenable. Thus the development of moral behavior and desirable traits is no simple process. Reflexes merge into patterns influenced by inner dynamic drives and modified throughout by the relationship between the outer and the inner consequences.

Thus, motivation for desirable or undesirable behavior is an evolving affair further complicated and affected by maturational needs. The idea that behavior is exclusively the product of the consequences of exterior and interior factors is a facile oversimplification. Maturation is a factor in all kinds of growth and development and cannot be ignored. It brings new desires into focus at certain stages and also enhances growth, both good and bad. Thus maturity itself can at times be held responsible for shifts in the pattern of behavior regardless of exterior-interior relationships.

Principle of Continuation. Another principle is that the achievement of maximum desirable, ethical behavior demands continuation of effective factors. Where influences remain constant, there is the tendency for moral behavior to continue in the established individual pattern. Woodworth points out that any activity in which an individual may be engaged provides temporary motivation (49). In reference to character or moral behavior, the motivation for a child to act one way or another depends considerably upon the chain or series of past experiences related to the behavior at hand.

Effect of Emotional Conditioning. In behavior of a moral or ethical nature the emotional effects of experiences have not been investigated fully. Emotional effects, because of the enhancement which they provide in the way of satisfaction or dissatisfaction, must be regarded as important. In clinical work, where behavior can be explained as a conditioning toward a secondary or alternate response regarded as deviational, delinquent, or bad, it is found that emotional satisfactions tend to perpetuate the pattern. It is also found in remedial work with such cases that reconditioning can produce results in which the earlier pattern causes dissatisfaction and thereby tends to obliterate the undesired series.

Principle of Subconscious Control. Less can be said about the subconscious. There is nothing in organismic or developmental psychology to support the idea that the subconscious mind plays a very important part in ethical or moral behavior. Developmentalists perhaps are more concerned with the primary causes of deviational behavior than they are with the psychological explanation of such action and thereby have not investigated sufficiently. It may be that repressions, conflicts, and complexes cause deviational behavior. Most organismic investigators accept this idea. What they are concerned with primarily, however, is the identification of causes. They believe that digression into unapproved behavior is the result of thwarting of the response which would be natural under more normal circumstances. Consequently it is easier to accept the idea that a deviational response, such as sexual satisfaction identified with stealing, is the result of factors other than subconscious drives.

Principle of Concept. Although research shows but little relationship between knowing and doing, it does indicate that genuine concepts of desirable behavior tend to produce desirable behavior. This might technically be called the influence of verbalized concepts. Such a paralleling of goal and action raises the level of behavior beyond blind conditioning or what might be referred to as a low-level response. Verbalization and understanding tend to strengthen the pattern so that resistance to secondary or deviational responses is more successful. Only through understanding can goal and action be made compatible.

IMPROVING MORAL AND ETHICAL BEHAVIOR

A. BASES FOR GENERAL IMPROVEMENT

The problem of what can be done by the school to improve moral and ethical behavior must be touched upon. Unquestionably the best approach would be a case-study analysis in which the principles and facts underlying behavior could be brought to light and the responsibility of the school in relation to the specific diagnosis pointed out. Limited space makes such an approach impossible. The only alternative is to outline general plans and procedures which may be followed in order to reduce to a minimum the number of problem, or deviational, children and facilitate the acquisition of desirable behavior patterns.

1. General Personality Factors

Good Health Desirable. The factor of health has been mentioned earlier. The child who is healthy, growing normally, well coordinated, and normally skilled in games has a much better chance of acquiring desirable behavior than a child deficient in these physical attributes.

Security Essential. The development of moral and ethical character is closely related to the child's personal-social development, to the role emotion plays in his problem of adjustment, to his general personality growth, and, most important, to the extent of security and belongingness that he has achieved. Security and belongingness make it unnecessary for the child to slide into behavior deviations at the slightest environmental provocation. For him there is no strong need for compensation, no revenge motive, no bitterness. Any child occasionally finds the conditions under which desirable behavior was learned considerably changed. Playing amicably with a group of children develops desirable behavior. But the harmony among groups frequently runs out and violence makes its appearance. The secure child is less easily influenced by the change and has the tendency to resist and continue in the desired direction.

Opportunity for Expression. Adequate occupation and pursuit of interests, as well as the establishment of outlets for creative expression, counterbalance tendencies toward undesirable behavior. These provide adequate areas for stimulating experiences so that the child does not need to cultivate deviational activity in order to free himself from boredom and obtain undesirable stimulation.

Experience in Self-control. The child who resists participation in activities leading to unethical or immoral acts is the child who has experience in self-control. The school and home must provide him with the opportunity for self-evaluation, for making decisions, for planning for himself and for others. Only through such environmental stimulation can desirable behavior be readily developed.

Broad Experiencing. The child with a narrow background of experience may continue on a path of desirable behavior as long as there are no new factors added to the environmental stimuli with which he is unfamiliar. On the other hand the child with narrow experience and background can be misled rather easily, other factors being equal. The school has a responsibility in making available a variety of experiences in which there are opportunities to apply codes and judgments regarding conduct which the child has accepted and which are satisfying. Such experiences will provide challenges within his range of ethical maturity. They will give him the opportunity to learn tolerance, sympathy, and understanding. Such experiences compromise differences and develop adjustments of individual patterns to emerging group patterns.

2. Cooperation between Home and School Necessary

All of those influences such as the home, the school, the church, and associates have been discussed and their importance noted as conditioners of ethical and moral behavior. Because there is a multiplicity of what might be referred to as institutional influences, it is obvious that the most effective results will be obtained where these agencies and influences can cooperate to produce desired effects. Parents and teachers must join forces and grow in understanding of what each expects from the other. This does not mean that school and home must establish ideals beyond the level of normal peer groups, nor does it mean that each cooperates in developing a combined pressure attempting to influence behavior at an adult level or even at a level beyond the maturity status of the child. Cooperation between the home and the school does, of course, imply a thoroughgoing study of the child's problems, an extremely careful consideration of all the aspects in which the home can possibly do more, and of those in which the school can more closely integrate its academic as well as its nonacademic program with the needs and the desires of the children.

3. Study of Child Groupings

One of the most important ways to discover the problems that help or hinder the development of desirable behavior traits is to study the group in which the child finds himself. Sociometric techniques furnish an approach, but something more than this is necessary, since sociometry is directed primarily toward a study of the child with the social grouping regarded mainly as a background (30). Group study can often provide the key to individual behavior, and consequently, efforts toward improving group morale frequently represent the best techniques for individual therapy.

B. ATTACKING SPECIFIC PROBLEMS

Respect for Property. One of the universal problems faced by parents and by all teachers in the lower elementary grades is that of teaching children respect for property. One of the best ways to do this is through cooperative use of property owned by all. The school is particularly adapted for presenting opportunity in learning this skill as contrasted with the home, where there may be only one or two children. Children who have few possessions and those who have many but lack the opportunity to share them benefit most from the school situation. Where facilities are sufficient to interest children and valuable enough to enable them to cherish possessions, the opportunity is greatest.

Respect for property cooperatively used is a quality developed after the child first learns that he must not take things that belong to someone else. Nearly every child must learn not to steal, since almost every child around five or six years of age has the experience of taking something which does not belong to him. Fortunately, such experiences usually occur first in the home and are normally corrected there. The most common experience is in taking coins from the family purse. The child learns at an early age that coins may be exchanged for things which are desirable — candy, food, presents, etc. The child in the normal home, once the money is taken, feels guilty and almost inevitably spends it for the first thing available rather than waiting and selecting something more desirable.

When a child takes money he should not be treated like a thief or told that he cannot be trusted. Developing a sense of trust-worthiness and family confidence in him is an important under-taking. A common approach is to explain the use of money, where it comes from, and where it must be used. It is also important, when the child learns what money is for, to establish a small budget for him and when possible to enable him to earn a part of it.

Learning of this kind does not prepare the child for respect of community property. Children who have clearly established a sense of honesty at home may take chalk because he sees it almost everywhere around the school and thinks it belongs to no one. Perhaps the reason children deface school property and are care-less with it is that it is given to them without any planning on their part or any request from them. Pupil participation in re-questing and in requisitioning, or group participation in earning the special things which they cherish, use, and need in their school activities are ways of developing respect toward community-owned facilities.

Certain warnings are in order in regard to stealing. First of-fenses should be regarded as mistakes. No moralizing is necessary in dealing with the child, and punishment as such is out of order. If replacement or payment is called for, it should be done with the child's own money or money from his allowance. If replacement calls for more than the child's funds permit, family assistance may be permitted. Perhaps, at best, the parent may share with the child in replacement. Second or third offenses call for assumption of more responsibility on the child's part. Frequently several offenses and corrections must be made before the child understands the property rights of others.

In school the treatment by the teacher follows similar lines. Apologies or return of material in face-to-face situations are very popular remedies used by teachers. In many instances they are bad for the child. The overly shy child or the one who is disturbingly conscience-stricken should not be required to make amends in such a manner. It is often best to settle the affair quietly and un-obtrusively without the offender being known. Other children can be best handled where real punishment of one kind or another is involved. Continued stealing cannot be cured by increasing the severity of the penalty. Treatment in such instances demands getting at the cause rather than the effect. Repeated offenses may be interpreted in two ways. Either the child's moral sense is immature and more functional situations for learning self-control are essential, or the child is responding to certain personal and emotional affects.

Respect for Truth. Another fundamental in the development of desirable behavior is respect for the truth. Children distort the truth or deliberately lie for a number of reasons. In the prekindergarten years children mix truth and fiction. At this stage, which in reality is only the beginning point in moral and ethical development, he has difficulty in determining the difference between what occurred and what he believes has occurred. Other children lie to see what will happen. They detect lies on the part of other children and not infrequently by their parents. When parents are obviously insincere in respect to the truth in relations with others, children follow this pattern. A child may lie to escape punishment for stealing and to satisfy the need for security. Probably the most frequent cases are of this kind. When a child lies to avoid punishment, the punishment should be evaluated in terms of the event. In the case of insecurity the child should be pitied rather than punished. Lying for such a reason demands an appraisal of the forces preventing him from achieving status.

C. THE DEVELOPMENT OF ATTITUDES

Important in the development of guides for behavior is the attitude of the individual child. Attitudes are in reality the sum of the inner and outer influences resulting in a conscious rationalization of specific behavior. Thus attitudes have multiple causes, since the response to stimulus situations utilize many aspects of the individual's psychophysical equipment. They are not merely a mental response.

Attitudes play a constant part in the entire process of reacting to a stimulus. They are important in the child's education and aid, positively or negatively, in the development of behavior patterns. In the sense described they are similar to what has been categorized by others as conscience. Consequently attitudes are important in determining how an individual will react in given situations. There are many explanations of how they may arise.

Related to Security. The amount of security obtained by an individual affects the kind of attitude he develops. To identify oneself with a minority attitude or prejudice, for example, causes most individuals to feel insecure unless the minority attitude developed gives the individual a privileged identification. It is easier to seek the wider approval that goes with accepting the attitudes and attributes of the majority. Children are more self-conscious than adults in identifying themselves with minority groups, even if they feel that the attitude of the minority is the right one.[3] This is one explanation of the difficulty of bringing about social reform.

For teachers there is considerable meaning in this fact. It indicates the need for developing group morale or group approval before one can be very effective in developing personalized acceptance of desirable behavior. It also explains progress in helping children develop desirable behavior in cases where group acceptance is first obtained. It also shows the potential remedial values to be obtained in dealing with an individual child who demonstrates deviational behavior when such a child can achieve group identification and be treated through group guidance activities.

This principle also explains why certain forms of school recognition, such as honor societies, high marks, the privilege of aiding the teacher or acting as a monitor, etc., so seldom have a broad appeal (46). In many instances such opportunities are not valued highly by the group. The child who is approved by the teacher for his reaction to such stimuli in groups where these are regarded as having little value probably has but little peer prestige. His reaction in such situations is deplored rather than approved. Unless the child is entirely rejected he will prefer the approval of his playmates to that of his teacher. Identification is distinctly pleasurable and represents good status and acceptance by the group (17). Hence the teacher represents a threat upon the individual security of each child when she opposes, or attempts to change, attitudes that are fairly well established. This is not to imply that

[3] This view is not contrary to the fact that children are also less conscious of minority groups or class lines than adults.

the teacher should not oppose the group at times or attempt to develop new attitudes. There are many times in life when the individual finds it necessary to oppose the views of the group. At times individual resistance to group opinion should be encouraged, since majority views are frequently biased and require challenge for correction and refinement.

Related to Prestige. The opportunity to gain prestige is also important in determining the kind of attitude a child may form. This factor is similar to that of obtaining security but varies enough to be considered separately.

Prestige can be good or bad in the development of behavior traits. Its effect explains why a child with outstanding status can influence others. It explains why a child may be willing to substitute teacher approval for peer approval. It explains how a gang leader can attract others. The result is that some attitudes are merely halo reflection and are not real or basic. This is true for both children and adults. It poses difficulty for the teacher in that although attitudes may be transient, they last sufficiently long to deny the child the opportunity for growth in more significant views. A child may devote several years to gaining prestige through his attitude toward, and efforts in, athletics and thereby deny himself exploration in other endeavors which are basically of more appeal to him.

Related to Emotional Trauma. Another important factor in the development of attitudes is the extent to which a given child has suffered emotional shock. What is called shock may result from extreme rejection by a desired group or a complete loss of prestige after having once been established within a desired social grouping. Thus emotional shock resulting in aggression toward social groupings is in reality more significant than the act of aggression.

Related to Acceptance of Facts. Young children are but slightly influenced in their attitude development by what is regarded as factual or objective evidence on critical issues. This is particularly true if the evidence runs contrary to group opinion. The child may rationalize in reference to the facts bearing on certain specific issues but act in the opposite way when involved in a group pattern of behavior. This principle explains mob action on the part of those who individually or apart from a specific situation may deplore such action. It also suggests that the way to use facts and objective evidence is in developing group attitudes.

Unfortunately, facts are difficult to obtain in connection with critical issues or they are obtained by propagandists who present only those facts that support their own attitudes. As children mature, however, facts assume increasing importance and should be utilized fully in activities directed toward the development of attitudes.

CONCLUSION

One of the most important ideas which one obtains from a study of the research on this problem is that ethical and moral development is a continuous process. The child at a very early age begins the behavior sequences which continue throughout his life. This idea negates the thought that morals and ideals can be developed only when the child is mature enough to rationalize and distinguish right from wrong. Concepts regarding moral and ethical behavior continue from early childhood throughout life. Consequently, the earlier the child is introduced to desirable learning situations, the earlier these concepts are ingrained and the earlier he begins to sort out his own ideas of relative values.

Teachers must realize the importance of personal satisfaction to the child in learning ethical behavior. In this connection the use of rewards and punishments must be fully understood. The former idea that the child should be severely punished for undesirable behavior is decidedly contrary to the available evidence. This does not imply that rewards and punishments are not useful in this kind of learning. They are important, and to be most effective they must be carefully designed to fit the child's maturity. What is proper at one stage is improper at another. Penalties should be imposed as deterrents to undesirable behavior rather than in a vindictive spirit.

There is much evidence that rewards for desirable behavior are much more effective than punishment for undesirable action. Rewards, however, may be overdone or given without desirable purpose. They should be regarded as permissible and desirable only when they are to be used less frequently as the child matures. Maturity in moral and ethical behavior can be said to result only when desirable action itself provides the necessary motivation and satisfaction. Within this framework those rewards are the most desirable which build security and status. To the teacher this implies judicious usage of compliments, increased responsibility, and personal acceptance.

And lastly, of importance to teachers, is the fact that the learning of desirable behavior becomes generalized only through the development and maturity of attitudes. This means that the teacher who would foster desirable behavior must provide practice in a variety of situations if transfer is to occur. Specifically, this means that trustworthiness cannot be developed merely by admonition not to cheat on tests or, for that matter, through a situation in which children actually do not cheat on tests. Trustworthiness can often be displayed in one situation and found wanting in quite a different one.

In this connection, conversely, where variety of response is provided, there should be provided also an almost unlimited opportunity for generalization. Experience is so often quoted as the proper means of learning. Experience without generalization is often ineffective and wasteful. Learning demands interpretation of experience. Without this attempt by teachers to help the child isolate and build into an attitude the generalized concept, the child is restrained from learning how to transfer this particular concept to another situation.

There is very little available research on how to carry out this process. Teachers should be encouraged to experiment with ways and means of helping children see elements in untried situations and experiences in which a particular concept applies. Thus the development of concepts and the identification of the concept in new situations result only when they parallel each other in the total learning situation.

SELECTED REFERENCES

1. BAKER, W. A., "Longitudinal Study of the Effect of Experience in the Character Research Project on the Learning of Concepts," *Union College Studies in Character Research,* Vol. 1, No. 4, 1954.

2. ANDERSON, J. E., "Parents' Attitudes on Child Behavior: A Report of Three Studies," *Child Development,* 17:91–97, 1946.

3. BARBU, Z., "Studies In Children's Honesty," *Quarterly Bulletin of British Psychology and Sociology,* 2:53–57, 1951.

4. BLUMER, H., AND HAUSER, P. M., *Movies, Delinquency and Crime.* New York: Macmillan, 1934.

5. BOSSARD, J. H. S., *The Sociology of Child Development.* New York: Harper, 1948.

6. BRECKENRIDGE, M. E., AND VINCENT, E. L., *Child Development.* Philadelphia: Saunders, 1943.

7. BROWN, W., MORRISON, JOAN, AND COUCH, G. B., "Influence of Affectional Family Relationships on Character Development," *Journal of Abnormal and Social Psychology,* 42:422–428, 1947.

8. BURT, C., *The Young Delinquent.* London: University of London Press, 1925.

9. BARKER, R. G., AND WRIGHT, H. F., *Midwest and Its Children.* Evanston, Illinois: Row, Peterson, 1955.

10. CHASSELL, C. F., E. B., AND L. M., "A Test of Ability to Weigh Foreseen Consequences. *Teachers College Record,* 25:39–50, 1924.

11. CARTWRIGHT, DORWIN, AND ZANDER, ALVIN, *Group Dynamics, Research and Theory.* Evanston, Illinois: Row, Peterson, 1953.

12. CRESSEY, P. G., AND THRASHER, F. M., *Boys, Movies, and City Streets.* New York: Macmillan, 1934.

13. DALE, EDGAR, *Attendance at Motion Pictures, and the Contents of Motion Pictures.* New York: Macmillan, 1935.

14. DIEDERICH, P. B., "Methods of Studying Ethical Development," *Religious Education,* Vol. 1, No. 3, 1955.

15. FREUD, S. A., *A General Introduction to Psychoanalysis.* New York: Boni, Liveright, 1920.

16. HAINES, T. H., "Diagnostic Value of Some Performance Tests," *Psychological Review,* 22:299–304, 1915.

17. HARTMANN, G. W., *Educational Psychology.* New York: American Book Co., 1941.

18. HARTSHORNE, HUGH, AND MAY, M. A., *Studies in Deceit.* New York: Macmillan, 1928.

19. ——, MAY, M. A., AND SHUTTLEWORTH, F. K., *Studies in the Organization of Character.* New York: Macmillan, 1930.

20. HEALY, W., AND FERNALD, G. M., *Tests for Practical Mental Classification,* Psychological Monographs, Vol. 13, No. 54, 1911.

21. ——, *The Individual Delinquent: A Textbook of Diagnosis and Prognosis for All Concerned in Understanding Offenders.* Boston: Little, Brown, 1915.

22. ——, AND BRONNER, A. F., *New Light on Delinquency and Its Treatment.* New Haven: Yale University Press, 1936.

23. EDUCATIONAL POLICIES COMMISSION, *Moral and Spiritual Values in the Public Schools.* Washington: Educational Policies Commission, 1951.

24. *The Growth and Development of Christian Personality.* A chart published by the Union College Character Research Project, Union College, Schenectady.

25. HARRIS, DALE B., GOUGH, HARRISON G., MARTIN, WILLIAM E., "Children's Ethnic Attitudes: II: Relationship to Parental Beliefs Concerning Child Training," *Child Development,* 21:169–181, 1950.

26. LIGON, E. M., *Dimensions of Character.* New York: Macmillan, 1956.

27. MacRAE, DUNCAN, JR., "A Test of Piaget's Theories of Moral Development," *Journal of Abnormal and Social Psychology,* 49:14–48, 1954.

28. JONES, VERNON, *Character and Citizenship Training in the Public School.* Chicago: University of Chicago Press, 1936.

29. ——, "Character Development in Children—An Objective Approach," *Manual of Child Psychology,* edited by Leonard Carmichael. New York: Wiley, 1946.

30. McGRAW, MYRTLE, "Later Development of Children Especially Trained During Infancy," *Readings in Child Psychology,* edited by Wayne Dennis. New York: Prentice-Hall, 1951.

31. MALLER, J. B., "Character Growth and Jewish Education," *Religious Education,* 25:627–630, 1930.

32. McDOUGALL, WILLIAM, *An Introduction to Social Psychology, Revised Edition,* Boston: Luce, 1926.

33. PAYNTER, R. H., AND BLANCHARD, P., *Educational Achievement of Children with Personality and Behavior Difficulties.* New York: The Commonwealth Fund, 1928.

34. PIAGET, J., *The Moral Judgment of the Child.* New York: Harcourt, Brace, 1924.

35. PRESSEY, S. L., AND ROBINSON, F. P., *Psychology and the New Education,* New York: Harper, 1944.

36. RAUBENHEIMER, A. S., "An Experimental Study of Some Behavior Traits of the Potentially Delinquent Boy," *Psychological Monographs,* Vol. 34, No. 159, 1923.

37. MASON, ROBERT E., *Moral Values and Secular Education.* New York: Columbia University Press, 1950.

38. PARSONS, TALCOTT, AND SHILS, E. A., *Toward a General Theory of Action.* Cambridge: Harvard University Press, 1951.

39. STRAUSS, ANSELM L., "The Development of Conceptions of Rules In Children," *Child Development,* 25:193–208, 1954.

40. UGUREL-SEMIN, REFIA, "Moral Behavior and Moral Judgment of Children," *Journal of Abnormal and Social Psychology,* 47:463–471, 1952.

41. WOLFENSTEIN, MARTHA, "Some Variants In Moral Training of Children," *The Psychoanalytic Study of the Child,* edited by Ruth S. Eissler *et al.,* International Universities Press: New York: Vol. V. 310–328, 1950.

42. TAYLOR, H. R., AND POWERS, F. F., "Bible Study and Character," *Journal of Genetic Psychology,* 35:294–302, 1928.

43. TROLAND, L. T., *The Fundamentals of Human Motivation.* New York: Van Nostrand, 1928.

44. VOELKER, P. F., *The Function of Ideals and Attitudes in Social Education,* Teachers College Contributions to Education, No. 112. New York: Teachers College, Columbia University, 1921.

45. WEBER, C. O., "Moral Judgments in Female Delinquents," *Journal of Applied Psychology,* 10:89–91, 1926.

46. WICKMAN, E. K., *Children's Behavior and Teachers' Attitudes.* New York: The Commonwealth Fund, 1929.

47. WILLEY, R. D., AND YOUNG, HELEN A., *Radio in Elementary Education.* Boston: Heath, 1948.

48. WITTY, PAUL, "An Analysis of the Personality Traits of the Effective Teacher," *Journal of Educational Research,* 40:622–671, 1947.

49. WOODWORTH, R. S., *Psychology.* New York: Holt, 1924.

13

THE DEVELOPMENT OF
PERSONALITY

INTRODUCTION

Some writers on personality appear to agree with Hartmann that ". . . a superior personality is also a superior character and that the term 'personality' contains all that 'character' connotes. . . ." (16). Breckenridge and Vincent show a similar tendency to identify personality development with the growth of certain other patterns, notably social development (5). Identification with one or more aspects of growth, but not with all, implies a lack of relationship with those not selected. But personality, if not a specific aspect of growth and development, is certainly related to all others. This is what justifies further treatment of the topic. Nevertheless, the approach is based upon the idea that personality is a total developmental concomitant rather than an isolated development. Consequently, personality must be studied and approached from the hereditary, physiological, and psychological backgrounds, all considered in a definite relationship with each other and with the environment in which the child exists.

DEFINITION

There have been many interesting definitions. Although no two agree in detail, there is much unanimity. Since "personality" is a term used freely and loosely by lay persons and since many teachers have not carefully studied certain of its implications, it seems justifiable to review critically several of the earlier definitions and to conclude the discussion by pointing out similarities and differences in the concepts currently held. It is not expected that teachers will entirely agree with the definition of this writer or necessarily with those of others. It does seem likely that concept differences already existing can be brought close enough together so that teachers may arrive at generally agreed upon goals in guiding personality development.

One of the first concepts was based upon the idea of personality as a spiritual characteristic of the individual. This concept was in vogue at a time when psychology was studied subjectively and mainly as a philosophical problem. Psychologists at that time believed that personality could not be further analyzed and that it was more or less mystic and vague, nevertheless giving direction to behavior and meaning to experience. Sufficient progress has been made today in our analysis to classify the concept as obsolete (33).

Modern Definitions. One of the first of the modern definitions considered personality in terms of instincts. This definition seemed appropriate in the early part of the century, when instincts seemed to provide a satisfactory explanation for behavior. A good illustrative definition from this school of thought is that of Morton Prince, who considered personality a product of experience and of preformed, inherited tendencies containing their own basic motivations (39).

Most other definitions developed during the 20's and 30's included some identification with what Thorpe calls the social-stimulus value of personality (45). Schwesinger provides a good illustration of this point of view, which considers personality in reference to dress, voice, and gesture and defines personality in respect to external aspects of the individual (41). Other psychologists have shown a readiness to accept a similar view. Allport claims that, with some exceptions, personality may be defined by the individual's reaction to various social stimuli, including the manner in which he adjusts to the social demands of the environment (1). May also describes personality in terms of effectiveness and influence over others in social contacts (30). In a somewhat different vein Woodworth describes it as a reflection of total behavior, stating that personality represents the qualitative and impressionistic aspects of the individual's total reactions (50). And Symonds says virtually the same thing — that personality is the totality of exterior qualities plus the kind of relationships established by the individual in his personal contacts (44).

These definitions, particularly the latter, illustrate the view that personality is the sum total or the integration of all the capacities of the individual in action. Such an idea is in accord with the concept of the organism as a unified mechanism acting in totality, which is considerably more than an additive concept of individuality.

Personality and Character not the Same. It is likely that the reader may accept the definition of personality as a reflection of general individuality. However, the question is sure to arise as to its difference with character. In the preceding chapter, character was definitely described as having moral and ethical connotations. In this sense character, although related to moral and ethical behavior, was given a general classification of which moral and ethical aspects are subcategories. In a similar scheme of organization, character may be viewed as one phase of the broader individual attributes referred to as "personality." Such a point of view is quite acceptable. Gilliland adopts this idea in designating character as a moral or ethical component of personality (15), and Symonds describes character as the habits and skills connected with total behavior, particularly such as are social and have reference to organization and consistency of conduct (44).

There is further question concerning the practical relationships between the two. The popularized viewpoint regards personality as having little or no bearing on an individual's real character. In other words, a person might exhibit a very charming personality and be an entirely unreliable or worthless character. In respect to the concept accepted here this could not be the case. Character, as viewed positively, contributes to personality development. The better the character, the better the personality. The contrary lay view of the character-personality relationship is due to the fact that certain elements of personality are dominant in one's total make-up. Limited contact with individuals results in judging them in terms of the more obvious aspects of their personality. This is particularly true with individuals whose observed social reactions cause them to be regarded as extroverts. Such persons on more careful observation may reveal, not true extroversion based on a genuine liking for other people, but rather a type of extroverted-egocentrism. These individuals do not genuinely like other people. They like themselves and can only be satisfied by admiration from others.

GENERAL VERSUS SPECIFIC CONCEPTS OF PERSONALITY

A consideration of the organization of personality raises a problem similar to the one presented by intelligence. Although many people look upon personality as the embodiment of individuality, there seems to be no way to get at the idea sufficiently to demonstrate the practicality of the concept. After we have once defined personality we seem to move, in further discussion, to a consideration of what has been called personality traits. One effort away from this trend, toward an appraisal of total personality, has been the attempt to classify the individual as to temperament, physique, and general social reactions. Such classifications have done little to clarify the concept of individuality but have been of some assistance in dealing with personality extremes, which are the result primarily of mental ills of one kind or another. Actually, most individuals fall too close to border lines to be satisfactorily placed in rigid categories. Probably the greatest contribution of recent research is the conclusion that all individuals contain many variations of different kinds of specific personality patterns. An individual may be dominant and aggressive in some kinds of situations and meek and submissive in others.

This viewpoint tends to identify itself with the specificity theory rather than with what has been called the theory of unitary or general trait in personality development. Actually this is not the case. Identification with either the general or the specific doctrine is difficult, since each places too much emphasis upon either heredity or environment, respectively, as the dominant factor in its emergence. Moreover, the contrasting viewpoints both seem to deal with traits but disagree mainly as to the kind and quality of organization involved. Both viewpoints regard traits as aspects of personality, but whereas one considers a personality trait to be fixed and unalterable, primarily the result of inheritance, the other regards traits as transient patterns dependent on the intensity of stress and strain or other influences at particular times (32).

Unitary View. Thus the unitary viewpoint describes personality as a semipermanent organization contingent upon inner regulatory mechanisms and resulting in a certain consistency of behavior. Allport, for example, defines a trait as a "generalized response unit that reflects personality" (2), and more recently as "dynamic and flexible dispositions, resulting, at least in part, from the integration of specific habits, expressing characteristic modes of adaptation to one's surroundings" (3).

Criticism of Unitary View. Psychologists today are very critical of this point of view. They have difficulty in accepting the idea of a "generalized and focalized neuropsychic system peculiar to a given individual" (3). The crux of the issue seems to arise in the idea of the earlier psychologists that behavior is primarily determined by innate dispositions to action and relatively independent of current stimulating situations (45).

Specificity View. The current viewpoint regards a personality trait as a more or less temporary combination of specific tendencies to act in characteristic ways (45). The key to action exists not in the child or in certain fixed traits but rather in the relation of the child to his environment. Or as Curti has stated, traits are "more or less loosely organized systems of habits and attitudes, which have been developed in the process of adjustment to the special and varying conditions of life" (10).

Arguments for Specificity. The main evidence for this idea is the lack of consistency of human behavior in situations which appear to involve the same traits. The studies of May, for example, are quoted as evidence that children will lie or cheat in one kind of situation but not in another. Thus, it is argued that behavior reactions vary according to the elements of a given stimulus and that predictions of behavior or performance are inaccurate when the individual is confronted with unfamiliar elements of given environmental patterns.

The work of Hartshorne and May, mentioned and quoted in the previous chapter, currently furnishes the evidence of the specificity idea (17). Therefore it seems logical to give some attention to an evaluation of the statements made, both favorable and critical. Attention to the controversy is pertinent, since the point of view to be advocated in this chapter favors neither one nor the other viewpoint exclusively.

Two outstanding and noteworthy comments have been made, one by Thorpe in defense of the specificity view and the other by Allport who, as has been previously mentioned, advocates the unitary viewpoint. According to Thorpe, when a child deceives he is reacting in a way which seeks the solution of a problem. He is not innately dishonest, nor does he necessarily have a tendency toward that kind of behavior (45). Behaving "honestly" is not an innate disposition independent of the situation in which the child finds himself, but rather a form of behavior related to specific situations.

Criticism of Specificity View. Allport, in general, attacks the methods used in the Hartshorne-May studies as well as certain of the findings (2). He criticizes their selection of children for studies involving social and ethical concepts. Because they are young, and therefore immature in their development of ideals and standards, they are much more likely than adults to exhibit variability in their reactions. Allport also criticizes the use of mass data, results based upon averages, and other statistical interpretations.

Compromise Necessary. There is much to be said in favor of Allport's argument. The evidence does not clearly prove that the trait concept of personality is entirely specific to a given situation. Nor is Allport's unity view any more convincing. Personality as reflected through what has been called "traits" is both general and specific. In situations in which the majority of elements are familiar and in which the balance of inner and outer motivations has been experienced, a previously established pattern of behavior can be expected to function. Where no familiar elements are found, or where the balance of inner and outer demands is disrupted, or where continued dissatisfaction with the old balance is experienced, new patterns or ways of acting may be produced.

In justification of a compromise view which gives some credence to generality or unity of trait behavior, it cannot be said that such acceptance necessarily implies that behavior is determined entirely from within or in reference to previously established modes of behavior. The compromise view expects uniformity of behavior in many kinds of situations where stimulatory elements are sufficiently familiar. It also recognizes that the most uniform pattern can be disrupted if the social or environmental pressures are strong enough to cause conflict, stress, and dissatisfaction with the old reactions. Everything else being equal, among individuals faced with the same pressures and motivations, the more practiced and the more satisfying pattern is the one which is more likely to recur in situations somewhat changed. Where two such individuals face a complete shifting of elements in the environment, differences in behavior may be credited to other factors. This view represents a similarity to Allport's point regarding low relationships in honesty traits when he says that such results show that among such children the tendency of one trait to express itself shows dominance and thereby governs action, rather than the idea that the child shows inconsistency because he acts one way in one situation and another way in a second kind of situation.

Compromise View Favors Educability. A combination of the two views has implications which are encouraging to the efforts of the school in the matter. The idea of personality as somewhat plastic and amenable during its period of growth, and the idea that experience does lead to the formation of a pattern or dominant trait behavior encourages the teacher to be helpful in personality development. If heredity or inherent determinations of response are dominant, then the school has little responsibility beyond helping individuals to adjust to the *status quo*. In such a case education, if concerned at all, would have the responsibility for determining what biological laws were operative and directing the application of them to accomplish its purpose.

If some plasticity of performance is to be expected then the school and those who direct the development of children can accept greater responsibility. Personality and trait conditioning may then become something more than a haphazard activity delegated to extracurricular hours and to after-school contact with other children.

And further, if experiences of a desirably conditioning nature may be looked upon as leading to a dominant pattern reaction to various stimuli, then much activity and school time is justified in meeting such a challenge.

PRINCIPLES OF PERSONALITY DEVELOPMENT

The discussion thus far would seem to indicate that personality is considerably more than an aggregate of specific components of individuality (33), and that it is not similar in its totality to what rightly or wrongly is implied by the I.Q. in relation to intelligence. Personality in essence is the totality of individuality which, for a given person in a given situation, may represent a balance or pattern in which certain traits assume dominance. Traits may shift in dominance according to the meaningfulness of a given situation to the individual concerned. For example, in a light, casual, social relationship the more extraneous traits like poise, physique, and appearance are more obvious than consideration for others, social attitudes, and ability to make sacrifices. In this setting an individual may be seen as quite charming, whereas in a setting involving infringement upon one's desires, for example, he would display other traits. The point to be made here is that personality is what one really *is* in a variety of reactions rather than what one *appears to be* in certain superficial or "one-sided" motivations.

Personality Grows and Develops. Personality can only be fully understood if it is looked upon as growing and developing individuality. It cannot be viewed accurately as inherent and fixed. Inheritance undoubtedly plays a part in determining ranges of development and in placing the individual in the kind of social inheritance which will promote maturity. The principles substantiating this viewpoint are discussed in the following paragraphs.

A. PERSONALITY INFLUENCED BY SOCIAL ENVIRONMENT

The first principle, generally agreed upon, is that personality is greatly affected by the child's social environment. This does not imply that heredity or the child's organic being has nothing to do with his future personality. Size, appearance, and other physical attributes, as well as intelligence, are powerful in their influences upon the kind of personality which the child will reflect as he grows and will eventually acquire. Nevertheless, the extent to which the child will achieve his maximum potentialities is contingent upon his social experiences, the pressures which people exert on him, and his response to them (11).

Even Early Behavior Learned. It is quite commonly believed by parents that the early behavior of children is indicative of inherited temperamental or personality characteristics. The child who cries lustily and is easily disturbed, in contrast to the child who is quiet, cries little, and seemingly has a "nice" disposition is often considered representative of innate differences. Laboratory experiments indicate that such differences furnish poor predictions for performance some years later. Differences may be regarded as the result of familiarized, learned, continuing pattern responses. Thus those traits that become differentiated at an early age and seemingly are fixed are nothing more than learned responses.

B. PERSONALITY TRAITS RAPIDLY BECOME DIFFERENTIATED

Differences among children may become obvious during the first days and weeks of life. The early appearance of learned individuality is the correct assumption rather than the idea that such differences as may be observed are basically inherent. The person unacquainted with the experimental literature can be forgiven for making this assumption. Only the investigator or the student of child development can become fully aware of how plastic and amenable is the emerging personality of the infant and how quickly he learns to parallel and mimic the personalities of those about him (56).

Evidence for Effect of Early Influences. There is also much evidence that eventual, mature personality characteristics have been considerably shaped even before the child begins school. Marston, for example, claims that children as young as five years of age begin to show clear enough personality patterns to be designated by the terms "extroversion-introversion" (28). Characteristics described as negativism or jealousy, for example, also become rather clearly differentiated before the child enters school.

C. PERSONALITY DEVELOPMENT — A COORDINATION OF GROWTH EFFECTS

Personality not an Isolated Development. The point must be made that personality development is not isolated from other aspects of growth in the developing child. The evidence for such a statement comes from a search of the literature dealing with personality development. Such treatment as is given considers personality from the standpoint of the child's personal-social development, his emotional status and development, his problems of learning self-control, and his creative opportunities. Somewhat on the fringes, but likewise interwoven, is its relation to physical and mental development. Thus personality can be seen only as a total growth effect, not as a separate entity or growth aspect (35, 51).

D. PERSONALITY DEVELOPMENT REQUIRES A MULTIPLICITY OF
   GUIDED EXPERIENCES

Generalization Requires Experience. In order to develop desirable consistency in the personality pattern as it reacts to given stimuli, there must be planned experiences in a multiplicity of situations. If the child is to exhibit trustworthiness he must be given the opportunity to do so in all possible contacts in which this trait can be employed. The Hartshorne-May investigations, on which this idea is based, do not necessarily underline the hopelessness of the task. What they actually show is the need for wider experiences than have previously been considered necessary. In many instances we attempt to develop desirable personality through imitation and exhortation. Our failure has resulted through the effort to accomplish generalization without experience. Only through a carefully planned sequence of experiences can the individual learn to apply generalized patterns.

E. PERSONALITY AFFECTED BY DEVELOPMENTAL STAGE
   OF THE INDIVIDUAL

Some Early Exaggerations. Certain investigators of personality traits in young children have popularized the idea that personality patterns become fixed and unalterable to such an extent, in the preschool years, that they are the chief determinants of behavior during adult years. This view likewise has considerable research substantiation. The highly regarded study of Lerner and Murphy encourages one to believe that constructive citizenship and satisfactory adult relationships depend entirely on preschool experiences (25). There is considerable new evidence to challenge possible exaggerations in such a theory. There is no question, however, that continued behavior of any kind tends to become permanent.

Prediction from Cycle to Cycle Difficult. Although any kind of behavior can be diverted somewhat from its usual course when the conditions or motivations act strongly enough on the individual, there is no evidence that performance can be accurately predicted from one cycle of growth to another. Two boys may grow similarly during preadolescence but deviate unexpectedly and establish quite unlike patterns during the adolescent years. This is true for height, weight, mental growth, growth in reading, and other measurable aspects of development. It seems reasonable to assume that arrival at new or more mature organismic stages results in shifts in the dominant motivational forces which produce behavior, and the result is behavior quite different from the previous pattern. Such shifts are aided by new inner forces which lie dormant until the proper stage of maturity enables them to function.

In view of the knowledge of the developmental curve of growth of children, one would seem justified in postulating that the greatest variability in behavior is exhibited at the beginning and end points of cycles of growth. Periods in between are periods of rapid growth during which the personality pattern in relation to its stage of maturity assumes definite shape and organization. During these times there may be a marked durability and consistency of response in comparison to performance at beginning and end points (12).

It is true that such a characterization of personality is quite theoretical; it is a generalization of the studies of Courtis and others regarding growth and is quite clear in the individual growth curves of children if measurements are taken frequently. One can, however, find some similarity between this concept of the relation of stage of maturity to consistency of performance (or reaction) in the idea advocated by psychologists relative to the awkwardness of boys and girls at the beginning of adolescence. If the theory is sound one might conclude, where performance and behavior are relatively consistent, that during the periods of rapid growth nothing much can be done in the way of helping the child. The answer to this is that the child only infrequently lives under conditions conducive to maximum growth and that environmental improvement is effective at all times and consequently can always be attempted.

The idea of cycle development also indicates the opportunity at the beginning of growth cycles for providing a good start in personality development. In general, in quite a number of schools, kindergarten and first-grade activities are well planned. At the junior high school level the current situation is deplorable. At a time when the child shows the greatest plasticity and lack of consistency in behavior he is given the greatest freedom that he has ever experienced. At this time, consequently, he resorts almost entirely to peer guidance for direction and standards of behavior.

New Maturities Susceptible to New Influences. This thought is based upon the idea that the influences that affect behavior at the beginning of a cycle of growth condition to a considerable degree the pattern to follow. On the other hand, it could be argued that inconsistency and unreliability do not necessarily respond any better to guidance and factor influence than does consistent behavior. One must concede, however, that new cycles of growth reflect new social and physical motivations. Old ways of behaving become outgrown and outmoded, and new goals and standards must be acquired.

CONDITIONING FACTORS

A. HEREDITARY FACTORS

Limitations of Heredity. As has been implied in the discussion to this point, students of growth have been concerned with the relative influence of congenital, versus environmental, influences in personality development. Since many investigators of the problem have definitely given dominant importance to gene transmittal in reference to such so-called personality traits as dullness, ambition, thrift, and — surprisingly — moral qualities, the issue deserves elaboration. The problem may be stated as a question: to what extent is personality inherited? Undoubtedly many teachers feel that inheritance is a major factor in determining the kind of personality a child may acquire. In contrast is the point of view of those committed to longitudinal study of children. Their thought concerning transmission adheres mainly to the view that organic structures only are inherited.

View on Heredity Determines School Practices. Conventional teachers, however, who stress rigid learning activities in terms of disciplinary objectives or in terms of acquisitional concepts of learning reflect the congenital emphasis. For them, activities for personality development may well be ignored by the schools. On the other hand the developmentalists in education regard the child's environment as providing the key to growth. This group would implement such an idea by directing efforts toward arranging the kind of social order that is thought to guarantee desirable growth and development.

Heredity Cannot Be Separated from Environment. Child developmentalists feel that both heredity and environment are important and complement one another. Neglect of one or the other is equally faulty. Neither may be regarded as having a dominating influence.

Such a viewpoint is not entirely original with recent investigators. More than twenty-five years ago it was pointed out that heredity and environment represented a team in which both were regarded as having equal influence. This thought also has been repeated over and over in the preceding chapters. The genes, although they carry hereditary capacity, are incapable of producing their effects where there is no environmental medium in which to carry on their work. On the other hand, the environment also must come into contact with some agent to produce its effects.

Revisions in Views on Heredity. The viewpoint represented above is generally accepted today — not entirely because of its simplicity of logic but also because of a better understanding of what is meant by heredity and what its implications are. Today we know that although gene inheritance is determined at conception, modification begins almost immediately as a result of the conditions under which the embryo is nourished. Development at any stage, even during the prenatal, is the result of relationships between gene potentiality and environmental forces. Capacity for development, then, is not a matter entirely of gene effect, but rather the result of inner gene constitution, reacting under given environmental conditions. In reference to personality this means that many of the traits commonly attributed exclusively to inheritance are to a considerable degree the result of inherited potentiality modified by environment.

B. PHYSIOLOGICAL FACTORS

1. The Question of Personality Types

Somewhat related to the belief of physiological factors as a determinant is the concept of personality types. The idea of type implies that a certain trait pattern is dominant throughout the reactions of a given individual. This is a rather common interpretation of personality and is usually related to belief in the dominance of heredity over environment. Popular illustrations are the business man type, the actor type, the administrative type, the homebody type, and in a somewhat more scientific vein, the introvert-extrovert type, and the dominant versus the submissive type. *Kretschmer's Types.* Classification of personality into types is not strictly modern. Hippocrates and Galen, before the birth of Christ, provided four categories — the choleric, the melancholic, the phlegmatic, and the sanguine. The choleric were strong and easily aroused; the melancholic were pessimistic and somewhat slow; the phlegmatic, of course, were stolid; and the sanguine, responsive, quick, and reactive. The most familiar of the modern semiscientific classifications is the well-known designation by Kretschmer. This classification identifies the personality with body build and perhaps accounts for the popular identification of physical attributes with personality. Kretschmer originally noted only two types — the *pyknic* and the *asthenic*. A little later he added what he called the *athletic* and the *dysplastic*. The pyknic represented the jolly, friendly, laughing individual who possesses a broad head, long trunk, short legs, broad hips, and considerable weight. The asthenic, temperamentally and physiologically, was at the other extreme. The athletic type, of course, was synonymous with the broad-shouldered, narrow-hipped person and the dysplastic category designated all individuals not specifically fitting the others. Of exceeding interest are Kretschmer's behavior predictions for the most contrasting. Whereas the pyknics were said to be inclined toward mental neuroses of the manic-depressive kind, the asthenic, when in emotional aberrations, contracted the dementia disorders. Also of interest was Kretschmer's neglect to apply such typing to women. Men alone could be so classified.

Other Classifications. Probably the most impressive of all personality categorizing is Jung's extrovert-introvert classification (22). Extroverts are described as intensely interested in the external world and in having an active social part in it. They are supposed to be generally free from worries, like to work with others, and do not dwell much on inner thoughts. The introvert is just the opposite. He is a man of thought rather than of action, likes to work alone, is inclined to worry, and is quite reserved. He stays in the background but has strong ideas and convictions regarding behavior.

Other attempts to classify personality are those of Spranger (43) and Sheldon and his associates (42). Neither of these has achieved the renown of the classifications of Kretschmer and of Jung, although Sheldon's work is probably the most thorough. Whereas Sheldon's classifications, like Kretschmer's, showed that physiological and temperamental characteristics are related to each other, the Spranger classification attempted to relate personality to general traits, attitudes, and behavior.

Evaluation of Type Classifications. There are many other theories and classification systems. In general, it is fairly well agreed today that such systems are inaccurate when applied to individuals. Although a person may show definite dominant characteristics which at first glance tend to place him in a given category, further analysis and study reveals other traits which make the classification invalid. Most individuals tend to straddle the classifications provided. Individuals show a spread of trait characteristic ranging throughout all categories but frequently demonstrating dominant traits which fit only one or more.[1] Among a large sampling of the population it would be found that a distribution occurs which approximates a normal spread. Categories therefore appear to be valid only for extremes. In general the tendency to type children should be discouraged. Categories and descriptive phrases are handy but can become unreliable and invalid instruments: (1) they are inaccurate and (2) they tend to encourage superficial analyses. The

---

[1] As a result of Sheldon's work one may say that we have as yet found no significant relationships between physique and personality qualities.

term *introvert,* applied to a child, carries a meaning descriptive of his whole personality. He may indeed show certain "introvertive" tendencies, but to dismiss analysis thus is to gloss over, or discourage search for, other personality characteristics less obvious and perhaps more meaningful. (3) Categorizing or typing of individuals is likely to imply too much dependence in the analysis on the idea of inherited traits (21).

2. Physiological Counterparts of Personality

There are other aspects of the physiological counterparts of personality that require clarification. This is necessary, since there are many other misconceptions, some of which are deeply rooted in lay thinking and in the minds of some teachers. On the other hand, there are physiological aspects of personality development which have very valid assumptions.

Some Misconceptions. Physical features have been used for centuries as keys to the kind of personality possessed by an individual. Among the most popular misinterpretations have been those which regard a prominent chin or a square jaw, for example, as synonymous with determination, reliability, and honesty. No better example could be provided than that of Dick Tracy, of the inevitable jutting jaw, pursuing criminals relentlessly. A receding chin conversely is supposed to indicate traits of a weak, "spineless," easily corrupted individual. Extensive research has generally failed to validate such popular conceptions of the relationship between specific personality traits and physiological counterparts.

Valid Generalizations. The relation of certain other physiological characteristics with personality is more valid. Relative size and maturity at all stages of children's development and even at adult maturity are positive factors in a good many instances influencing the direction a trait may take. The large boy or man may easily become either a bully or a protector. General appearance, beauty, and health are also significant. The undersized child is often at a disadvantage. Unless other influences provide positive compensating drives, he may easily become reticent, shy, bitter, and inferior.

Influence of Physiological Defects. Other influential negative physiological factors are such defects as speech disorders, skin blemishes, a crippled arm or leg, and defective vision or hearing. Children so affected may develop feelings of inadequacy and inferiority, eventually culminating in harmful compensatory activity. Opportunities for acquiring wholesome skills are needed by these children if their personalities are to develop in a more wholesome social direction.

Effect of Illness. Ultimate personality distortion may also be comparatively easily attained by children who are ill and sickly. Such children are more readily disturbed, become angry and emotional with their playmates, and tend to become aggressive. One of the great risks sick children encounter is the quite natural pampering they receive from their parents and friends. Such treatment while momentarily giving satisfaction also develops an increasing state of insecurity.

3. Glandular Effects

Much has been written concerning the effect of glandular activity upon personality development. Some of this is quite accurate, whereas much more is mere speculation. There are two kinds of effects which glandular activity may have on the child's growing personality. The first may be called the indirect, through which personality is influenced by physiological change resulting from abnormal glandular action. The second may be considered as a more direct effect where disturbed glandular action upsets the metabolic or general activity ratio of the child.

Indirect Effects. The entire glandular system functions cooperatively in the establishment of necessary chemical balances which are essential for normal drives, urges, and ways of reacting to stimuli of various kinds. The correct balance guarantees regular physical growth, a proper metabolic ratio, and the stimulation and development of normal sex characteristics and behavior. The glands responsible for such an indirect effect on personality are the pituitary, the thymus, and the pineal. When these glands fail to maintain their normal relationship with the total organism, or when they otherwise malfunction, they produce abnormalities in physical growth. Such extremes as dwarfism and giantism result from an imbalance in the functioning of the pituitary gland. Precocious sex development results from a malfunctioning of the thymus and pineal glands. Deviations such as these in physiological growth and development have a profound influence on the child's personality. This effect is not directly the cause of undesirable personality trait development but indirectly a cause through the resulting deviational physical growth.

Direct Effects. Direct effects may come about from a thyroid malfunctioning which produces a highstrung or hyperactive condition. An individual so constituted finds it difficult to rest or relax and responds to the slightest stimuli in his environment. An opposite type of reaction on the part of the child may be activated by what is called a hypofunctioning of this gland. Such a reaction is accompanied by a retarded metabolism, by marked indolence, and by extreme apathy.

Other Relations. The relationships suggested should not be taken to mean that personality traits are most affected in their development by glandular action, direct or indirect, without accompanying environmental or social stimuli. The feeling of inferiority, lack of belongingness and security are the factors, in the last analysis, which make it possible for glandular effects to condition behavior most severely. Although endocrine researchers point out that deviational behavior is associated with glandular malfunctioning, such association is not necessarily inevitable. As a matter of fact, behavior deviations and undesirable personality traits are often manifested without any evidence of a glandular relationship. Quite frequently the association seems, in the light of our present knowledge, to be merely coincidental.

Another thought is most important. This is the idea that glandular malfunctioning itself may be the result of personality deviation brought about by entirely different forces in the environment. Physicians and endocrinologists tend more and more to discount the affective influence of the thyroid and are pointing out with greater frequency that personality and emotional instability are causal in glandular and other organic malfunctioning. There is, of course, no conclusive proof of this, but there is a respectable body of evidence to justify this theory.

C. ENVIRONMENTAL FACTORS

1. The Biophysical versus the Bisocial Viewpoint

Undoubtedly this chapter emphasizes the behavior response in a social situation as the dominant factor in personality development. This viewpoint cannot be harmonized entirely with the biophysical concept, which regards personality in terms of what might be called the "inner man," nor can it be too closely identified with the bisocial view, which regards personality chiefly as an individual behavior pattern seen by others in various situations.

In order to explain the viewpoint to be taken and to show its relation to environmental factors, a short sketch will be given of the two contrasting theories mentioned.

Biophysical Viewpoint. The biophysical explanation emphasizes the inner, rather than the outer, manifestations of personality. According to this theory, the personality remains the same even when it is not in action or observable. Or, as stated by Allport, it may be viewed as a "solid organization of dispositions and sentiments" (3). Or, in Sandiford's words, "when a person gives rapt attention to a performance of beautiful music, there are few overt acts which give outsiders a clue to the ecstatic babblings of the personality within, yet the personality is undoubtedly there, and . . . is known to himself." (40). This viewpoint is entirely acceptable. What is not acceptable is the hypothesis that personality is, in the main, inwardly determined and quite uninfluenced by environmental factors.

Bisocial Viewpoint. The bisocial hypothesis considers personality almost entirely from the standpoint of what has been called its social-stimulus value. Its advocates regard personality as having but little meaning when out of contact with external social stimuli — the same person presents differing personality clues to different people. Or, stated in another way, personality is the potentiality for making impressions rather than a representation of inherited qualities or reaction tendencies.

Actually, considered in terms of their basic meanings, the two viewpoints are not entirely in conflict with one another. It is true that the combined effect of social situations and the individual's potentiality to react produces responses which eventually build into rather definite patterns. However, a constant pattern may seem to show variation. A continued demonstration of identical behavior may appear in one light to one person, in another light to others. One approves a reaction; another condemns it. It is difficult to accept the bisocial concept in sufficient entirety to state that because there are two contrasting impressions the basic personality producing the impressions is not the same in each instance. Such a conclusion would be absurd.

It is difficult to accept entirely either theory. Each has certain logical aspects which together give considerable insight into the problem.

Compromise View. A compromise viewpoint considers personality as a product of potentiality and environment. Repetitive experiences build up pattern reactions, whereas new situations tend to produce variations. To the extent that the stimuli of a new situation are familiar, the response becomes increasingly automatic and through continuance tends to become permanent. This view regards the individual as having a given response potential which can be induced to produce limited changes in the behavior pattern when the individual meets with change in the environmental stimuli.

2. Experience Provides Modification

Potential Behavior Modifiable. Students of child development are not inclined to consider personality as the result of an inherent, carefully organized potential. They do recognize general potentiality as well as individual differences in potentials. Personality itself emerges and forms response patterns only through experience (4). Personality and its components — attitudes, ideals, character, etc. — are due in no small part to the environment. Thus the particular personality reaction at any given time is the product of the environment and the organismic potential. A compromise view of this kind does not ignore the reality and importance of the inner organismic inheritance but holds that it is modified by the social environment.

Modification Depends on Experience. In accord with the idea of specificity of response, already noted, this doctrine implies that behavior patterns are modified as the various social situations vary.

The emphasis on the situational aspect can be justified by the great weight of evidence in support of the belief that conduct seems to be modified more by external stimuli than by inner organismic mechanisms.

3. Cultural Influences

Culture Limits Experience. Of considerable importance to the general environmental effect is the cultural background of the individual. This is what might be called the background for environmental organization. Although behavior and personality reactions are produced by environmental forces acting on the organism and providing motivation, both the inner organismic mechanisms and the social environment have a cultural background and meaning. The evidence for considering the culture as an influence in determining or modifying behavior lies in the thought that ideas, beliefs, prejudices, opinions, and attitudes are to a great extent the result of racial and social customs, codes, and standards. The culture may be found in the language, art, fashions, mores, religion, etc., of all groups and thereby gives meaning and direction to what is expected of an individual in a given environment. Cultural patterns obviously condition personality. The child is born within a specific background and is conditioned to the demands of that culture. Mead points out instances in which cultural patterns influence the development of behavior along lines quite the reverse of what we think of as normal. She reports that Arapesh men show a cooperative, unaggressive, and gentle nature quite unlike what we think of as manly qualities. Among certain women of other cultural groups she reports violent, hostile, aggressive, and competitive characteristics. Among certain groups, sex roles are reversed. Women are powerful, do the fishing, and produce the most important trade articles, whereas the men confine themselves to more artistic, nonutilitarian roles. The women tend to be very efficient and practical, while the men are shy, sensitive, and tend to be extremely dependent on their women. As in more modern cultures, deviation from the accepted roles is regarded as a sexual perversion. In every phase of existence, the prevailing culture emphasizes prohibitions that sharply limit experience.

D. MATURATIONAL FACTORS

Limitations in the Evidence. Although the effect of maturation has been studied in connection with various types of learning very little attention has been given to its influence on personality development. The greatest obstacle to clear-cut generalization is the fact that personality appraisal has been approached entirely from the status, rather than from the longitudinal, consideration of data. Experiments have been concerned with how a child behaves in relation to other children. Very little attention has been given to the question of how the child's personality changes in relation to his own developmental trends (31).

Reason for Limitations. The lack of attention to this problem might also spring from the earlier ideas that personality is mainly hereditary and susceptible to but slight modification. The furore caused by the Iowa studies dealing with shifts in intelligence in connection with environmental change illustrates the confidence in the earlier procedure. Unfortunately, in reference to arriving at acceptable conclusions, neither the Iowa group nor the conventionalists have given full consideration to the effect of maturation. Not until the effect of maturation on mental growth has been studied and determined can the influence of environmental factors be adequately appraised.

Basis of Attack. As a result of such limitations in the study of personality, it is entirely necessary to generalize from the limited available evidence in which the effect of maturation has been viewed in connection with aspects or phases of personality and from evidence where generalizations can be formulated from observed relationships between maturation and general growth aspects which have a bearing on personality.

1. The General Relationship of Growth and Learning

In a previous section considerable attention was directed to the relationships between learning and maturation. It seems desirable here to consider the matter further and to answer such challenges as have been made. This is particularly essential if generalizations are to be formulated regarding personality, where the evidence is general rather than specific.

Early Concepts of Maturation. The term *maturation* was originally used by geneticists and embryologists to indicate the period prior to fertilization during which process an immature germ cell is converted into a mature cell. Although the term was originally limited to this meaning, psychologists and biologists have since given it a more general connotation. Gesell in 1925 defined maturation as the regulatory mechanism which preserves inter-growth relationships and gives direction to emerging patterns (13). Since that time the word has been used rather loosely without any common acceptance. McGraw uses the term to refer to any phenomenon in the process of growth without reference to physical or genetic associations (31). She seems to oppose usage of the term in a situation in which growth and learning are considered as complementary aspects.

A definition which McGraw lists as "loose" and applicable to any "phenomena in the process of completion without reference to physiological or genetic correlates" is that of Courtis (9):

> Maturation may be defined precisely as the progress of an immature organism toward a mature, or terminal, state — a progress produced by constant forces acting under constant conditions. The organism itself may be either individual or social, and the mature state may be either that of the organism as a whole or that of any of its parts or functions.

This definition incidentally illustrates how the use of the term *maturation* has broadened from its original meaning. In answer to McGraw, Courtis implies "physiological or genetic correlates" in his reference to "constant forces acting under constant conditions."

Further Authority concerning Interrelation of Growth and Learning. The argument for a maturational effect on personality rests primarily on the general relationship between maturation and learning. This seems logical, since personality is basically a product of potentiality conditioned by environment. Conditioning in this sense is synonymous with learning, or what has familiarly been called the adjustment of the individual to his environment. If personality can be thought of as plastic and modifiable, it is subject to the laws of maturation, cycle effects, drives, motivations, and needs, as are learning to read, learning to spell, learning social behavior, learning emotional control, etc. Carmichael seems to agree to this when he states that it is impossible to say at any point that growth has stopped and learning has begun (7). According to him, maturation plays a part in all learning. Marquis does not differ fundamentally from Carmichael's point of view but insists that any definition of maturation must show its dependence on inner, rather than outer, motivations (27). According to him, both are the product of organism and environment. Learning, however, has a specific function which distinguishes it from maturation. Learning in this sense represents a modification resulting from specific outer stimuli. In contrast, maturation represents modification in response to internal stimuli. Regardless of differences in definition, both men recognize some kind of relationship between maturation and learning. This point of view is shared by the majority of current writers and gives validity to the idea that learning of all kinds is closely associated with maturation.

2. Learning-Maturation Relationship of Importance in
   Personality Development

Learning Most Effective at Given Periods. One of the findings, verified by many investigators, about the maturation-learning relationship is that there are certain periods in the developmental cycle of a specific growth during which learning is most effective. An experiment by Hilgard effectively illustrates this point (5). Utilizing control and experimental groups over a period of twelve weeks, he found that the experimental or special-practice group excelled the control group on all tests. The tasks learned involved such activities as buttoning, climbing, and cutting with scissors. However, at the end of the period the control group achieved equal efficiency, with only one week of practice at the later age. Thus the increased maturity reduced the period of learning from twelve weeks to one. Many other experiments could be cited, particularly those involving the child's introduction to reading and the effects thereof. The results in this area also indicate that learning is more efficient when it takes place at the proper period of maturation. In many schools reading and certain other subject-matter skills are not introduced as early as formerly. Nevertheless there is no evidence to show that these children do not mature in these skills at as high a level as formerly and at about the same age. Consequently, the skill is learned in a shorter period of time.

Other Evidences of Savings. In learning certain manipulatory skills, Gesell and Thompson also point out that the child's maturity has a significant influence on the efficiency of learning. According to these investigators, there is no conclusive data to indicate that practice and experience are especially effective when incompatible with maturity (14). Their conclusion is that the time of appearance of certain skills is dependent upon the "ripeness" of neural structures.

3. Implications for Personality Promotion

To what extent does such a relationship have meaning for those who are to direct the development of personality? There are several implications of the conclusions drawn from every investigation dealing with growth.

Need for Time. In the first place, time is needed for personality development. The teacher can do little in a short period. If teachers are to be constructively and positively helpful, they must work with a child for longer periods than are now allowed by the conventional school, where the teacher remains with the child for only one year. If maturation has a bearing on personality, comparable with the effect it has been shown to have on physical, mental, motor, personal, social, and other aspects of growth, there is likely to be a given rhythm in specific phases or periods of growth. In a specific period or cycle of development, all aspects of growth settle into a pattern or definite relationship characteristic only of that period. The emerging pattern probably lasts beyond the time in which a child has contact with a single teacher. The teacher's contact is too brief for her to do more than ascertain, or become sensitive to, a given child's rhythm of growth. By the time such understanding is established, the child passes on to another teacher.

Development Is Rhythmic. In reference to the need for time, there is the fact that growth relationships once established in a particular developmental period continue quite uninterruptedly unless the situation becomes drastically changed through shock, trauma, or extreme deprivation. Accordingly, then, immediate and temporary teacher effect has little significance. If personalities are to be changed for the better, or even for the worse, something more than mediocre teacher stimulation and motivation is necessary.

There is sufficient evidence about the relationship between maturation and learning to postulate the idea that personality traits appear, grow, and mature in relation to the developmental cycles of the child and according to the complexity of the trait involved. Appearance and continuity of growth are the result of maturation and need, both of which are the product of capacity or potentiality plus environmental and organic stimuli. The implication here is that the sudden appearance of new traits, from egocentric to social attitudes for example, or from general friendliness to intense interest in particular peer cliques, is the result of reaching developmental maxima or of potentiality asserting itself in terms of organismic and environmental demands.

Change Requires Continued Effort. In this same connection another point may be made which is quite contrary to the theories of those who have given little attention to maturational effects on behavior. Personality, although flexible, indefinite in its periphery, and constantly subject to modification can be influenced only by considerable effort and diligence on the part of teachers. The effect of teaching is a part of the general motivational pattern, but in relation to the total stimulus, a very small part. Much needs to be done in developing and organizing the total school environmental influence before the work of a single teacher can be particularly significant.

Critical Periods Demand Extra Attention. A third point to be made is that there are critical periods in a child's developmental pattern when the organism is more responsive and sensitive to environmental stimuli. Such points in the developmental pattern are at the beginning of new phases or growth cycles. In terms of school age and grade these periods are the period extending from kindergarten to the first grade and the beginning of adolescence at the sixth-, seventh-, or eighth-grade level, depending on the child's maturity. It would seem, then, that the most sensitive, alert, and understanding teachers should be available at these periods, if teachers are to continue on the one-year-tenure basis with children.

SOME SUGGESTIONS FOR DIRECTING PERSONALITY DEVELOPMENT

Limitations of Viewpoint. The theory that personality is modifiable by various inner and outer influences enables the teacher to play a positive role in the maximum development of the personalities of her pupils. Personality grows and develops under many kinds of circumstances. Under perfectly normal conditions it grows, develops new patterns, discards old patterns, and eventually emerges into adult behavior. The purpose of this section is to show ways and means by which the teacher can be helpful in guiding development to its highest possible positive expression. Little attention will be given here to the problem of providing guidance and direction of a remedial nature. Extreme personality disorders and the teacher's responsibility in handling them will be given consideration in a later chapter. The attention here will be confined to suggestions for dealing with personality problems within what might be thought of as a normal range of behavior.

A. AN ELABORATION OF THE IDEA OF FLEXIBILITY

A Concept of Individuality. It is obvious that if the school, and particularly the teacher, are to influence the course of personality development, personality itself must be considered capable of reacting to such an influence. The arguments for and against this viewpoint have been reviewed and further validation scarcely seems necessary. As a result of the various factors governing behavior, both inner and outer, and the varying consistency of stimulus, practice, and need, some personalities are far more modifiable than others and respond to changed external stimuli more readily than others. Other personalities, probably because of consistency of strength of motivating stimuli, appear to be inflexible and rigid. We tend incorrectly to say that such a personality reflects "character." Within normal ranges all personalities, both the consistent and the varying, possess a pattern of dominant trait behavior or what might be called a personality *core*. Even the most variable possess a stability or balance of one kind or another. This is what is referred to as *pattern*. The details of the pattern consist of a range of response and a series or sequence of trait behavior.

Traits may be closely related or widespread. In the concept of the amount of variability of response of specific traits and in the number and range of trait reactions lies the idea of individuality. Throughout normal development new traits are added and old ones dropped according to the individual's organismic needs in relation to his social environment. The range of response shifts as the individual moves through various developmental periods, tending toward more consistency as maturity is approached. Such is the picture of a flexible maturing personality. Individuality represents, then, not merely the core, or the sum of the dominant traits consistently reflected, but also the potentiality for modification.

Role of the Teacher. As has been stated throughout each of the preceding chapters, the teacher's role is that of indirect control and guidance. The teacher is powerless to effect change directly. The teacher can only modify, enrich, aid in developing situations in which needs can be better met, and help provide the child with more beneficial stimuli. Only this procedure, plus the effect of such organic changes as are operative in the individual, can aid in personality development (24).

This thought suggests certain do's and don'ts in connection with the matter. In the first place, it should discourage teachers from plunging into a situation between the child and his stimuli and from attempting through nagging, preaching, or punishing to change his behavior according to her preconceived ideas as to how he should act. Obviously the core, or pattern, around which attitudes and habits have been built prevents this kind of action from having anything but a bad effect. And this kind of activity is never justified except temporarily in emergency situations or when the personality is so maladjusted as to need treatment of this kind. Where such is the case a clinician is needed. Teachers who fail to heed this kind of warning are ignoring the fact that efforts to modify basic traits must take into consideration the relation of this activity to other traits, habits, and attitudes.

B. RECOGNIZE PRIMARY NEEDS

Most basic of all in aiding children to achieve maximum personality development is constant sensitivity to the child's primary needs. The emergence of a properly maturing personality with freedom from disintegrating conflict and frustration may be found by meeting physiological, social, and psychological demands.

Physiological Needs. Essential physiological effects depend upon such ordinary essentials as air, food, shelter, and clothing. Inability to obtain any of these in sufficient quantity will not only result in personality malformation and abnormal adjustive behavior but, in cases of extreme deprivation, in death (38). In connection with these are the needs for ridding the body of waste products, abstinence from bad food and excessive drinking of alcoholic beverages, and freedom from focal infection. A lack of satisfaction in respect to any of these can result in ill health, an irritable and neurotic personality and at times in complete mental aberration. Physicians today are more than ever concerned with the interrelations of mental and physical ills and are more and more frequently treating physical ailments from the mental or psychological aspect of personality.

Rhythm of Action and Rest. Where basic physiological needs are supplied, there must follow some control of energy which the organism must expend. Without activity and without control of that activity the end-point objective is never realized. Body structures, in order to develop and mature properly, need frequent exercise in reference to their structure and function. Another phase of meeting physiological needs adequately is securing activity and rest in proper proportions. A pattern relationship between the two is essential for adequate physiological expression and function as well as for balance and integration. It is in this connection that the American people present the incongruity of almost religious insistence and adherence to this principle in reference to their children and almost complete neglect of the idea for themselves. To obtain results with children which can carry into adulthood will require some adherence to this principle. If the child is to grow into an adult personality able to dismiss tensions and worries during sleep and recreation periods, he must become accustomed to the necessary rhythm of rest and activity. And the habit must be strongly rooted through the various developmental periods.

The importance of meeting the social needs of the individual has been mentioned in previous sections. It is mentioned again because the importance of satisfying social activity is dominant in personality development. Necessary outcomes of such activity are the acquisition of love and affection, the establishment of prestige and security in selected small groups, and sufficient identification with peer patterns to find group belongingness.

The need for love and affection appears very early in the lives of children and continues throughout maturity. Status and prestige require social participation with the objective of acceptance by successively larger groupings. This can be obtained only by contributing to the group and eventually by realization and satisfaction of acceptance by the group. What has not been mentioned previously is that the sign of a maturing personality is indicated by an ability to shift from the earlier home and small group relationships to the wider community groupings. In this connection the individual must learn to develop the necessary balance between his group identifications and his special individual differentiation from others.

Effect of Differences. The child who is different, even desirably so, frequently has a very trying time in establishing security and belongingness among his peers. All of us, children particularly, need to show personality traits that identify us with peers. The problem of teacher and parent is to help children preserve individuality while outwardly reflecting customs, habits, and the approved social practices of their group. This is not an easy task.

The purpose of teaching, guiding, and directing behavior is to help children achieve maximum development. The realization of this goal should result in extending acceptable differences in group behavior. On the other hand, teachers and parents must help children at the same time to establish sufficient conformity to be acceptable to their peers. It is only by ignoring the problem of conformity that exhibition of individual specialized abilities causes difficulty. Where the child can display special abilities in connection with cooperative group activities, the best possible kind of balance has been achieved.

Psychological Needs. The meeting of psychological needs is as important as aiding the child in realizing physiological and social satisfactions. The word "psychological" is used here somewhat advisedly for want of a better word. It refers to the creative, recreative, and emotional urges. The individual requires a certain amount of spontaneity, freedom, and imagination in his behavior. The need for free, spontaneous play is one illustration. The need to plan and execute is another. Quite obviously this thought has implications for teachers which have been mentioned previously. Briefly, each child needs the opportunity to do some planning for himself and to be allowed to work plans out in the best possible manner.

Use of the Environment. The achievement of these objectives depends in great part upon the kind of environment provided. All normal children are born with the potentiality for desirable personality development. In the environment with its multiplicity of factors, its mores, its good and bad influences, and its motivating and frustrating effects are to be found the materials which will eventually determine the kind of personality the child achieves. The job of the teacher or parent is to provide the controls through which can emerge the kind of personality which finds satisfactions in cooperative and constructive endeavor. Such control does not necessarily imply a by-passing of reality in the organismic-environmental relationship. The implication to be drawn is that each child deserves as rich and varied an experience as his environment can place at his disposal. From the standpoint of learning, it must afford him the opportunity to discover the nature of social processes, forces, pressures, and cultural offerings. It must afford him opportunities to encounter reality and authority in its varied forms. And most important, it must give the child an opportunity to suffer reasonable failure as well as reasonable success. Pain as well as pleasure, frustration as well as satisfying creative effort are necessary in achieving personality maturity. The conventional school does little in this respect. Errors and mistakes are considered something to be avoided and, incorrectly, their appearance provides the exclusive means for much educational evaluation. The right, as well as the need, to be wrong should loom high in the learning criteria held by teachers.

Balance between Failure and Success. The child needs the opportunity to achieve a satisfactory balance between success and failure. The present school allows little opportunity for the child to say that he doesn't understand. He must understand or fail, and the quicker he understands, the better the mark or reward he receives. Learning would be much more effective if errors could be corrected and mistakes explained. The right to succeed is likewise a basic, fundamental need and right. The environment for maximum personality development must be so ordered as to enable all children to feel adequate in ability, in skills, and in meeting ordinary and universal situations. A balance between success and failure is essential to a realization of the needs leading to maximum potential fulfillment (38).

C. CHILDREN BENEFIT FROM TEACHER ASSISTANCE

Trainability of Personality. There is considerable evidence that certain efforts to meet children's needs result in positive personality change. Jack, for example, had considerable success in aiding submissive children to become more normally aggressive and dominant in dealing with other children (20). This study was one of the first to deal with possibilities in modifying personality reactions. In this particular instance change was brought about by teaching each of the children in the experimental group to do three different things in which the control-group children were not skilled. Since these children were four-year-old children, the skills learned were rather simple, involving block building, familiarity with certain stories, etc. These children, usually meek and submissive, either became normally dominant or increased their efforts in this direction. Such studies indicate that a little help and attention from parents and teachers can produce marked results. Teachers must overcome their reluctance to seek the assistance of children other than those who so aggressively and successfully gain their attention and favor as helpers. Much more training should be provided for the less conspicuous children.

There is also evidence that a child who is having difficulty in contributing to a group and thereby feels a lack of status, may, when once started on the right path, proceed very rapidly. Such evidence has been presented by Page, who points out that ascendant behavior is modifiable and that training results appear to be cumulative (37). One must infer from results of such experimentation that when the child begins to acquire poise and ability in certain skills or activities, he is motivated to try other areas of expression. It must be kept in mind that a series of related situations must be provided before anything like a general "trait" of confidence, poise, and security is achieved. Poor guidance can easily lead early successes into injurious and critical failures.

Children Need Assistance. This point of view has considerable significance for the type of situation called "free-play." Recess periods, play periods after school, during the noon hour, etc., are frequently unsupervised because teachers feel that children need the freedom the situation seems to offer. Or free play may be justified on the basis that the children are given the opportunity to plan their play and then carry it out under their own direction. Opportunities to do this are fine but should be available as testing situations rather than as everyday occurrences. Children are selfish, cruel, dominant, aggressive, and in many situations quite insensitive to the personality needs of other children. Leadership, even where children plan, results through the interplay of certain dominative-submissive relationships. And domination is not necessarily of the bullying, unpleasant type. Domination frequently results through the desire of children to please certain individuals in the group. Status and prestige are often the criterion used rather than ability or the needs of the child. Therefore it seems advisable to shift many free-play opportunities into situations where adult influence can exert its share of planning. This does not mean that the teacher shall force children into a preconceived plan based on what she thinks is good for them. It means that, to the advantages of the free, rough and tumble interplay of personalities that permit children to go as far as possible in achieving their goals, there should be added the adult leader who can help children develop necessary special abilities as occasion demands. The adult participant will find it necessary at times to withdraw an incompetent child from the center of attention and perhaps give him special assistance later.

Elimination of Failure Complexes. Many children develop a sense of failure very early in school. Updegraff and Keister have reported optimistically on the chances for counteracting this kind of personality blighting (47). In this experiment children were selected who clearly demonstrated undesirable or immature reactions to failure. Such reactions included more than a normal number of requests for help in specific test situations, exaggerated reactions and responses, and more than normal rationalizations in reference to specific responsibilities. Training periods in which (1) easy success was obtained, followed by (2) periods of more practice in situations in which chances for success were reasonably within their range resulted in remarkable progress. Emotional behavior diminished steadily, sulking and crying were reduced to a minimum, and interest and effort were notably higher.

These children were handled in accordance with the best clinical practices. They were actually taught how best to obtain success in situations within their ability range. As they succeeded, the range of difficulty was slightly increased.

OF IMPORTANCE TO TEACHERS

A. ESSENTIAL TO STUDY NEEDS

Considerable emphasis has been placed upon the many possible ways in which the child's personality can be distorted or made to deviate from what for him is his highest potential. It should also be emphasized that there is much in the school program which fails to impress or to impinge upon his personality in any way whatever. In many instances it is recognized that only certain items of experience have possibilities for personality motivation, since needs appear to determine whether learning experiences are meaningful to the child or not. It must be admitted that when fear comes between the child and the instructional offering, the child then, at least temporarily, attends to the situation at hand. The test of the importance of the opportunity can be determined only when fear is removed and the child and the opportunity either merge or remain apart.

Criteria of Instructional Challenge. Children will accept instructional opportunity according to various criteria. If the situation offers the chance to establish group prestige and belongingness the child is motivated and reacts accordingly. If he is attempting to reinforce his inner ego, which has been threatened by failure, he will also become interested. And according to many other conditions of belongingness, prestige, value concepts, and the like, the

child responds. The child who is dominated by inner turmoil —
and at times all children are — will avoid and ignore all instructional motivations unless he is threatened with more of what he is
already suffering. Needs are an important consideration in determining ways and means of building desirable personalities. Unmet
or neglected, they form the dominant background for daydreaming, brooding, and preoccupation.

The Conventional School Negligent. Teachers as a group have
been concerned only incidentally with coordinating instructional
and personality motivating procedures. School programs have
been devoted traditionally to the task of teaching fundamental
skills. And traditionally, the approach to method has been based
on a logical organization of the material to be learned. A logical
consideration of how the child learns has been entirely secondary
and only in recent years has been given attention. Even when tradition has been threatened by such potential improvements as individualization, it has remained pretty solidly intrenched. The
implementation of generalizations concerning individualization
has involved mainly quantitative changes rather than changes in
content. And measurement has done little toward breaking the
old and illogical relationship between need and instructional offering. In many ways it has tended to re-emphasize skill learning
as an end, rather than as a means to an end.

Implications in the Challenge. If the school is to accept the challenge implied in its fundamental objective of citizenship training, freedom, and well-being of all individuals, it must mend many
of its ways of doing things. Certain elementary principles pertain-
ing to the establishment of security, prestige, and belongingness,
to mention only a few, must be made compatible with content and
method of instruction. Relationships between children and teachers should be based on mutual respect, not alone on the child's
respect for the teacher. If we utilize what we know about individual differences, it is obvious that much more can be done for children at the extremes. The dull child needs a multitude of successful experiences and the bright child the opportunity to participate
at a higher, much enriched level. Skills may be treated as means
to an end and emphasis placed on activities that motivate organization of knowledge, on making generalizations based on experience,

and on experiences that motivate the development of values in human relationships.

B. THE PROBLEM OF THE SCHOOL

It is clearly indicated that much reorganization is necessary if the school is to assume responsibility for the guidance and direction of personality development. If this responsibility is to be assumed, how much attention should be devoted to the problem and what are the chances of success with the wide range of behavior exhibited by children?

Opportunities in the Conventional School. As has already been indicated, not much can be achieved in the very rigid type of conventional school. On the other hand, one can be quite optimistic about what can be accomplished even in this type of school, if some elasticity can be allowed. The question will never be solved as long as educators insist upon an "either-or" attitude toward some of the experimental results and implications which seem so promising. Schools must move toward more integrative practices. Carefully planned evaluation of even simple deviations in procedure can be made the content for public relations programs. It must be remembered that any change which is pointed toward more security for the child may also provide security for parents. Only if parents understand and approve the efforts of the school in this direction can real instructional planning for personality development make permanent and satisfying progress.

Need for Parent Cooperation. Within the framework of parent-teacher cooperation certain steps may be taken. Although most children will move toward eventual satisfying personality maturity without much special attention, certain others need more assistance. The problem child whose personality weaknesses drive him to aggressiveness and rebellion is acutely apparent. The parent may have difficulty in identifying symptoms with cause and may himself be demanding and aggressive in his relation with the school. Such a parent will blame teachers and the school or will attempt to point out weaknesses in the school program in order to hide or avoid recognizing the problems of his child. This kind of situation is very difficult. Some way must be found to obtain parent cooperation and to attack the real, rather than the substituted, problem. Obtaining the cooperation of parents in helping children whose behavior is characterized by withdrawal or by completely submissive behavior is even more difficult. Such behavior is only infrequently recognized by teachers as serious and is overlooked by compensating approval of some kind of substitute behavior such as high scholarship.

In addition to the problem of recognition, there is the even more complex need of doing something about it. There is evidence that improvement can be effected and changes made in the personality pattern. Reconditioning has been shown to be helpful in the elimination of fear, and in other situations a reorientation of value concepts has helped to eliminate the child's feeling of insecurity. If the results of such research are to be accepted, then there is much that the school can do to assist with the problem.

Regulation versus Personality Development. On the other hand, teachers must not become too confident. They must realize that little is now known about procedures for eliminating emotional tensions, strengthening desirable traits, and eliminating those that are undesirable. Throwing aside every possible administrative and instructional routine in order not to "handicap" the child is a very questionable procedure. It must be remembered that the child is so strongly motivated by the total environmental influence that merely requiring him to march in line, for example, is not exactly devastating to his personality. Such a requirement may, or may not, be foolish, but beyond that its affective influence is very mild. And it must be remembered that children need and seek guidance. It is only with maturity that authority can be completely released. Many decisions can desirably be made for children, while they are in the process of maturing. The question of what decisions and when is, of course, another problem.

Need for Experimentation. In the field of personality development there is a real need for experimentation. It is true that many educators are afraid to experiment because of conventional ideas against it, because of uninformed parents, or political-minded school boards. Undoubtedly there is a great lack of centers where experimentation can be planned, unhampered by convention or prejudice. On the other hand, the validity and reliability of the results of experimental studies and schools is not too well accepted.

Real improvement can come only where parents and teachers work together. The schools, after all, reflect the culture of a given locale, are of the people, by the people, and for the people. This assignment is more difficult than that given the experimental school. The isolated, volitional, experimental school can light the way, but for universal enlightenment there must be much duplication of experiment which merits parent participation, approval, and faith.

SELECTED REFERENCES

1. ALLPORT, F. H., *Social Psychology*. Boston: Houghton Mifflin, 1924.
2. ALLPORT, G. W., "What Is a Trait of Personality?" *Journal of Abnormal and Social Psychology*, 25:368–372, 1931.
3. ——, *Personality, A Psychological Interpretation*. New York: Holt, 1937.
4. ALSCHULER, ROSE H., AND HATTWICK, LABERTA W., *Painting and Personality, A Study of Young Children*, Vol. I and Vol. II. Chicago: University of Chicago Press, 1947.
5. BRECKENRIDGE, M. E., AND VINCENT, E. L., *Child Development*. Philadelphia: Saunders, 1943.
6. ALEXANDER, THERON, AND ALEXANDER, MARIE, "A Study of Personality and Social Status," *Child Development*, 23:207–213, September, 1952.
7. CARMICHAEL, LEONARD, "Origin and Prenatal Growth of Behavior," *A Handbook of Child Psychology*, edited by Carl Murchison. Worcester: Clark University Press, 1933.
8. AMATORA, MARY, "Similarity in Teacher and Pupil Personality," *Journal of Psychology*, 37:45–50, 1954.
9. COURTIS, S. A., "Maturation as a Factor in Diagnosis," *Thirty-Fourth Yearbook, National Society for the Study of Education*, 169–187, 1935.
10. CURTI, M. W., *Child Psychology*. New York: Longmans, Green, 1938.
11. AUSUBEL, DAVID P., "A Preliminary Study of Developmental Trends in Socioempathy," *Child Development*, 23:111–126, 1952.
12. CATTELL, RAYMOND B., AND GREEN, WALTER, "The Personality Factor Structure of Eleven Year Old Children in Terms of Behavior Rating Data," *Journal of Clinical Psychology*, 9:256–266, 1953.
13. GESELL, ARNOLD, *The Mental Growth of the Pre-School Child: A Psychological Outline of Normal Development from Birth to the Sixth Year, Including a System of Developmental Analysis*. New York: Macmillan, 1925.
14. ——, AND THOMPSON, HELEN, "Learning and Growth in Identical Infant Twins: An Experimental Study of the Method of Co-Twin Control," *Genetic Psychology Monographs*, 6:1–124, 1929.
15. GILLILAND, A. R., *Genetic Psychology*. New York: Ronald Press, 1933.
16. HARTMANN, G. W., *Educational Psychology*. New York: American Book Co., 1941.

17. HARTSHORNE, H., AND MAY, M. A., *Studies in Deceit.* New York: Macmillan, 1928.

18. CATTELL, RAYMOND B., BLEWETT, D. B., AND BELOFF, J. R., "The Inheritance of Personality. A Multiple Variance Analysis Determination of Approximate Nature-Nurture Ratios for Primary Personality Factor in Q-Data," *American Journal of Human Genetics,* 7:122–146, 1955.

19. GALLAGHER, BUELL G., "Personality Under Pressure," *Child Study,* 30: No. 3, 9–13, 1953.

20. JACK, L. M., *An Experimental Study of Ascendant Behavior in Preschool Children.* Iowa City: University of Iowa Studies in Child Welfare, Vol. 9, No. 3, 1934.

21. HARRIS, D. B., ROSE, A. M., CLARK, K. E., AND VALASEK, F., "Personality Differences between Responsible and Less Responsible Children," *Journal of Genetic Psychology,* 87:103–109, 1955.

22. JUNG, C. G., *Psychological Types.* New York: Harcourt Brace, 1923.

23. HINKELMAN, E. A., "Relation of Certain Personality Variables to High School Achievement," *School Review,* 60:532–534, December, 1952.

24. JACKSON, JOSEPH, "Effect of Classroom Organization and Guidance Practice on Personality Adjustment and Academic Growth of Students," *Journal of Genetic Psychology,* 83:159–170, September, 1953.

25. LERNER, E., AND MURPHY, L. B., *Methods for the Study of Personality in Young Children,* Monographs of the Society for Research in Child Development, Vol. VI, No. 4. Washington: National Research Council, 1941.

26. KLUCKHOHN, CLYDE, AND MURRAY, H. A., *Personality in Nature, Society, and Culture.* Second Edition. New York: Knopf, 1953.

27. MARQUIS, D. G., "The Criterion of Innate Behavior," *Psychological Review,* 37:334–349, 1930.

28. MARSTON, L. R., *The Emotions of Young Children, An Experimental Study in Introversion and Extroversion.* Iowa City: University of Iowa Studies in Child Welfare, Vol. 3, 1925.

29. KRALL, VITA, "Personality Characteristics of Accident Repeating Children," *Journal of Abnormal and Social Psychology,* 48:99–107, January, 1953.

30. MAY, M. A., "The Foundations of Personality," *Psychology at Work,* edited by P. S. Achilles. New York: Whittlesey House, 1932.

31. McGRAW, MYRTLE B., "Maturation of Behavior," *Manual of Child Psychology,* edited by Leonard Carmichael. New York: Wiley, 1946.

32. LONG, L. M. K., "Alfred Adler and Gordon W. Allport: A Comparison of Certain Topics in Personality Theory," *American Journal of Individual Psychology,* 10:43–53, Nos. 1 and 2, 1953.

33. MURPHY, GARDNER, *Personality.* New York: Harper, 1947.

34. NAPOLI, P. J., "Finger-Painting and Personality Diagnosis," *Genetic Psychology Monographs,* 34:129–230, 1946.

35. MACFARLANE, JEAN W., ALLEN, LUCILLE, AND HONZIK, MARJORIE P., "A

Developmental Study of the Behavior Problems of Normal Children between Twenty-One Months and Fourteen Years," *University of California Studies in Child Development,* Vol. II. Berkeley: University of California Press, 1954.

36. MEAD, MARGARET, AND WOLFENSTEIN, MARTHA (Editors). *Childhood in Contemporary Cultures.* Chicago: University of Chicago Press, 1954.

37. PAGE, M. L., *The Modification of Ascendant Behavior in Preschool Children.* Iowa City: University of Iowa Studies in Child Welfare, Vol. XII, No. 3, 1936.

38. PRESCOTT, DANIEL, *Emotion and the Educative Process.* Washington: The American Council on Education, 1938.

39. PRINCE, MORTON, *The Unconscious.* New York: Macmillan, 1921.

40. SANDIFORD, P., *Foundations of Educational Psychology.* New York: Longmans, Green, 1938.

41. SCHWESINGER, G. C., *Heredity and Environment.* New York: Macmillan, 1933.

42. SHELDON, W. H., STEVENS, S. S., AND TUCKER, W. B., *The Varieties of Human Physique.* New York: Harper, 1940.

43. SPRANGER, E., *Types of Men.* New York: Niemeyer, 1928.

44. SYMONDS, P. M., *Diagnosing Personality and Conduct.* New York: Appleton-Century, 1931.

45. THORPE, L. P., *Psychological Foundations of Personality.* New York: McGraw-Hill, 1938.

46. MORRIS, WOODROW WILBERT, AND NICHOLAS, ALMA L., "Intra-Familial Personality Configurations among Children with Primary Behavior Disorders and Their Parents: A Rorschach Investigation," *Journal of Clinical Psychology,* 6:309–319, 1950.

47. UPDEGRAFF, R., AND KEISTER, M. E., *A Study of Children's Reactions to Failure and an Experimental Attempt to Modify Them.* Iowa City: University of Iowa Studies in Child Welfare, Vol. XIII, No. 4, 1937.

48. MUSSEN, P. H., AND CONGER, J. J., *Child Development and Personality.* New York: Harper, 1956.

49. OJEMANN, R. H., *Personality Adjustment of Individual Children.* What Research Says to the Teacher, No. 5. Washington: National Education Association, October, 1954.

50. WOODWORTH, R. S., *Psychology.* New York: Holt, 1924.

51. PAULSEN, ALMA A., "Personality Development in the Middle Years of Childhood: A Ten Year Longitudinal Study of Thirty Public School Children By Means of Rorschach Test and Social Histories," *American Journal of Orthopsychiatry,* 24:336–350, 1954.

52. ROTHNEY, J. W. M., AND HEIMANN, R. A., "Development and Applications of Projective Tests of Personality," *Review of Educational Research,* 23:70–84, February, 1953.

53. SAPPENFIELD, B. R., *Personality Dynamics.* New York: Knopf, 1954.

54. SEARS, R. R. AND OTHERS, "Some Child-Rearing Antecedents of Aggression

and Dependency in Young Children," *Genetic Psychology Monographs*, 47:135–236, May, 1953.

55. SMOCK, C. D., AND THOMPSON, G. G., "An Inferred Relationship Between Early Childhood Conflicts and Anxiety Responses in Adult Life," *Journal of Personality*, 23:88–98, 1954.

56. SMITH, MADORAH E., "A Comparison of Certain Personality Traits in the Same Individuals in Childhood and Fifty Years Later," *Child Development*, 23:159–180, 1952.

57. SONTAG, L. W., CRANDALL, V., AND LACEY, J. I., "Dynamics of Personality Resolution of Infantile Dependent Need," *American Journal of Orthopsychiatry*, 22:534–541, 1952.

14

DISCIPLINE AND THE
GROWTH PROCESS

INTRODUCTION — THE PROBLEM

Individual and Group Problems. The problems of discipline will be discussed from two standpoints: (1) that of solving group problems and (2) that of solving the problems of the individual. The chapter is not divided into sections dealing with each category separately. It seems advisable to illustrate, whenever pertinent, the relation of the material to either or both of the problems of group and individual behavior.

Limitations of Treatment. Certain limitations need to be understood. Much of the material in the previous chapters, particularly on the emotions, personality, and moral behavior, has a bearing on discipline. In the chapter following, on mental hygiene practices, attention is given to procedures somewhat related to this topic. Therefore this chapter will adhere quite rigidly to the idea of discipline as the development of individual freedom and self-direction in relation to the increasing maturity of the child.

A. DEFINITION

Definition of Discipline. The word *discipline* comes from the Latin verb *discere,* meaning *to learn.* This probably explains why certain academic subjects are frequently referred to, particularly at the university level, as "disciplines." In the days of Greek and Latin glory the word also implied individual responsibility for directing oneself in the learning process. The term and meaning later became distorted to such an extent that discipline and learning, although still synonymous, implied not free, self-directed learning but learning imposed from without. To provide disciplinary values, the task must be difficult — the more difficult the better. Discipline meant not freedom in learning but rather a process by which the mind of the individual became disciplined. A mind so trained was enabled to approach a task quite apart from individual interests or worldly significance. It was humble and never questioned authority.

Discipline May Vary in Same Classroom. Regardless of the kind of classroom setting provided, either one or both of these two viewpoints may be found. In certain schoolrooms one attitude toward discipline may prevail during one part of the school day and another attitude at another hour or period. Where a varying philosophy is found, it is likely that the more rigid is associated with the academic subjects. The kind of discipline which allows choice is associated with the less academic classes like arts and crafts or gymnasium and playground activity. No one knows why this should be true. If rigid discipline marked by meek acceptance of direction and authority is good for arithmetic and spelling there is no reason why it isn't also good for physical education, art, music, and industrial arts. The only excuse for a mixed philosophy is that "it is done that way."

Difference between Philosophies. One distinction between the two philosophies seems to be that of goal. In the one instance, the goal is a personal goal of the individual who subjects himself to restraint, the better to achieve his objectives. In the other, the goal is that of someone else who dominates those under his charge toward the accomplishment of objectives as he sees them. The only aspect of uniformity of the two philosophies as seen at this point is that discipline is not isolated but is always associated with the achievement of objectives. Thus, in this sense, discipline refers to some sort of behavior organization undertaken in order to attain more effectively a specific goal. With group discipline the behavior of several or many must be organized for efficient attainment of a group objective. And at times there must be group organization of behavior so that individuals may most effectively realize individual goals.

Behavior Good or Bad according to Goal. An example of individual discipline in respect to achieving a group goal is that of participating in a game, perhaps, when one is not much interested in

playing. The point to be made is that discipline is always associated with a goal. But it should be remembered that an activity
can be proper at one time with one goal and improper at another
time with a different goal. Teachers and principals fail to take this
into account in deciding whether behavior is "good" or "bad."
Sheviakov points out that when a group of boys run through the
hall on a Saturday in order to get to a Scout meeting on time they
are acting appropriately. The same behavior during a recess period
may represent poor discipline if it interferes with the group desire (20). The act itself is indicative of poor discipline only when
it interferes with the achievement of a goal.

B. CONTRASTING PATTERNS

Dominative Approach. In one of the groups studied by Anderson,
kindergarten children were making May baskets (1). They had
been given material with lines drawn on by the teacher in order
to direct their construction. The teacher also distributed to each
child four diamond-shaped pieces to be pasted horizontally on the
baskets for decorative purposes. One of the children, Terry, had
followed the lines according to instructions but had pasted the dia-
monds vertically rather than horizontally.

> "Oh, oh, Terry," the teacher said, "the decorations are to
> be pasted on lying down and not standing up."
> "But I want to paste mine this way," said Terry.
> "Well, that isn't the way they are supposed to go. Here now,
> just paste it this way." [1]

The teacher then took the basket and pasted the diamond before Terry had a chance to say anything. Under her direction the
boy then pasted on two others. She went on to another child assuming that Terry would follow her directions for the final diamond. At the end of the period the fourth diamond was still missing. Upon inquiry Terry said he did not want the other one.

> "Oh, but every basket should have four. Here is one your
> color. We'll just paste it on quickly." [2]

[1] From *Child Behavior and Development,* edited by Barker, Kounin, and Wright,
1943. Courtesy of McGraw-Hill Book Company.
[2] From *Child Behavior and Development,* edited by Barker, Kounin, and Wright,
1943. Courtesy of McGraw-Hill Book Company.

Another child, Mary Lou, having trouble with the handles of the basket decided she didn't want a handle. Instead she cut the material into pieces and added them as decorations. The teacher said,

> "Oh, you've spoiled yours, Mary Lou; yours is all messy and doesn't have a handle." [3]

As Anderson notes, both of these children indicated spontaneity of action. As in many other instances familiar to the reader their spontaneity was squelched because their ideas differed somewhat from the teacher's. These children were unquestionably creative and were thinking for themselves — generally a desirable activity. The boy was completely frustrated in his desire, and the girl's idea in the matter was completely disapproved (1).

The Integrative Approach. Professor Anderson provides a contrasting illustration, which he terms the integrative or democratic approach to child direction. In one of his second grades under observation the children chose the song about the organ-grinder and the monkey. After the song was sung, the teacher asked the children if they would like to dramatize it. There was general agreement, and the boy who had suggested the song was given the opportunity to select the organ-grinders. He chose three, who in turn were to choose their "monkeys." The third boy was slow.

> "Why don't you choose, James?" the teacher asked.
> "I want a little person and I want somebody who wants to be a monkey."

A child volunteered, the song was sung, and organ-grinders and monkeys performed their functions. Finally one child asked if they shouldn't march down the street. Whereupon the aisles became the street and more dramatization followed involving playing, performing, and imaginary dropping of pennies into cups. At the end the teacher said,

> "Well, I hope you enjoyed their song, and that the monkeys received lots of pennies."

In this situation there is considerable evidence of friendly teacher-pupil contact resulting in natural behavior on the part of

[3] *Ibid.*

the children. The children easily expressed their real interests, had ideas, and were allowed to act accordingly. As indicated by Anderson, to the extent that child behavior is flexible, creative, and elastic, the social interplay between teacher and pupil is harmonious and encouraging. Naturalness leads to understanding by others. When children are natural, they are better understood and all the children in the group become more efficient in adjusting personal needs and desires to those of others.

On the other hand, according to Anderson, teacher domination stifles differences in others, reduces the interplay which results in cooperation, and hinders the achievement of understanding (2).

Advantages of Integrative Discipline. It might seem to some that the illustrations have little bearing on the question of discipline. There are three ways, however, in which the illustrations relate to this problem.

1. There is no denying the fact that the satisfaction children derive from achieving a self-imposed goal contributes to good discipline. Of course this implies that choice leads to a goal which both teacher and child see as worthy. In an assigned task which has little or no meaning for the child but where choice is possible, the opportunity may result in superficial action in which the child boasts that he did something valueless and thereby "put it over on" the teacher. In assigned tasks where choices are available, there must be some acceptance of the worth-whileness of the activity or some identification with what the child feels is a real interest or need.

2. Where choice can be made under the conditions noted, the total activity leads to better pupil-teacher relationships and thereby minimizes the opportunity for bad disciplinary situations to arise. There is also the danger here of the teacher "putting something over on" the child. An extremely genial, personable, likable teacher can frequently "sell" the child on an activity and through acceptance of himself guide choices. Even though such pupil-teacher relationships are just as dominative as those involving fear and reprisal, at least they do not lead, from the conventional point of view, to disciplinary situations. Nevertheless where this technique is used it should be substituted as soon as possible by pupil planning and group organization of learning activities (21).

3. Children without experience in integrative relationships easily become disciplinary risks. Dissatisfaction, competition, and the resulting frustration provide a readiness for rebellious disturbing behavior which appears at the slightest possible opportunity (14).

C. DISADVANTAGES IN CONVENTIONAL DISCIPLINE

Problem of Discipline in Conventional Schools. What Anderson refers to as "dominative" teaching is in reality the kind of instructional organization in which conventionally problems of discipline easily arise (2). Such classrooms are in the great majority in schools throughout the world. How did such a condition arise? Why do nearly all beginning teachers point out that their main instructional problems center around the maintenance of good discipline?

In the first place, at the time when elementary schools first came into being the idea was prevalent that what was forced on the child, if difficult and demanding of sacrifice, was good for him. This thought came out of the concept of education associated with the disciplinary ideas of the Protestant Reformation. And this philosophy was clearly reflected in the early Puritan schools in this country. As America became industrialized, the position shifted somewhat to the belief that children should be taught to acquire skill, industry, neatness, respect, obedience, and efficiency — the accoutrements of the acknowledged gentleman. From that day to this, efficiency, neatness, and dispatch have been valued more highly than the prime objective — desirable individual change. Sometimes this kind of thinking backfires. Records of institutions at all educational levels contain hosts of names of individuals who were deemed unfit by virtue of the process but who nevertheless eventually acquired success and acclaim. However, the old standards still persist and form the basis on which behavior is judged.

Difficulty of Achieving Conventional Discipline. The child, of course, makes good discipline hard to achieve. Conventional teachers see children, especially the younger ones, as just the opposite of what they would like them to be. They are filled with impulses, mostly wrong, are self-centered, willful, and resistant to school objectives. Teaching, conventionally, has become a "conflict of wills." Year in and year out the ceaseless struggle takes place to convert children into something which adults would like them to be (7).

As a result of this kind of strife, year after year, the word "discipline" has come to denote a means of getting children to do whatever the course of study or the teacher prescribes. Even so-called "sugar-coating" has come in for its share of criticism. Education is effective and sound only if it succeeds in direct proportion to the amount of resistance offered. Gaining the child's approval and cooperation is unfair and soft pedagogy. No teacher is judged good who cannot *make* children study and learn under the most adverse conditions.

A whole system of accompanying rewards and punishments has come to be a teacher's stock in trade. These range all the way from John Locke's "Rules for the Rod" to the techniques of the Michigan superintendent who instructed his teachers in judo so that they could in all emergencies take care of disciplinary situations. As stated by Courtis (8) :

> It is not strange, therefore, that in many a classroom where the teacher stands in the place of parents, she like the Creator Himself, determines what consequences in terms of rewards and punishments shall follow each specific act of child behavior. Hitler, disciplining a conquered nation, is not more ruthless in spirit than some of the dictators who rule the nation's classrooms.

D. SOME CURRENT CONTRASTS

Rise of Progressive Philosophy. The new progressive philosophy presents a contrast which is just as bad for the child as the old rigid discipline. Paralleling the developing disciplinary viewpoint but gaining prestige only during the last few decades, there evolved a new concept of how children should behave. First to go was corporal punishment. Without this threat to the child, teachers developed ways and means to punish mildly or to give commendation. Gold stars, sarcasm, ridicule, and demerits were brought into being. After some experimentation teachers became dissatisfied with the the workings of these newer disciplinary devices. They then began to be interested in the child study movement. Motivation became the stock in trade, and teachers attempted to assign and instruct in a manner to catch the child's interest. The movement gained momentum, and eventually many schools and educators went to the extreme as reflected by complete freedom of the child. Nothing that could be identified with adult standards was acceptable, and the only satisfactory criterion in teacher-pupil relationships was complete release of children from all disciplinary procedures. Democracy could be practiced only where there was complete freedom. Such was the attitude of many in this school of thought.

This point of view is just as faulty as the heavy, dogmatic, autocratic, compelling discipline at the other extreme. The abandonment of all rules, teacher authority, grade levels, and marking is not the answer to how the child can best grow and develop. Nor is it the answer to how he can achieve freedom and democratic living (28).

New Attitude toward Discipline. Child development research indicates that qualitative behavior is learned in accordance with the child's capacities. At birth his potentialities are unorganized, and it is education's opportunity to guide these into patterns for dynamic, creative, and social living. Thus the school has a dual purpose: (1) to provide the means of facilitating growth, and (2) to encourage practice in those aspects of behavior where sufficient maturity has been achieved to guarantee purposeful activity. This does not mean, however, that there should not be a fringe area in which children's behavior should be spontaneous and experimental. In this kind of setting improvement and growth rather than perfection are the goals to be sought.

THE GOAL OF SELF–DISCIPLINE

It cannot be too strongly emphasized that the achievement of self-discipline, based on growth and eventuating in a high level of self-control is an exceedingly complex and difficult task. Dynamic, self-directed, creative living can result only through fully developing in each individual the capacity for self-direction and self-evaluation of his conduct. If discipline is the process through which this is to be achieved, it demands not blind, submissive obedience to authority but practice in self-direction and self-control of individual and group activities without the need for threat, fear, or irrational authority. This ideal can be justified by pointing out that only in a free society can such a standard be achieved and maximum potentials realized.

This thought is not entirely new. An equally high ideal of individuality, of its responsibilities, and how to achieve it occupied the minds of free men at the beginning of western civilization. From that time to this it has come down through the ages as an ideal for all human behavior.

Transitional Beliefs. The complexity of current life again threatens its acceptance. Many today regard the young child as innately depraved and wicked, susceptible to evil and bad influences, and thereby needing to be diverted or directed by fear, punishment, or precept.

This return to a reactionary view does not imply that parents love their children any less than those with any other viewpoint. It simply implies that in addition to love there is authority, obedience, and, when necessary, punishment. In this confusion of thought, parent and child relationships alternate between affectionate play and love in large doses and equal portions of threat, painful discipline, and continuous authoritative command. Others maintain about the same ratio but go to lesser extremes in both directions (10).

Thus there is much talk about discipline. Teachers and parents in reality face a situation that is disturbing because of current social problems. In a former era many individuals became emotionally insecure and frustrated although outwardly conforming and regular. Those who showed their reactions to authority by extreme deviations in behavior were regarded as wayward or sinful and were allowed to suffer consequences accordingly. Incidentally many survived this kind of treatment. Although the old method may have motivated greater contrasts of success and failure in human endeavor than in any other period of civilization, nearly everyone followed uniform practices and the problem was little discussed.

Dominative Discipline Challenged. Advances in social research, experimentation, and studies of cause and result have about abolished all evidence of the value of dominative discipline. The increase of problem children, delinquency, sex offenders, maladjusted adults, and the increasing frequency of poor marital relationships far outstripping the increase in the number of schools using more modern methods have engendered skepticism as to the effectiveness of the traditionally autocratic child-adult relationships. Experimentalists report remarkable results in dealing with many problem cases where authority becomes a resource for guidance or is self-imposed by the individual concerned (13).

Progressive Schools Not Responsible for Current Delinquency.
Many naïve reporters and uninformed speakers, writers, and lay persons blame the increasing incidence of maladjustment on schools and frequently on "progressive" schools. The correlation between the universality of the incidence and the number and influence of progressive schools is so slight as to render such a statement ridiculous. Actually, if delinquency is a product of schools, it is probably much more closely associated with schools where discipline has its roots in the former ways of "directing and guiding" child behavior (21). Among the more enlightened parents and teachers there is developing a realization that purely autocratic practices are failing in their goal of orienting children to their social inheritance, and a suspicion is growing that perhaps such dominative procedures are more than coincidentally related to delinquent behavior (18).

Experimental Results. The experimental centers for child study are producing an increasing volume of evidence on the subject. In general they agree that the demands on children to conform to adult standards are rendering greater damage to the child by inhibiting many phases of desired behavior than has hitherto been believed possible.

The New Problem. There is no question regarding the need to learn patterns of behavior, of speech, and of beliefs and ideals of a given culture. This is especially true within a society that places human rights, responsibilities, and freedom above all other goals. Children must be helped to understand and appreciate what is good in a culture. They must accomplish these goals in a way that is not only satisfying but that will lead to fulfillment of their goals as men and women of tomorrow.

This manner of aiding adjustment requires delicate rearing and handling. The objective and the means are equally important. The achievement of this goal can best result through the ideal of self-controlled action, where each individual behaves in accordance with what is best for the social order. In a democratic society individual satisfaction and achievement are just as important as the group goal. Each member of the group must go as far as possible in accepting his own personal worth and sense of dignity and in having respect for the worth of others (10).

Self-discipline Only Acceptable Kind. To achieve this goal the only valuable kind of discipline is self-discipline — a viewpoint which becomes even more valid in the face of crumbling traditions. There is no question that the former methods have proved ineffective and that the newer ideal has not yet been put into general practice. Until experimentation validates our present beliefs, teachers and parents must proceed cautiously, since not enough is known to provide clear and distinct guideposts.

First Steps. On the other hand there is little doubt as to what the first steps should be. It is reasonable to assume belief in human nature. Working on this assumption, one can give the child love and affection as well as a sense of belongingness and worth. The complexity of current social organization presents greater difficulties than have heretofore been faced in achieving satisfying adjustments. But if the child is consistently encouraged to have confidence in himself he can achieve the kind of self-discipline inherent in this kind of goal.

THE ROLE OF MATURITY IN THE ACHIEVEMENT OF FREEDOM AND SELF–DISCIPLINE

A. THE NEED OF THE TIMES

Transmission Not Enough. One of the greatest obstacles in the way of achieving better ways of handling children is that offered by parents and teachers who fail to see that the school should have some connection with what is going on in the world. The problems our children are to face are much more complex than those which so distress us today. In a recent editorial a group of parents, protesting the work of the schools, resolved that the schools should exist for the primary purpose of training children in the essentials of knowledge — reading, writing, arithmetic, spelling, and so on.

However worthy such an objective may be some way must be found to convince parents that mere transmission of knowledge is an inadequate preparation for the future. If schools and education are to have a part in training individuals to bring about an improved social order, other skills than the three R's must also be taken seriously as educational objectives. Adequate training for this role will require the development of originality, initiative, and creativeness as well as the ability to apply facts, to solve problems, and — more important than any of these — to apply the techniques of effective group cooperation. Such a task, incidentally, will require the full exploration of individual differences rather than the old pattern of conformity and narrowing of individuality.

B. FREEDOM, NOT LICENSE

Some interest has been shown in this idea. In a good many instances, parents and teachers have gotten together and decided to try the newer methods in which the child is released from the former "preventive" form of adult control. New school programs have emerged, and in many homes there has been increased freedom and responsibility in family affairs. On the other hand, many more educators have gone "overboard." Carefully planned programs for giving a child greater freedom and developing in him a sense of responsibility in using it properly have been ignored or abandoned in favor of erratic eccentricity and complete freedom of movement and action. As a result, what was planned as freedom becomes mere license, and creativeness drops to the level of egocentric expression. The publicity given this kind of experimentation has resulted in counter reactionary measures and a questioning of the whole concept of self-discipline.

The answer to the difficulty may be found in an analysis by parents and teachers of the relation of domination to increasing maturity. Only thus can a satisfactory program for achieving freedom and independence be worked out.

C. THE PLACE OF DOMINATION

Domination Necessary. Educators who feel that any restriction of the child is bad for him have forgotten or else ignore the fact that domination properly handled plays an important role in the teaching of self-discipline. Although no one likes to be dominated or restrained, one must recognize the fact that at certain stages of the child's development, domination and rigid control are quite essential. The infant at birth must be fed, dressed, and cared for in many ways in which he has no choice. If domination were not exercised, the child would die.

Illustrations of Proper Domination. Two illustrations have been provided by Courtis (7):

> . . . the individual wishing to learn to fly purchases an airplane, but makes it part of the bargain that he be given proper and adequate instruction. At first, he obeys his instructor's orders implicitly because he recognizes his own immaturity with respect to flying control. Also he does not permit the instructor to dismiss himself before he is convinced of his own competency. Further, to prevent the social consequences of too hasty assumption of maturity by the learner, the government requires that proof of maturity of control be given before the individual is licensed to fly by himself. Domination of the immature by the able not only may be a benefit, but may also be desired by the immature.

> .   .   .   .

> . . . if a perfect stranger suddenly and forcibly prevents our stepping from the curb into the street, we tend to resent his domination, but if later we perceive that by his action he has saved us from being run over by an automobile we had not seen, our anger turns to gratitude. If we are injured because someone who saw what was about to happen failed to exercise such domination, we punish him for his negligence. The greater the emergency, the more one excuses and accepts even violent forms of compulsion.

Disadvantages of Domination. But there are disadvantages in autocratic, compelling action. Teachers often through their own deliberate action deprive the child of the opportunity for learning. No child learns arithmetic through the experiences of teacher or parent. Nor does a child learn by having all decisions made for him. Domination of this kind limits, and at worst, completely prevents learning.

In addition to its effects on learning is the effect on the child's emotional outlook. The amount of surrender normally demanded is tremendous when it is fully analyzed. Adults, for example, require the child to regulate his very physiological being to their demands — to eat food which they have ordered and to control the release of body waste where and when they prescribe. In the words of Frank, adults constantly say . . . " 'don't touch, don't take, don't hit, don't handle, don't, don't, don't,' whenever he approaches . . . inviting objects or persons" (10). In the civilization in which we live the child must learn the prescribed forms of conduct of his social class. He must learn its manners, its customs, and the proper way to address people. He must learn his approved sex role, how to speak correctly, and how to perform the rituals of his social grouping.

Regardless of all this, the desire for choice and freedom is synonymous with creative individuality and is considered a primary drive in the dynamics of life. Even animals resent restraint on their freedom and area of action. The reactions of the human being are even more rebellious.

D. FROM DOMINATION TO FREEDOM

By growth and development the individual is enabled to escape from the completely dominating authority of parents at infancy to potentially complete freedom of choice and action at maturity. In the words of Courtis, then, ". . . growth and domination are thus, apparently, two opposing principles. Each tends to eliminate the other" (7).

Misconception of Maturity. They are opposed only when a working relationship between the two is not provided. It is because of misunderstanding of this relationship that either of the two extremes seems to become necessary. A part of this difficulty is that the meaning of maturity is not clear. We tend to believe that maturity is something achieved all at once. In the lay mind the individual is considered either mature or immature in reference to a phase of behavior. He is scarcely ever regarded as "maturing." Our laws recognize maturity as status achieved — the age required for voting, for example. Maturity in citizenship is not seen as something achieved or becoming but rather as status attained at some specific time.

New Definition of Domination. The apparent stalemate between growth and domination may be resolved by redefining domination. In this context domination may be seen as a child-adult relationship whose function is to facilitate growth. The kind of domination which leads to freedom or growth is desirable and good; that which frustrates growth or a developing freedom is bad. By this standard domination becomes the converse of freedom, and freedom is good if it contributes to growth and bad if it retards growth.

Contrasting Views toward the Idea. This is a fairly new thought (7). Too few parents are guided by the idea when they make decisions for children. Actually, perhaps because of present-day complexities and problems, most parents deliberately or unconsciously dominate children in order to keep them from growing up. Many teachers do the same deliberately, since more mature persons would not subject themselves to the techniques of authority prevalent in many classrooms. And many teachers would become confused in this situation, since domination so conceived has for its goal the elimination of the need for teaching.

This new idea, however, gives greater opportunity to the creative teacher. Domination so conceived is much more readily and happily accepted. Any child or adult will approve domination which leads to achievement, choice, decision, and satisfactory social relationships.

Why the Idea Has Failed. If the idea is so simple why hasn't it been applied more generally by parents and teachers, and why has it failed when tried? This question is reasonable. The answer may be found in the failure of teachers to see that the child's development and maturation is many-sided and that children, before assuming control in a given area of expression, must show sufficient maturity in related areas. A child may be physiologically and mentally mature but lack emotional and moral maturity. A parent frequently grants the use of a car to a child who is old enough physiologically and mentally but who is immature in his ability to assume responsibility for the welfare of others. And teachers have wrongly freed children for creative expression, where the opportunity for social and emotional relationships is beyond their experience and generalizations.

Criteria for Domination. 1. This error can be corrected by a broader conception of guidance. The teacher who assumes responsibility for facilitating the child's maturation is moving in the right direction. The person who does this need be motivated only by the idea of helping the child instead of exploiting him or using him as a pawn to perpetuate his own ideas either forcibly or with "sugar-coating." To do this, however, is difficult. Teachers are often tempted to dominate so as to solve their own problems. Some teachers gain great satisfaction from seeing achievement in terms of their own purposes and criteria. A neat, well-planned lesson, put over with dispatch according to prearranged plans, is a powerful motivation to continue with this procedure. Pupils frequently are impressed and demand more of this kind of teaching because they are confused and upset by first teacher efforts in meeting "children's needs." A parent finds it much easier to send his young son to bed than to spend the time answering the boy's questions or playing with him. Incongruously, such a habit pattern, which disposes of children neatly, makes the child want to grow up and do the same with *his* children. It is hard not to dominate somebody when to do so gives one an opportunity to show superiority or to further one's own ends.

2. Domination which aims at promoting maturity must be based as far as possible on a reasoned conclusion about the probable relationship of particular procedures to the end in view. Parents and teachers are frequently called upon to make decisions for children. Their first inclination is to decide in terms of their own convenience in respect to the problem or to decide on the basis of how the action may look to others. When a young man unexpectedly asks for the family car, the father is likely to refuse because he himself intends to use it. He should examine his own motives in reference to those of the child. If the boy greatly needs prestige, the parent should readjust his own plans. Objective weighing of the situation, examination of the motives of both the dominator and the "dominee" should be taken into consideration.

3. Domination requires understanding on the part of the child. Too many parents and teachers answer, "Because I said so," or the like, when children ask why a request can't be granted. Often this is implied if not said. A sensible rule fully understood is much

more effective in promoting maturation of social behavior than a complete lack of rules, with behavior governed entirely on the basis of children's whims, frequently referred to as "needs."

Or, as stated by Courtis (7):

> One individual by force can compel another to take a certain action, or move him by affection, or bamboozle him by trickery and craft, but this is not true cooperation; this does not minister directly to maturation.

4. Domination should be reduced as soon as possible. The amount of domination necessary at any given time should be inversely proportional to the proven relationship between experience and maturity. As experience develops an understanding of the problems involved and develops abilities to make decisions in terms of those experiences, more and more freedom should be given the child. Rules and restrictions should be kept in force only until the child so dominated demonstrates ability to make mature decisions. As freedom of action is judged successful both by the child and the teacher, the area for action may be extended.

E. RELATION OF DOMINATION TO MATURITY

Domination Necessary for Maturation. Progressives and liberals in education under other names may regard domination as something very evil and not to be used except in extraordinary circumstances. The point to be made here is that not only is it necessary to enable individuals to attain well-rounded maturity, but it is the duty and privilege of teachers. From this point of view, it is the real problem of teaching, and it is unfortunate that more attention has not been given to understanding its relation to achievement, its rationale, and its techniques.

Child's Need of Domination. The primary function of domination, or discipline, is to make more effective the process of learning, in which the learner is subject to the effects of all kinds of factors which are not understood and are at best only partially controlled. Individuals can learn discipline and control the hard way. Man's behavior is frequently the result of impulse, bias, and selfishness. There is no reason why schools should be so conducted, nor is there a good reason for conducting them in a way which protects the child while holding him fast to the decisions of the "competent." He must learn self-control which leads to cooperative, reasoned, group control.

Domination Needed by Society. Biologically the child is born self-centered: his only guide for action is the satisfaction of his basic desires. As he grows older he wants a greater expansion and satisfaction of personal goals as well as freedom and self-expression. Society has established guides and institutions for limiting complete freedom of behavior at the adult level. It has also used the school as a means of teaching the child to adjust his personal drives and needs to those of others and of fostering the union of individuals in evolving group goals and techniques for achieving them.

Appreciation Also Necessary. Rewards and punishments have been devised as a means of achieving mature social behavior. While we suppress, in relation to maturity on the one hand, we must create appreciations and understandings on the other. A small child refrains from stealing for fear of punishment long before he refrains because of his appreciation of the issues involved. Delinquent sex behavior may be prevented by social mores before it becomes restrained through understanding of its moral and emotional implications. In this connection it may be said that the greater the need for domination, the greater the excuse for rewards and punishments. It is only the continuance of these beyond the point of need or to an extent which unreasonably limits experience that is bad. The high school level of experience reflects much greater maturity of behavior if these principles have been operative throughout the elementary school period.

Criticisms of Progressive Educators. Many liberals in educational thinking will protest this attitude toward discipline. To them, restraint is regarded as frustrating and evil at any level of maturity. There is a certain amount of truth in the criticism, since domination undeniably limits experience. Nevertheless experience in itself is not educational; the generalization which always follows effective experimenting is limited if a child lacks guidance, and it is especially limited when experience is guided only by the egoistic whims of the immature. Egoistic behavior is always the antithesis of social behavior and more often than not is a sign of immaturity. Intelligent domination is the only means by which the shift can be made from egoistic to social action. Domination, then, becomes necessary if the child is to achieve freedom.

F. DOMINATION NOT NECESSARILY AUTOCRATIC

Modern Domination Different from the Old. The liberals will also question how such discipline differs from the old-fashioned primitive attitudes. Even the most punitive of teachers, except those who seek sadistic satisfaction or express their own inferiorities through disciplining children, believe that what they do to prevent "bad" behavior is for the good of the child. They *know* what he needs and they *see* that he gets it. The main difference is in the criteria previously discussed. The old-fashioned method may be identical at times with the methods of the viewpoint expressed here. They are similar in that both justify themselves on the basis of the child's "welfare." The main difference is that the old viewpoint approved a continuance of dominance at all age levels, regarded maturity as something achieved all at once, and was never postulated on the premise that its purpose was to make itself unnecessary.

Other Differences. Certain other characteristics of its administration reflect fundamental differences. 1. The handling of disciplinary problems must be impersonal. Teachers who feel that undesirable behavior is an attack on them will have difficulty in practicing this newer method. Undesirable behavior at times does represent a personal attack on the teacher. When it does, a counterattack may be essential in emergencies but under no other circumstances is it justified. The teacher who becomes emotional, who feels that teacher-pupil relationships are constantly the cause of difficulty, should examine the total situation. If she does not like children, cannot be accepted by them with respect and affection, she should abandon teaching as soon as possible.

2. Incentives, rewards, punishments should be assigned as natural consequences rather than as devices of the teacher to get children to do what she wants them to do. And the child should respond because he sees the real benefits of an act instead of because he will be punished if he does not do as told. It is only at the most immature levels of child growth that fear of punishment is justified. Thus children generally must understand the reasons

for the limitations placed on them as well as the consequences of not obeying, both for themselves and for the group.

Use of Appraisal. 3. Effective appraisal is necessary if disciplinary measures are to achieve the goal outlined — not the kind of appraisal which satisfies the teacher that the situation is well in hand but that which seeks to determine whether the child is growing toward self-direction. This sort of appraisal must be made at all times, particularly in situations where discipline *seems* to be good and where there is no outright aggressive rebellion. Where this is the case, the best test is to provide broader areas of freedom for choice or to extend the opportunities for choice within the area. Where individual or group rebellion results, it is obvious that something is wrong. Quick appraisal is then necessary in order to make the best of an emergency solution to the problem.

General Appraisal Approaches. In judging effects, a teacher should first question her own motives. Are the children being exploited or repressed because she is tired or nervous, or because she is expected to repress? Where individual aggressiveness and rebellion take place, is the child merely being irrational? Is his rebellion temporary, or is it the result of a building-up of some kind of frustration? Have purpose, reasonableness, and acceptance been thoroughly established?

EARMARKS OF GOOD DISCIPLINE

In all kinds of good disciplinary situations there are certain common characteristics. In the main, these characteristics are implied in the previous discussion of the relation of dominance to maturity, but it seems advisable to restate certain thoughts in another kind of framework.

There are certain limitations to the applicability of these ideas. They do not apply to the situation in which potential teacher-pupil compatibility, so necessary for solving disagreeable disciplinary situations, has completely disappeared. Everything recommended is for the teacher who has a fair chance of developing a desirable disciplinary relationship with the pupils.

Group Morale Basic. One of the most outstanding characteristics of a good disciplinary situation is the presence of good group

morale. This is usually evidenced by a happy working relationship between teacher and pupils. Children know and accept the
goals toward which they are working, and they also know when a
particular child does something undesirable. Discipline is not only
the will of the teacher, it is their will as well. At best it is their
will which governs the attitude and actions of the teacher. If high
group morale is established, the disciplinary problems which do
arise cluster around a few individuals who are motivated by some
influence outside the classroom to protest and rebel.

Group morale can be established and maintained only if there
are activities for bringing the group together in a sort of spiritual
unity. A previous chapter pointed out how individual children
reflect the attitudes of their classmates. Group morale demands
group achievements, group pride, and a feeling of unity, at best
enhanced through experience which offers the opportunity for
sharing, which does not penalize certain children because of differences, and which demands, for a successful outcome, whole-
hearted cooperation.

Individuality Must Be Recognized and Respected. Good discipline
is frequently characterized by some naïve teachers as giving all
children a "square deal." This implies a lack of favoritism and
gives the teacher an opportunity to boast that she "treats all children alike." As a matter of fact the only kind of situation in which
such discipline can flourish is in an iron-clad, harsh treatment of
children. Children differ greatly. They respond to discipline differently. Whereas one child needs scarcely more than a suggestion,
another child may need a spanking. Another child would be severely shocked and develop deep-rooted fears as a result of punishment of this kind.

The problem, of course, is to justify differentiated handling of
the same children. Actually this is not too difficult. Children view
a disciplinary situation in terms of the behavior which follows. A
child may boast to others about being let off rather easily, but if
his behavior deviates from the approved pattern the other children
scoff at his boast. It isn't likely that he will do much boasting to
children who disapprove of his behavior. Such an attitude is likely
to lead to recriminative measures from the children themselves
(21). If the group approves of what the child has done the situa-

tion indicates a lack of morale. This demands an entirely different handling. In other words, where rebellion is approved by the group it is foolish to punish the individual offender.

In dealing with children individually, the teacher must be concerned with the particular teacher-pupil relationship involved, with the child's sensitivity to punishment, and with the amount needed for corrective purposes. If the teacher is highly regarded, liked, greatly admired, or loved, she must carefully consider this relationship in planning punishment. The same caution holds true if there is particular dislike, mutual disrespect, or incompatibility between teacher and pupil (5).

Corporal Punishment Usually Unnecessary. It seems rather superfluous to be discussing this point. Much has been made of the problem of corporal punishment. There are children who can be punished effectively, and there are children who will be greatly disturbed not only by being punished but by seeing another child punished. Where love or mutual respect exists between teacher and pupil, or parent and child, corporal punishment may be used without particular fear. This is also true in situations where the child realizes that the situation calls for punishment. Corporal punishment is particularly undignified in school and sometimes shocking to other children. And the bond between teachers and pupils is ordinarily insufficient to risk this kind of treatment. Pushing, shoving, and slapping are even more crude. The situation seldom demands this treatment. Corporal punishment is likely to represent an emotional affect on the part of the teacher which is undignified as well as disturbing. No teacher, except the sadist, feels very proud or noble after this kind of an episode.

School Work a Poor Disciplinary Device. One of the most common bad practices is that of assigning "extra" school work as a disciplinary measure. School work has reached a pitifully low estate when it can be regarded as a fitting punishment (19). The instructional program plays a very important part in determining group morale, probably the most important after that of teacher-pupil compatibility. To give extra assignments is to block the development of basic desirable instructional opportunities.

This is a good place to discuss the problem of homework which indirectly can assume a disciplinary coloring. Unless homework can be regarded as a natural responsibility, the outgrowth of a need, it cannot be undertaken with optimism. If the child is made to feel that he must do this because he is failing, he is likely to react quite negatively to the task. Fear of failure will do little toward motivating effective extra study. Homework usually should be assigned after the pupil has discovered his cause of difficulty and gladly sees the extra work and effort as an opportunity to succeed where he has failed before.

Treat Child according to Background. In order to know how punishment should be varied to suit the varying needs of individual children, there must be records on the child. It is possible, of course, that an alert teacher can be aware of the different sensitivities and temperaments of children and can vary punishment accordingly, even if records have not been kept or are not available.

Nothing aids a teacher more in making decisions than some kind of record which attempts to evaluate the child's developing personality as well as the effectiveness of past treatments. Such data also protect the teacher from relying too heavily on hunches, especially those that may be unconsciously distorted by her liking for, or dislike of, a particular child. Records also help the teacher interpret the relationships involved when disciplinary action is needed by individuals who strongly influence group morale. Records will provide a more accurate analysis of the effects of previous punishment and the kind of action to be taken. Teachers need to be guided in their disciplinary techniques by the sociometric relations of the individual and the group. This does not imply that the teacher should discipline only the insecure and the unattached child while allowing those with prestige to go unnoticed. It implies that sociometric relationships are very important and should be given full consideration in determining a plan of action for realizing maximum disciplinary benefits.

Admit Lack of Knowledge. Too many teachers give lip service to this thought, but at heart they are insincere. When the average teacher in dealing with little Johnny says, "Now, Johnny, you are a bad boy, what shall I do with you?" she is not really admitting that she does not know what to do but is frequently indulging in a sadistic device to humiliate and confuse Johnny. Or she may be distraught and say, "Oh, Johnny, I don't know what to do with you." This is not an invitation for Johnny to make suggestions. It immediately gives him the cue that he needn't worry much and that the punishment will not be severe. The teacher should not use either of these techniques as an introduction to a friendly little conversation eventually leading to no punishment, to postponement, and consequently, to an opportunity for the same situation to occur all over again. This does not mean that a heart-to-heart talk, utilizing available knowledge of the child, and handled objectively on a cooperative basis, should not frequently lead to the conclusion that nothing further need be done.

The point is that teachers often need to explain to the child that they do not have the answer. Under many circumstances it will prove effective to tell this to the child and to tell him also that the situation will be considered and acted on later. All of this must be sincere and should not reflect a general unwillingness to face the situation but a rationalized decision on the best disposal of the case.

Use Positive Methods. The person who continuously nags children is not a good disciplinarian under any set of instructional conditions. Children get accustomed to the idea and soon discover that the constant voice of the teacher is part of the general confusion. Thus, frequently, the teacher herself contributes to poor discipline. If restrictions are necessary, they must be generally recognized and accepted. Only infrequently should restrictive commands be issued and then in a manner that is friendly and helpful rather than hysterical, discourteous, or humiliating. The teacher who maintains discipline by constant restrictive remarks discovers that the group soon gets out of hand. At this point all disciplinary possibilities are completely exhausted.

Do Not Sidestep the Problem. Only the teacher who finds herself at her wit's end sends children to the principal. The teacher who does this is usually incompetent, finds her own security threatened, or is thereby demonstrating emotional insecurity, which may suggest that her need for help is greater than that of the child.

Teachers who complain that the principal does not "back them up" may often be found in one of the above categories. Those who claim the opposite are probably identifying themselves with a sit-

uation in which the teacher gets satisfaction out of the more punitive and sadistic action of the principal, or, in finding such a resource in the principal, wash their hands entirely of disciplinary
problems and thereby knowingly or unknowingly proclaim their
incompetence. They are also denying themselves the opportunity
for providing creative guidance and thus denying themselves one
of the great satisfactions in teaching.

Ask for Help When Needed. This does not mean, however, that
when a problem emerges in which the teacher feels incompetent
she should not ask for the principal's assistance or that of others
who are far enough removed to be objective rather than emotional
in offering a solution.

The wise disciplinarian frequently needs help. The teacher
needs information about the child. This can be obtained from
parents, from other teachers, from tests, and from such specialists
as may be available. In this sense, aid and guidance are desirable.

CAUSES OF POOR DISCIPLINE

The discussion to be developed here is closely related to the
problem of discipline as a means for developing freedom and self-
direction and is regarded as a device for making teacher-imposed
domination unnecessary as soon as possible. Very few teachers have
the opportunity to work under conditions which favor the application of high-level procedures. As a matter of fact, there are far
too few teachers who themselves — mature, trained individuals —
have the chance to be self-directive in their own lives and in their
general instructional procedures. Good discipline is also indicated
where pupil-teacher relationships are just beginning to shift from
complete teacher-controlled behavior toward more cooperative
measures.

The suggestions and points made, however, will have little
bearing on those instructional situations where complete adult
control continues relentlessly without overt rebellion or reaction
unfavorable to the teachers concerned. As Redl and Sheviakov
state, what is frequently referred to as a "discipline case" is an illustration of a situation where real discipline has completely disappeared (20).

A. INSTRUCTIONAL ORGANIZATION

Uninspiring Curriculum. One of the most important contributing causes of disciplinary problems is faulty instructional organization. Both the progressives and conventionalists will agree with this, since both are inclined to view the "learning" organization as the primary basis for unsatisfactory pupil behavior and reaction. The progressives will feel that there should be no problem if the curriculum is properly organized and administered. They believe that there are no potentialities within the child which make for trying situations, and are inclined to direct their efforts toward better discipline on the instructional level. Conventionalists, although not in agreement with this point of view, also find that most of their problems arise in connection with learning requirements. This is true, since about all of the school day is taken up with getting children to learn what they are taught. The conventionalists hardly ever question the curriculum. The fault lies with the child. "How can I get him interested in division, in drill, in getting his assignments in on time?" is a common question. Other causes are an excessive number of children to be handled, faulty room facilities, or lack of equipment and materials.

Difficulty of Material. The subject matter offering may be either too difficult or too easy. If it is too easy it fails to challenge the child, and he finds time to follow unapproved pursuits. If it is too difficult, he becomes worried, frustrated, and must find some other way to strive for prestige and status. This, as pointed out previously, may lead to a wide range of undesired behavior (19).

Inadequate Teaching. Teachers may have little interest in, or understanding of, what they are teaching. They may be unable to express themselves adequately or to develop and utilize instructional aids and resources for effective teaching. All of these contribute to disciplinary inadequacies. The children get bored, fail to understand, fail to know and understand objectives.

Lack of Stimulating Activity. A situation, somewhat similar to the two preceding, is one in which instruction day after day is mere verbalism. Children need variety. Nothing makes even interesting subject matter so boring as constant reading, talking, and writing. Dramatization, trips, and the utilization of some creative activity will do much to raise the potential level of disciplinary climates.

Influence of Fatigue. Teacher and pupil fatigue, related to the instructional offering, gives rise to many kinds of disciplinary problems. The school day which offers no break from the continuous all-day contact between children and teacher does as much as anything else to break morale, create aggressive teacher-pupil incompatibility and render both teacher and pupils ready for emotional reactions to each other. Some of the suggestions already made will prove helpful. Teachers must try to obtain some opportunity for relaxation during the school day and must seek time to make and study children's records. As in any other profession, there must be time for diagnosis. Remedy and treatment must be planned and studied in order to be effective.

B. FAULTY RELATIONSHIPS WITHIN THE GROUP

The relationships to be explored between children in a given grade are great in number. There is a pattern to be expected at each grade level, but there are such differences in the same grade groups that variety may always be anticipated. Teachers who feel that instruction is the cause of *all* disciplinary problems are wrong. Children's classroom behavior is affected by home relationships and by their relationships with children outside of school. And conversely their behavior outside of school is influenced by relationships developed within the classroom (11). In school and out they form attachments to some individuals and they reject others. In school and out they form cliques and subgroups within a clique. Most interesting of all, they experiment with each other. They experiment with love, with hate, with cooperation, and with domination. The most conventional teacher would be amazed by the web of intrigue, devotion, and criss-crosses in their life patterns (18). Obviously these relationships have a bearing on every kind of disciplinary situation.

Pupil to Pupil Relations. One of the relationships which may give rise to unexpected reaction to instructional or teacher authority is an intense child-to-child response, either of friendship or of animosity. In the one case the second child in a pupil pair may react in defense of the other child if the latter's status is threatened or involved. In the conflicting pair relationship, one child may rebel if he suspects the teacher of showing favoritism or improving the status and prestige of the other child. Many other strong pair relationships may be involved as well as those of a lesser nature. This indicates that much more than a teacher-pupil reaction climate is basic in what is conventionally regarded as an instructional situation. Incidentally the stereotyped recitation of assignments offers much less than the broadened out curriculum for reducing the intensity of pupil-to-pupil emotional behavior reaction. At best it can control such relationships but because of its rigidity it can do nothing toward resolving tensions through the opportunity to plan, execute, and appraise together.

Group and Subgroup Relations. One need only realize the potential affectiveness of personal relations between several children to estimate what might be the effect where greater numbers are involved. The teacher, although she may fear the possible outcome of allowing group freedom, can never promote the complete maturation of children without permitting considerable group freedom for action. Group and subgroup stratifications are the basis for cooperative community life at the child and the adult level. As in adult life one group or subgroup may oppose another. In the school there is an opportunity to do something about it, a phenomenon in community life which can happen only through outstanding leadership, understanding, and untiring effort. Such a result at the adult level is an exception that frequently requires years of effort along with considerable membership shifting.

Fights, social snobbery, and other degrees of rejection may be manifested in strong subgroup relations. Specific issues that cause difficulty may be favoritism, developmental age factors, the incompatibility of school and peer codes of behavior, differences in nationalities, and social differences. The teacher can do either of two things. Group rebellion may be repressed and balance maintained by teacher weight thrown in the right direction, or the conflicting issues may be recognized, groups merged, and differences ironed out through combined teacher and pupil effort.

Teacher-Pupil Relations. The teacher who recognizes personality incompatibility between herself and a given child and wants to do something about it is likely to know how to handle the problem. The danger on the part of an intelligent teacher in dealing with such a child is that of "bending over backwards" in relations with him and allowing such a child to go undisciplined. For the teacher who does not realize that she and Johnny do not like each other, there is the danger that her discipline will suppress him at the slightest opportunity. All teachers have considerable difficulty in realizing the differences in their attitudes toward individual children and how such attitudes affect their reactions to them.

Another situation which has not been fully explored is that in which the child presents aggression, nonconformity, or general apathy because through the teacher he is attacking his parental relationships. Schools and teachers almost invariably reflect parental ideals and attitudes toward child behavior. Where this is the case a child who is confused, inhibited, severely dominated by parents without reason is sure to cause trouble. There are two contrasting types of children with this background. One is the child who may show leadership ability. He may be competent, attractive, and interesting. The teacher may desire his friendship but be totally unable to attract him. The only outside indication of his problem is his rejection of all adults. He is in difficulty and his main reactions are inner and thereby serious. The other type is the child who faces the same kind of parental relationships but lacks ability and does not have the respect of his classmates. His reaction is outer rebellion and aggression. With the first type the teacher is patient and responds in a friendly manner. If possible she works with the parents toward improvement of their attitudes toward the child. With the second patience is required as well as effort toward helping the child gain status. Working with parents is also necessary for a complete solution.

C. TEACHER-GROUP RELATIONSHIPS

Repressive Effects. The discussion of teacher-pupil reactions leads naturally to a discussion of the effects of certain teacher-group relationships. This aspect of causal background has been hinted at under previous points, particularly in reference to the need for group morale. Further discussion hinges around certain patterns which are especially affective. The first of these is what is called the repressive climate. This word is preferred over such other descriptive words as "punitive," for example, since in this kind of classroom there is little actual punishment.

Of all the techniques followed by teachers, the repressive is the most destructive of creative activity and of group morale. Invariably it is characterized by the teacher's lack of respect for the children. The teacher feels so sure that she can manage the group through threat and fear that she ignores them as human beings (20). The children know that they must either accept the situation or rebel. Consequently two groups develop. One group fights back at every opportunity, and the other group bows to the teacher's wishes. Through fear, many in the latter group identify themselves with the teacher, since this is the only way they can gain status or approval. They remain submissive in the presence of the teacher, act as her spies, and develop a superior attitude toward the others.

This situation prevails in many classrooms. And frequently this kind of classroom gives overt "evidence" of teaching good citizenship, as seen by some, and very frequently provides ratings on citizenship. Obviously these are determined by the extent to which the child falls in line with the teacher's dictates (27).

There is little question that this situation not only does not develop a readiness for good citizenship but breeds superficiality and a disrespect for authority. In addition it provides the motivation for such deviational behavior as bullying and other kinds of egoistic, compensating action. The weaker the background stimuli for desirable behavior, the greater the influence of this atmosphere in promoting undesirable behavior. More normal children will protest and become frequent victims of the teacher's displeasure.

Emotional Exhortation. There are teachers who can obtain "good discipline" without force, and at the same time, surprisingly, without democratic group and individual action. This type of discipline is the kind achieved by what often appears to be a very good teacher. Such a person shows an outer personality which is interesting and attractive to others, particularly to children. This teacher is the type who may have indulged too long herself in baby talk or have suffered from either a father or mother complex and consequently never quite achieved emotional maturity.

She prevents, rather than solves, discipline problems. This teacher "puts herself out" with children; the better they behave, the more she does for them. She lets the children know that she likes them, and does many things to prove it. Where she fools them and where she has her appeal is in the fact that emotionally she is not much more than their equal. Otherwise she is superior in intelligence, looks, and range of action. With these assets she is able to successfully utilize trickery.

Disciplinary cases in this kind of emotional affectation result in extended periods of "hurt" feelings on the part of the teacher. Because of her often demonstrated love for the children, the offending child feels guilty and is taken to task by the others. Unfortunately, unless principals and supervisors have more than a surface interpretation of what is going on between the children and the teacher, the situation is entirely misunderstood. Discipline seems good, no one else is bothered, and the relationships appear to be of a high order. Incidentally this kind of room gives an outer appearance of a democratic climate with almost no occurrence of physical or otherwise violent disrupting behavior.

The weakness of this kind of discipline lies in its restriction on maturation. The children are denied even the normal opportunity of rebelling. Their problems will become more serious when they reach the next grade. Being accustomed to overindulgence and to having someone solve all their problems, they are especially likely to have serious difficulties in the near future.

Competitive Effects. Another type of teacher-group relationship is one which in a mild form of competition exists in all conventional instructional activity. This is the case where considerable emphasis is placed on academic achievement. Overemphasis on this is responsible for many disciplinary problems. This is because many classrooms unconsciously tighten up if the teacher stresses three-R achievement and if scores in achievement tests are recognized as the main criterion of teaching efficiency.

It is not too difficult for children to accept a reasonable amount of pressure in their school work. If it is properly handled, they can gain satisfaction in competing with norms and in competing as members of a group. When too much of it is provided, habits of envy, hatred, and dishonesty will appear. Other results are a breakdown in group morale, an unwillingness to help each other, and complete rejection by the group of those borderline or failure individuals who are incapable of achievement approaching that of the other children.

Exaggerated School Spirit. Another type, which in a way is similar to what has been called "emotional exhortation," is the "school-spirit" climate, where an entire classroom is overmotivated in terms of class pride. This is similar to the others in that direct punishment of a child by the teacher is an exception and on the surface there is a high degree of group morale and good behavior. A clever teacher can carry this technique to great lengths, particularly at the upper elementary grade levels. Children are becoming more social-minded and when encouraged and baited will rise to this kind of challenge.

Its evil lies in its superficiality. In it children do not learn independent individuality nor do they learn cooperative group action. The teacher's role as a member of the group is characterized by successful promotion of her ideas. This situation tends to penalize borderline children; they become permanent rejectees and react accordingly with frequent fights and compensating behavior outside of school.

SOME THINGS TO DO

A. APPRAISE THE SITUATION

Look at Goals. If a teacher is having difficulty with a disciplinary situation, the first thing she must do is appraise accurately the objectives and purposes involved. Is the problem actually a disciplinary problem in which efforts are directed toward helping children develop independence, group cooperation, and creative learning? Or is the objective merely that of maintaining order and control? If it is the latter, the teacher should select one of the devices previously noted. She should be warned, however, of the consequences of her acts, also previously noted. If the objective is true discipline, a long-time program is involved, but it can be approached optimistically.

Look at Techniques. Secondly, the teacher needs to know which type of problem actually exists in her classroom. Is the basic problem one of facilities and instructional organization? Or is it primarily the result of faulty individual or group-teacher relationships? Whatever the answer, what general trend of working with children is the teacher tending to develop? Nothing will clarify thinking on objectives or enable a teacher to realize the problem to be solved quite so much as this procedure of objectively looking at the relationships involved. An honest appraisal of the difficulty represents the first step toward solving the problem (16).

B. DEVELOP A WORKING RELATIONSHIP BETWEEN INDIVIDUAL AND GROUP NEEDS

It is not easy to develop a working relationship between individual and group needs. Sending Johnny out of the room because he is disturbing the other children may be all right. If the punishment fits the "deed," everything works out satisfactorily. If the punishment merely raises his prestige with the other children, it is a waste of effort. If the teacher is merely avoiding the problem of punishing Johnny by sending him out, another problem arises. Is it then the right thing to do?

Principles for Judging. Certain principles may be applied in obtaining the answer to whether the individual or the group is of greater concern. (1) The child may be completely dominated and inhibited in emergency situations as a part of an overall plan in dealing with that child. In most circumstances the child will later recognize the emergency, particularly if he has had some friendly, helpful experiences with teacher guidance. (2) Some incidents of group behavior are more significant than others. The same is true of individual behavior. The two come into conflict only infrequently. Knowing which to regard as more important is more often than not revealed by knowledge of both the group and the individual. (3) Insofar as possible, the technique used on an individual should be harmless to group morale, and conversely the teacher must be sure that techniques used on the group do not act adversely on certain individual children. Where the teacher is really trying to develop group morale, the decision is easier, since programs for improving group morale almost invariably bring universal individual benefits.

C. MANIPULATION OR GUIDANCE?

The most important question of all is whether the teacher is to become a real expert in aiding children to mature effectively in all aspects of growth, or whether discipline is to be regarded merely as manipulation of children to achieve one's own personal ends.

Strong Arm or Strong Mind. When the teacher explores all of the available data on group structures and the possibilities revealed therein for love, hatred, rebellion, and the many diversified compensatory patterns, she may be completely confused by the complexity of the situation or she may be challenged by the wonderful opportunity for providing guidance. If the teacher has the strength and drive to dissociate herself occasionally from complete absorption with instructional detail, there can be a neverending challenge for learning something about the behavior of children within a group. For the teacher who remains tired, bored, completely enmeshed in instructional trivia, and constantly involved emotionally in the behavior pattern, there is only one possible answer: she must manipulate it.

Long-term Goals Should Dominate. If the teacher is ready to make the effort, the question of manipulation versus guidance can have another answer. Manipulation may fit a specific situation, but the long haul must be projected on the basis of providing guidance which will eventually lead to freedom and self-direction. With this philosophy the teacher may ignore the need for manipulatory handling, especially where the teaching of attitudes is deemed more important. Frequently under such circumstances surface behavior may not appear to change. In this choice, attention must be given to surface or chance behavior only when it really threatens the greater, long-term plan (17).

D. STUDY BEHAVIOR

The answer to all discipline problems may be found in a study of the behavior of children. Insensitive observation is of little help. Only a few teachers have sufficient insight to understand its hidden meanings. Not much can be said which will prove helpful.

The teacher herself is the only one who can find the answers to the problem. It is believed, however, that some of the following hints will prove beneficial. They are basic for both the beginner and the experienced teacher. Constant reference to these or similar suggestions enables one to be objective in appraisal (6).

Study Depth of Behavior. 1. Behavior should be studied for its depth of meaning. Is an act a chance reaction, a deviational expression within the normal range of the individual, or does it have depth and significance? The basic criterion of a disciplinary problem is not overt behavior. The real problem is deep underneath and may be far removed from its obvious expression. To what extent is the diagnosed problem related to the past behavior of the particular child? To what extent does it reflect other basic relationships established outside the school? How is it enhanced and aided by a particular school or instructional relationship?

Study Effects of Treatment. 2. The teacher should estimate the potential effects of her treatment of a problem on the individual and on the group. Which should receive greater consideration at a particular time, the individual or the group? If one or the other is significantly ignored how can the proper equilibrium be established? These questions must be answered before effective discipline can be promoted and can be answered only by the person involved.

SUMMARY

True discipline is education. Compulsion and domination, without a long-time goal leading to self-direction, are undemocratic, ineffective, and without satisfying rewards for teacher or pupil. On the other hand, this chapter proposes the view that the consequences of self-expression and other evidences of lack of discipline are even more dangerous and threatening to the development of children. In this respect it can even be said that the traditionalists are justified in the emphasis which they place on discipline. Order, restraint, and frustration are less undesirable than self-will and its accompanying conflict with group will. Many teachers are not competent to analyze or develop a program of discipline based on maturation and leading to freedom and self-direction. The best they can hope for is to develop a modified means for solving a problem temporarily.

Better Means Can Be Learned. There is no excuse, however, for the teacher who is sufficiently intelligent and competent to learn better procedures. For her there must be improvement both in the means and the end. Such teachers must be helped with the materials they need to study children, to understand their emerging developmental patterns, and to guide them in terms of their individual potentialities and abilities.

Teacher Growth in Self-direction Necessary. This is a difficult task. To reorient oneself, to discard familiar workable procedures, and to learn anew requires courage, optimism, and effort. Achieving true discipline is much more difficult than achieving discipline as a means of maintaining law and order. One of the factors which complicate the matter is the fact that it can be achieved only by a person who has himself acquired reasonable self-control, freedom, and a satisfying social adjustment.

As each child is unique and individual, so is each teacher. Effective discipline cannot be purchased, nor can it be handed on from one person to another. There are no ready-made patterns for guiding children. A teacher who is democratically minded and who herself has achieved emotional maturity and a considerable degree of self-direction can go far. Such a teacher, with a fund of information on children and a sensitivity to their problems, can develop ways and means that are best for her and for them. This is the way to achieve desirable teacher-pupil relationships, which, after all, are the most important factors in successfully disciplining children.

SELECTED REFERENCES

1. ANDERSON, H. H., "Dominative and Socially Integrative Behavior," from *Child Behavior and Development,* edited by Roger G. Barker, J. S. Kounin, and H. F. Wright. New York: McGraw-Hill, 1943.

2. ——, AND BREWER, J. E., "I. Studies of Teachers' Classroom Personalities, II. Effects of Teachers' Dominative and Integrative Contacts on Children's Classroom Behavior," *Applied Psychology Monographs,* No. 8, 1946.

3. BARUCH, DOROTHY, *New Ways in Discipline*. New York: McGraw-Hill, 1949.

4. BÜHLER, CHARLOTTE, SMITTER, FAITH, AND RICHARDSON, SYBIL, *Childhood Problems and the Teacher*. New York: Holt, 1952.

5. CLARK, ELMER J., "The Relationship between Personality Traits of Elementary School Teachers and Their Evaluation of Objectionable Pupil Behavior," *Journal of Educational Research*, 45:61–66, 1951.

6. GRIFFITHS, WM., *Behavior Difficulties of Children as Perceived and Judged by Parents, Teachers, and Children Themselves*. Minneapolis: University of Minnesota Press, 1952.

7. COURTIS, S. A., *Philosophy of Education*. Ann Arbor: Brumfield and Brumfield (mimeographed), 1943.

8. ——, "Discipline," *Child Growth in an Era of Conflict*, edited by C. V. Millard, 15th Yearbook, Department of Elementary School Principals. Lansing: Michigan Education Association, 1944.

9. HALL, WM. E., AND OTHERS, "Multi-Factor Effect in Change in Human Behavior," *Journal of Educational Research*, 45:49–54, 1951.

10. FRANK, L. K., "Discipline in Our Time," *Discipline: An Interpretation*. Washington: Association for Childhood Education, 1948.

11. LANE, HOWARD A., "Discipline in Today's Education," *Discipline: An Interpretation*. Washington: Association for Childhood Education, 1948.

12. HOOKER, DAVENPORT, *The Prenatal Origin of Behavior*. Lawrence, Kansas: University of Kansas Press, 1952.

13. LIPPITT, RONALD, AND WHITE, R. K., "The Social Climate of Children's Groups," from *Child Behavior and Development*, edited by Roger G. Barker, J. S. Kounin, and H. F. Wright. New York: McGraw-Hill, 1943.

14. HOPKINS, L. THOMAS, "How Children Develop Discipline," *Childhood Education*, 31:260–269, February, 1955.

15. HYMES, JAMES, *Discipline*. New York: Teachers College, Columbia University, 1949.

16. JONES, J. CHARLES, "Reactions of Prospective Teachers to Pupil Behavior Problems," *Educational Administration and Supervision*, 38:283–292, 1952.

17. KAPLAN, LOUIS, "The Annoyances of Elementary School Teachers," *Journal of Educational Research*, 45:649–665, 1952.

18. REDL, FRITZ, "Delinquency Prevention and the Role of Love," *Discipline: An Interpretation*. Washington: Association for Childhood Education, 1948.

19. SEARS, PAULINE S., "Levels of Aspiration in Academically Successful and Unsuccessful Children," *Journal of Abnormal and Social Psychology*, 35:498–536, 1940.

20. SHEVIAKOV, G. V., AND REDL, FRITZ, *Discipline for Today's Children and Youth*. Washington: Department of Supervision and Curriculum Development, National Education Association, 1944.

21. THORNDIKE, R. L., LOFTERS, J. J., AND GOLDMAN, BERNARD, "Observations of the Behavior of Children in Activity and Control Schools," *Journal of Experimental Education*, 10:138–145, 1941.

22. LANGDON, GRACE, AND STOUT, IRVING W., *The Discipline of Well-Adjusted Children*. New York: John Day, 1952.

23. LYLE, WILLIAM H., AND LEVITT, EUGENE E., "Punitiveness, Authoritarianism, and Parental Discipline of Grade School Children," *Journal of Abnormal and Social Psychology*, 51:42–46, 1955.

24. MARTIN, MILDRED H., "Some Reactions of Pre-School Children to Discipline," *Nervous Child*, 9:125–130, 1951.

25. SLOBETZ, FRANK, "Elementary Teachers' Reactions to School Situations," *Journal of Educational Research*, 44:81–90, 1950.

26. SNYGG, D., "Discipline," *Childhood Education*, Vol. 31:258–259, February, 1955.

27. WANDT, EDWIN, AND OSTREICHER, LEONARD M., "Validity of Samples of Classroom Behavior," *Psychological Monographs*, 68 (5), No. 376, 1954.

28. WOLF, KATHERINE M., *The Controversial Problem of Discipline*. New York: Child Study Association of America, 1953.

15

MENTAL HYGIENE FROM THE STANDPOINT OF GROWTH

THE PROBLEM

A. AN ANALYSIS OF EXISTING TEACHER REACTIONS

Parents and teachers formerly looked upon temper tantrums, truancy, incorrigibility, delinquency, and other forms of asocial and antisocial traits as outward manifestations of meanness, obstinacy, selfishness, or laziness. And in the main, these were thought to have a hereditary background. Today this point of view is somewhat changed, but schools have not moved very far in the direction of doing something about it. *Adjustment* and *integration* have become catch words of certain educators, but such words have generally been given implementation and meaning only in academic areas and for academic purposes.

Need for Better Practices. At present we know that we have to go much further. We realize that behavior, previously dismissed with a shrug or solved by counterattack, may not helpfully be so simply handled. We realize that behavior may be the expression of deep-rooted, undetermined fears, of growth confusion, or the random effort of a normal child to cope with his problems. Thus teachers are beginning to see that good mental hygiene implies something more than classification and grouping of children on the basis of their educational attainment (24).

Teachers and Clinicians Disagree. How badly the schools need this kind of reorientation was shown in a study by Wickman (45), who had teachers and mental hygienists rate typical behavior patterns in the order of their seriousness. Whereas teachers considered shyness, sensitiveness, lack of sociability, fearfulness, and dreaminess among the least serious of all problems, the clinicians ranked these, together with unhappiness, depression, resentfulness, cowardice, suggestibility, and an overly critical attitude as the most serious problems of childhood. Heterosexual activity, which topped the teachers' listing, was ranked midway, while masturbation appeared very nearly at the bottom. Teachers classified shyness as least important, but the clinicians considered it equivalent in seriousness to stealing. Items appearing at the end of the clinicians' ranking were such things as minor defiance of authority, impertinence, disobedience, impudence, the problems of smoking, profanity, and defacing of school property. These items were considered by teachers as most serious. Wickman found, in general, that teachers stress the importance of problems relating to sex, dishonesty, disobedience, disorderliness, and failure to learn, while the problems indicative of withdrawal are considered to be comparatively insignificant.

Cause of Teacher Difficulty. If teachers are wrong on these rankings they are not entirely to blame. They are often placed in charge of large classes, where their paramount responsibility is the preservation of law and order — a complicated and difficult procedure at best and one which often deprives them of the opportunity to know and understand children as real individuals. Many teachers lack the experience and training necessary to enable them to identify problems except as nuisances. Consequently they become fixed in their attitudes, inelastic, prejudiced, prone to moral judgments, and ready to solve problems by counterattack. Teachers often fail to see that much so-called "bad" behavior is perfectly normal and that the child's resistance to rigid authority is often essentially wholesome. The average teacher often fails to recognize that the child is a sensitive personality, passing through innumerable phases of development with natural disturbances in growth.

Purpose of the Chapter. Good mental hygiene practices depend considerably on experience and training. Much gain has been made since Wickman's study. Teachers certainly need to know more about behavior and how to treat it more effectively. Nevertheless they now possess sufficient knowledge to do the job better.

This chapter then does not need to assume responsibility for an exhaustive treatment of the problems involved in achieving better mental hygiene. Its purpose, rather, is to review pertinent findings, which will be new for some, and to approach the problem from the standpoint of growth. To indicate clearly the relationship of mental hygiene to behavior and to show its implications for diagnosis and treatment are the main objectives.

B. DEFINITION

Like *child development,* the term *mental hygiene* occurs frequently in the professional discourse of teachers. Dr. Ryan states that it refers to the encouragement of wholesome human relationships (35). A somewhat different definition has been presented by Washburne, who describes mental hygiene as an approach to the problems of personality and behavior that provide the background for action (44).

Both Ryan's and Washburne's definitions are rather general and somewhat lacking in suggestions for the kind of activity that produces good mental hygiene. Like many others, Washburne brings in its emotional aspects. This is entirely as it should be, but emotions, although certainly indicative of the mental hygiene status of an individual, are likely to be symptoms rather than causes of behavior.

Proposed Definition. A simpler definition, and one which seemingly doesn't ignore important factors or aspects of development, may be stated as follows:

> Mental hygiene is the condition which results when the factors for growth are favorable for reasonably achieving maximum potentials.

Physical, mental, and emotional growth and all other aspects of development are involved (16). They are not only involved as they contribute singly but as they become integrated into a unified whole, which characterizes individual behavior. Stated in still simpler terms, good mental hygiene occurs when all aspects of growth are given proper encouragement and facilitation for progressing toward maximum levels. Poor mental hygiene occurs when the influences for maximum growth are not present. Such a definition is practical only to a certain point. It assumes a normal inheritance and a normal environmental encouragement. Some children as we well know may reach their maximum potentials and yet not achieve a satisfactory mental hygiene status. Let us suppose that such a child may normally be unusually short. Shortness of stature may be his congenital heritage. Thus he achieves his growth potential in this phase of development but because other children are so much bigger he may feel inferior and finally insecure and rebellious. This child, then, demonstrates an unsatisfactory mental hygiene condition. Treatment involves for him not an "enriching" of the environment but help in solving the problem of adjusting to his limitations. In a sense the problem of limitations and of helping individuals to adjust to them is what is most often referred to as mental hygiene activity. It should be regarded, however, as a secondary, rather than a primary, responsibility of those working in this field. The assumption is twofold: (1) that for many individuals all the teacher and parent need do is provide the best facilities for all kinds of growth and development; (2) that those whose environmental stimuli are limited or hindering need a special type of guidance and help pointed directly toward the development of attitudes and adjustments to those attitudes.

The Teacher's Job. In spite of the fact that parents are scarcely ever critical of schools that fail to function in this area of well-being, it is a legitimate responsibility of the school. This requires training which enables all teachers to direct growth in such a way as to avoid aggravation of simple problems present throughout the developmental pattern of all children, to give each child with more complex problems the opportunity to resolve his conflicts, to adjust to the group, and to provide satisfying experiences and socially desirable relationships with other children.

Teacher training institutions are reluctant to provide the training necessary. Should they be encouraged to revise their training programs and give adequate preparation for facilitating maximum child growth and provide the kind of training that enables teachers to identify the beginnings and the causes of behavior? Is such activity a legitimate teacher function or should it be dealt with exclusively by specialists? Many undoubtedly believe that the school already has a job big enough to occupy its entire attention, namely, the teaching of reading, arithmetic, writing, and history. Certainly many parents believe that mental hygiene is merely a frill and should not directly occupy the attention of teachers.

Partial Recognition of the Problem. On the other hand, there is a constantly enlarging group which believes that each child has the right to develop personally, socially, and emotionally as well as academically. The public is awake to the need, but only partially so. Much attention is being given on a national level to the problems of old-age security, to the need for adults to learn hobbies. to the need for institutions for the mentally diseased, to group insurance, etc. Most of these, however, operate at the adult level. Some attention is also being given to youth centers as a cure for juvenile delinquency, but the barn door in many instances is being locked after the horse has been stolen. Nevertheless the interest in the problem is encouraging. Perhaps when this kind of attention flows down to the school-age level it may occur to the general public that time and energy might be given to cause as well as to correction. Juvenile delinquency today is generally looked upon as a type of behavior which is somewhat inherent rather than as a developmental product brought about according to factor effect. Perhaps parents and others engaged in popular and well publicized community welfare activities will eventually realize that the behavior problems that they attempt to cure by evening school programs are certainly aggravated, if not entirely caused in many instances by what happens in that same room during school hours.

Evidence of Further Need. There is much evidence that there should be more corrective work during school hours. The school is the only social institution that has the opportunity to do the job. And as opportunity for high school and college education becomes more and more universal, the point accumulates added meaning. No one questions the legitimacy of the school's involvement with the problem. It is the urgency of the matter that concerns us here. Mental hygiene must become as important to the schools as, for example, physical health. The two are closely identified and one cannot be treated apart from the other. Neither can full growth and learning in the three-R areas be fully achieved without attention to the mental hygiene of the child.

TYPES OF MALADJUSTIVE BEHAVIOR

If mental hygiene is to become a part of school practice and organization, one of the first needs for teachers is to understand and recognize types of behavior which give clues to the growth demands of the child. It is better to aid development in such a way that characteristic maladaptive behavior may be prevented and the need for remedial treatment greatly lessened. Nevertheless, it must be said that there will always exist the opportunity to help children and adults face their life-adjustment problems.

There are many generally recognized adjustive patterns. Some of these are rather simple and quite harmless accompaniments of solving life's problems; others are more serious and may generally be regarded as a type of mental set which provides hazards and difficulties. It is these latter which are constantly referred to as hindrances and frustrations to growth and learning. Our discussion in this section includes (1) a description of commonly agreed upon ways of reacting, and (2) a consideration of various proposed classifications of these behavior patterns.

A. BEHAVIOR MECHANISMS

1. Compartmentalization

A common form of behavior is what is called *compartmentalization*. This is one of the more unfamiliar terms and not necessarily indicative of serious maladjustment. The individual who shifts attitudes according to the situation or the difficulty involved illustrates this type of behavior. The child who is honest in one kind of situation but dishonest in another is also showing this type of behavior. A third example is the child who is cooperative and helpful in the classroom but mean, egoistic, and destructive on the playground.

In most cases of this kind the child acts as he does because he is insecure, fearful, or has not established confidence in himself. The seeming inconsistency should be expected under such circumstances and can be overcome only where security and confidence can be established.

2. Compensation

Compensation is one of the best known and understood of all mental hygiene terms. It probably demonstrates itself in more outlets of expression than any of the other types. And it is likely that it is exhibited in the behavior of all individuals. Thus it shows a range of expression from normal desirable behavior to the more serious outlets detrimental to both the individual and society. Most demonstrations of this kind are motivated by either one of the following conditions: (1) to hide what is only imagined by the individual to be a serious deficiency of one kind or another, or (2) to make adjustment for what is obviously an undesirable characteristic. The second generally is related to some form of congenital inheritance such as race or physical malformation. The two frequently overlap.

This kind of adjustive behavior may be conscious and deliberate, or it may be represented by an unconscious automatic response. The fact that the motivating trait or defect may be either real or unreal complicates diagnosis. To the individual concerned, of course, it is always real. Differentiation is possible only to the outside diagnostician.

Examples Numerous. Examples are numerous. One of the most common is the child who doesn't do well in school and compensates by assuming leadership in unapproved activities, by bullying if he is physically competent enough, or by bothersome and annoying activity with younger children. Or the child may compensate by excessive effort in certain approved modes of expression such as music, athletics, and social affairs. Another common demonstration is provided by the child who compensates by excessive "cooperation" with the teacher, or by scholastic achievement if he is incompetent in peer-approved activity.

May Be Normal or Abnormal. Compensation is both a normal and an abnormal behavior adjustment. To the degree that it provides satisfaction which does not require effort and ability beyond the individual's capacity and is attended by broad social approval, it is good and desirable. To the degree to which it leads to antisocial aggressiveness, exploits other individuals harmfully, and demands effort beyond the individual's potentials, it is bad and harmful.

3. Daydreaming

A Form of Compensation. Mild daydreaming and serious fantasy are extremes of the same kind of escape from reality. They are harmful in that they rarely lead to action. The kind of thought which may appear to be daydreaming but which leads to experimentation and action is not included under this category.

A typical case is the child who refuses to face the task at hand, or defers facing it, by dreaming up a much more difficult situation in which he is hailed as a hero and receives the plaudits of those he would like to number among his friends. Questionable as an illustration is the child who sits and looks out the window and does nothing while sitting at his desk. Before categorizing him as a daydreaming adjustor, one should check his home behavior to determine its relationship to the situation. If he daydreams at home instead of doing things, or if he is consistently reluctant to approach the solution of his problems, he is typical. On the other hand if he is cheerful, active, responsive, and friendly, he may appear to be a daydreamer at school for the simple reason that he is bored. The conventional school without challenging alternates to teacher requirements, without opportunity to do something interesting when the assignment is completed, is likely to nourish a listless, daydreaming attitude. Children who have slight difficulty with assignments may choose to defer them or to ignore time limits when their interests are not challenged, but when they get outside of school show no evidence of this kind of escape. They, of course, are not serious cases.

4. Displacement

A not too familiar term descriptive of behavior is *displacement*. This form of behavior is the kind in which an emotional response to one element in a situation is carried over to all kinds of situations in which the same element is found. Except for the emotional accompaniment it could be referred to as a simple matter of conditioned learning. The child, for example, who has been

frightened by a furry animal and subsequently shows an emotional reaction to toy replicas, to fur coats, etc., provides an illustration of this kind. Another illustration is the individual who reacts unfavorably to a person who is associated in some way with
another person with whom unhappy relationships and attitudes
have been established. The adult who does not like the man next
door frequently dislikes the man's whole family.

5. Distortion or sour-grapes behavior

Commonly known is the *sour-grapes* type of behavior. The individual concerned is frustrated in attaining his goal and decides
that it was not worth attaining. Or an individual belittles someone who has achieved what he himself has been unable to accomplish. Another illustration is that of the child or adult who refuses
to participate or to play a game because he is not very skilled in
that particular activity. He expresses his refusal, not by saying that
he is quite unskilled, but by saying that the game isn't any fun or
is a waste of time. The difficulty in dealing with this type of reaction is often that the individual tends to believe what he is saying
rather than recognize his own limitations.

6. Identification

Identification is another illustration of a psychic phenomenon
which may be either good or bad. As a matter of fact, complete
freedom from this type of behavior is an indication of difficulty in
adjustment to basic drives and needs and to demands of society.
Essential for All. No one is so constituted for life in a social world
that he can entirely refrain from it. There are many illustrations
and variations of its existence. The child who mimics another,
either parent or friend, represents a common type. Where mim-
icry is not outgrown it can constitute a serious developmental
problem. By and large it appears most frequently at certain stages
of development and disappears at other stages. The young, fully
mature adult, however, should have outgrown all need for exaggerated expression of this kind.

Other types are thoroughly natural at certain preadolescent and
early adolescent levels. At these stages, identification aids social
development. During adolescence particularly it enables peer

groups to form around common interests. Identification is desirable at adult stages for the same reason. It provides a common interest for clusters within a community. Lodges, clubs, fraternities furnish a mutual interest and opportunity for group identification. *Bad Effects.* Identification which is something other than the manifestation of a basic need, such as that motivated by insecurity or frustration in establishing one's prestige at a desired level, is quite bad, since persons so motivated are rarely satisfied in their achievement. Reaching one level requires establishment of another. While such activity is not necessarily harmful in itself, it limits the individual in his opportunity for establishing satisfaction in the more basic and simpler routines of daily living. Families are often neglected, and worthwhile community activity and participation are passed up in favor of more superficial, egoistic behavior. Charities are supported, for example, which leads to headlines and social approval, but an activity which might make charity unnecessary is completely ignored or rationalized as undesirable.

7. Negativism

Negativism is one of the most serious of all types of mental adjustments. The individual becomes unresponsive in terms of group participation and refuses all outlets and opportunities for cooperative expression. Such reactions approach the sour-grapes type of behavior. Negativism is harmful because the total reaction is a response to situations usually accompanied by emotional feelings. It is likely that such response leads to more serious forms of adjustment motivated by fear and frustration.

8. Projection

The most familiar and common illustration of *projection* is that of blaming someone else for one's own failures. Another form of quite common projection is the act of persuading someone else to do what an individual cannot do himself because of inability or fear. Adolescents, particularly, may demonstrate this type of behavior. Actually the situation is such that the child has the vicarious satisfaction of doing wrong and at the same time receives social approval by refraining from the overt wrongdoing itself. Such demonstrations range all the way from sex manifestations to mere simple outbreaks of rebellion in which someone else takes the consequences of the act.

One of the most difficult types of projection for the teacher to handle is that of the parent who makes his child an unconscious victim in sustaining the parental ego. Some children may suffer little in the immediate relationship but will be handicapped in developing fully their own creative desires and needs. When the child is unable to carry out and maintain the responsibilities necessary for giving parental satisfaction the situation is immediately serious. The possible evils are then of two kinds — that which diminishes opportunity for growth or that which sets up a pattern of frustration and confusion.

Desirable Effects. A form which is desirable is that in which individuals project themselves as "members of the team." This is somewhat more of an emotional relationship than simple identification. If not carried too far it can result in desirable group morale.

9. Rationalization

Rationalization is common. It may be defined as the process of providing reasons for an act or an attitude that is fundamentally the result of other thinking, reasons, or attitudes than those given. One of the difficulties in dealing with this kind of behavior is the fact that the individual may not be aware that he is rationalizing. Such a situation represents a severe case. Equally difficult to solve is the problem of the child who deliberately, time and time again, rationalizes his behavior. A lack of security is the cause of this action, and rationalization may be only a symptom of something far more serious. A cure cannot possibly be achieved in this instance by requesting the child to tell the truth, or by telling him that he is lying, or by punishing him. Treatment must be developed over a period of time, the cause of insecurity established, and steps taken to eradicate it.

Harmful Effects. Rationalization is bad for other reasons than those related to an individual's mental state. It sidetracks and slows down the process of arriving at truths and developing cooperative effort in solving problems. It allows emotional motivation to supply an answer and then proceeds to seek evidence to substantiate the decision or answer given. It is bad because it fails to weigh the evidence and to propose hypotheses accordingly. This is done because the individual needs to justify behavior not in accord with social standards. As in projection it enables him to follow his emotional drives without having to face squarely the consequences of his acts.

Examples of Rationalization. Many typical examples are available. One child may attempt to explain his failure to be elected to a class office as the jealousy of others toward his own accomplishments. Another child may rationalize his failure as the result of a particular teacher's dislike toward him. At the adult level illustrations are equally available. A businessman fails because his competitor uses questionable ethics and procedures. A specific legislative proposal is ridiculed and criticized because it is "new dealish," will discourage "free enterprise," or encourage "unemployment." Adults also frequently rationalize their personal habits. Smoking and drinking are often advocated as desirable for reducing tensions or for providing relaxation. Such claims may be debated and discovered to be true. The point, however, is that some other reason than the one given motivates the particular argument given.

Probably everyone rationalizes at one time or another. Infrequent manifestations are relatively harmless, but the well-adjusted individual should be able to recognize these in his behavior and realize that emotion rather than thinking is governing his action. Rationalization plays an important part in face-to-face reactions between close friends, members of a family, and in teacher-pupil relationships. Friendship and marital relations may be threatened by a constant demonstration of this kind of behavior on the part of one or other of the two concerned. The elimination of rationalization requires a calmness and a sense of security big enough to acknowledge wrongdoing or to face consequences, which are usually minor.

10. Regression

Regression is an immature mode of response to frustrating circumstances. With children, throwing a tantrum is a common illustration. With adults, slamming a door or kicking something out of the way is characteristic. It is undesirable, since it represents a return to an earlier stage of maturity and if indulged in frequently completely handicaps emotional growth and development and completely eliminates the use of reason in solving personal problems.

Hinders Maturation. Regression occurs at times without strong emotional accompaniment. A child may be skilled in side-stepping situations which cause fear or challenge his security and status. He may protest that he is incompetent or that he has to do something else at the time. All such response is harmful in that it hinders the development of capacity and ability at a higher stage of maturity.

Parents and teachers frequently miscalculate ability and force children into situations in which emotion and hysteria throw them far back into an earlier response pattern such as crying, getting sick, or even running away. Children must be eased into higher levels of action and problem solving so that security and satisfaction of accomplishment are brought into harmony with each other (4).

11. Sublimation

Sublimation is often regarded as the process of substituting certain approved social practices for sexual drive and motivation. The individual, of course, must seek approved outlets for his sexual impulses. Nevertheless he is much more involved in adapting his individual goals and objectives to the goals and objectives of a social grouping. The latter involves the whole process of getting along from birth to death. In this sense it is more general and includes much more than adjusting to sexual motivation.

Often Desirable. Sublimation is desirable and part of the everyday living of every individual. It resolves conflict and dissatisfaction and contributes to the development of the individual. It is detrimental when the substituted activity takes a deviational turn and inhibits the process of maturing.

B. CLASSIFICATION OF BEHAVIOR PROBLEMS

The types of behavior just described are ways and means of seeking satisfaction and prestige in the face of obstacles to achieving personal goals. Since all individuals meet barriers of various kinds, it is essential that some way be provided to bring about a satisfactory adjustment. This is what nature has done in establishing psychic mechanisms. Thus, adjustment to problems, to limitations, and to barriers is not indicative of abnormal behavior except in extreme cases. The great problem is to determine where the borderline lies. It varies from individual to individual and can be ascertained only by expert observation. Most children may be found within normal ranges so that teacher effort is only occasionally concerned with determining abnormality. Teacher effort is usually devoted to preventive measures and to eliminating frequent escape mechanisms, preventing minor adjustment problems from becoming more serious, and helping children achieve satisfactorily so that there is a constantly diminishing need for escape behavior.

Classification Helpful. The various forms of adjustive behavior described, all of which are quite uniformly accepted as definite patterns, have been classified by those who treat the problem through psychoanalytic techniques. Many of them are intermingled in the behavior of a given individual, and several of them may appear at any one time. To show the various relationships involved it is possible to categorize them under several general headings. None of the classifications are hard and fast, and consequently no one classification holds superiority as indicated by general acceptance. The only purpose achieved in such classification is in the attempt to relate a particular kind of behavior, in reality a symptom of the kind of adjustment attempted, to its cause, or to the type of avoidance being made. In other words, a classification provides a somewhat better insight into the problem.

Shaffer's Classification. Three very satisfactory classifications have been made. The first to be described is that of Shaffer. He provides five main headings (38) :

1. Adjustment by defense
   a. Compensation
   b. Rationalization
2. Adjustment by withdrawing
   a. Negativism
   b. Fantasy
   c. Retrogression
3. Adjustments involving fear and repression
   a. Phobias
   b. Repression

4. Adjustment by ailments
   a. Hysteria
   b. Psychoneurosis
5. Adjustment through persistent nonadjustive reactions
   a. Anxiety
   b. Worry
   c. Nervousness

Seashore and Katz. Seashore and Katz show relationships from an entirely different approach. Their classification is organized in terms of the reactions of society to the kind of behavior manifested (37) :

1. Socially approved
   a. Compensation
   b. Rationalization
   c. Substitution
2. Socially tolerated
   a. Identification
   b. Projection
   c. Egocentrism
3. Socially criticized
   a. Sympathism
   b. Regression
   c. Dissociation
4. Socially disapproved
   a. Regression
   b. Negativism
   c. Fantasy

This classification gives insight into the seriousness of the behavior demonstrated and its ensuing annoyance and threat to society. It is assumed that the sub-listings are ranked in accordance with their seriousness.

Thorpe's Classification. Thorpe presents a third classification based on the way in which the individual faces reality (42) :

1. Forgetting reality
   a. Conquering hero
   b. Suffering hero
   c. Identification

    2. Distorting reality
        a. Projection
        b. Sour-grapes
        c. Sweet-lemon
    3. Atoning for reality
        a. Overcompensation
        b. Compensatory identification
        c. Malingering
        d. Regression
    4. Retreating from reality (hysteria)
        a. War neurosis
        b. Dual personality
    5. Attacking reality [1]
        a. Defiance
        b. Delinquency
        c. Lying
        d. Stealing
    6. Facing reality [1]
        a. Recognition of problem
        b. Cooperation with others

Aside from providing a means of definition and discussion, the various classifications are of little help to teachers in interpreting behavior. In a sense they represent a status classification without an accompanying qualitative definition. The child who is defiant once a year is quite different from the child who is defiant every day. And on the other hand, any of the number one items in any of the three classifications which are implied as mild or benign may, on the part of some children, represent serious behavior maladjustments. Consequently, it is impossible to categorize behavior in a sequence from mild to bad except in a specific trait reaction. In other words *compensation* may be represented in a mild form at first but may later represent serious maladjustment. With this assumption the following descriptive phrases may be used to further describe adjustive behavior: (1) *exploratory,* (2) *developmental,* (3) *persisting.* These terms may be used to describe development of maladjustment which conforms to the pattern of growth and may be applied to any one or more of the behavior mechanisms previously described. They are said to con-

---

[1] Subdivisions taken from the content. Not listed by Thorpe.

form to the growth pattern in the belief that the development of any type of maladjustment proceeds from an immature to a fully mature characteristic. It would appear that without maturation and the problems which accompany its progress in the social environment, a mild, benign adjustive pattern would be immobilized and remain static. In this sense the progress of maladjustment is similar to any other growth pattern. It begins slowly with considerable variation, proceeds rapidly in a definite pattern, and gradually materializes with the behavior characteristics of a given child.

Exploratory Period. The exploratory period is roughly similar to the beginning points in the various growth cycles. When the child is very young he begins to demonstrate adjustive behavior related to his problems and needs. Many psychologists point out the importance of the first few months in the behavior of the child throughout his entire babyhood cycle. In a sense many of his adjustive reactions are experimental, random, or better described as exploratory. The child is inconsistent in his behavior. Reactions which do not help him or provide satisfaction are dropped and those which bring success are retained. If frustration is never adequately solved for a given individual, he evolves new criteria by which to judge success, and adjustive behavior begins.

Developmental Period. The developmental period represents the period of rapid growth in which satisfactory or acceptable adjustive behavior begins to emerge as a pattern. It is at this stage that individual differences become most obvious. One child characteristically adjusts in one way, and another reacts differently. The child who faces no basic adjustment difficulties, who is not frustrated or has learned behavior in which adjustment represents no problem, proceeds normally in a well-integrated manner.

Persisting Period. The culmination of the previous period leads to what is described as the period of persisting behavior. Behavior becomes more fixed than ever and without further maturational or environmental change is quite predictable. This period presents a leveling-off of experimental behavior. Random explorations and new reactions are at a minimum, and the whole period is characterized by maximum consistency. It is here that change is most successfully pushed aside and the attempt of the school toward improvement most successfully resisted.

Change from Cycle to Cycle. There are certain principles on which this concept of developing adjustive behavior is based. 1. The idea of cycle importance must again be stressed. As in aspects of development in which the whole growth sequence is measurable, there is both continuity and difference in the total design. There is undoubtedly a strand of individuality in all kinds of growth sequences from birth to maturity and even beyond. On the other hand, little recognition has been given to differentiation in growth or behavior from one maturational period to another. This certainly is the case with mental growth and it has been equally ignored in the pattern of adjustive behavior of individuals. The hypothesis has been quite well accepted, for example, that the total life behavior pattern of the individual becomes fixed in his early years. Such a concept is just as unreasonable as the idea that physical development is uninfluenced by maturational effects. No one can deny that maturational periods bring new problems, which demand new adjustive mechanisms.

Continuity, nevertheless, cannot be denied. When a child reaches new maturational periods he faces new problems but tends to explore and experiment with familiar tactics. To the extent that these bring continued success he tends to employ them in the new situation.

Beginning Point of New Patterns. 2. The beginning point of new adjustment mechanisms is more likely than not to be found at the beginning of developmental cycles. This is a logical deduction, since this is the time when growth needs produce new problems. Where the situation becomes altered, change and experimental behavior are much more likely to develop than during a time when the situation has been appraised and become familiar.

New Cycles Produce New Problems. 3. The maturational concept of adjustment is sound in view of the widely recognized fact that new maturational periods bring new problems. In some instances a change in the physical growth pattern, resulting in an attitude of superiority, may alleviate problems which a child faced previously. Conversely, a change in the other direction brings problems the child has never had to face.

4. Most tentative of all is the idea that desirable change can best be produced at the beginning of growth periods. From this concept one may infer, less tentatively, that guidance and as-

sistance, properly handled, are most effective at these periods. Certainly it is true that these periods are most important in determining the child's later reactions. Assuming the existence of three developmental cycles, the most important periods are the first months in the child's early life, his introduction at five or six years of age to school, where he first learns to make broad social adjustments, and the beginning of the adolescent cycle, when his adjustive behavior is affected by new interests in sex.

The idea that change or improvement or proper conditioning for later years can be produced most effectively at these times has implications regarding the kind of teachers a child should have at the corresponding school years, namely, the kindergarten or first grade, and the beginning junior high school years. Understanding, elasticity, resource, and creativity are priority competencies for those who guide children at these ages.

5. Most important in reference to the teacher's role is the idea that adjustive behavior is never entirely fixed and can be modified according to circumstances and the child's potentiality. If this were not true, mental hygiene would be unimportant and could be disregarded by teachers. This assumption is based upon the thought that whereas behavior seemingly emerges according to a specific design it can always be improved upon and diverted more nearly toward the individual's maximum potentiality. Life at best provides frustrations and obstacles to maximum achievement. It is the thought here that constant efforts to improve the environmental effect can bring about improvement and progress toward maximum goals.

CAUSES OF MALADJUSTIVE BEHAVIOR

A. GOAL AND NEED IN DESIRABLE BEHAVIOR

Integration is achieved when an individual adequately meets the personal and social requirements of everyday living. This is not easy. Everyone has his own problems, and the individual who adjusts satisfactorily not only adjusts in reference to his own problems but in reference to the problems of everyone else. Behavior is never the same. Two people may live in harmony with each other at times, but when one is acting in a compensatory or an escape manner his personality pattern becomes more complex and confusing to the other individual, who is attempting to develop his own pattern in relation to the other. When both deviate, conflict results. When two or three other personality patterns enter the action level of the two, the problem is intensified. This is the kind of situation which prevails in the typical family. If one multiplies this situation many times, one gains an idea of the complexity and difficulty of getting along satisfactorily with others in a social grouping. No one person is able to meet all adjustment problems adequately. Some adjust readily and proceed toward their goals; others succumb. A large third group proceeds in a haphazard and uncontrolled way without a goal based on ideals but toward an adapted goal which may be given some social approval but may provide little personal satisfaction.

Seriousness of the Problem. Few achieve complete adjustment, and an approximately equal number become completely maladjusted. This number, although small in terms of the total population, is large and growing larger. No one really knows the total, since the public is not well accustomed to seek mental treatment and consequently many individuals are restricted at home without treatment.

Families who do not have the income or resources for private treatment and isolation, in the main, furnish the patients for mental hospitals. The number is large. According to a report on the subject (34):

> The number of hospital beds devoted to the care of mental cases exceeds in many countries the number of hospital beds for all other diseases put together. If there were any way of knowing the number of hospital patients whose apparent bodily illnesses are the result or concomitant of mental disorders, the picture would expose even more vividly the discrepancy in our effectiveness against "diseases of the mind" as contrasted with "diseases of the body. . . ."

Nor does the situation involve only adults. Children develop early the patterns which may lead to later neuroses, and many show symptoms of serious maladjustment during the elementary school years.

B. ENVIRONMENTAL EFFECTS

Hindrances to Good Adjustment. What hindrances and barriers frustrate children by preventing them from achieving their goals and lead to one or several adjustive or compensatory types of behavior? Without classifying these, or noting their frequency, Hirdansky lists the following as background effects (19) :

1. Poverty
2. Ignorance
3. Lack of skilled preparation for earning a livelihood on the part of parents
4. Immigration involving the lack of knowledge of the English language and American customs
5. Crowding
6. Bad companionship
7. Neurotic parents or guardians
8. Overprotection
9. Neglect
10. Death of one or both parents
11. Parental discord
12. Chronic toxemia
13. Disease — mental or physical
14. Mental retardation unrecognized and untreated
15. Unsupervised recreation
16. Poor heredity
17. Mental conflict

Influence of Parents. An interesting study, which attempted to get at the causes of maladjustment in children, surveyed the diseases and problems of parents of nondelinquent and delinquent groups. The data show some significance of parental influence (Table XV) (11).

This point is particularly significant in reference to psychoneuroses and feeblemindedness in parents as well as in the case of sex problems and temper demonstrations. In comparing the percentages shown it should be pointed out that the nondelinquent children were sufficiently maladjusted to be brought to the clinic, although their behavior had not yet reached the stage of delinquency. Undoubtedly a comparison between parents of delinquents and parents of children with lesser delinquency trends than the nondelinquents studied would show an even greater discrepancy (27).

Other investigators have also found that overprotection or repression, neglect, and discord are factors in parental behavior

TABLE XV

PREVALENCE OF DISEASE AND PERSONALITY DIFFICULTIES AMONG PARENTS OF DELINQUENT AND NONDELINQUENT CHILDREN (11)

	NONDELINQUENTS 1397 *Cases*	154 *Metropolitan*	DELINQUENTS 120 *Cases*
Disease			
TUBERCULOSIS	3.4	2.6	4.6
CARDIORENAL DISEASE	3.4	3.5	5.4
EPILEPSY	1.8	2.5	1.7
OBESITY	.8	1.9	2.5
INSANITY	4.1	6.8	6.5
PSYCHONEUROSES	25.3	23.1	30.8
FEEBLEMINDEDNESS	16.7	17.8	42.9
Personality Difficulties			
SEX	8.1	9.7	15.3
TEMPER	10.3	10.7	15.3
ALCOHOLISM	12.1	18.1	19.2
CRIMINALITY	.9	1.9	1.2
WANDERLUST	1.7	2.5	2.1

which are related to maladjustment in children. In studying overprotection and repression, Levy concluded that this kind of relationship frequently produced an aggressive-egocentric type of behavior (27).

On the positive side recent research points out the effects of family relations which cut through class lines. Brown, Morrison, and Couch show that children who have experienced democratic participation in the home in solving family problems tend to be rated by their classmates as friendly, responsible, and honest (12). Arriving at a similar conclusion, approached somewhat differently, Baruch reports that the parents of the well-adjusted children in a given nursery school had a minimum of conflicts and tensions related to sex, health, work, and relatives (7). These parents likewise reported greater unanimity in methods of handling the child and in training techniques. Anderson similarly reports that children who claimed that their parents nagged, criticized, and punished were identified by "Guess-Who" techniques as children who were unpleasant, bullying, and quarrelsome (3).

The Broken Home. Closely related to these causes is the broken home. From this statement one should not infer that every home in which parents are merely living together is influential for good behavior. The criterion of a broken home is not actual physical separation of parents but more significantly the separation of parents in their love and understanding of each other. Either kind of separation contributes to a feeling of inadequacy and insecurity among children.

There is some evidence that certain maladjusted behavior is directly traceable to doubt about parentage. A child's sudden discovery, for example, that he is adopted frequently results in harmful emotional conditioning. The repression following such a discovery gives rise to undesirable behavior outbreaks. Such cases show an intensive inner turmoil frequently with a definite compulsion toward deviational and harmful action.

Status Necessary for Good Adjustment. Failure to obtain satisfactory status in a group is a cause of maladjustment. To a certain extent desirable social membership is a form of inheritance. In many cases, satisfactory social security is denied by parental status, and the child must acquire by his own interplay of interests and abilities the level he desires to obtain. Failure to establish belongingness with desired groups may result in significant deviations or it may motivate an ingrown, festering type of brooding.

C. PERSONAL EFFECTS

Factors of a more personal nature are (1) the child's physiological heritage, (2) his physical make-up, (3) his mental equipment, and (4) the effect of disease.

Biological Inheritance. The biologically defective child is handicapped from the very start in the process of social integration. He has difficulty in conforming and must make unusual compensatory efforts. Physical make-up and the child's own attitude toward it are also important. If a child despises or even dislikes himself because of his size, looks, or abilities, he indulges in self-pity or develops a feeling of inferiority. He may become bitter and anti-social or he may sink into a listless, introverted type of behavior. *Effect of Intelligence.* Intelligence is an important factor in the adjustment of an individual to the demands of society. Intelligence utilized to achieve personal success and desirable and satisfying group relationships is a decided asset, but without control and balance it can produce trouble. Where other factors motivate the individual toward maladjustive behavior, intelligence intensifies it. The "bright" criminal is much more harmful both to himself and society than the unintelligent one. On the positive side the use of intelligence can be called into play in analyzing a situation and in calling up resources for its proper solution. And the intelligent person can respond much more profitably and effectively to guidance applied in his behalf.

Effect of Disease. Disease may be considered a very important direct and indirect contributor to maladjustment. Many behavior problems are the result of certain diseases including chronic toxemias, post-encephalitic states, debilitating childhood infections, and traumata of various sorts. Severe infections of the central nervous system are not uncommon causes of abnormal behavior. A child so affected may recover from the disease, but his later behavior may range from minor mischievousness to serious delinquency.

In analyzing 120 cases of psychopathic personalities, or what he calls abnormalities of the unstable egocentric type, Kasanin reports that approximately ten per cent had serious cerebral injuries, skull fractures, or severe concussion of the brain (22). He found that personality changes following brain injuries are similar to those found with epidemic encephalitis, such cases showing extreme emotional instability, tantrums, egocentricity, and lack of control. According to Kasanin severe brain injury and encephalitis do not cause the specific behavior reaction but they do result in a diffusing process in the central nervous system which disrupts normal inhibitory influences. According to this theory, then, children so affected do not have stronger compulsions to act abnormally, but are handicapped by an underdeveloped inhibitory mechanism toward harmful activity.

Other traumata which may contribute to behavior irregularities are birth injuries, accidents, and shock brought on by accident. Many of these conditions develop a feeling of inferiority, which is most important in determining the manner in which the child will make adjustments to the problems of daily living.

Behavior — Cause and Effect. All of this is to say that maladjusted behavior is a matter of causation manifested in either organic or psychological ways, or both. Children acting under the effect of such causes can hardly be blamed for their behavior. Teachers, who wish to be helpful and to redirect children to paths where they may continue natural maturation, must look into the relations between cause and effect (26).

SOME EXTREME EFFECTS OF MALADJUSTMENT

A. GENERAL SYMPTOMS

In discussing this problem it must be kept in mind that the reactions of the maladjusted child are somewhat different from those of the maladjusted adult (13). The job of the parent, teacher, and others concerned is to detect the connection between early and mature behavior. Many adults are committed to institutions for mental treatment and isolation. To the casual, naïve observer these individuals during their school years undoubtedly did not exhibit behavior which would have justified prediction of their ultimate outcome. To the trained observer they may have shown evidences of deviation and warning signs of future serious trouble. It is the task of those concerned to learn to identify the kind of landmarks that warn of this kind of future (10).

1. Psychoneuroses

Symptoms of Psychoneuroses. The nervous or psychoneurotic child is the victim of fears, obsessions, repressions, and indecisive action. Symptoms of this kind have been summarized by Lowrey as (28):

> 1. Habit formation including thumb-sucking, enuresis, temper tantrums, finicky food habits, sleep disturbances, speech

disturbances, nail biting, masturbation, negativism, and over-submissiveness.

2. Personality reactions including seclusiveness, timidity, sensitiveness, fears, excessive imagination, fanciful lying, excessive unhappiness and crying, selfishness, restlessness, overactivity, sullenness, revengefulness, excessive irritability, and the like.

3. Social reactions such as fighting, teasing, bullying, impudence, disobedience, show-off behavior, lying, stealing, cruelty, unpopularity.

The symptoms listed are likely to develop before the child is six years of age. The neurotic child tends to allow his emotions to dominate his behavior, frequently showing a history of an outburst of one kind followed by an outburst of a different kind.

This classification should probably also include the neurasthenic child who appears alert and interested for a short period of time but is unable to react with sustained attention. In many instances this child presents an anemic appearance, is pale and underweight, and has aches and pains. He tires easily, especially after mental effort, and becomes quickly fatigued at play. This condition may be attributed to malnutrition, too little sleep, too much excitement, bad personal habits, long school hours, and little healthful exercise.

2. Personality Disorders

The term *personality difficulty* is used to refer to certain other well-defined behavior patterns. This classification would include the neurotic and psychopathic child as well as the seclusive, overactive, emotional, egocentric, and inadequate personality type. In point of comparison these kinds of maladjustments are somewhat more serious in nature than those in the previous classification.

Symptoms of Personality Difficulty. Personality disorders frequently occur in children. The shy, retiring, oversensitive youngsters who tend toward seclusiveness and introversion may be classified under this grouping. Included also is the aggressive, self-assertive, domineering child. When behavior in this latter category becomes sufficiently serious for referral to a clinic, the specific behavior pattern most frequently shown is that of pugnacity, hyperactivity, excitability, destructiveness, and general extroversion (18). Extroversion, however, rather than being a cause is an aid in the process of getting into trouble. The more extroverted a troublesome child, the more likely he is to get into trouble with constituted authority.

3. Psychoses

It is believed that fantasies occupy a great part of the emotional life of children with psychotic tendencies. Some of the more common are those relating to a return to an earlier period of childhood. Others are concerned with death, rebirth, and even reincarnation, replacing or displacing a parent, and fantasies involving wealth and power. In general, fantasies represent an escape from reality (8).

General Characteristics of Psychoses. In the more serious psychoses distinct hallucinations may be found. Many boys in this category hear voices accusing them of various perversions, chiefly of a sexual nature. In studying 114 clinic cases, 19 of which were definitely schizoid, Childers found the following contrasts (Table XVI) (13).

TABLE XVI

COMPARISON OF SCHIZOID AND NONSCHIZOID CHILDREN (13).

Fantasy	Nonschizoid	Schizoid
EXCESSIVE DAYDREAMS	57.8	100.0
PURIFICATION	27.2	47.4
WEALTH AND POWER	39.5	42.1
WISHES COMING TRUE	6.1	15.8
MAN OF THE HOUSE (BOYS)	26.3	36.8
WOMAN OF THE HOUSE (GIRLS)	14.9	26.3
PARENTAGE	27.2	42.1
EXCESSIVE SEX PRACTICE	28.4	52.6
RETURN TO EARLIER LIFE	52.6	78.9
REBIRTH	34.2	57.9
REINCARNATION	6.1	26.3
DEATH OF SELF	43.8	68.4
LIFE IN ANOTHER WORLD	33.3	42.1
NONACCEPTANCE OF PRESENT	48.2	63.2
DESIRE FOR BEING OLDER	35.1	15.8

The percentages in the table are impressive. All contrasts between the two groups are definitely in favor of the schizoid in reference to the frequency of fantasy. Particularly interesting is the marked difference concerning a desire to be older. This strongly implies a lack of natural maturing on the part of the maladjusted children. Other findings, not shown here but particularly characteristic, are the following: eighty-four per cent of the schizoid cases showed a definite withdrawal from group life, sixty-three per cent were labeled queer by others, and sixty-eight per cent achieved more poorly in school than their ability would indicate.

In another study an analysis was made of 160 cases under sixteen years of age (23). Of this group sixty-five were diagnosed as definitely psychotic, while the remaining ninety-five were non-psychotic but displayed symptoms of a psychopathic personality, conduct disorders, mental deficiencies, etc. The psychotic children were characterized by little interest in, and lack of adaptation to, the ordinary world, increased interest in fantasies, frequent hallucinations, odd and fragmentary behavior, and utterances of no meaning. The general conclusion regarding symptoms of children at this level of maladjustment is that there is marked withdrawal from reality. Children at this age — adolescence — are preoccupied with sex topics, but this is not regarded as necessarily of etiological significance.

Relation to Earlier Behavior Unknown. In these cases there is nothing to show that behavior in their early school years was markedly different from that of other children. The occasional presence of such traits as restlessness, night terrors, impatience, and enuresis cannot necessarily be accepted as early signs of mental disorder. The development of seclusiveness, of odd conduct, the lack of social elasticity, the peculiarities of thought processes are more important clues in the early school years.

B. EARLY EXPLORATORY BEHAVIOR WITH SERIOUS LATER POSSIBILITIES

The lack of relationship, noted above, between serious mental disturbances and earlier behavior patterns should not imply that we cannot draw some connecting links between early behavior and serious later maladjustment.

1. Unsocial Action

One of the first cues to potential maladjustment is continuation past the proper terminal point of basically unsocial activity. Such action may follow one or more of a variety of trends.

Center of Attention. One of the most frequent is the eagerness of the child to be the center of attention at all times. Most children who are bright and attractive have many opportunities to develop this trait. Their parents think that they are cute and are forever urging them to sing or dance, and since they are attractive, their parents take every opportunity to grant them the center of the stage. Nearly all parents find it difficult to refrain from following this urge. More often than not, good sense tells them that they are making a bore of themselves and that others are not as interested in their children as they are. The normal child begins to resist and thereby helps correct this tendency. Other children with other parents are never discouraged. They find it necessary to seek the center of attention continuously and are very unhappy and restless when left alone or ignored by others. Such children find it difficult to apply themselves, do little or nothing for others, and attempt to achieve success through trickery, clowning, or easy effort.

As they become adolescent and older they become risks in situations which lead them continuously into more serious maladjustive reactions. If they live on an upper social scale they avoid work that involves any personal self-sacrifice; they cheat, gamble, and steal. If they come from a lower social background, they may commit crimes for the sole purpose of receiving glamorized publicity.

As has been pointed out in an earlier chapter, the child who has everything or nothing is a behavior risk. Many parents either completely suppress or fully indulge the child's wants. Either course can lead to stealing or unusual sexual exploration and experimentation. This, of course, does not help the child to learn to make a living or to learn cooperative social techniques. The child who has too little is handicapped. He will resist working toward a goal which provides a community dividend. The child who has had too much cannot easily see the value of working with someone else because he has always obtained his own goals without any effort.

Where behavior is represented as maladjustive simply because it is continued past a given stage of maturity, certain personality demonstrations may be linked with later serious behavior for the same reason. They are bad because they are continued as a mode of expression when something more mature is called for.

Effect of Fear and Anxiety. Some of the most common traits in this category are shyness, fear, and anxiety. All children develop some of these at one time or another. They are rather easily eliminated under wise guidance, provided there is no deepseated reason for their appearance. Such behavior as anxiety or fear not only precludes the opportunity for social and emotional maturation but, when continued into adolescence and later, may lead to deviational response as a solution to many problems. Instead of solving a problem straightforwardly, the child may lie, cheat, or prove his courage in certain irrational ways (2).

Aggression and Hatred. Another type of persisting behavior is aggression and hatred. Young children very easily develop animosities (3). Continuance of this trait at an age when they should be developing social behavior is prognostic of trouble. Quite frequently this is the result of bad treatment by a parent, teacher, or older child. The hatred and animosity developed can carry over into their relations with other children. They may act cruelly and bully younger children, or show intense anger and hatred toward anyone who holds a superior position. These children have not been encouraged to analyze and develop personal controls. A spoiled child with this kind of background becomes aggressive at the slightest provocation.

2. Social Immaturity

Lack of Social Sensitivity. A kind of social insensitivity is a type of abnormal development in childhood which can lead to trouble in later life. Most children develop a strong awareness of the implications of their behavior with other children. Some children grow up socially clumsy, totally unable to see how what they say and do affects others. Some are naturally awkward in this respect; others cultivate this kind of behavior. The child who is greatly surprised and hurt by retribution directed at him for some provocative act of his is an illustration. The inability to develop social sensitivity may lead to the most serious types of delinquent behavior, or where expression remains within the law, may lead to serious personal maladjustment and difficulty in getting along with other people (47).

Regression to Lower Social Level. Another type of social immaturity which results in aggressiveness and other forms of maladjustment is demonstrated by the child who in trying to establish security and belongingness identifies himself with groups somewhat below his own social level. Where such identification and struggle for status culminate in the child's stepping into a role which for him represents misbehavior or delinquent action, he is started on a road leading to much trouble. Where limited regression in group identification results in wholesome satisfying behavior it is wise for the individual to attempt it. Where the child achieves no real satisfaction but recognizes his inferiority the more because of such identification, he tends toward aggressive, delinquent action.

Identification with Social Rejectees. Closely allied with this kind of identification is identification with social rejectees because of too strong parent pressure for alliance with children of friends and adherence to parental behavior standards regarded by the child as somewhat prim and old-fashioned. It is a common failing for parents to be too concerned about the companions of their children. If children are isolated from those with whom they would like to associate they become either meek or rebellious. Either response is bad. If the child feels seriously hindered he will openly rebel against his parents by deliberately seeking companionships which neither child nor parent approves. If such parent and child relationships are not corrected the conflict becomes more and more serious until a break is made. The child will leave home, run away, or become involved in some misdemeanor. Where a milder form of conflict is involved which goes on and on the child becomes more insecure, achieves little peer prestige and status, and is well on the way toward forming any number of maladjustment patterns.

3. Lack of Values Leads to Maladjustment

Causes of Value Immaturity. Another factor which prepares children for maladjustment patterns is what might be referred to as *value immaturity.* Some children have no sense of values at all. They may know that a certain act is right or wrong because someone has said that it is wrong. On the other hand they have no ability to generalize rightness or wrongness because they have had no experience in forming generalizations. All of their lives they have been protected. When they have done something wrong they were punished. When they did something right they were rewarded. Some children have had no chance to be naturally punished or rewarded for their behavior, having always had someone around to make decisions for them.

Effect of Value Immaturity. These children usually appear to be very well behaved. They may go through life without any serious problems. If they continue to be protected by living in a sheltered environment and have the good fortune to face no critical problems or decisions, they will consider themselves, and will appear to be, individuals of strong character and great stability. On the other hand, if they are thrown off the familiar protected pathway they run into all sorts of trouble. They may become seriously delinquent, neurotic, and completely maladjusted.

Does Not Accept Restrictions. Another early symptom of later maladjustment is the kind of behavior wherein the child rationalizes that something is wrong, but not for him. This kind of behavior can easily carry through adolescence and into adulthood. When it does it provides a very unstable basis for developing satisfactory human relationships, so essential for personal adjustment and well-being.

THE RELATION OF MATURITY TO GOOD MENTAL HYGIENE

As in all kinds of growth, increasing maturity is a factor which must be taken into consideration in developing satisfactory mental hygiene conditions. For many children growth which deviates from what is considered normal is the result of physiological limitations. The teacher or parent must then recognize the task of aiding the child to adjust to these. With most children, however, good mental hygiene involves the more complex but less spectacular activity of helping them properly achieve their potential limits.

Increased Self-control with Maturity. Probably no other factor is more significant in providing an adequate mental hygiene status than that of acquiring increased self-control with increased maturity. To do this requires guided opportunity to plan, to evaluate, and to have experience in judging the consequences of acts in terms of their effect on the welfare of others. To do all this successfully requires a feeling of security and adequacy, a group consciousness, and the achievement of satisfaction.

From Egoistic to Social Behavior. Maladjustment can be avoided or minimized only by substituting social behavior for egocentric. For some children this is very difficult; for others it is easy. Children must be acceptable to the group to which they would like to belong, and the group must be of the right sort to provide the kind of normal satisfactions compatible with the child's basic drives and social background. Where these conditions can be met it is not difficult for him to modify his behavior to fit the role he must play.

Evils in Homogeneous Grouping. So-called "homogeneous" grouping lends itself to a continuation of egocentric behavior beyond the age where it should be expected. Where children are academically incompetent and are placed in groups recognized as incompetent, they suffer loss of prestige and status and tend to be shunned. The child who is slightly insecure and who, instead of seeking his salvation through an intelligent effort to achieve social status, compensates by doting on his teacher's nod of approval or by seeking satisfaction through high scholarship, is also limited in his developmental opportunity.

Increased Knowledge of Needs. A point which has not received a great deal of attention is the fact that the child requires an increasing understanding of his own personal developmental needs as he grows older. Nothing will help him more to achieve a satisfactory adjustment than a recognition of his capabilities and weaknesses.

Mistakes Made by Guidance Experts. In this respect too many wrong things have been done. Guidance personnel in many instances have played fast and loose with inventories of one kind or another, and the individual seeking assistance has taken his test scores very seriously — much more seriously than even those

who understand such inventories and work with them. Achievement test scores, I.Q.'s, and like data have been handed out to
teachers as gospel truths or as a basis on which important judgments should be made. All of this is bad because no one yet knows
very much about what they mean.

Significant errors are also made by parents. When a child is immature, afraid, or unable to compete successfully, many parents
help him rationalize that the achievement accomplished by
others is not worthwhile or that he would be foolish to try it anyway. And there is also the parent who encourages disparagement
of all other children while approving the petty and minor accomplishments of his own child. Many children who fail in their
struggle for status are encouraged toward maladjustment in this
way. The child should learn to get satisfaction out of group effort,
even where he plays a minor or inconsequential role. Playing the
game should give the main satisfaction rather than being able to
achieve satisfaction only by playing the game well.

Defects in Guidance. Teachers and parents have gone too far in
excessive encouragement of compensatory activity. Child guidance in the schools has in the past rested primarily on the idea that
the child must do something well. Failure in one task is generally
taken as the cue for attempting some other task. Thus we have in
school and in our guidance and adjustment clinics a tendency to
shift the child from one failure experience to another in the hope
that eventually he will find something in which he is an outstanding success. We have ignored the fact that a failure complex toward a certain activity is usually the conditioning effect of a poor
environment, poor teaching, or an unreadiness for the experience.
The increasing interest in art and music which is manifesting itself throughout the country finds many of its participants among
those who in school considered themselves inept in these fields.
This is the result of the failure of educators to encourage children
and adults to experiment in areas in which they are interested but
somewhat handicapped in ability. The idea of finding the "proper
niche" for the individual, which is scarcely more than professional
encouragement to accept failure but to compensate for it, is diminishing. It is generally recognized that everyone can be creative
to a degree in art, music, or writing if he has the proper guidance.

There is no reason why any child shouldn't be expertly competent at a limited level of mathematics instead of half-competent at several levels. Guidance is beginning to recognize that general competency which leads to self-analytical, integrated behavior is a much better preparation for a vocation than the results obtained by identifying specific potentiality with a specific job demand. General ability in solving many types of problems is much more desirable than intensive knowledge of a very limited skill. If this be debated in relation to vocational benefits, it cannot be debated in terms of adjustment and integrative personality.

Balanced Growth Necessary. Similar to this point is the attitude toward integration and adjustment which regards a good mental hygiene program as one in which there is balanced growth. The child who has satisfactory maturity in one aspect of his development but lacks it in another is an illustration of status incompatibility which may lead to serious maladjustive behavior. It is questionable whether the school has done much from this viewpoint to aid adjustment. The typical school is little concerned with emotional or social immaturity as long as these do not perceptibly hinder academic achievement. And the school has been guilty too in failing to provide a balanced academic diet. The elective system allows the student to avoid subjects which he may need if he has experienced what seemingly is a failure background in these fields. Consequently there has been guidance pressure to identify need with easy success. Much of this is wrong. Undoubtedly there should be a personal emphasis upon certain well-chosen areas, but the selection for emphasis should take much more into consideration than past academic records and highly unreliable "aptitude" results.

Variation Normal for Some. Children's growth patterns vary considerably. Some children show a range of development within which there are but slight differences between various kinds of growth. In the usual growth-analysis chart such children present no more than a two- or three-year range in growth aspects at any one time, whereas another child will show a ten-year difference. Research is not yet available to validate this point entirely, but it is believed that where different types of growth proceed on comparable developmental levels, with advancing maturity, the chances for good adjustment and integrative social behavior are very likely to be considerably greater than in instances where there is a wide range.

If instruction could be geared toward maximum individual development the problem of curriculum selection would be greatly minimized. Equally minimized would be the need for a marking system based on the relative performance of different individuals. In the sense implied here the child with better than normal potentiality would be motivated to go beyond a complacent grade average and proceed far enough beyond to come close to achieving his best performances.

Individuality in Range of Behavior. Another growth factor of importance to teachers in guiding development is the question of what constitutes deviational behavior. For some children activities which seem to be on the borderline of bad behavior are normal, whereas for other children the same behavior represents a tendency toward maladjustment and delinquency. Mixed in with the problem of determining whether a given child's level of behavior is good or bad is the problem of determining whether deviations are a chance affair or the indication of a trend. The child who dips to a lower level than might justifiably be expected does not necessarily represent a risk, and his participation may indicate only a "chance" deviation from his true pattern.

The problem of consistency in terms of total behavior has some connotations and raises some questions as to the significance of performance on such measurable aspects of growth as can be portrayed on a growth-analysis chart. Some children show consistency in their variation, either great or small; others show more uniformity with only occasional variation. For some it is small; for others it is greater. The question can be raised, then, as to the probability of a general stability or reliability factor. Indications that slight variation in the pattern of measurable aspects of growth means strong chances of social progress without much maladjustment would be a great interpretive aid to teachers. A thorough study of this problem will surely throw much more light on emotional and social growth.

SOME GENERAL ATTITUDES FOR DEALING WITH MALADJUSTIVE BEHAVIOR

A. TECHNIQUES TO AVOID

Avoid Impulsive Action. As stated in the chapter dealing with disciplinary problems, the teacher must be warned about acting on impulse. 1. Impulsive action indicates that the teacher is involved emotionally some way or another. 2. Maladjustive behavior takes a long time to develop into serious mental difficulty. Therefore there is sufficient time to deal with a situation after giving it thought and study. And if maladjustment is well started it will take time to correct it. Teachers who wish to change behavior often feel that unless immediate attention is given the problem the child will be lost. 3. Impulsive action is ineffective and perhaps even harmful because it fails to give complete consideration to all the details involved. Because it is impulsive it cannot be studied and well planned according to the needs of the case.

Avoid Personally Satisfying Action. Another error made by those who attempt to change behavior is that of judging the benefit of treatment in terms of teacher satisfaction. A teacher may feel very happy as a result of having induced a group of extroverted children to adopt a lone-wolf type of child. Or, through a study of a sociometric chart she may feel very happy about her efforts in transplanting a rejected child to a group whose members are mutually interested in each other. Where this is hastily done neither the group nor the individual is prepared for the move and the child is likely to become even more isolated and rejected although daily coming within the area of this group's social action. Or the teacher may feel that a completely frustrating action on her part toward a child who is compensating or regressing in his behavior is a very good thing. Such a teacher fails to realize that maladjustive behavior is but slightly beyond the range of adjustive and beneficial behavior. Blocking such action may be personally satisfying, but it is scarcely ever good for the child.

Avoid Superficial and Thwarting Action. In a similar vein teachers should be warned about using techniques which prevent the obvious action but divert the drive into other channels. Many teachers are guilty of this kind of treatment. They see the symptom rather than the cause, and treating the symptom usually means an outbreak in a new spot. In dealing with certain social and psychological ills it is desirable to keep the symptom in the open where it may be observed and the cause determined, rather than driving it "underground" where both symptom and cause are more elusive.

On the positive side such a warning implies that when treatment, direction, or guidance is given, it should be of the kind that can be checked in reference to what else it does for the child. As Redl says (32), "No doctor would brag about a medicine which does away with headaches in an hour but after a week destroys the patient's kidneys."

B. POSITIVE HINTS

Study Less "Serious" Behavior. Wickman's study indicates that teachers are quite insensitive to those behavior patterns which have the most serious implications (45). This has been explained as a matter of tradition, the effect of overcrowded classrooms, or other factors, but it can also result in a teacher's faulty assumption that what appears most serious now will become most serious later. As a matter of fact if any ratio exists between preadolescent behavior and postadolescent behavior and mental disturbance, it is in an inverse ratio, namely, that that behavior which seems the least serious now may have the most serious later consequences. This, of course, is not entirely true. It is stated in order to exaggerate the point that later serious maladjustment only infrequently demonstrates its beginnings in those many noisy rebellious acts that bother teachers the most.

Therefore children who are introverts, daydreamers, and unusually quiet, shy, or polite should be given much more attention. Teachers should look for attitudes and signs of activity which seem only remotely concerned with the situation at hand. Neurotic and maladjustive behavior with serious later consequences usually appears in disguise as mild and innocuous, and sometimes even as desirable behavior.

Professional Attitudes Defined. It is questionable whether a teacher can accept, like, or even love a child without becoming emotionally involved. When teachers are advised to act professionally toward children, the warning usually carries the implication that emotions should not enter into the relationship. And while a teacher should be warned against letting emotion interfere with judgment when dealing with the child in terms of behavior, still there is almost uniform belief that the teacher must like children, be accepted by them, and accept them fully. Thus the confusion arises.

Teaching Involves Emotions. It seems logical that the apparent conflict — and it is more apparent than real — should be cleared up. First, teaching, to be creative, involves some sort of emotional accompaniment. Such emotion is mild, of the type to provide verve, impetus, and creative action. Teaching can never be completely and exclusively rational. Nor can the relations between child and teacher be completely cold, objective, and impersonal. For best results there must exist a mutual understanding, respect, and affection. Without this the teacher would be egocentric — an individual interested only in her own power to provide change, and gaining satisfaction only in seeing personal power in action rather than in making a child happy.

It is difficult to develop a friendly attitude toward all children. It is difficult to be friendly, interested, and affectionate toward a dull, dirty child, or toward the one who is lifeless, or the one who is universally considered a pest. Then there is the child who lies, dislikes the teacher, cheats, does everything possible to make teaching difficult. And yet these are the children that need acceptance, friendship, and attention (20).

C. THE ROLE OF THE GROUP IN CORRECTIVE BEHAVIOR

The chapter on disciplinary problems gave considerable attention to the effect of group morale on individual behavior. The point was made that the group is very influential in reference to unapproved modes of acting. A similar point can be made regarding the influence of the group on the individual in respect to the need for maladjustive behavior, its frequency and extent, and its seriousness in terms of consequences.

The Individual a Group Member. Whereas much attention is given to the individual in discussions such as this, the point must be made that the teacher never deals exclusively with the individual child. This is true for the reason that the individual never exists entirely in terms of his own achievement and potentiality. His limitations, his worries, his problems, all become real only because he exists in society, where he is surrounded by varying capacities, interests, worries, doubts, and codes. The guidance of children in school is in a setting in which the individual is studied and appraised in and through the group to which he belongs (40).

Writers almost invariably rate the importance of gang groupings outside of school as more natural than those in school. There is much to be said, however, concerning the opportunity of the school for supplementing desirable outside school grouping, for blocking and for counteracting undesirable influences, and for providing an experimental area in which teachers can study the effectiveness of gang groupings by deliberately, but judiciously, changing the pattern in school.

Kind of Experimentation Needed. From the standpoint of good mental hygiene the most promising areas of experimentation are to be found in this kind of strategy. Certain principles are basic and suggestive. In the first place the grade placement or grouping within a room, club activity, and all other opportunities available within the school for getting children together in groups, should be handled from an entirely different point of view than is done currently. Grade placement is more or less automatic except for very immature or very slow children. When the so-called normal child starts a given grade with a group of children he continues with this group unless he fails or at some stage of development is promoted because he is superior or too mature. It is almost unheard of to make a child repeat a grade with the motive of placing him in a situation where he would be superior, more aggressive, and hence more active in some leadership roles. Nor is it usual to promote a borderline or near-failing child to the next grade or allow him to skip a grade, thereby putting him in a group where his deficiency is about the same but where he feels more satisfied to assume his usual unimportant role. Many children would be benefited by this type of treatment. Such children are happy to be followers in a group regarded as superior.

D. THE ROLE OF THE TEACHER IN CORRECTING MALADJUSTIVE BEHAVIOR

Much is being written currently about the teacher's responsibility in directing child development toward its highest possible level. This role is played through individual guidance, group administration and organization, and attempts to restore deviational behavior to normal. There is no question regarding the responsibility of the teacher in this connection. Many suggestions for getting the most effective results have already been made. There are certain other points which need clarification.

Proper Use of Consultants. The first concern is the use of technical advice. Supplementary assistants have been provided throughout the nation's schools to aid in dealing with many of the kinds of maladjustment peculiar to school children. In the main the consultants provided can be classified under three headings — visiting teacher service, counseling and guidance personnel, and technical and professional consultants who are available but usually not connected with the school organization.

Unfortunately as special services have been established there has been a tendency to relieve the teacher of the problem by delegating responsibility to the special agents. And, also unfortunately, a look at many school systems indicates that the more rigid, inelastic, and uncompromising the curriculum, the more comprehensive and specialized the staff of special consultants.

Cannot Delegate Guidance. The teacher should not be freed of the responsibility of handling maladjustive behavior when correction involves creative, ongoing social relationships. Where the problem involves behavior sufficiently serious to involve other agencies and institutions, special agents may advisedly assume greater responsibility. Court cases, juvenile delinquents, and serious maladjustments are in this category. In these instances direction and planning will be delegated to other hands. However, as long as the child remains in school, social organization related to solving the problem is the teacher's responsibility.

Guidance Experts as Consultants. Visiting teachers and special guidance personnel should exist in general as consultants to the classroom teacher. They may render services in providing her with information which she is unable to obtain. At best the teacher briefs them on the kind of information needed, since she is the person who best understands a child's total behavior. Initiating and obtaining complete case data when a child comes to her attention is wasteful for the counselor or visiting teacher and is an indictment of the child study program. The teacher is in the best situation to maintain this type of information and supplement the picture already at hand by utilizing data collected by consultant interview or testing.

Interview Overemphasized in Guidance Activity. Too much importance has been given by counseling personnel to the place of the interview in child guidance. Interviews held for the purpose of changing behavior through making decisions, "seeing mistakes," etc., are wasteful and time-consuming. In order to change behavior it is necessary to study the cause and make a shift in the child's motivational environment. Interviews by special personnel should be held to a minimum. If the child is seeking information he should turn to the person most familiar with his total developmental pattern.

The teacher may well place the greatest emphasis on group study in identifying maladjustive behavior. Group activity greatly influences individual behavior (43).

The opportunity of the teacher in this connection is tremendous. No matter how well the child adjusts to problems outside of school, six hours of social maltreatment in school can do much to upset the balance. And, conversely, six hours of happy, successful adjustment in school can do much to counterbalance disturbing influences at home and out of school. It must be realized, however, that one cannot expect too much. Home conflict, bad neighborhood associations, and daily contacts with delinquents are powerful influences. The school is a "balancer." It can aid materially in negating bad effects and where it can become compatible with desirable, positive home trends, its influence is at its best.

Teacher Must Be Well Adjusted. The teacher who becomes efficient in dealing with problems of mental hygiene must have achieved satisfactory status in her own adjustment. Many teachers are troubled with chronic personality difficulties which tend to exaggerate children's emotional problems and create blind spots in recognizing their difficulties. These teachers hinder maximum achievement, although appearing to do the opposite, and they may even create the very kind of problem which it is their responsibility to solve.

Extent of Teacher Maladjustment. A hint as to the number of teachers so affected comes from a review of Fenton's study (16). Among 241 teachers 77.6 per cent were considered adequately adjusted. These teachers were amiable, easy to get along with, and participated in community life. Among the total group, 22.5 per cent were not only maladjusted but in need of special clinical attention. Their difficulties were of a psychoneurotic order, including personality problems sufficiently serious to hinder teaching efficiency. Of the total group, 15.4 per cent were seriously enough afflicted to be definitely incompetent.

In another study Peck inventoried one hundred women teachers attending summer school (31). Of this number, 33 per cent were discovered to be maladjusted, with 12 per cent definitely in need of clinical attention.

An enlightening investigation dealing with the kind of mental disorder shown by teachers was made by Mason (29). Over 65 per cent of the number needing treatment were institutionalized before the age of forty-five. Dementia praecox ranked first with 37.3 per cent, manic-depressive psychoses second with 23.8 per cent, and paranoia third with 6.1 per cent. Most interesting is the finding that in only a small per cent of the cases involved was the difficulty associated with the school situation.

SUMMARY

Before mental hygiene practices can gain much headway in the schools much research is needed.

Longitudinal Study Needed. In the first place, there is a great lack of longitudinal study directed toward appraising the developmental pattern of the child in relation to his adjustment and emotional problems. Thousands of superficial case studies have been prepared which outline temporary remedial handling and its effects. What is needed, however, is a type of long-time individual case-study research, in which data is collected, prognosis made, and handling prescribed. Those who study children must evaluate data and predict the chances for good adjustment. Remedial treatment, as well as preventive and corrective handling, must be planned in terms of such prediction with the object of increasing the child's adjustment opportunities. Research of this type would then demonstrate to all concerned that attention to adjustment problems pays high dividends and that it is worthwhile to divert teacher activity from the more conventional instructional effort to the handling of behavior problems.

There is too much of an attitude among parents and others interested in the schools that all the talk about maladjustment, democracy, pupil planning, etc., is merely an alibi for neglecting "fundamental" teaching and implies nothing more basic than giving way to children's whims.

It seems fitting to close this discussion with the comment that mental hygiene in the schools is not merely an added frill or secondary service to be wedged into the teacher's already overcrowded calendar. It has far-reaching implications for complete betterment of our culture in reference to human needs and values. The attitude toward those needing attention is characterized by much more understanding than it was only a decade or so ago. Charlatans and well-meaning, but poorly prepared, individuals have done much to impede its progress. More support, therefore, is needed. The gains made must be extended and new techniques discovered and applied. As this is done, the prestige of mental hygiene work in the schools will improve, and the public will demand teachers who are genuinely concerned with the adjustment problems of children and not merely interested in their academic skills. We will then continuously recognize the emotional and personality needs of children and learn techniques to deal with them.

SELECTED REFERENCES

1. BRILL, NORMAN, "Solving The Problems of Emotional Illness," *Mental Health*, 38:594–603, October, 1954.
2. BURNS, CHARLES, "Pre-Schizophrenic Symptoms in Pre-Adolescents' Withdrawal and Sensitivity," *Nervous Child*, 10:120–128, 1952.
3. ANDERSON, H. H., "Experimental Study of Dominative and Integrative

    Behavior in Children of Pre-School Age," *Journal of Social Psychology*, 8:335–345, 1937.

4. ELLINGSON, R. J., "Response to Physiological Stress in Normal and Behavior Problem Children," *Journal of Genetic Psychology*, 83:19–29, March, 1953.

5. FARNHAM, MARYNIA F., "Cases of Hysteria in Childhood," *Nervous Child*, 10:232–237, 1953.

6. FOX, W. H., AND SEGEL, DAVID, "The Validity of the Choice of Friends Method of Measuring Social Adjustment," *Journal of Educational Research*, 47:389–394, January, 1954.

7. BARUCH, DOROTHY W., "Therapeutic Procedures as Part of the Educative Process," *Journal of Consulting Psychology*, 4:165–172, 1940.

8. FRAZEE, HELEN E., "Children Who Later Become Schizophrenic," *Smith College Studies in Social Work*, 23:125–149, February, 1953.

9. GARDNER, GEORGE E. (Editor), *Case Studies in Childhood Emotional Disabilities*, Vol. I., New York: American Orthopsychiatric Association, Inc., 1953.

10. GERARD, MARGARET WILSON, *The Emotionally Disturbed Child. Papers on Diagnosis, Treatment and Care*. Child Welfare League of America, 1956.

11. BRANHAM, V. C., "An Analysis of 1671 Cases Brought to the Child Guidance Clinics of the New York State Department of Mental Hygiene," *Psychiatric Quarterly*, 3:569–589, 1929.

12. BROWN, W., MORRISON, JOAN, AND COUCH, GERTRUDE B., "Influence of Affectional Family Relationships on Character Development," *Journal of Abnormal and Social Psychology*, 42:422–428, 1947.

13. CHILDERS, A. T., "A Study of Some Schizoid Children," *Mental Hygiene*, 15:106–133, 1931.

14. HEATHERS, GLEN, "Emotional Dependence and Independence in a Physical Threat Situation," *Child Development*, 24:169–179, 1953.

15. HULSE, WILFRED C., "Childhood Conflict Expressed through Family Drawings," *Journal of Projective Techniques*, 16:66–79, 1952.

16. FENTON, N., *Mental Hygiene in School Practice*. Palo Alto: Stanford University Press, 1943.

17. KNAPP, IRWIN J., AND RICHARDS, T. W., "The Child's Differentiation of Sex as Reflected in Drawings of the Human Figure," *Journal of Genetic Psychology*, 81:99–111, 1952.

18. LORR, MAURICE, AND JENKINS, R. L., "Patterns of Maladjustment in Children," *Journal of Clinical Psychology*, 9:16–19, January, 1953.

19. HIRDANSKY, S., "Problems Associated with Maladjusted Children," *Psychiatric Quarterly*, 5:278–286, 1931.

20. MARTIN, W. E., "Identifying the Insecure Child: II. The Validity of Some Suggested Methods," *Journal of Genetic Psychology*, 80:25–33, March, 1952.

21. MEAD, MARGARET, "Technological Change and Child Development," *Understanding the Child,* 21:109–112, October, 1952.
22. KASANIN, J., "Personality Changes in Children Following Cerebral Trauma," *Journal of Nervous and Mental Disorders,* 69:385–406, 1929.
23. ——, AND KAUFMAN, M. R., "A Study of the Functional Psychoses in Childhood," *American Journal of Psychiatry,* 9:307–384, 1929.
24. NATIONAL SOCIETY FOR THE STUDY OF EDUCATION. *Mental Health in Modern Education, Fifty-Fourth Yearbook, Part I.* Chicago: University of Chicago Press, 1955.
25. PENNELL, MARYLAND Y., CAMERON, DALE C., AND KRAMER, MORTON, "Mental Health Clinic Services for Children in the United States, 1950," *Public Health Reports,* 66:1559–1572, 1951.
26. PLANT, JAMES S., *The Envelope. A Study of the Impact of the World Upon the Child.* New York: The Commonwealth Fund, 1950.
27. LEVY, D. M., "Maternal Overprotection and Rejection," *Journal of Nervous and Mental Disorders,* 73:65–77, 1931.
28. LOWREY, L. G., "Some Principles in the Treatment of Behavior Problems in Children," *Journal of Nervous and Mental Disorders,* 73:62–65, 1931.
29. MASON, F. V., "A Study of Seven Hundred Maladjusted School Teachers," *Mental Hygiene,* 15:576–599, 1931.
30. RABINOVITCH, RALPH D., AND FISCHOFF, JOSEPH, "Feeding Children to Meet Their Emotional Needs," *Journal of American Dietetics,* 28:614–621, 1952.
31. PECK, L., "Study of the Adjustment Difficulties of a Group of Women Teachers," *Journal of Educational Psychology,* 27:401–416, 1926.
32. REDL, FRITZ, "Deviations Tending toward Delinquency," *Child Growth in an Era of Conflict,* edited by C. V. Millard, 15th Yearbook, Department of Elementary School Principals. Lansing: Michigan Education Association, 1944.
33. ——, AND WATTENBERG, WILLIAM W., *Mental Hygiene in Teaching,* New York: Harcourt, Brace, 1951.
34. ROCKEFELLER FOUNDATION, *The World of the Mind,* Annual Report, 1936.
35. RYAN, W. C., "Mental Hygiene," *Elementary Educational Psychology,* edited by C. E. Skinner. New York: Prentice-Hall, 1945.
36. REDL, FRITZ, AND WINEMAN, DAVID, *Children Who Hate.* Glencoe, Illinois: The Free Press, 1951.
37. SEASHORE, R. H., AND KATZ, B., "An Operational Definition and Classification of Mental Mechanisms," *Psychological Record,* 1:3–24, 1937.
38. SHAFFER, L. F., *The Psychology of Adjustment.* Boston: Houghton Mifflin, 1936.
39. REDL, FRITZ, AND WINEMAN, DAVID, *Controls from Within.* Glencoe, Illinois: The Free Press, 1952.
40. ROSENTHAL, SHELDON, "A Fifth-Grade Classroom Experience in Fostering Mental Health," *Journal of Child Psychiatry,* 2:302–329, 1952.

41. SCHEIDLINGER, SAUL, "Group Factors in Promoting School Children's Mental Health," *American Journal of Orthopsychiatry*, 22:394–404, 1952.

42. THORPE, L. P., *Child Psychology and Development*. New York: Ronald Press, 1946.

43. SLAVSON, S. R., *Analytic Group Psychotherapy—Its Use with Children, Adolescents and Adults*. New York: Drexler Book Co., 1950.

44. WASHBURNE, CARLETON, "Training Teachers to Use Mental Hygiene," *Education*, 1934 (Reprint).

45. WICKMAN, E. K., *Children's Behavior and Teacher's Attitudes*. New York: The Commonwealth Fund, 1928.

46. SODDY, KENNETH (Editor), *Mental Health and Infant Development. Vol. I: Papers and Discussions: Vol. II: Case Histories*. London: Basic Books: 1956.

47. STEWART, R. S., AND WORKMAN, R. S., *Children and Other People*. New York: Dryden, 1956.

48. STOUFFER, GEORGE A. W., "Behavior Problems of Children as Viewed by Teachers and Mental Hygienists," *Mental Hygiene*, New York: 36:271–285, 1952.

49. SUESSMILCH, F. S., "A Long Term Maladjustment Culminating in Catatonic Episodes during Adolescence," (a case study), *Journal of Projective Techniques*, 15:461–479, 1951.

50. WITMER, HELEN (Editor), *Psychiatric Interviews With Children*. Cambridge: Harvard University Press, 1946.

INDEX

Abernethy, M. E., 32, 53
Ackerson, L., 136, 145
Acquisition, learning as, 282
Activity and rest, rhythm of, 395
Adler, Alfred, theory of motivation, 350
Adolescence:
  conflicts in moral and ethical behavior, 333
  effect on pattern of learning, 272
  effect on personal-social development, 216
  growth differences in, 77
  growth in, 62
Aggression:
  contrasting theories, 237
  defined, 236
  development of, 231
  potential effect of, 475
  secondary facts, 238
Alexander, Marie, 404
Alexander, Theron, 404
Allen, Lucille, 376, 405
Allen, R. M., 324
Allport, F. H., 294, 317, 368, 404
Allport, G. W., 324, 371, 372, 385, 404
Almy, Millie, 293, 324
Alschuler, Rose H., 386, 404
Altus, Grace Thompson, 142
Amatora, Mary, 404
Ames, Louise Bates, 172, 324
Anastasi, Anne, 143
Anatomists, contributions to organismic viewpoint, 2
Anderson, H. H., 256, 285, 286, 323, 410, 411, 412, 413, 443, 468, 475, 489
Anderson, J. E., 8, 364
Ansbacher, H. L., 123, 143
Anxiety, potential effect of, 475
Appreciation:
  as creative development, 199
  emotion and understanding in, 200
  role of environment, 201
Arey, L. B., 94, 97
Armstrong, Charles M., 129, 143

Art, creative development in:
  developmental sequences, 191
  inhibiting effects, 192
  use of tools, 192
Asmussen, Erling, 53
Associates, influence on moral and ethical behavior, 339
Asthenic, personality type, 380
Athletic, personality type, 380
Attitudes:
  development of, 317
  in moral and ethical behavior, 359–362
    acceptance of facts, 361
    emotional trauma, 361
    prestige, 361
    security, 360
    redirection, 318
    role of school, 318
Ausubel, David P., 214, 250, 374, 404

Bahrick, H. P., 286
Baker, W. A., 363
Bal, M. E. P., 118
Baldwin, B. T., 18, 29
Barbu, Z., 364
Barker, R. G., 1, 2, 8, 364
Barton, E., 102, 117
Baruch, Dorothy W., 324, 434, 444, 467, 490
Bayley, Nancy, 25, 28, 34, 53, 54, 81, 97, 104, 117, 123, 143
Bedoian, Vagharsh H., 250
Behavior:
  compensatory, 241
  deviational, 481
  effect of moral knowledge on, 340
  emotional, control of, 313–320
    by attitudes, 317
    by avoidance, 314
    by conditioning, 315
    by discipline, 314
    by relaxation, 314
    trainability, 313
  emotions as clues to, 303
  See also Mental hygiene, Moral and ethical behavior, Personal-social development

493

Behaviorism, 256, 316, 349, 351
Bell, John Elderkin, 205
Beloff, J. R., 405
Belongingness:
  as factor in moral and ethical behavior, 355
  sense of, 209
  See also Security
Berenda, R. W., 250
Bergman, Garnet W., 51
Berne, E. V. C., 209, 230, 250
Betts test, 108
Biehler, Robert F., 250
Binet, Alfred, definition of intelligence, 119
Binocular vision, 91
Blanchard, P., 338, 365
Blanton-Stinchfield Articulation Test, 164
Blatz, W. E., 229, 250
Blewett, D. B., 123, 143, 405
Bliss, C. I., 97
Blum, L. H., 97, 104, 117
Blumer, H., 346, 364
Body development:
  ears and eyes, 91–92
  framework, 79–82
    bone development, 79
    bones as protective agency, 79
    characteristics of children's bones, 79
    characteristics of maturity, 81
    differences in skeletal maturation, 81
    methods of study, 80
    qualitative aspects of skeletal growth, 81
    skeletal development, 80
    X-ray studies, 80
  growth of head, 82
  growth of organs, 90
    heart, 90
  posture, 86–90
    constituents of good, 87
    defined, 86
    effect of poor, 86
    importance of observation, 86
    pairing of muscles, 88
    phases of control, 88
    proper interpretation, 88
    relation to personality, 87

reproductive system, 92–94
  effect on personality, 92
  immaturity during childhood, 92
  menstruation, 93
teeth and jaw, 82–86
  effect of growth differences, 85
  effect on personality, 84
  eruption of teeth, 84
  growth of teeth, 82
  growth pattern in tooth eruption, 82
  individual differences, 85
  meaning of integration, 83
  necessity for growth record, 85
  sequence of eruption, 84
Bones:
  characteristics of children's, 79
  characteristics of maturity, 81
  development, 79
  differences in skeletal maturation, 81
  methods of study, 80
  as protective agency, 79
  qualitative aspects of skeletal growth, 81
  skeletal development, 80
  X-ray studies, 80
Bonney, M. E., 229, 250
Book, W. F., 255, 258, 260, 261, 286
Books, influence on moral and ethical behavior, 347
Bookwalter, K. M., 97
Bossard, J. H. S., 330, 337, 364
Bousfield, W. A., 324
Boy Scouts, 344
Boynton, P. L., 32, 53
Bradbury, D. E., 8
Brandt, R. M., 27, 28
Branham, V. C., 466, 490
Breckenfield, I. J., 103, 118
Breckenridge, M. E., 11, 28, 29, 191, 193, 198, 205, 238, 331, 334, 364, 367, 390, 404
Bregman, E. O., 292, 305, 324
Brewer, J. E., 412, 413, 443
Bridges, K. M. B., 292, 295, 324
Brill, Norman, 489
Brodbeck, A. J., 162, 172
Brody, Samuel, 39, 53
Bronner, A. F., 339, 342, 346, 348, 364, 365

Broom, M. E., 122, 143
Brothers, influence on personal-social development, 220
Brown, George, 272, 286
Brown, W., 337, 364, 467, 490
Brown, William H., 324, 325
Bruce, W. F., 260, 261, 265, 286, 296, 324
Brueckner, L. J., 192, 193, 205
Bruner, J. S., 278, 286
Bryan, A. H., 63, 97
Bryan, W. L., 255, 258, 260, 261, 286
Bühler, Charlotte, 444
Buell, Charles, 117
Buker, Mae E., 251
Bullock, Burleen L., 324
Burge, Ivar, 109, 117
Burlingham, Dorothy, 324
Burns, Charles, 475, 489
Burt, Cyril, 346, 364
Burton, W. H., 286
Buswell, G. T., 118
Buswell, Margaret M., 250, 286

Caille, R. K., 236, 250
Calcium, 79
California, University of, clinical center, 58
California Pre-School Mental Scale, 32
Calvin, A. D., 286
Cameron, Dale C., 491
Cane, Florence, 205
Cannon, Kenneth L., 250
Cannon, W. B., 297, 301, 324
Carlson, Irene, 250
Carmichael, Leonard, 390, 404
Carpenter, Aileen, 102, 117
Carr, H. A., 255
Cartwright, Dorwin, 333, 364
Cassel, Russell N., 250
Catalona, Frank L., 143
Cattell, P., 154, 172
Cattell, Raymond B., 377, 404, 405
Center for Research in Child Health and Development, Harvard, 58
Center of attention, 474
Cermak, Ethel B., 318, 327
Chains, in school groupings, 212
Chambers, O. R., 309, 324

Change:
quantitative characteristic of growth, 10
study of, in individual child, 4
Chant, S. N. F., 229, 250
Character:
personality distinguished from, 369
See also Moral and ethical behavior
Chassell, C. F., 341, 342, 364
Chassell, E. B., 341, 342, 364
Chassell, L. M., 341, 342, 364
Chicago, University of, clinical center, 58
Child Development Abstracts and Monographs, 57, 97
Child groupings, study of, 357
Child study centers, growth of, 4
Childers, A. T., 470, 472, 490
Church, influence on moral and ethical behavior, 339
Clark, Elmer J., 429, 444
Clark, K. E., 382, 405
Classroom, requisites for, 243, 249
Clements, E. M. B., 97
Clinical centers, 58. See also Guidance clinics
Club membership, influence on moral and ethical behavior, 344
Comenius, John Amos, 278
Communication. See Language development
Companionships, imaginary, 199
Compartmentalization, 451
Compensation, 452
Competition, overemphasis of, 438
Competitiveness, development of, 231
Conditioning:
control of emotions by, 315
emotional, effect on motivation, 353
as type of learning, 256
Conflict, emotions as causes of, 312.
See also Aggression
Conger, J. J., 406
Consultants, in maladjustment, 486
Cooperation:
between home and school, 245
sense of, 231, 233
Core, personality, 393
Cornell, Ethel L., 119, 129, 143

Development, distinguished from growth, 9. *See also* Growth
Dewey, John, 278, 341
Diederich, P. B., 364
Dimock, H. S., 63, 98
Discipline:
causes of poor discipline, 432–439
faulty instructional organization, 433
faulty relationships, 434
teacher-group relationships, 436
earmarks of good discipline, 427–432
admitting lack of knowledge, 431
asking help when needed, 432
avoidance of sidestepping, 431
consideration of background, 430
group morale, 427
positive methods, 431
problem of corporal punishment, 429
respect for individuality, 428
school work as disciplinary device, 429
goal of self-discipline, 415–418
achievement, 418
dominative discipline challenged, 416
experimental results, 417
first steps, 418
new problem, 417
progressive schools, 417
transitional beliefs, 416
to manage emotional behavior, 314
maturity in achievement of self-discipline, 418–427
freedom, not license, 419
from domination to freedom, 421
need of the times, 418
place of domination, 419
relation of domination to maturity, 424
problem of, 408–418
contrasting patterns, 410
current contrasts, 414
definition, 408
disadvantages in conventional, 413
selected references, 443

summary, 442
things to do, 439–442
appraise situation, 439
develop working relationship, 440
manipulation or guidance, 441
study behavior, 441
Disease, influence on maladjustment, 469
Displacement, 453
Distortion, 454
Domination:
criteria for, 423
defined, 422
freedom and, 421
in teaching of self-discipline, 419
not necessarily autocratic, 426
relation to maturity, 424
Dreger, Ralph Mason, 172
Drill, effective, 264
Drives. *See* Emotion
Dumas, Georges, 295, 311, 325
Dunbar, H. Flanders, 320, 325
Dunklin, H. T., 276, 286
Dusenberry, Lois, 111, 117
Dymond, Rosalind F., 250
Dysplastic, personality type, 380

Ears, 91
Ebbinghaus, Hermann, 255, 258, 260, 263
Educational Policies Commission, 365
Eels, K., 124, 143
Elder, Rachel A., 206
Ellingson, R. J., 458, 490
Elliott, M. H., 212, 251
Elwood, Mary Isabel, 136, 143
Elzi, Anna, 250
Emotion:
control of emotional behavior, 313–320
by attitude, 317
by avoidance, 314
by conditioning, 315
by discipline, 314
by relaxation, 315
trainability, 313
defined, 293–298
disintegrative, 297
mild, 295
relation to feelings, 298

497

Heredity:
effect on intelligence, 123, 141
environment and, 379
factor in growth and achievement, 21
factor in maladjustive behavior, 468
of musical talent, 190
in personality development, 378
See also Personal-social development
Herrick, V. E., 124, 143
Hersey, R. B., 310, 325
Hightower, P. R., 339
Hildreth, Gertrude H., 172
Hilgard, Josephine, 260, 261, 390
Hinkelman, E. A., 405
Hippocrates, 380
Hirdansky, S., 466, 490
Holmes, Carlotta R., 325
Home:
broken, 468
cooperation with school, 356
influence on moral and ethical behavior, 337
influence on personal-social development, 227
relations with school, 244
See also Family
Homework, 429
Homogeneous groupings, 478
Honzik, M. P., 32, 54, 144, 376, 405
Hooker, Davenport, 444
Hopkins, L. Thomas, 413, 444
Horace Mann-Lincoln Institute of School Experimentation, 251
Horrocks, John, 251
Howard, P. J., 322, 326
Huggett, A. J., 177, 180, 181, 186, 203, 204, 206
Hughes, B. O., 35, 51, 54, 123, 143
Hugles, Anne S., 250
Hulse, Wilfred C., 490
Hunter, N., 173
Hymes, James, 444

Identification, type of behavior, 454
Iliff, A., 90, 98
Illness, effect on personality, 383
Imagination:
in creative thought, 197–199
dangers and possibilities, 197
defined, 197
developmental phases, 198
uncreative situations, 199
Immaturity, social, potential effect of, 475
Incidental learning, 270
Individuality:
concept of, 393
in growth, 13–18
maximum, 16
rate, 15
status, 14
timing, 14
respect for, 24, 428
See also Personality
Insight, in problem solving, 265, 266
Instinct, as basis of motivation, 351
Institutions, language retardation in, 162
Instruction:
implications of growth for, 24–28
importance of principles, 27–28
study of cycles, 26–27
unfairness of conventional interpretations, 25–26
Integration, meaning of, 83
Intelligence:
constancy of intelligence quotient, 134
distribution, 126
as factor in adjustment, 469
as factor in language growth, 159
factors affecting, 123–126
environment, 124
environment *vs.* heredity, 124, 141
inheritance, 123
race, 125
implications for teachers, 140–142
recent experimentation, 141
revised attitude necessary, 140
weakness in Iowa studies, 140
meaning of mental age, 136
mental growth curve, 127–134
adequacy of equations, 129
composite picture, 130
composite sex differences, 131
data available, 127
other factors, 133
nature of, 119–122

McCraw, L. W., 117
McCurry, William H., 148, 173
McDougall, William, 294, 326, 349, 351, 365
McFarland, M. B., 220, 230, 251
McFarlane, Margaret, 103, 118
McGraw, Myrtle B., 224–225, 331, 365, 388, 389, 405
McLean, Dorothy, 3, 8
McNemar, Quinn, 122
Magazines, influence on moral and ethical behavior, 347
Maladjustment. *See* Mental hygiene
Maller, J. B., 340, 365
Manipulation. *See* Skills
Marquis, D. G., 390, 405
Marschak, Marian, 119, 143
Marston, L. R., 375, 405–406
Martin, Mildred H., 445
Martin, William E., 8, 206, 251, 365, 484, 490
Mason, Beverly Derksen, 251
Mason, F. V., 488, 491
Mason, Robert E., 365
Massler, M., 99
Mateer, Florence, 316, 326
Matter, Jean, 278, 286
Maturation:
effect on emotions, 304
effect on height and weight patterns, 77
effect on personal-social development, 226–229
changing behavior patterns, 228
changing family needs, 227
relation to need, 226
influence on personality, 388–392
implications for promotion of, 391
learning-maturation relationship, 390
relationship of growth and learning, 388
in language development, 149
role of, in motor skills, 105
of skeletal structure, 81
teaching and, 269–278
incidental learning, 270
pressure teaching, 269
remedial instruction, 273
special effects, 272

Maturity:
and achievement of self-discipline, 418–427
freedom, not license, 419
from domination to freedom, 421
need of the times, 418
place of domination, 419
relation of domination to maturity, 424
emotional, 309
motor development as index of, 115
relation to good mental hygiene, 477–481
balanced growth, 480
deviational behavior, 481
growth variations, 480
homogeneous groupings, 478
increased knowledge of needs, 478
increased self-control, 478
mistakes in guidance, 478
social behavior, 478
stages in moral and ethical, 331–333
blind obedience, 331
interpretation of rules, 331
understanding of acts, 332
Mauer, Katherine M., 135, 143
Maximum, in growth cycle, 16, 21
May, M. A., 338, 339, 341, 342, 343, 364, 368, 371, 372, 376, 405
Mead, Margaret, 406, 491
Meek, L. H., 209, 210, 217, 251
Memorization, as type of learning, 262
Memory span, 263
Menarche, 63–64
Menstruation, 63–64, 93–94
Mental age. *See* Intelligence
Mental growth. *See* Growth, Intelligence
Mental hygiene:
causes of maladjustive behavior, 464–470
environmental effects, 466
goal and need, 464
personal effects, 468
classification of behavior problems, 458–464
change from cycle to cycle, 463
developmental period, 461, 462

509